T0342239

The Meddlers

SOVEREIGNTY, EMPIRE, AND THE BIRTH
OF GLOBAL ECONOMIC GOVERNANCE

Jamie Martin

Harvard University Press

CAMBRIDGE, MASSACHUSETTS
LONDON, ENGLAND

2022

For my parents
Janet Whelan and Roger Martin
And for Katrina

Second printing

Library of Congress Cataloging-in-Publication Data
Names: Martin, Jamie, 1984– author.
Title: The meddlers : sovereignty, empire, and the birth of global
economic governance / Jamie Martin.
Description: Cambridge, Massachusetts : Harvard University Press, 2022. |
Includes index. |
Identifiers: LCCN 2021047323 | ISBN 9780674976542 (cloth)
Subjects: LCSH: International Monetary Fund—History. |
International finance— History—20th century. | Economic councils—
History—20th century. | Economic history—1918- | World War, 1914-1918—
Economic aspects. | Sovereignty—Economic aspects—History—
20th century. | Capitalism—History—20th century.
Classification: LCC HG3881 .M338 2022 | DDC 332.4/5— dc23/eng/20220105
LC record available at https://lccn.loc.gov/2021047323

CONTENTS

Introduction

B Y THE END OF the twentieth century, a small number of international institutions had come to wield great influence over the domestic
economic policies of many states around the world. The International
Monetary Fund (IMF) and World Bank made assistance to member states
conditional on them enacting a broad suite of reforms, often with far-
reaching political and social consequences. From Africa to Latin America
to Asia, loans were tied to the balancing of government budgets, the privatization of state-owned industries, the removal of regulations, and the lowering of tariffs. The World Trade Organization (WTO) targeted not only
outright barriers to trade but also an array of domestic laws and regulations concerning health and safety, industrial and agricultural policy, and
the environment. Working alongside powerful governments, central banks,
and private corporations, these institutions exercised powers of "global
economic governance" that unsettled long-standing norms of sovereignty,
which, at least in theory, were meant to safeguard national institutions
and policy-making from outside interference.

There is a well-known story about the twentieth-century origins and
development of these powers of global economic governance. It begins with
the Bretton Woods Conference of July 1944, when, just as the Allied invasion of Western Europe was unfolding, representatives from forty-four
countries met to reshape the rules of the international monetary system and
create two new institutions, the IMF and World Bank, to govern the world
economy. Within a few years, these institutions were joined by the General
Agreement on Tariffs and Trade (GATT), a legal agreement between twenty-
three states to encourage a return to freer trade.[1] This unique postwar

arrangement lasted for two and a half decades. When the Bretton Woods system fell apart in the early 1970s, the IMF and World Bank, having lost their original mandates, began to exercise greater powers over the domestic policies of some of their members. Using the incredible leverage of access to foreign capital, they enforced austerity and structural adjustment reforms, which dramatically reshaped the economies and institutions of many countries. In 1995, when the more interventionist WTO replaced GATT, it also began to deal with problems once assumed to reside within the exclusive jurisdiction of sovereign states.

The increasingly intrusive powers of these institutions damaged their legitimacy. They were criticized around the world for interfering in domestic politics and imposing neoliberal policies on states in the Global South and former communist bloc. Even their supporters raised difficult questions about their compatibility with traditional conceptions of sovereignty and democracy. If representative politics remained an exclusively national affair, how could institutions beyond the state legitimately make such extensive demands on domestic policy? What was the difference between a voluntary act of delegation to such an institution and an act of submission to the powerful foreign governments and private interests that set its agendas?

These questions are often considered unique to an era of late twentieth-century neoliberal globalization. But they are in fact quite old. Their origins date to the end of the First World War, when international economic institutions—for the first time in history—began to intervene in the most consequential domestic economic decisions of some of their member states. In the process, these institutions oversaw a major transformation in sovereignty and international order, as they reshaped tools of informal empire for a new era of self-determination. *The Meddlers* tells the story of this transformation. In doing so, it offers a political history of the birth of global economic governance at a moment of profound flux in the relationship of empire and global capitalism.

The first international economic institutions were designed to defend capitalism and stabilize a European-dominated international order that the First World War had thrown into turmoil. Their powers were shaped according to the prerogatives of a few European governments and central banks—primarily those of the victorious Allied powers and, above all, Britain. But US private interests and occasionally public authorities also played a role in their genesis. The most important such institution was the League of Nations. In 1920, the League established the first standing intergovernmental economic and financial bodies, modeled on wartime councils used by the Allied powers to regulate global trade and shipping. A few years later, the world's first international bank, the Bank for International Settlements, was established to facilitate the cooperation of European central banks and help resolve the destabilizing problem of German reparations. Various intergovernmental bodies were created to control the global production and exchange of raw materials and agricultural goods. These institutions worked alongside private international cartels; the International Chamber of Commerce, a business lobbying group; and the International Labour Organization, which was dedicated to expanding labor laws and worker protections in member states. Across various domains, international intervention in economic processes became routine, as global markets were embedded in new legal and institutional frameworks, underwritten by a handful of powerful states, empires, and banks. At the Bretton Woods Conference in 1944, a second wave of innovation in international economic governance began, which both built on and departed from this earlier one. The twentieth-century history of global capitalism runs through these international institutions.[2]

During the interwar years, these bodies developed novel powers over once-insulated domestic realms of economic policy-making. They tied loans to commitments to austerity or development practices; coordinated the policies of independent central banks beyond the direct control of national governments; and imposed restrictions on the production and export of certain raw materials and agricultural goods. These new powers involved demands to open policies, resources, and information to the reach of actors beyond the sovereign borders of states and empires. Such demands always faced fierce opposition, since they were widely seen as challenges to a long-established norm of international law and diplomacy: that formal sovereignty provided protection from any kind of "foreign interference." There were many areas of policy that were designated problems of domestic administration alone, including immigration and religious and civil matters. But few were as significant in their implications as economic policies like tariffs, taxation and public spending, the management of currencies, and the regulation of raw material and agricultural production. Any state that allowed a power beyond its realm to weigh in authoritatively on such economic issues was said, in effect, to be relinquishing its full sovereignty.

Beyond Europe's borders, few states had ever enjoyed such insulation. For centuries, one empire after another had violently laid claim to the wealth and resources of the non-European world. Even when their incursions fell short of colonial annexation, these empires, along with the United States, forced many countries to open up domestic spaces to the reach of foreign officials, militaries, bankers, and businesses—whether in China, the Middle East and North Africa, Latin America, the Caribbean, or on Europe's Balkan periphery. In the nineteenth century, banks and the empires that protected their interests perfected the art of meddling in the affairs of others without needing to formally colonize them. At the end of the First World War, there was no shortage of precedents for the sovereignty of the weak being violated by the strong for the sake of power and profits.

But it was precisely these imperial precedents that made the earliest innovations in global economic governance so controversial. In a profoundly unequal world, how could a sovereign state open its internal affairs to outside intervention without admitting to a loss of status, power, and autonomy? How could it allow an institution representing the interests of rival governments, central banks, or capitalists any influence over policies of strategic significance or with important distributional and political consequences? In the wake of the First World War, the stakes of answering these questions were extremely high, given the dangerous interstate rivalries and volatile transformations in national mass politics to which the war had led. Claims to self-determination were more influential than ever. The collapse of old empires like the Russian and Austro-Hungarian had given rise to new states that guarded their sovereignty warily.[3] Powerful European countries, demoted by an ascendant United States from the summit of global hierarchies, went from fraught coexistence in the 1920s to the outbreak of another war in the 1930s. At the same time, many governments were becoming more democratic as class and gender barriers to suffrage fell and socialist parties gained a foothold in parliaments. Far-right, far-left, and nationalist movements innovated new forms of nondemocratic politics that were nonetheless rooted in mass mobilization.[4]

Against the backdrop of these transformations, and across a range of sovereign countries and colonies, resistance to the interference of external actors in domestic economic policies provided a global lingua franca of opposition to the earliest attempts to govern the world's capitalist economy. The opponents of international economic institutions criticized them as meddlers. In many cases, the charge was justified—though not always.

What was undeniably true was that during an era of empire—when the sovereignty of many countries was partial, contested, and new—the question of which countries allowed the involvement of outside actors in their domestic affairs was always a question of their relative power and status in a hierarchical international system. This fact made international cooperation extremely difficult to realize—and the charge of meddling a highly resonant one. To many contemporary observers, it was obvious that the interventionist powers of these institutions were rooted in practices of empire. But this created a problem: Unlike preventing a war, governing an interdependent world economy could not only involve managing the relations between states. Doing so also appeared to require reaching deeply into their interior realms—to adjust their budgets, currencies, or tariffs. How could this be done in ways that did not simply recapitulate practices of informal empire and gunboat diplomacy?

The Meddlers explains how the first international economic institutions developed the power to open the internal economic spaces of sovereign states to the involvement of "outsiders," while attempting to legitimate their actions as a reproducible form of international cooperation, not outright coercion. The challenge faced by the architects of these institutions was to transform potential insults to sovereignty and self-governance into practices of international cooperation that could win broad acceptance, even when these institutions were clearly used for the sake of the strategic interests of rival empires or the profit-making of powerful capitalists.

The First Wave of International Economic Institution-Building

The years following the conclusion of the First World War were some of the most tumultuous in the history of global capitalism. They have long been described as the moment when a vibrant wave of globalization came to a disastrous end. In the second half of the nineteenth century, the world economy had reached unparalleled levels of interconnection as tariffs were lowered, beginning with Britain in the 1840s. Technological innovations, the expansion of empires, and the integration of financial markets increasingly knit the entire earth into a single system of exchange. Even after many countries began to raise tariffs from the 1870s onward, this did not seriously interrupt a worldwide process of market integration made possible by the introduction of new transportation technologies, including the steamship and railways, which dramatically lowered the costs of doing business over vast distances. By the turn of the twentieth century, most large economies had fixed the value of their currencies to gold, greasing the wheels of trade between them. The telegraph transmitted information around the world in the blink of an eye. Staggering volumes of capital flowed out of wealthy countries into investments abroad, such as the new rail lines crisscrossing Europe's growing colonial empires, which brought agricultural goods and raw materials from once isolated rural areas to coastal outlets. Millions of migrants moved around the world. The total volume of global trade grew at a blistering pace. At the same time, a new division of labor solidified between industrialized economies, mainly in Europe and the United States, and producers of primary commodities. This deepened global inequalities and accelerated the "great divergence" that had begun in the late eighteenth and early nineteenth centuries between the "core" regions of global capitalism and its "peripheries."[5] Governments at this time did little to manage their national economies. Nor did they offer much protection to their populations from the turbulence of this expanding global capitalist system, which since the 1820s had experienced major crises every ten years, on a schedule of almost metronomic predictability—"as regularly as the comets," as Friedrich Engels once put it.[6]

Although the First World War did not bring all of these globalizing trends to a screeching halt, it did throw the world economy into disarray.[7] When Austria-Hungary issued its ultimatum to Serbia in late July 1914, stock exchanges were shuttered from Johannesburg to Amsterdam, and bank runs broke out from the Dutch East Indies to Peru.[8] The gold standard was suspended, trade and exchange restrictions were implemented in the belligerents, and the infrastructures of global shipping and commerce were weaponized for the sake of wartime blockades. At the end of the war, much of Europe was exhausted economically. The vanquished owed painful reparations, and the victors had crushing debts to their allies. Trade and finance were in tatters. Many efforts to recreate a durable and stable world economy, like that of the prewar "golden age" of capitalism, were unsuccessful.[9] Some observers have described these efforts as signature cases of the limits of interwar internationalism, foiled by interstate rivalries, US isolationism, and the turn to militaristic nationalism in the 1930s.[10] When the global Depression arrived, it aggravated existing instabilities and created new ones. Long-distance trade shriveled, foreign investment dried up, and millions of industrial and agricultural workers were thrown out of employment. Tariffs, exchange controls, and imperial economic blocs proliferated. States ran a range of experiments in managing their national economies, from the US New Deal to the Soviet Five Year Plan. The globalized world economy that had emerged in the late nineteenth century, bruised but not broken by the First World War, was dashed on the rocks of economic nationalism. Another world war approached.[11]

Many accounts of the interwar "collapse of globalization" focus on a story about the difficulty of restoring the classical gold standard. The gold standard was the financial linchpin of the prewar world economy, but it posed external constraints on national economies and politics that proved over time to be increasingly incompatible with representative politics.[12] Before the First World War, the gold standard had encouraged the growth of world trade by providing stable exchange rates. But it required constant fiscal discipline and periodic doses of domestic deflation. Central banks adjusted interest rates with little input from governments and mostly insulated from the political consequences of the recessions they engineered to protect the currency's peg to gold, even when these recessions brought wrenching unemployment. After the war, the political costs of prioritizing the stability of exchange rates over the livelihoods of industrial workers and farmers became much higher as the possibilities for political resistance proliferated in democratizing societies. The increased power of labor and the rise of socialist parties made wages stickier and the threat of strikes more palpable. Vitriolic and often deadlocked parliamentary conflict raised the stakes of decisions about taxation and public spending. Mass unemployment brought by the Depression made it more difficult than ever for governments to prioritize maintaining the gold standard if this meant avoiding expansive monetary or fiscal powers to deal with the crisis.[13] When the fetters of gold were removed, beginning with the devaluation of sterling in late 1931, recovery from the Depression began.[14] This lesson was taken to heart in the 1940s. At the Bretton Woods Conference, the interwar gold standard was replaced with a system of fixed but adjustable exchange rates. This allowed governments greater autonomy to pursue the expansive economic and welfare policies needed to maintain their legitimacy without resorting to the extreme economic nationalism that had so destabilized global capitalism in the 1930s.[15] The idea that the world economy was to be shaped in light of domestic social and economic priorities, not the other way around, marked a dramatic reversal from the assumptions that had guided policy for decades.[16] For this reason, some claim that the Bretton Woods system allowed national sovereignty, democracy, and global capitalism to be made compatible in a stable synthesis for the first time ever—if only for a few short decades.[17]

But the gold standard was not the only external constraint on the economic policies of governments after 1918. The first wave of international economic institutions enabled foreign governments, central banks, and private interests to exercise a voice in the internal affairs of a range of sovereign states. This power was distinct from that of the gold standard, since it involved institutions making discretionary decisions on the basis of varying political or economic criteria. The rules of gold required states to forgo policies that jeopardized the stability of their currencies, like running up budget deficits or adjusting monetary policy to rescue economies from recession. This proved to be incompatible with robust democracy during an era in which citizens could better defend their interests through political parties and labor unions. But the gold standard did not involve any formal relinquishment of national policy discretion to external authorities—who could back up their demands, whatever they might be, with threats of discipline and even punishment. Its maintenance did not require any international institutions at all.[18] Committing to the gold standard, moreover, was widely considered a marker of a country's "civilizational" status and national prestige. Allowing foreign actors to have a voice in its domestic policies was universally seen to be the opposite.[19]

The importance of this emerging international power over domestic economic policy-making in the wake of the First World War has long been downplayed. In large part, this is because the international institutions of this era were for decades considered failures. If measured against their goals of rescuing the world from depression and preventing the outbreak of war, no other conclusion can be reached. But recent scholarship has revisited the internationalist experiments of these years with an eye to understanding how they laid important foundations for the institutions of the liberal international order of the post-1945 period.[20] Alongside developments in the international regulation of public health, migration, refugees, and the policing of contraband, the League of Nations' long-neglected Economic and Financial Organization, in particular, has been rediscovered and credited with giving rise to an entirely new conception of "international economic regulation."[21] In the words of one of the League's greatest historians, the Economic and Financial Organization made "efforts to support global capitalism" one of the League's central aims.[22] It harmonized regulations concerning trade and played a

The Economic and Financial Section of the League of Nations. *United Nations Archives at Geneva.*

critical role in saving several European countries from financial collapse in the 1920s.[23] It sponsored some of the era's most influential economic research, including studies that helped give shape to the very idea of "the national economy" itself—an idea that was not, until the interwar period, the common sense it is now.[24] It gathered so much data that it made another new idea, "the world economy," statistically legible for the first time.[25]

But a crucial aspect of the political origins of these early international economic institutions has remained in the dark. How did they develop powers to intervene in traditionally domestic arenas of economic policy-making? This book explains how this dramatic innovation in international governance took place—in the face of widespread opposition to it. To do so, *The Meddlers* tells a history of institutional design alongside one of political struggles over legitimacy, representation, and ideology. It charts the development of a range of new practices during the interwar years—from conditional lending to international development. What was so novel about these institutions was that their interventionist powers had to be differentiated from the kind of unwanted meddling that empires had long visited on semi-sovereign countries—from North Africa to Asia to the Caribbean. The task of these institutions was to make their powers compatible with the legal fiction of sovereign equality and the mass politics of self-determination.

The era following the conclusion of the First World War was not the first time that foreign ministries, businesses, and banks had worked together across national lines. The integration of the world economy in the nineteenth century had involved many instances of public and private cooperation for the sake of promoting international commerce. Nor was this the first time that financial advisers had been sent from some countries to help reform the domestic laws and institutions of others.[26] Powerful states, of course, had long coerced weaker ones into relinquishing their autonomy and assets. But until this point, there were almost no examples of the government of a sovereign state willingly relinquishing control over vital economic matters to an external body that claimed to represent its interests—and in which it enjoyed at least some representation.

In the nineteenth century, the two kinds of international institutions that dealt with problems related to the integration of global capitalism had either avoided exercising such interventionist powers or had done so in ways that were unmistakably imperial. The first were the international public unions established from the 1860s onward to coordinate regulations over technical matters related to international commerce—such as telegraphs, the post, railways, and river navigability—as part of broader efforts to standardize measures, statistics, and global timekeeping.[27] These bodies did not play any role in major domestic economic policies and were restricted to handling what were deemed uncontroversial issues.[28] Even their attempts to deal with supposedly apolitical problems, however, were denounced as threats to sovereignty and national pride. More controversial policies, such as tariffs, were off limits to them. While many bilateral trade treaties were signed in the second half of the nineteenth century, tariffs were generally considered matters for domestic jurisdiction alone, not international law or administration.[29] Some have described these technical unions as precursors to twentieth-century institutions of global governance.[30] But this was true only in a limited sense. Although these international public unions standardized regulations and facilitated the collection of statistics, they were prevented from touching domestic policies with important strategic or distributional implications.[31]

Much more powerful were the multinational debt commissions created at the behest of European investors in North Africa and the Middle East beginning in the 1860s, and then later in Balkan states like Bulgaria, Serbia, Macedonia, and Greece. These debt commissions, usually staffed by representatives of various European banks and governments, wielded extensive powers over the revenues and budgets of sovereign borrowers said to be at a high risk of default. They vetoed decisions over public spending and removed sources of revenue from domestic control to ensure that foreign lenders were repaid. They were later seen as models for compelling sovereign states to accede to demands imposed from the outside. But these debt commissions were clearly instruments of informal empire, which made it difficult to adapt them to international forms of governance. At first, these commissions were established outside Europe and were considered appropriate only for countries deemed by European bankers and governments to be at a lower level of "development" or on a lower rung of civilizational hierarchy. After these commissions were brought to the Balkans in the 1890s, some claimed a boundary had been crossed: institutions once generally restricted to Muslim-majority countries were now being used in Christian Europe—though still only in what many considered its underdeveloped post-Ottoman periphery.[32]

These earlier arrangements provided clear precedents for twentieth-century institution-builders. But in the aftermath of the First World War, international efforts to govern the world economy involved a new challenge: compelling governments of sovereign states to relinquish full autonomy over policies, resources, and institutions without insulting their claims to self-governance and national pride in the process. One of the principal aims of these institutions was to serve as legitimation machines, making older imperial practices acceptable for a new era. But nearly every attempt to reach beyond the barriers of sovereignty resulted in fierce resistance—whether from political elites, bankers, workers, or businesses, who, in fighting their own battles, debated whether these institutions offered a new kind of internationalism or simply an ingenious method for laundering empire.

The Architects

The architects of these first international economic institutions came from a very specific and narrow milieu. Most of them were men born around the 1870s–1880s in Britain, the United States, and continental Europe.[33]

Their careers straddled the public and private, the national and international. Some were officials in treasuries, foreign ministries, and colonial offices; others were bankers, whether on Wall Street or in the City of London, or at the world's most powerful central banks. Most of their careers took off during the First World War through their involvement in the economic mobilization of the Allied powers—whether in the supply of raw materials or food, the production of munitions, or the allocation of shipping. After the war, several played a role in the League of Nations or Bank for International Settlements. Many shuffled between institutional settings, whose borders at this time were often porous. They all shared a basic internationalist orientation, though their political commitments varied: some were conservatives, others moderate socialists.[34] They included some famous figures, such as the British economist John Maynard Keynes, the French internationalist and financier Jean Monnet, and the Bank of England Governor Montagu Norman. But they also included many quietly effective technocrats working at the intersection of banks, governments, and international bodies. Their efforts all shared the basic aim of preserving and stabilizing capitalism at a moment of increasing challenges to it. At times, they were engaged in fierce struggle—often, though not always, due to national rivalries. Whether it was for the sake of promoting British, US, or French interests, however, the institutions they designed all functioned to project the economic power of empires in new ways during an era of rising nationalism and shifting global hierarchies.

The transnational network of these architects was very small. It was no coincidence that most of them sat at the nexus of political and financial power in Britain and the United States, the two most powerful capitalist empires the world had ever seen. Although the US government did not take as central a role in international and European political affairs during the interwar period as it would later, various US citizens were involved in institutions like the League of Nations, and Wall Street loomed over many decisions taken in Europe during this time.[35] Until the 1940s, the burdens of international stabilization fell heavily on the British Empire and the Bank of England. This gave British elites outsized influence in these international institutions, which they used to advance a new kind of economic imperialism in Europe and abroad, at a moment when Britain's global power, at least in relation to its longtime US rival, was on the wane.[36]

Although a small network of people formulated these novel practices, their work was not part of a unified and self-conscious project of worldmaking. Instead, they responded to different crises and with varying aims. The first time that an international institution ever made loans conditional on a government committing to a program of domestic austerity and central bank independence, for example, was in former Ottoman and Habsburg lands in the early 1920s. The goal of doing so was to prevent financial chaos, the westward march of Bolshevism, and the outbreak of another war in Central Europe and the Balkans that would jeopardize the fragile peace settlement of 1919. The first time that private investments were channeled to an international development program was to address the huge refugee problem that Greece faced in the wake of its 1919–1922 war with Turkey and the population exchange that followed in 1923, not to build up the industrial capacity of a "modernizing" state, as would later become the standard aim of development programs. The first major experiment in intergovernmental commodity governance, later elaborated more fully by the Organization of the Petroleum Exporting Countries (OPEC), was pioneered in the case of one specific raw material: tin. Its aim was to contain worker uprisings in British and Dutch Southeast Asian colonies and respond to the demands of a lobbying group in London dominated by a multinational mining conglomerate. Taken together, however, these experiments led to the establishment of institutions that collectively exercised a type of power recognizable today as that of an early form of global economic governance. Although this term was not used at the time, many contemporaries saw these novel public and private institutional innovations as part of the same trend: toward increasing international control over the world economy.[37]

Sovereignty and Foreign Interference

One of the most effective and widely deployed methods for resisting the powers of international institutions during the interwar period was to claim they were exercising an illegitimate form of "interference" in the domestic affairs of a sovereign state. This was a popular tactic for an opposition party to use against a sitting government, for example—particularly in countries with new or partial sovereignty, or where claims to self-determination had potent mobilizing effects. In powerful European countries and the United States, opposition to interference was also used by public and private actors to counter threats to their interests or autonomy. A convincing charge of interference did not only have rhetorical effects, but posed real political barriers to the powers these new institutions could develop. There was, of course, nothing new to mobilizing against the "foreigner," whether in arenas of popular politics or elite realms of diplomacy and jurisprudence. Denunciations of interference were also sometimes little more than conspiracy theories, or thinly veiled expressions of anti-Semitism or xenophobia. Yet the charge of interference also explicitly appealed to a set of legal claims about sovereignty and the insulation it was supposed to provide from the reach of external entities. This charge provided a diverse set of actors with a globally recognizable way of framing resistance to international institutions—one with a legal and diplomatic pedigree but also with the potential for mass mobilization. Understanding the conflicts that attended the birth of global economic governance thus requires a multi-scalar approach, moving beyond the halls of international institutions to consider political struggle at the national and local levels as well.[38]

At the end of the First World War, the norm of non-interference was deeply rooted in international law and diplomacy. Its earliest programmatic declarations were made by the German philosopher Christian Wolff and the Swiss international lawyer Emmerich de Vattel in the mid-eighteenth century. In his 1758 *Law of Nations,* Vattel influentially argued that one sovereign could not legitimately interfere in the domestic affairs of another.[39] Immanuel Kant developed a broader account of this right in his 1795 guidelines for "perpetual peace," in which he claimed that no country could lawfully meddle with the constitution or government of another.[40] Non-interference was subsequently elaborated into a fuller legal doctrine. It was said to be the guarantor of true sovereign equality and the independence of states.[41]

This norm was widely debated in the nineteenth century, particularly after the Napoleonic Wars, in large part due to the development of counterrevolutionary practices of interference during the era of the European Congress System. In the wake of the wars, members of the Holy Alliance—Prussia, Russia, and Austria—claimed a right to suppress revolutionary uprisings and unwanted constitutional changes in other states. Their attempts to normalize a taboo practice were never universally accepted. Efforts by some powers to quash rebellions in others, to get involved in their civil wars and dynastic disputes, or to police the global trade in enslaved people were resisted as forms of illegitimate interference in their internal affairs.[42] It was not only members of the Holy Alliance, moreover, that were seen as meddlers. The question of the legitimacy of interference was also at the center of British foreign policy.[43] At the end of the

Napoleonic Wars, it had been the British who had sought to avoid any international system that involved the "Superintendence of the Internal Affairs of Other States," as the British Foreign Secretary Lord Castlereagh put it in 1820. But this principle was inconsistently maintained in the years to come, as Britain's global imperial expansion accelerated.[44] In the case of relations between most European powers, legal and diplomatic opinion swung against the legality of intervention in the second half of the nineteenth century, even for the sake of counterrevolution.[45] The same was not true for places brought under direct European domination, such as India or Algeria, or for the sake of certain humanitarian causes, like protecting the Christian subjects of the Ottoman Empire.[46] However, in relations between the self-anointed "civilized" states of Christendom, sovereignty was supposed to prevent a wide array of abuses—from unwanted military interventions to more subtle forms of meddling by one sovereign in the domains of another.[47] By the early twentieth century, the right to non-interference was widely seen to extend to various economic policies, even when they affected the welfare of other countries. These included tariffs, subsidies for domestic industries or shipping, export taxes, controls over natural resources, intra-imperial preferential trade arrangements, and taxation and public spending.[48]

Defining these policies as strictly domestic, however, created a problem for those who first sought to endow international institutions with extensive economic powers. This was because stabilizing global capitalism appeared to necessitate intervention into precisely those realms that were said to be off limits: preventing the imprudence of governments that spent more money than ever on arms and alms, encouraging a retreat from rising trade barriers, or overseeing sound monetary policies. This challenge reflected a new reality about the politics of international commerce. Over the second half of the nineteenth century, political struggles over trade had moved from the exclusive plane of international relations to the intranational level as well: that is, competition between rival mercantilist powers was now joined by conflict between interest groups, classes, and political parties.[49] The world economy became a domestic political issue. The birth of the first institutions of global economic governance involved a series of challenges to the idea that these political and distributional conflicts could be kept hidden behind sovereign walls.

For much of the world, the right to economic non-interference was rarely respected. It had never been recognized in territories brought under European colonial rule or countries subjected to foreign financial controls, concessions, and the removal of their tariff autonomy. The establishment of the sovereign debt commission in Egypt in 1876, for example, was described by contemporaries as London and Paris claiming a "right of interference" in Egypt's domestic affairs.[50] Even when lip service was paid to the idea of non-interference, it carried little weight when it conflicted with the prerogatives of the powerful. Just before the outbreak of the First Opium War in 1839, for example, the British Foreign Secretary Lord Palmerston had attempted to diffuse tensions between British merchants and Chinese authorities by insisting the Crown would not come to the former's defense if this meant interfering with Chinese efforts to outlaw opium.[51] But Britain was soon at war with China for precisely this reason. After the war, the British developed new means of institutionalizing their involvement in Chinese affairs through the Maritime Customs Service, treaty ports, and laws of extraterritoriality. Similar semi-colonial tools were brought to other countries, such as Siam and the Ottoman Empire, to subject them to external controls without forcing them to formally relinquish their independence.[52] In the case of the US empire, the Monroe Doctrine was said to represent a scaling up of the principle of non-interference to the hemispheric level. But the Monroe Doctrine facilitated frequent US meddling in the affairs of its southern neighbors.[53] The 1904 Roosevelt Corollary, which stated that the United States could, in fact, interfere in Western Hemisphere countries if they did not pay their debts or maintain law and order, formalized what was already clear: The Monroe Doctrine did not articulate a generalizable principle of non-interference but instead demarcated a zone in which the United States alone was allowed to meddle.[54]

During the decade before the outbreak of the First World War, disputes over sovereign debt involved worldwide controversy over questions of interference.[55] The Roosevelt Corollary had been prompted in part by the attempts of European powers to violently force the Venezuelan government in 1902 to pay debts in arrears to European creditors. But this crisis also had another outcome. In its wake, the Argentinian Foreign Minister Luis Drago, drawing on a long tradition of argument about non-interference in Latin America, led a campaign to instantiate a new international norm prohibiting sovereign debtors from being forced by threats of violence to repay their foreign bondholders.[56] Drago's efforts, culminating in an agreement reached at the 1907 Hague Peace Conference, showed that claiming a right to non-interference offered a tool for subordinate countries to resist the incursions of stronger empires—or, at least, for bringing international attention to these abuses. But it did little to prevent the US government from inaugurating a new era of interventionist foreign policy in Latin America and the Caribbean, ranging from outright military occupations to the establishment of financial receiverships in countries like Haiti and Nicaragua.[57] At the same time that the United States expanded its power to override the sovereignty of other countries, however, US political and economic elites also claimed a right to non-interference to oppose international arrangements that jeopardized their interests or autonomy.

The fundamental political indeterminacy of these claims at the moment when the history told in this book begins can be seen in the drafting of the Covenant of the League of Nations in 1919. The "domestic jurisdiction" clause of Article 15 clarified that the League's Council or Assembly could not make recommendations in any dispute concerning the strictly domestic affairs of a member state. It was proposed at the Paris Peace Conference by US delegates, who faced intense pressure from Republican lawmakers not to allow the institution to touch US trade or anti-Asian immigration policies. But Chinese delegates also attempted to shape the meaning of this clause to prevent the League from enabling foreign powers to further erode Chinese sovereignty.[58] Countries that had full or only partial sovereignty thus both claimed a right to non-interference. But it was usually only the former that enjoyed it. To some contemporary observers, it was clear that protection from meddling was always a "question of power and politics rather than a rule of law."[59] Whatever the norms about sovereign equality, the new international institutions risked acting like the great powers that dominated them always had: only respecting the right of some states to full autonomy.[60] The fact that not all states, in practice, enjoyed the same features of statehood was obvious to the representatives of "weak" states during the foundation of the League.[61]

The inclusion of the domestic jurisdiction clause in the Covenant of the League of Nations was novel in how it formalized a right to non-interference in the constitution of an international institution. While its immediate effects were limited, it sparked wide debate about how to draw clear and legitimate borders around the domestic spaces whose protection sovereignty was said to guarantee. The vagueness of the clause complicated this task. For Article 15 did not clarify what, exactly, a purely domestic issue was. According to some legal experts, the only plausible interpretation of it was that it covered any issue not already governed by international law.[62] Some of its implications were clear: The League was not authorized, for example, to make any pronouncement about a country's decision concerning democratic or authoritarian political institutions.[63] But what about in economics? Here, the issue was murkier. While most economic policies were at this time considered exclusively domestic matters, they could have major consequences across an interdependent world economy. This fact was clear to US opponents of the League of Nations, who recognized that the conceptual blurriness between the economic borders of the domestic and the international when it came to policies like tariffs meant that what was today an issue for a sovereign state alone could tomorrow become one for the international community.[64] That the League's Council was to have the final say about what counted as a purely domestic issue was one of the principal charges made against the League during the congressional debates that decided the United States would not be allowed to join it.[65]

At the same time, the ambiguities of the domestic jurisdiction clause also troubled many liberal internationalists, who worried that it allowed an ill-defined set of issues to remain outside the domains of international law and cooperation, even when these issues jeopardized international stability and peace.[66] Many of these same internationalists, however, also recognized that a convincing charge of foreign interference could jeopardize the legitimacy of an existing international institution or doom the creation of a new one. There was no disputing that international cooperation required national governments to relinquish some freedom of action, just as they did when they signed a treaty. But interference went beyond this. It involved an external authority targeting the space within states, not the space between them.[67] Many internationalists writing during and after the First World War agreed that the first great experiment in international government—the Concert of Europe—had been doomed by its members' penchant for meddling.[68] A century before, such meddling had aimed to protect monarchical order and religious orthodoxy; now, the challenge was to stabilize capitalism itself.

The story told here focuses on how questions about sovereignty and interference became key to international political struggles about the world economy and its governance after the First World War. But similar questions were also crucial for issues of rights and humanitarianism. In debates at the Paris Peace Conference about whether the League of Nations could adopt robust protections for religious and ethnic minorities, some of the organization's architects worried that the degree of interference this would entail would jeopardize support for the League plans.[69] When Japanese delegates attempted to include explicit provision in the Covenant for promoting racial equality, or even watered-down claims about the "equality of Nations," British delegates framed their opposition to these efforts in terms of preventing unwanted interference in their domestic politics.[70] The question of women's rights and suffrage was similarly coded by delegates as a domestic issue that could not be opened to negotiation.[71]

The minority rights treaty regime that was established after the First World War was successful in turning some previously domestic questions about the treatment of nationals into issues of international concern, but only in a select number of places—primarily in new or recently defeated states in Central and Eastern Europe.[72] This treaty regime was frequently attacked by governments for enabling external supervision of their affairs and for the unevenness of its application. Its asymmetries were said to be a violation of sovereign equality and a humiliating burden for those states that were pressured into adopting its rules.[73] For more powerful countries, by contrast—particularly those with extensive segregationist regimes and exclusionary immigration policies—the doctrine of non-interference provided a tool for preventing external scrutiny of these policies. None of the Great Powers allowed their own national minority populations to be placed under international supervision after the First World War. These double standards continued for years. One of the reasons that the US designers of the United Nations (UN) insisted on a broad interpretation of the domestic jurisdiction clause in the UN Charter—which was modeled directly on the corresponding section of the League's Covenant—was to reassure southern senators that the inclusion of human rights language in the Charter would not expose Jim Crow laws to external challenge. This decision sparked fierce but ultimately unsuccessful efforts by African American political groups to overturn this clause.[74] The birth of the UN human rights regime, as several historians have shown, was accompanied by compromises that prevented its enforcement.[75]

As it turned out, there were few direct appeals to Article 15(8) of the League's Covenant in disputes between member states—and no successful ones.[76] But the principle of non-interference it formalized was constantly invoked, whether concerning economic issues or questions of rights—and often with significant effects. As we shall see, it provided a powerful and widely intelligible way for many different actors to prevent international institutions from reaching into areas where they were unwelcome. The charge of foreign interference was not only made by diplomats and lawyers, who took constitutions and legal precedent seriously. It was also used by politicians to make the abstract ideal of sovereignty more concrete in the arenas of mass politics. In the years surrounding the First World War, this charge had explosive resonance on the street. It was then common to claim that the proximate cause of the war had been a dispute over interference exacerbated by the frenzied politics of nationalism. When the Serbian government rejected Austria-Hungary's demands to allow foreign oversight of its investigation of the assassination of Franz Ferdinand in July 1914, precipitating the outbreak of war, this had shown how much "domestic administration" had become the "most precious flower and fruit of sovereignty," as the British internationalist Leonard Woolf wrote. "[W]hatever the real causes which would induce civilised men to massacre one another by the hundred thousand," Woolf claimed, "the men themselves must believe that a demand had been made by one independent sovereign State to interfere in the administration of another independent sovereign State before the process could begin."[77]

In the aftermath of the war, an era of competitive nationalism and extremist politics, particularly on the right, the charge of interference was deployed to potent effect.[78] But its political and normative implications were not uniform. It was used by both liberals and fascists, and by the governments of newly independent states and the representatives of empires. The fact that this claim for autonomy could be put into the service of such disparate political projects showed how much the boundary between the national and the international had become a frontline in struggles for power.

This book charts how the architects of the first wave of international economic institutions responded to these charges of trespassing. While the resistance they faced set political limits to their efforts, they nonetheless managed to gradually oversee a revolutionary development in international order, despite the setbacks of the 1930s. This innovation was on a par with later transformations in international governance, such as the establishment of the first effective international human rights regime, which similarly involved domestic realms becoming targets of external intervention.[79] For those who attempted to legitimate this transformation, the challenge was how to encourage states to voluntarily delegate powers. One way was to make such requests for delegation undemanding, leaving them full of carve outs and limited to "nonpolitical" issues unlikely to drum up public passions or alienate private interests. Another was to argue that membership in an international institution was sufficient on its own to turn an act of interference into a benevolent form of assistance, even if it came at a steep cost to a state's autonomy. Yet another approach involved convincing a government that discipline imposed from the outside could cement its power, allowing it to claim that it had been forced into painful reforms that simultaneously helped to stabilize its rule. This was similar to the strategies of "encasement" advocated by early neoliberals: blocking opposition to unpopular policies needed to liberate markets by removing these policies from public contestation and control.[80] But the antidemocratic ideal of encasement was not limited to neoliberals. The strategy of preventing interest groups and voters from overturning policies demanded by external authorities was used by actors of diverse ideological commitments to protect investments, prevent financial instability, and preserve capitalism. As we shall see, political elites sometimes willingly accepted this discipline to curb the power of their opponents at home. But this was always risky, since it provided an obvious line of attack on a sitting government: that it had sold out the national interests to foreign rivals and allowed a grave insult to national pride.

Organization of the Book

The history told here unfolds over six chapters. It opens with the origins of the first intergovernmental organizations to wield real powers over domestic economic policies. These were created during the First World War for the sake of the Allied war effort. After the war, they provided foundations for the economic organs of the League of Nations. The book then charts the development of the earliest and most effective powers of global economic governance: enforcing austerity, coordinating politically independent central banks, overseeing a small set of international development projects, and stabilizing commodity prices. Some of these powers long outlived their institutional origins; all remained in existence, at least in related forms, into the early twenty-first century. Each chapter considers a constitutive act—either of a new institution or a new set of powers at an existing institution, as well as the resistance it faced. This resistance was not always waged most successfully by labor or social movements. Powerful political actors, banks, and businesses also stoked antagonism to the outsider for their own ends—sometimes out of political convictions, sometimes to protect their narrow interests. The book concludes with the opening of a second wave of international economic institution-building in the 1940s, and with the creation of the IMF in particular. It shows how the Bretton Woods agreements did not conclusively result in a form of international economic cooperation without interference, but instead opened a new phase in struggles over whether this was possible at all. Despite efforts by some of its architects to ensure that the IMF could not intervene in the domestic fiscal and monetary policies of its members, the institution developed the powers to do so not long after it was established.

Chapter 1 opens in the last year of the First World War, when the Allied powers created wartime councils to manage the supply of raw materials, foodstuffs, and ships for their war effort against the Central Powers. Over the course of 1918, some of these bodies developed unprecedented powers to coordinate the policies of wartime national economic ministries; others set prices and made purchases of primary commodities, such as nitrates from Chile, a Latin American neutral that experienced extensive encroachments on its economic sovereignty during the war. In 1918–1919, an array of public and private actors in Europe and the United States—from governments and businesses to socialist parties and women's movements—hoped these bodies could be transformed into a postwar institution that controlled resources, whether to implement economic sanctions against Germany or to take charge of postwar reconstruction. But the most ambitious versions of these ideas floundered in the face of opposition from US businesses, the Wilson administration, and ultimately British authorities as well, who claimed that these plans threatened to violate the sovereignty of the Allied empires. Nonetheless, these wartime efforts provided templates for many future experiments in international economic institution-building and laid direct foundations for the economic work of the League of Nations.

Chapter 2 shows how the League of Nations Economic and Financial Organization, while formally prohibited from interfering in the domestic affairs of member states, developed powers to do so in the 1920s by innovating new forms of conditional lending. The League implemented financial stabilization loans that involved the empowerment of foreign advisers to enforce programs of austerity. What had once been a form of foreign financial control reserved for sovereign debtors outside Europe, or on its supposedly underdeveloped Balkan periphery, was now extended to other parts of Europe, particularly to the lands of the vanquished Central Powers. This led to resistance wherever it was attempted, such as in Albania and Austria, as well as where it was suggested and rejected, such as in Portugal, Yugoslavia, Poland, and Liberia. Anxious comparisons were drawn between the kinds of states that could expect to enjoy real autonomy on the basis of their confessional, political, and "civilizational" status. But a new and lasting practice of international governance was born.

The creation of the Bank for International Settlements in 1929–1930, an important innovation in the history of global economic governance, is the subject of Chapter 3. On the eve of the global Depression, this institution attempted to coordinate the work of national central banks beyond the control or oversight of national governments and to replace aspects of the German reparations regime that were widely criticized for allowing foreign actors to interfere in domestic German economic affairs. The establishment of this bank involved a double demand for delegation: First, governments were to affirm that national central banks could operate free from their control, and then that these banks could work with their foreign counterparts to shape policies with potentially major domestic consequences. But the idea of turning central bank independence into a norm of international organization was opposed by right and left parties across Europe and elsewhere, who claimed their governments were leaving domestic spaces defenseless against the reach of unaccountable bankers. These disputes turned on a question with vital stakes for norms of sovereignty: Who, in the end, had the final say over monetary policy—governments or "nonpolitical" financial institutions?

Chapter 4 takes up the innovation of international development. While international development is more commonly associated with the Cold War, its origins can also be traced to the interwar period. This chapter looks at how the League of Nations undertook two very different projects of development in two very different member states—Greece and China—both of which raised fraught questions about how much more autonomy these countries with constrained sovereignty could be asked to relinquish in exchange for private development loans or technical assistance. In Greece, the settlement of more than a million Greek Orthodox refugees after the 1919–1922 war with Turkey and 1923 population exchange entailed an extraordinary degree of external involvement in Greek affairs. This led to conflict with the Greek government and the refugees themselves, from whom repayment for the loan was demanded. In the early 1930s, the elaboration of a League development project in Nationalist China, by contrast, was not paired with any major international loan, in part due to the resistance posed by the Nationalist government to any further erosion of Chinese sovereignty. While these two early international development programs were distinct in their aims, they both involved similar conflicts over how an international institution could channel private capital for development and empower foreign experts to oversee its use.

Chapter 5 focuses on the final interwar innovation in economic governance: the regulation of the global production and exchange of commodities. The first successful experiment with this form of governance was with tin—a valuable raw material produced predominantly in British colonial territories, Malaya above all. It involved the creation of an international institution to coordinate the enforcement of strict production controls by member governments, both in colonies and sovereign states. It was resisted by the British and Chinese private firms it threatened, the workers it threw out of employment, and the colonial authorities that were pressured by interest groups to remove regulations that benefitted foreign governments and business competitors. But this too was a lasting innovation: After 1945, such controls were used to regulate the prices of many different goods, most famously by OPEC with oil. They were widely advocated as a means of improving the terms of trade faced by commodity exporting countries, largely in the Global South. The case of tin marked another departure in the politics of interference: By allowing the economic policy of British colonies like Malaya to be put into the hands of an international institution, even one dominated by London, the resources of colonial territories were opened to the involvement of non-British governments and businesses.

In Chapter 6, the book revisits efforts in the 1940s to create a new set of international economic institutions, with a focus on the IMF. The beginning of this second wave of institution-building involved continued struggles over the meaning of legitimate international cooperation and illegitimate violations of sovereignty. In the years following the First World War, it was largely countries with partial sovereignty or the vanquished that faced the prospect of interference; now, in a recasting of global hierarchies, it was the United Kingdom itself. This chapter shows how the well-known context of the Bretton Woods negotiations opened a new phase in disputes about what constituted "meddling." Soon after the end of the Second World War, the IMF began to wield leverage over the fiscal and monetary policies of various member states, and in ways that some of its architects had hoped it would avoid. It did not take the rise of neoliberalism for these powers to be deployed. They had always been latent in the IMF's design. These powers would subsequently be developed more fully in practices of conditional lending and, later, structural adjustment.

The question of how to differentiate coercive meddling from voluntary international economic cooperation, which became a crucial feature of international politics in 1918, continued for decades to come—even as different international regimes rose and fell and global capitalism itself underwent dramatic transformations. The four major new powers of global economic governance first developed in the 1920s and 1930s—enforcing austerity, coordinating the policies of independent central banks, providing loans and expertise for development projects, and regulating commodity prices—proved highly adaptable to later contexts.

To understand the political origins of these powers, this book focuses on institutions that had some governmental or central bank involvement. It also focuses on their efforts to develop control over domestic policies, rather than on other less interventionist endeavors characteristic of pre-1914 forms of internationalism, such as collecting data, organizing conferences, or standardizing regulations. Some of these institutions were strictly intergovernmental, others had quasi-private public forms; some had broad portfolios, others more specific "functionalist" aims. What institutions like the League's Financial Committee, the Bank for International Settlements, and intergovernmental commodity organizations all shared, however, was their ability to shape domestic economic policies with far-reaching public effects, whether concerning fiscal and monetary policy or commodity production. The same was not true of private organizations like cartels or institutions handling legal and regulatory problems about workers' rights, intellectual property, or infrastructure—at least not to the same extent. One area of policy that remained much harder to influence during these years was trade. States remained more sovereign over trade than they did over finance. While the League attempted to facilitate a return to freer trade, its efforts had limited immediate results other than concerning a handful of specific regulatory issues. The organization struggled with the hard problem of tariffs.[81] For decades to come, trade remained one of the most challenging areas of policy for international institutions, in large part due to the explosive domestic political conflicts it involved. At the end of the Second World War, proposals for an International Trade Organization were defeated, leaving GATT, a legal agreement with a bare-bones secretariat, as alternative until the creation of the WTO a half century later.

This history of the birth and evolution of global economic governance offers a new way to understand the shifting terrain of international hierarchies during the first half of the twentieth century. These processes of institution-building revealed and reconfigured inequalities of status and power, as countries that allowed intervention into their domestic economies showed their condition to be one of sovereignty without standing. Initially, the states where the League of Nations could exercise real economic power were limited to those with partial, novel, or contested sovereignty. These included the vanquished—Austria, Bulgaria, and Hungary; new states, particularly those that had already been under international administration, like Albania; and ones with restricted sovereignty, like Greece and China. At the beginning of this era, the British Empire refused to allow any arrangement that allowed outside bodies to intervene in metropolitan or colonial economic affairs. But over time, some of these barriers began to weaken. By the early 1940s, the British Parliament accepted US designs for an IMF that entailed the possibility of more international involvement in the political economy of the United Kingdom than ever before. Tracing the changing politics of interference thus offers a way to chart the decline of British power, the rise of US power, and the shifting status and capacities of many other states caught between the poles of this process of hegemonic transition.[82] It also shows how the original asymmetry of this form of international governance ensured it would face a lasting problem of legitimacy.

Another aim of this story is to recast how we understand the period that follows its conclusion. The two and a half decades after the end of the Second World War have long been seen as an era of "embedded liberalism," when the Bretton Woods system allowed states a large degree of national autonomy to undertake national experiments in social welfare and Keynesianism while maintaining some openness to the world economy.[83] There are several reasons to regard this description of the world with some skepticism. After 1945, much of the world continued to reside within the bounds of colonial empires, not sovereign nation-states, where there was little policy autonomy to speak of. Countries that achieved formal independence rarely saw their new legal status translate immediately into freedom from external pressures. Moreover, few countries followed the rules of the Bretton Woods agreements until well into the 1950s, and the entire arrangement was discarded in the early 1970s.[84] Most of all, the new Bretton Woods institutions never, in practice, gave up powers to reach into internal policies. Almost as soon as the IMF began to provide financial assistance to member states, particularly in Latin America, their receipt of aid was made conditional on austere and anti-inflationary reforms. Even after the classical gold standard was abandoned, some countries thus continued to face external disciplinary pressures, now enforced by intergovernmental institutions exercising discretionary judgments that were inescapably political. Stark depictions of the caesura between the international regimes of embedded liberalism and neoliberalism risk understating these continuities and reifying a myth of a golden era of autonomy that never existed.

This book explains how the economic borders between the domestic and the international were clarified, contested, and consolidated during an era of imperial warfare, capitalist crisis, and self-determination. These were struggles over whether new international institutions could embody universal ideals of internationalism, even as they repackaged old tools of empire and affirmed existing global hierarchies. What this history shows is how efforts to govern the world economy have long been jeopardized by problems of legitimacy and violations of autonomy. As such, it reminds us how difficult it has always been to achieve real international cooperation, but also how dangerous giving up on it can be.

CHAPTER I

Managing the Global Economy during the First World War

THE OUTBREAK OF THE First World War appeared to bring an era of global economic integration to a disastrous end.[1] The establishment of wartime exchange controls, the suspension of the gold standard, and the weaponization of commerce severed ties that linked merchants and bankers around the world and precipitated a slump in the total volume of global trade, which had grown exponentially in the decades before. But the war itself was also a profoundly global event. It was waged with soldiers, workers, and resources from around the world and led to the establishment of the first international institutions to wield real governmental powers over the global capitalist system.[2]

These institutions emerged out of imperial efforts to organize the world economy for the sake of the Allied war effort against the Central Powers. They were established over the course of the war, and with accelerated speed in 1918, to ensure the Allies a steady supply of energy resources, raw materials, and food, and an efficient means of arranging their transport from all corners of the earth. Well before the outbreak of the war, it had become obvious that the dependence of European powers on overseas sources of important goods left them vulnerable to blockade.[3] During the First World War, Britain exploited this vulnerability by targeting Germany with a comprehensive seaborne strategy of resource denial; Germany countered with a campaign of submarine warfare designed to starve Britain into defeat before it brought the United States into the war. With the resumption of unrestricted attacks on Allied and neutral shipping by German U-boats in early 1917, competition between the Allies over scarce goods and ships began to jeopardize their war effort. Waging total war in a globalized world economy required radically new institutions. The innovation of the Allies was to replace the market-driven allocation of goods and ships with a system of government purchasing, price-fixing, distribution, and transport. This was, in effect, a system of international economic planning. After the United States entered the war, this system provided an institutional framework for managing what was, until that point, the single greatest concentration of economic power in human history. It offered the Allies a crucial strategic advantage and laid the foundations for the first postwar experiments in governing the world economy.[4]

These Allied arrangements raised fraught questions about the degree of autonomy that governments were willing to relinquish and the sacrifices that they could be expected to demand of private interests. Conflict broke out among governments over the stakes of opening metropolitan and colonial resources, merchant shipping, and the activities of domestic firms to the reach of other powers. Private firms, chafing under new regulations, fought against them. Still, many in the European Allied countries saw these bodies as laying the foundations for something new: a postwar international institution that could be used to enforce economic sanctions against Germany, facilitate industrial reconstruction, and prevent unemployment at home. Such an institution would need to exercise real powers over the domestic economic policies of sovereign states: setting prices for strategic resources, deciding export and import rules, and coordinating global transport. Whether these arrangements would be possible or desirable after the emergency conditions of the war had passed was a question that affected governments, businesses, and workers from Europe to Latin America, and that led to disputes among liberals, socialists, and conservatives.

By 1920, however, the transformation of the wartime Allied bodies into a postwar international institution had, in part, been realized. These bodies provided a direct institutional foundation for the creation of the Economic and Financial Organization of the League of Nations—the world's first peacetime intergovernmental economic institution.[5] But this transformation played out in ways that were distinct from what many had imagined during the war. The League inherited from the wartime bodies new procedures for intergovernmental cooperation: the coordination of national bureaucracies through a standing international body that did not itself wield executive powers over domestic policy-making. This form of intergovernmental cooperation lay at the heart of the League's many technical agencies, as well as future institutions of the European Union; it was no coincidence that one of founders of the Allied system, Jean Monnet, later became one of the pioneers of European integration.[6] Yet this foundational moment of technocratic internationalism also marked a significant departure and a chastening of ambitions. The creation of the League involved the abandonment of far more interventionist plans for a system of international resource control that would have entailed an unprecedented degree of external involvement in the domestic production and trade policies of the resource-rich Allied empires and the United States.

Allied economic cooperation in 1918 offered postwar planners two competing lessons. First, the international coordination of national bureaucracies could be used to solve complex international economic problems in ways that could be sold to national governments anxious about foreign interference in their domestic affairs. Second, an international institution controlling global supplies of raw materials and foodstuffs could be used as a powerful tool to punish enemies and reward friends. After the war, the League of Nations was designed with the first lesson in mind, in part to avoid the sacrifices demanded by the second. The birth of the first peacetime institution of global economic governance was made possible only once its jurisdictional reach was clarified: It would not be permitted to encroach on the domestic affairs of the Great Powers, even as they continued to exercise similar powers over many other countries around the world.

The Evolution of Inter-Allied Economic Cooperation

Wartime Allied experiments in controlling global trade and shipping were inaugurated in response to the unprecedented logistical challenges of an industrialized conflict that was waged from East Africa to Flanders to Mesopotamia and that by 1918 had come to involve nearly every sovereign country on the earth. They were made possible by the prior expansion of national economic powers in all major European belligerents, as well as in the colonial territories of the Allied empires. This process began in 1914–1915. As hopes for a short conflict fizzled, attritional warfare along the Western Front required extraordinary levels of industrial mobilization. In August 1914, a raw materials office was set up in the Prussian War Ministry under the German industrialist Walther Rathenau to requisition and allocate goods for war production. It is widely considered the world's first experiment in national economic planning.[7] In Britain and France, new ministries were created in 1915 to direct the production of munitions after a severe shortage of shells exposed the need for further government intervention in industry. As the war continued, states developed additional economic powers, including controls over imports and exports, shipping, and supplies of food and raw materials. New forms of taxation were introduced. Central banks, many of which had long enjoyed de facto political independence, were mobilized to help finance the costs of war. This was true in the United States as well. After it joined the war in April 1917, Bernard Baruch, a financier and adviser to Woodrow Wilson, was put in charge of a controversial public-private institution to coordinate US industrial mobilization: the War Industries Board.[8]

The Allied powers gradually coordinated some of these national economic controls to establish new forms of intergovernmental economic cooperation. This was done in response to two related problems: first, the inflation of prices for key goods caused by competitive purchasing between the Allies; and second, a shortage of ships needed to transport raw materials; food; energy resources; and later, US troops to Europe. The first Allied supply organization was created at the beginning of the war to coordinate Allied orders for purchases in Britain in order to prevent competitive bidding from pushing up the prices of important goods too high. Another was set up in 1916 to arrange the joint purchase, allocation, and transportation of wheat. The so-called Wheat Executive was designed, as one French account later put it, to replace a "chaotic system" with "a rational and complete organization."[9] As the war became more complex in 1917–1918, controlling global supply chains moved to the center of Allied strategy.

The development of new institutions of inter-Allied economic cooperation accelerated in 1917 as the lethality of the German submarine campaign led to a crisis of Allied shipping. Throughout the war, France and Italy had relied heavily on Britain's merchant fleet to carry their imports. In the first months of 1917, the resumption of unrestricted submarine warfare complicated the ad hoc provision of British ships. Even after the development of the convoy system later that year reduced losses of tonnage, unexpectedly poor harvests in France and Italy exacerbated these countries' dependence on imports of food. The US entry into the war in April 1917 threatened to place additional burdens on transport. That summer, French officials pleaded with their British counterparts to establish a system for pooling all available ships according to need.[10] They claimed that France faced the prospect of a "food revolution" that would force it out of the war—a clear reference to the revolution that had broken out that winter among a Russian population radicalized by hunger. From the vantage point of the British War Cabinet, the dire situation faced by France and Italy was fundamentally a problem of shipping. Any solution to it required a tough choice between prioritizing the feeding of civilians or the supply of raw materials and munitions.[11]

The French request for a shipping pool reflected the importance by 1917 of controlling the seas, and the resources carried across them, to a conflict that is remembered most vividly as a grinding war of attrition in the trenches.[12] While solving these supply problems was critical to Allied success, the French request had dramatic implications for the British Empire. It was, in effect, a demand for Britain to relinquish full sovereign control over a principal source of its national strength: its unrivaled shipping capacity. At first, the British government rebuffed this demand. But in late 1917, an agreement was reached with France and Italy to allocate Allied shipping according to national food-import requirements. A more extensive system of shipping control involving the US government was finalized in the final weeks of the year. At inter-Allied meetings in Paris, which took place just after the Bolsheviks seized power in Petrograd, an agreement was reached to establish an Allied shipping council. Its purpose was to arrange the most efficient allocation of all available tonnage on the basis of each country's import requirements, whether of raw materials, food, energy resources, or munitions.[13]

The plans for this organization were guided by the ideas of two young French and British technocrats. One was Jean Monnet, then in his twenties, who before the war had worked in his family's cognac business before joining the French state and becoming an influential deputy to the minister of commerce, Étienne Clémentel. The other was Arthur Salter, an ambitious career civil servant in his thirties, who had risen up the ranks of the British Admiralty and Ministry of Shipping. Their efforts to create the Allied Maritime Transport Council were guided by a simple but profound insight: It was easier to deal with international economic problems if they were removed from the politicized domain of diplomacy and given to ostensibly nonpolitical bureaucrats who could coordinate their work across national lines. Their attempts to put this insight into practice launched their intertwined, decades-long careers, as they became the leading lights of a generation of European economic internationalists—collaborating as architects in the foundation and early economic work of the League of Nations, overseeing development work in Nationalist China, and again managing problems of Allied supply and shipping during the Second World War.[14]

Their first act of collaboration in 1917–1918 involved navigating a thorny political question: how to create an international institution powerful enough to be effective on the national level without appearing to threaten governments with the prospect of foreign involvement in domestic policies that implicated problems of security or distribution. While the British had been the first to drag their feet over plans for a shipping pool when the French proposed it in the summer of 1917, it was the Wilson administration that objected most vehemently to any organization that wielded executive powers over the US government. During the Paris negotiations, US delegates, led by one of Wilson's closest advisers, Edward House, insisted that no government would ever willingly give up any control of its nationals' ships to another. The "surrender of ships by one nation to another" was "both unpalatable and difficult," as the US Shipping Board official Bainbridge Colby echoed this point. While the Americans moved closer to the more ambitious plans of their European counterparts, they refused to consider an intergovernmental body to which Washington relinquished real powers. In addition to threatening US sovereignty, this body would be out of touch with national administrations, they claimed, and lack the legitimate authority to work effectively. The agreement reached in Paris was thus limited by the fact that neither government was willing to "delegate absolute power to dispose of its tonnage . . . to a representative on an International Board on which he might be out-voted." The Allied shipping committee, while voicing the needs of France and Italy, would not be allowed to interfere with British or US decisions about how to employ the ships under their national control.[15]

When the Allied Maritime Transport Council was inaugurated in London in March 1918, it was designed to appease such fears about foreign actors making binding decisions over national policies. But it was not a toothless advisory body. It provided a forum where officials of ministerial rank with responsibility for supply and shipping policies from each major Ally could collectively plan the most economical use of Allied ships based on need and availability. Because these officials were in charge of national ministries, the decisions they reached together could be executed on the domestic level with relative ease. The British members, for example, were the minister of shipping, the Glaswegian shipping magnate Joseph Maclay, and the minister of blockade, Robert Cecil. The French were the minister of munitions, Louis Loucheur, and the minister of commerce, Clémentel. The reason this institution wielded any powers at all was because of the authority vested in these national ministries, which by 1918 had come to wield extraordinary command over the Allied war economies. Coordinating their work was relatively straightforward once proper lines of communication were established between them—though in the case of US members, this was complicated by the delay and confusion that came from transmitting decisions for approval across the Atlantic and by the suspicion with which Wilson regarded this European-dominated body in London.[16] As the remit of this system expanded, its US members had to gingerly remind Wilson that no inter-Allied committee would ever be given the power to "control policies."[17]

The council also gathered and shared economic information in ways that had never before been attempted on this scale. While the council of cabinet-level ministers met only a few times before the war ended, an executive body run by Salter, Monnet, the Italian diplomat Bernardo Attolico, and the Wilson adviser George Rublee oversaw the routine work of planning and adjusting the allocation of Allied ships on the basis of data provided by governments that normally guarded such information jealously (or in some cases, barely collected it all). This information included detailed estimates of total imports and shipping requirements.[18] Responsibility for putting the decisions of the council and executive into effect was given to a standing secretariat, which was designed to be an international bureaucracy staffed by individuals who were to "divest themselves of any national point of view."[19] To allocate shipping across more efficient routes, the location of all British, Allied, and neutral ships was tracked with a color-coordinated card catalog system provided by the British Ministry of Shipping. It was so large that it occupied an entire floor of a large building and required an around-the-clock staff to keep it updated.[20] Information was collected from many sources, including telegrams from naval and intelligence officers and customs officials from ports around the world. These statistics were tabulated into a balance sheet of Allied shipping, showing availability against need, which was used to direct ships to the most dire shortages.[21] It functioned as an analogue computer for the Allied war machine—or, as the head of the US Shipping Board Edward Hurley later described it, a "single set of brains."[22] It was used to solve logistical problems of supply and transport that, left in private hands, would have compounded the delay and waste jeopardizing the Allied war effort.

This Allied shipping council never became an "economic generalissimo," as Salter later explained.[23] What he meant was that it lacked the power wielded by the French general Ferdinand Foch over the joint Allied military command. But still, it was a radical innovation. It was empowered to crack open the black boxes of sovereign states and colonies and use the information it gathered about the worldwide distribution of resources, the supply requirements of each Ally, and the location of Allied and neutral ships to coordinate the work of national ministries that were themselves of unprecedented power. In some ways, the problems it dealt with were no different from those of any major war: how to overcome shortages, geography, and the logistical complexities of transport. But never before had responsibility for solving these problems been handed to an international bureaucracy that made decisions affecting the economic well-being of millions of people around the world. In early 1918, the Allies had created the first intergovernmental system of economic planning for the sake of an industrialized war on a global scale. This system involved inter-imperial controls over the sinews of shipping and trade that before 1914 would have been unthinkable. The assumptions it was premised on were that national policies could be coordinated without being directed by an external authority and that supply problems could be depoliticized for the sake of a shared aim.[24] This was the dream of economic internationalism: cooperation, coordination, and the control of knowledge and resources. But it turned out that the specter of politics was far more difficult to exorcise than the architects of this system had imagined.

The Powers of the Raw Material Executives

As Allied economic cooperation moved from the coordination of shipping to the purchase of specific commodities, it began to generate greater friction among governments and private firms. At the same time, a new vision of managing the global exchange of raw materials and foodstuffs took shape. During 1918, along with the inter-Allied shipping council, a series of commodity bodies were established to coordinate national import programs to free up shipping, mitigate shortages, and prevent US credits from being wasted on a war effort that was heavily financed by Americans.[25] Some of these bodies were authorized to make joint purchases of scarce goods to prevent their prices from rising further and to decide allocation among the Allies.[26] In the summer of 1918, the committees handling foodstuffs were put under the authority of US Food

Administrator Herbert Hoover, who had spent the first years of the war heading international food relief efforts for German-occupied Belgium. Committees dealing with munitions and raw materials were put under the control of an inter-Allied Munitions Council, run mostly by members of the European munitions councils, including the British minister of munitions, Winston Churchill, and his deputy, Walter Layton, an economist and former editor of *The Economist* magazine.[27] These commodity bodies posed more difficult questions than the shipping council did about whether external bodies could reach into sensitive domestic realms of business, trade policy, strategic resource control, and colonial administration.

These controversies first became clear with the establishment of a raw material executive in early 1918 to deal exclusively with a single neutral country in South America: Chile. This executive was designed to control the purchasing and allocation of nitrate, a crucial raw material for the manufacture of explosives and agricultural fertilizers. Nearly all of the world's supply of natural nitrate came from the Atacama Desert of northern Chile. While a process for fixing atmospheric nitrogen developed by the German chemist Fritz Haber allowed the Central Powers to overcome their dependence on overseas sources of this good, equivalent efforts by the Allies were not as successful. This left them reliant on Chilean sources of a raw material that was indispensable for the industrial production of explosives. As the war progressed, competition among importers and speculators for this key resource drove up its price.[28] A breakdown in the flow of Chilean nitrates to Europe threatened to have serious effects, potentially crippling the supply of explosives to the Allied forces.[29] By January 1918, nitrate stocks in France were estimated to last for only a month; in Italy, for a few days.[30]

At the inter-Allied meetings in Paris where the agreement for the Allied shipping council had been reached, a decision was also taken to create a Nitrate of Soda Executive in London to control the purchase of all Chilean nitrate at fixed prices for Allied use. It was to be staffed by government representatives of the European Allies and the United States but headed by a private merchant, Herbert Gibbs of Antony Gibbs & Sons, a British firm that had long played a leading role in the Chilean nitrate trade. By joining the executive, countries agreed to prevent their nationals from making any purchases of nitrate that did not go through their representative on this body. The total global supply of this raw material was considered a pool from which each country was assigned a quota. Through the "mutual consent" of its member governments, the executive could reduce the quota allotted to each member as dictated by overall needs and the availability of sources and ships.[31] The executive was also authorized to collect data from each member on its consumption and recommend measures to economize. While such recommendations did not come with powers of enforcement, this innovation was nonetheless significant: an intergovernmental board was to monitor the domestic use of a strategic raw material and suggest policy adjustments for the sake of a collective aim. As with the Allied shipping council, the creation of the Nitrate of Soda Executive was made possible by a corresponding extension of economic controls on the national level. In Britain, the Ministry of Munitions had declared in October 1917 that all dealing in nitrates was prohibited without license.[32] In the United States, a public-private nitrate committee, made up of representatives of importers, was set up under the War Industries Board to coordinate imports and distribution and to arrange transport.[33]

The Nitrate of Soda Executive was a remarkable institution. It was a London-based international body, headed by a powerful British merchant, that was authorized to directly purchase Chilean nitrates at prices it fixed, or, in the case of US importers, to approve or deny purchases made by private companies.[34] In the US case, allowing purchasing to remain in private hands was a concession to the chemical companies DuPont; Wessel, Duval, and Company; and W. R. Grace. These companies were reassured that their positions in the Chilean trade would not be jeopardized, though their activities would now need to be approved and overseen by Gibbs.[35] This arrangement still led to great frustration among these companies, which played significant roles in the war effort.[36] For DuPont, the war was incredibly profitable, as demand rose precipitously for its munitions-related products. But the war also led to increasingly difficult relations with the Wilson administration.[37] The creation of the Nitrate Executive joined the company's list of grievances. Its representatives claimed that empowering Gibbs would force US companies to play second fiddle to a foreign rival that could use the executive's powers to drive them out of business.[38] This complaint, as we shall see, became one of the sticking points about this institution. In Britain, importers also balked at the executive's power to sell to their customers at lower prices than they could offer. As it took centralized control over a once-free market, it would put dealers and merchants out of business.[39] To prevent Gibbs from becoming too powerful, US officials insisted that his duties be limited to those of a transmitting agent for purchases that were otherwise conducted as ordinary commercial transactions.[40]

A magazine produced by DuPont celebrating the company's role in the US war effort.
Hagley Museum and Library.

Another reason this international executive was so controversial was because Chilean nitrate was also in high demand among US agricultural producers. When the executive was established, US officials insisted that 100,000 tons be specially earmarked for the exclusive use of the Department of Agriculture.[41] This rule was included because of a recent amendment to a law advocated by the South Carolina Democratic Senator Ellison D. Smith, an arch segregationist and defender of cotton interests, which forced the Department of Agriculture to purchase a set amount of nitrate to make available to cotton growers.[42] Allocating this good for European munitions manufacture involved the executive acting through its US member, Robert Skinner, to compel US authorities to "take away nitrates from farmers," as one British official put it bluntly.[43] This placed Skinner in the position of asking his own government to prioritize European munitions manufacturing over the demands of a powerful domestic interest group.[44]

The most extensive powers of the Nitrate of Soda Executive, however, were those it exercised over the Chilean government and national economy. By combining all purchasing of Chilean nitrate under one roof, it effectively became the sole customer for Chile's most important product. Alongside the by-product of iodine, nitrate accounted for almost 80 percent of the country's total exports on the eve of the war, which provided a major source of foreign earnings that were used to settle debts and purchase imports. Taxes on nitrate exports also provided around 50 percent of government revenue.[45] The executive attempted to push down the price of nitrate and threatened to cease purchases if its demands were not met. This led to resistance in Chile. Private producers, led by the Compañía de Salitres de Antofagasta, lobbied the government to take control of the sale of domestic stocks and begin negotiations with the executive to reach a higher price. These talks, led by Churchill on the Allied side, continued until war's end. This arrangement also provided leverage for the Allied governments to pressure the Chilean government into requisitioning German ships held in Chilean ports. They backed up this demand with threats to halt purchases, while recognizing their bluff could be called, given the dependence of Allied munition production on this one raw material. The British and US governments also blacklisted a large number of German firms in Chile and cut off imports of oil and jute to force them out of business.[46]

The wartime economic measures exercised by Britain and the United States over this South American neutral generated hostility for the violations of economic sovereignty that they involved. Like many countries in the region, Chile was profoundly affected by a war it never joined. The outbreak of hostilities in the summer of 1914 led to a serious financial crisis and widespread unemployment. The German market for Chilean nitrate, the largest before the war, was cut off by the blockade, leading to a slump in prices and production. By late 1915, Allied demand for nitrate had pulled Chile out of depression. But this had demonstrated how much the Chilean state and national economy depended on external demand for this single commodity. As in most Latin American countries, foreign companies controlled the production and marketing of large quantities of Chilean natural resources, which made this neutral country, like neighboring Argentina, a site of extensive economic warfare. Before the war, British companies alone had produced almost half of Chile's nitrate exports.[47] The wartime penetration of British and US official and private power into Chile through the use of boycotts, blacklists, and blockades was thus not unlike the other kinds of foreign interference that Chile had long faced. What was so new in 1918 was that the nitrate market had, in effect, been put under the control of an international institution, which used its extraordinary powers of monopsony to pressure the government of Juan Luis Sanfuentes into agreeing to a

Nitrate workers in the Oficina Buenaventura in Tarapacá, Chile, January 1918. *Reproduction © Colección Museo Histórico Nacional.*

lower price for a commodity that it depended on heavily for revenue.[48] Even some US officials worried these "bulldosing methods" would alienate Chile. The Wheat Executive exercised similar powers when it became Argentina's sole customer by blocking grain sales to other countries. This was a new kind of international power. As those hoping to transform these wartime bodies into postwar international institutions soon discovered, this kind of power, wielded in this case over subordinate Latin American neutrals, could not be easily universalized as a practice of international cooperation at war's end—certainly not when it came to purchasing and distributing resources found within the borders of the United States or the British Empire.

But while the war was still raging, the establishment of the Nitrate of Soda Executive appeared to Allied officials to offer a means of preventing capitalist competition, unregulated and uncoordinated government purchasing, and speculation from raising the price of a scarce good so high that it imperiled the production of munitions and the overall war effort. Baruch called for the creation of equivalent bodies to handle

The other side of the global nitrate supply chain. Women loading a nitration pan for the manufacture of cordite in Gretna, Scotland, July 1918. *Science & Society Picture Library via Getty Images.*

the purchasing, allocation, and shipping of goods from all over the world, especially the various scarce raw materials over which the Allies competed—such as rubber, palm oil, platinum, manganese, mica, molybdenite, pyrites, and tin.[49]

Efforts to reach these agreements, however, led to controversies over questions of jurisdiction and profit. This was true for proposals for an executive to control tungsten, a metal used primarily to make high-speed tool steel. This executive was designed to eliminate competitive bidding and speculation from driving up tungsten prices, while freeing up scarce ships for other uses.[50] But the idea immediately faced resistance from private and public interests. US mining companies in Portugal, a country rich in tungsten deposits, fought against being forced to sell to France and Italy at prices lower than what they could fetch in the United States, where imports of Portuguese ores would now be embargoed. Earmarking the products of US-owned mines in Portugal for the exclusive use of France and Italy obviated the need for unnecessary trans-Atlantic passages. But representatives of US firms claimed this arrangement both hurt their profits and jeopardized their control over a strategic mineral. Taking orders from an institution designed to benefit French and Italian manufacturing meant admitting defeat to European competitors that for years had been attempting to prevent US mining companies from gaining a foothold in Portugal.[51]

The tungsten purchasing executive was also opposed by the Department of the Interior, the arm of the US federal government that was charged with strategic mineral policy.[52] Its members echoed private worries by denouncing an executive that allowed foreign governments to remove control from US firms: "the foreign trade for which we have been striving during the past ten or twelve years must now be either left in status quo or given up altogether," one official warned. Tungsten producers in South America would resist demands to sell at prices "arbitrarily fixed as if for children or dependents," which would jeopardize US commercial expansion southward.[53] This was precisely what the Nitrate Executive had done in Chile, where by fixing nitrate prices, it had put the Chilean government and economy into a deeper state of dependency.

Questions of jurisdiction also became sources of conflict. In the case of neutral countries like Chile with a long history of foreign interference, a single powerful executive could be established to direct purchasing and decide allocation of a key raw material. But this could not be done so easily for goods produced within the bounds of the Great Powers, whether in the United States or in British or French territories like India, Australia, and

Indochina. While the executive considered the world's total production of tungsten a "common pool" for Allied use, any tungsten that was found within the bounds of the British and French colonial empires was reserved exclusively for British or French use. The same was true for US sources.[54] Among the European Allies and the United States, domestic jurisdiction over resources was still considered inviolable. This left the proposed tungsten executive with powers to fix prices and direct purchases only in subordinate noncombatant countries like Bolivia or in semi-sovereign cobelligerents like China.[55]

Similar problems arose during negotiations for an international tin executive. Tin was used not only to manufacture the cans from which soldiers ate bully beef in the trenches, but also automobiles and various armaments, like artillery and grenades.[56] In the spring of 1918, Baruch proposed an inter-Allied tin bureau to supervise purchasing agents, fix prices, and decide national allocations to prevent competition over a raw material that, unlike most, was almost completely unavailable on US territory.[57] But unlike nitrate produced in neutral Chile, much of the world's supply of tin was produced in British colonies, such as Malaya. Its smelting and marketing were dominated by British firms. This made Baruch's proposal appear to British eyes as a US government plot to seize a dominant position in the Southeast Asian tin trade.[58] Alarms were raised by members of the Colonial Office, who opposed any international executive becoming directly involved in the domestic economic affairs of a colony. This went against the legal and diplomatic precedent of British colonies meriting complete insulation from the unwanted reach of rival empires. In the case of Malaya, the world's largest tin producer, the Colonial Office had established export controls to keep this strategic raw material out of German hands, which resulted in a significant expansion of metropolitan control over the colonial Malayan economy.[59] But the problem was not government intervention itself: It was giving an authority external to the empire influence over how the resources of a colony were stripped and fed into a war machine thousands of miles away. Malaya, in other words, did not have the same status as Chile, a sovereign neutral power in which foreign actors had long competed for influence. In Malaya, colonial capitalism and resource extraction were to be kept insulated from the reach of any other powers. To the Colonial Office, Baruch's proposal for an international body making purchases of Malayan resources at fixed prices was thus a nonstarter.[60] One member of the Colonial Office insisted that a colonial government could not be "asked to regulate any local industry in accordance with instructions emanating from any body or persons other than His Majesty's Government." The "allocation of Straits tin or of any other material produced in a British Colony by an inter-allied council, bureau, or committee is out of the question."[61] The British government agreed to a tin executive only with the assurance that it would have no executive powers over Malayan production. Instead, it would only appoint purchasing agents in neutral countries.[62]

These raw material executives entailed two fraught forms of interference. First, they restricted the autonomy of private firms to buy and sell without direction; and second, they laid claim to resources that metropolitan and colonial governments insisted were under their exclusive control. Both issues got folded into questions about postwar Anglo-American global commercial expansion and competition over resources, markets, and customers. Even at the height of wartime collaboration and technocratic enthusiasm for bringing governmental control over resources and markets, these issues were never far from the surface.

Postwar Planning for International Raw Materials Control

While there were clear signs during 1918 that the end of the war would bring renewed competition among the European Allies and the United States, many contemporaries nevertheless saw in the creation of these inter-Allied bodies the outlines of a postwar system of international economic cooperation. Like the many new state economic controls on the national level, these bodies appeared to augur a dramatic transformation in how governments planned and regulated the world economy. Between 1916 and 1919, the idea of establishing a system to control global raw material and food supplies was advocated by a wide range of actors in Europe and the United States. The supporters of this idea generally imagined two aims for this system: first, to threaten Germany with economic sanctions; and second, to supply countries with scarce goods at favorable prices to facilitate reconstruction and prevent unemployment. These two goals, it was hoped, could be combined in an institution that promised the carrot of aid and the stick of sanctions. But doing so required winning the support of domestic public and private interests, from which this institution would ask real sacrifices of autonomy and profit.

These plans evolved well before the establishment of the inter-Allied system, particularly in the context of discussions of a long-term economic war against Germany after the military conflict came to an end. This idea was popular in France among a broad array of public and private actors and in Britain among Conservative protectionists.[63] Proposals for a protracted economic offensive against Germany took on concrete form in the wake of an economic conference held in Paris in June 1916, where representatives of the Allied governments met to discuss the possibility of reshaping the rules of postwar trade to subordinate Germany and facilitate the economic cooperation and reconstruction of the Allies. The resolutions of the Paris conference called for new measures of trade discrimination against Germany, the exchange of raw materials among the Allies on favorable terms, and the exclusion of Germany from most-favored-nation treatment.[64] They were shaped by the vehemently anti-German views of the French minister of commerce, Clémentel, a career politician of the Radical Republican and Independent Radical parties who had risen through provincial offices until being appointed by Prime Minister Aristide Briand in late 1915 to take charge of the French war economy.[65] Throughout the war, Clémentel called for a system of Allied control over the global trade in primary products to pool goods at favorable prices and according to need. This system was supposed to aid French reconstruction and prevent what he and many in France and Britain feared were German expansionist aims, including the creation of a German-dominated imperial bloc, stretching from Belgium to the Middle East.[66] Up through the Paris Peace Conference of 1919, Clémentel advocated international raw material controls as the best way to weaken Germany and mitigate the decline of French power. While he described these plans in the language of a brutal imperial struggle, Clémentel was also an internationalist who sought to make these plans compatible with Wilson's vision of a league of nations.[67] It was only when these proposals were decisively rejected at the end of the war by the British and US governments that the French turned to reparations as an alternative means of containing Germany and rebuilding France.[68]

Before this point, the resolutions of the 1916 Paris conference were greeted with horror by liberal observers around the world, who saw them as signaling a decision to abandon free trade and divide the world into rival blocs.[69] In the United States, they led to panic among business elites, lawmakers, and members of the Wilson administration, who worried they were designed to contain the postwar expansion of the United States as much as that of Germany. To them, the Paris Resolutions were emblematic of the kind of European imperialism and protectionism to be overcome in the new postwar international order.[70] In Britain, support within

H. H. Asquith's Liberal government for the Paris Resolutions exacerbated a long-standing conflict between free traders and protectionists and contributed to a split in the Liberal Party that set the stage for Asquith's fall in late 1916.[71] Many Conservatives supported these ideas, however, and attempted to link patriotic anti-German feeling to proposals for a general tariff in order to produce broad support for an economically punitive peace.[72]

Despite their controversial nature, the Paris Resolutions shaped the context in which postwar planning unfolded in both countries. While France led the way in pushing for the most far-reaching approach to raw material controls, there was a clear audience in Britain for the idea of "weaponizing" Britain's control over the infrastructures of global exchange to weaken Germany.[73] Before the war, plans to effectively engineer Germany's economic collapse were debated at high levels of the government, led by the Admiralty, though after its outbreak, they were abandoned for narrower blockade plans.[74] In the wake of the Paris Economic Conference, radical visions returned. British debates about international raw material controls took place against the background of broader discussions about the postwar—concerning imperial preference, trade, and the courting of working-class support through promises to rebuild industry and prevent unemployment. In late 1917, a special War Cabinet committee set up under the conservative Irish Unionist politician Edward Carson, a fierce supporter of the Paris Resolutions, investigated how to use the emerging system of inter-Allied raw material controls to contain Germany and pressure it to quit the war and agree to Allied peace terms.[75] In 1912–1913, the Allied powers had accounted for nearly all of the world's production of cotton and nickel, as well as most of its rubber, wool, lead, copper, and petroleum. This meant they could, as one report put it, "cripple, or even completely paralyse, the restoration of German industry."[76]

Official reconstruction planning in Britain also began against the backdrop of debates about the Paris Resolutions. When Prime Minister David Lloyd George set up a Ministry of Reconstruction in the summer of 1917—designed in part to ensure working-class support was not lost to challengers from the left—its directorship was given to the left Liberal Christopher Addison. Until then, Addison had worked at the Ministry of Munitions on raw material problems, including on plans to establish an imperial system for controlling strategic minerals.[77] In the face of what was bound at war's end to be a dangerous shortage of goods like timber, sugar, cotton, tin, lead, and wheat, Addison's ministry proposed using an "inter-Allied Board" to prevent international competition from leading to inflation and thereby jeopardizing a return to normal economic life in Britain. Maintaining secure access to scarce raw materials was important to ensure that domestic manufacturing could absorb demobilized soldiers, which was key to preventing postwar economic instability from leading to unrest. This required the continuation and adaptation of wartime inter-Allied controls.[78] This was a rather different justification for these controls than the "anti-German economics" common in the government. But such ideas were put forward by the same civil servants working multiple briefs, such as Addison, who was also a member of Carson's Economic Offensive Committee.[79] The Ministry of Reconstruction similarly focused on how to use Allied controls to inflict profound economic distress on Germany by coordinating export licenses and joint purchasing arrangements to engineer the collapse of German agriculture.[80] Planning for reconstruction and protracted economic warfare went hand in hand.

These visions of raw materials controls were also crucial to the elaboration of wartime blueprints for a league of nations. Using economic sanctions as an enforcement mechanism for a league had been proposed since the beginning of the war by influential French and British advocates of a peacekeeping body.[81] When Clémentel attempted to win over Wilson to his plans for continued Allied raw material controls in late 1917, he described them as a humane tool for enforcing the rules of the league.[82] (Such efforts to "camouflage" the Paris Resolutions, however, were transparent to US observers.)[83] In Britain, the idea of an "economic weapon" was crucial to official league planning from late 1916, in large part due to the efforts of Robert Cecil, a free trade–supporting Conservative and parliamentary undersecretary of state for foreign affairs, who earlier that year had become minister of blockade (from which position he also served as member of the Allied Maritime Transport Council).[84] Other British backers of a league insisted that it inherit the "many-handed giant" of the inter-Allied economic organization, which held "in its grasp the economic power of nine-tenths of the world."[85] This was not only for the sake of an economic weapon, but also to ensure that member states were supplied with scarce raw materials and foodstuffs, at least for the period of reconstruction.[86]

These plans for empowering an international institution to control the global exchange of raw materials, energy resources, and foodstuffs, however, even if just for a limited period, were far more radical than many of their supporters openly admitted. Doing so required the perpetuation of import and export licensing regimes and shipping controls by national governments as well as by the governments of the Dominions and colonies. It also required the coordination of such regulations with other governments through a standing international bureaucracy and the marketing of commodities at fixed prices to countries in need. One memorandum by the Economic Offensive Committee suggested an inter-Allied council that monitored each country's trade to ensure it was conducted according to the export and import restrictions mandated by its government. Legally, such rules over imports and exports were widely considered matters of exclusive domestic jurisdiction, which meant this form of cooperation went well beyond the scope of any kind of prewar international economic cooperation. This system also necessitated the strengthening and centralization of government control over trade as well as the creation of new bureaus to estimate the national production and consumption of various commodities and to organize the internal distribution of the rationed goods. In their strongest form, such proposals, the memo admitted, demanded a "complete change of commercial and industrial opinion throughout the world."[87]

From the point of view of private companies, empowering a national government to enforce such regulations was hard enough to tolerate. The idea of allowing an external body to do so was yet more explosive. Why would the United States allow decisions about its vast wealth of resources and expanding maritime power to be made by an institution representing the interests of the British Empire, its principal rival on the seas and over the future of world trade? The maximalist French vision of this system was also clearly antithetical to basic liberal conceptions of trade. It was premised on the idea of commodities being redistributed by an international institution, not being bought and sold at prices determined by markets.[88] The US socialist Jessie Hughan put this point bluntly. The kind of wartime Allied executive on which a postwar institution would be based had functioned according to a "simple communist method:" allocating goods, she wrote, "to each according to his needs."[89] This kind of quasi-socialist internationalism was a very popular vision of international order in 1918–1919. But after the Clemenceau government was forced to drop it in early 1919, the idea lost its most powerful official sponsor. In any case, it was not yet guaranteed that plans for a league of nations would be successful. As we shall see, one of the reasons the architects of the League dropped ideas for raw material controls was to prevent the United States from abandoning the institution altogether. As soon as the war ended, traditional claims of a right to non-interference in domestic questions of resources, trade, and the regulation of business were mobilized to prevent any plans that entailed a far-reaching destabilization of the existing relationship of sovereignty, empire, and global capitalism.

Before this point, however, the remarkable evolution of the inter-Allied system in the last year of the war gave hope to its backers that a standing international economic institution was close to realization. What the foundation of a league of nations required, as the British War Cabinet member Maurice Hankey wrote in early 1918, was simply moving the existing inter-Allied bodies into a single enormous building, perhaps the Palace of Versailles. After all, Hankey wrote, the material foundations of a league were now in place: Allied control over "all trans-oceanic supplies and their transportation."[90]

The End of Controls after the War

When the war with Germany ended in November 1918, there was uncertainty about what would happen to the inter-Allied supply institutions. Clémentel continued to call for them to be turned into an "Atlantic Economic Union" of Western European and American democracies.[91] Without pooling scarce goods and providing favorable access to British and US resources and ships, inflation would jeopardize French reconstruction and the reincorporation of the economically valuable regions occupied by Germany.[92] The French and Italian governments had the most to gain from an international system of resource control. They made the loudest demands for it.

The British were unsure about the proper course of action. Whatever enthusiasm there had been in the War Cabinet about the Paris Resolutions and a punitive peace had been fading, as tensions with France resurfaced and the need to placate the Americans, who were antagonistic to these ideas, became more pressing.[93] But still, there was wide support in London for using the inter-Allied institutions to handle the transition to peace. Late that summer, Cecil had proposed merging the inter-Allied bodies into an overarching economic council, an idea the French government eagerly backed.[94] And there was much talk of the inter-Allied bodies forming a "skeleton" for the economic organization of a peacekeeping

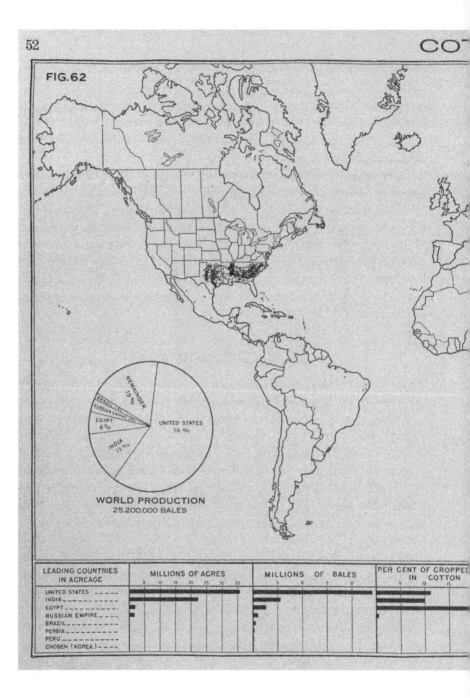

FIG. 62

WORLD PRODUCTION
25,200,000 BALES

UNITED STATES
58 %

INDIA
13 %

EGYPT
6 %

RUSSIAN EMPIRE 3%

BRAZIL 1.5%

REMAINDER
19 %

LEADING COUNTRIES IN ACREAGE	MILLIONS OF ACRES							MILLIONS OF BALES				PER CENT OF CROPPED IN COTTON			
	5	10	15	20	25	30	35	3	6	9	12	5	10	15	
UNITED STATES _ _ _ _ _ _															
INDIA _ _ _ _ _ _ _ _ _ _															
EGYPT _ _ _ _ _ _ _ _ _ _															
RUSSIAN EMPIRE _ _ _ _															
BRAZIL _ _ _ _ _ _ _ _ _															
PERSIA _ _ _ _ _ _ _ _ _															
PERU _ _ _ _ _ _ _ _ _ _															
CHOSEN (KOREA) _ _ _ _															

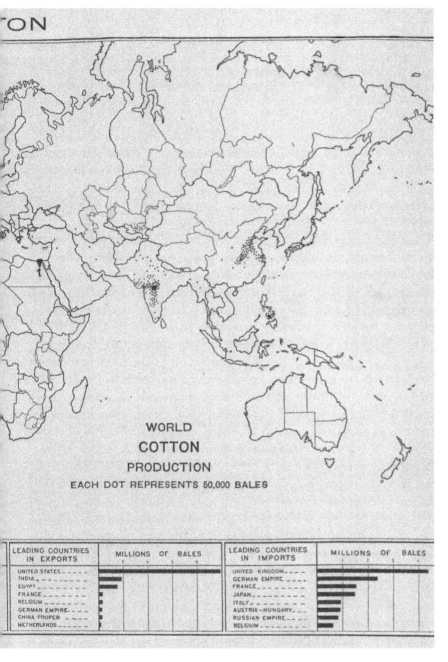

WORLD

COTTON

PRODUCTION

EACH DOT REPRESENTS 50,000 BALES

LEADING COUNTRIES IN EXPORTS	MILLIONS OF BALES				LEADING COUNTRIES IN IMPORTS	MILLIONS OF BALES			
UNITED STATES					UNITED KINGDOM				
INDIA					GERMAN EMPIRE				
EGYPT					FRANCE				
FRANCE					JAPAN				
BELGIUM					ITALY				
GERMAN EMPIRE					AUSTRIA-HUNGARY				
CHINA PROPER					RUSSIAN EMPIRE				
NETHERLANDS					BELGIUM				

Map published by the US Department of Agriculture in 1917 showing cotton production around the world. The US government paid close attention to problems concerning the global distribution of raw materials during the war. *US Department of Agriculture*, Geography of the World's Agriculture.

51

body.[95] But there was also anxiety in the British government about the nature of French demands. Just days before the armistice, one British member of the inter-Allied Munitions Council responded to a French suggestion for extending the council's powers by claiming this threatened to fasten "International Control on Trade and Industry for all time, before the Governments interested had even decided in principle whether such a policy were desirable." The continuation of any controls, moreover, depended on the support of the US government. And it was unlikely to want "to shackle its merchants and manufacturers and to prevent them from making profits to which, no doubt, they will consider themselves entitled."[96]

These suspicions were well founded. As soon as the war on the Western Front came to an end, Washington withdrew its support from the inter-Allied councils as quickly as possible. Wilson, poised to shape the peace settlement, did not want to be bound by the demands of needier European governments in any way that limited his freedom of action or that jeopardized the ideal of equality in postwar trade. Among US postwar planners, there were worries that the French government was attempting to win a US commitment to the Paris Resolutions, which were antithetical to Wilson's commitment to nondiscrimination in trade, "while the passions aroused by the war are hot."[97] Republican gains in congressional elections held just days before the armistice had, in any case, imperiled any ambitious plans for a postwar international economic institution. On November 16, Baruch set into motion the end of US participation in the nitrate and tin executives, and he called for the return of War Industries Board personnel from abroad.[98] Within months, most wartime controls in the United States were removed.[99]

The opposition of the US government to the continuation of Allied economic cooperation after the armistice was later seen as a kind of original sin of the interwar period, one that was emblematic of the Wilson administration's devotion to "economic unilateralism" and laissez faire and its unwillingness to back up the peace settlement with economic guarantees.[100] Even Wilson's faithful biographer and former press secretary, Ray Stannard Baker, admitted his boss had erred in demanding an end to the Allied experiment in "economic world government."[101] The US government's abandonment of these institutions provided a cautionary tale to internationalists for years to come and a lesson about how to shape a more stable peace after the next world war.[102] In the 1940s, some US postwar planners claimed that Wilson's refusal to consider continued Allied economic cooperation had been a tragic mistake.[103]

A long backward glance from the Second World War to the First, however, and accounts of Wilson's decision that see it in terms of a broader narrative about US unilateralism, risk understating how radical these European designs really were. The aim of the French Ministry of Commerce was to create institutions that allowed the French state to make privileged claims on US resources and ships. This would have involved a system of price fixing and import and export controls that jeopardized the bottom line and autonomy of US businesses. These plans entailed a much further degree of external involvement in US domestic markets and policy-making than what the Roosevelt administration would agree to in the 1940s, at the height of US internationalism. Hoover articulated official opposition to these ideas in a message he sent to House just days before the armistice: "After peace over one-half of the whole export of food supplies of the world will come from the United States and for the buyers of these supplies to sit in majority in dictation to us as to prices and distribution is wholly inconceivable. The same applies to raw materials."[104] Continued Allied cooperation also imperiled the global expansion of US commercial and strategic power. After the war, Britain was as much a competitor as a partner—certainly from the vantage point of US firms eager to wrest customers and markets from their British rivals and to remove the shackles that prevented them from doing so. Both governments had prepared for a postwar struggle for commercial dominance, particularly in Latin America.[105] In the case of nitrate, the US Departments of State and Commerce sought to ensure that US firms were well positioned to displace their British competitors in Chile—a strategic aim that had shaped the establishment of the Nitrate of Soda Executive in the first place. Just days after the armistice, a member of Wessel, Duval, and Company wrote to Chandler Anderson, general consul to the War Industries Bord, to demand an end to this arrangement. He warned Anderson that Gibbs was using the executive to cement control over the Chilean nitrate trade in perpetuity, leaving US companies to pay "tribute" to him. The British Board of Trade, he claimed, had aimed all along to use this body to give British firms an upper hand in Chile.[106] These complaints were taken seriously. The executive was to be disbanded as soon as its business for the year was finished.[107]

Yet there were pockets of support for continued international economic cooperation, at least for the period of reconstruction, in and around the wartime US state, particularly among the economic and scientific experts advising the Wilson administration. Members of the American Section of the Allied Maritime Transport Council joined their European colleagues in supporting the creation of a "General Economic Board" as the war approached its end. They wrote missives back to the United States about the dangers of allowing inter-Allied cooperation to give way to Anglo-American competition.[108] One of the two economists that Wilson brought to the Paris Peace Conference, the Harvard professor Frank Taussig, urged the president in October 1918 to establish an international board to allocate scarce goods like tin, rubber, and cotton among the Allies, neutrals, and Central Powers to prevent competition from raising prices to dangerous levels.[109] The geologist brought to the Paris Peace Conference, C. K. Leith, was similarly disappointed when Wilson rejected European plans to ration scarce minerals. But Leith recognized that the United States, which boasted an export surplus in most raw materials, would have to make the greatest sacrifices for this new kind of international cooperation.[110] Though some in the United States continued to dream of a new era of economic internationalism, the reality of the wartime institutions was that they had depended on external intervention in domestic economic policies that the US government was never likely to accept at war's end. The institutions with the most extensive powers to control the purchasing and distribution of raw materials had been applicable only to non-European neutrals, moreover—certainly not to a US empire on the rise.

The Legacies of the Wartime System

The institutions of international economic cooperation that were established after 1918 were to be quite different from these wartime visions. This became clear by the summer of 1919. During the armistice period, the Wilson administration granted the European Allies a small concession: The inter-Allied institutions would remain in place for a limited time, though stripped of most of their powers. After several months of delay, the existing bodies were merged into a single organization, the Supreme Economic Council (SEC), in February 1919. The SEC was given temporary responsibility for shipping, food relief in Eastern Europe and Germany, and management of the blockade, which was expanded to cover Soviet Russia and kept in place on Germany and Hungary after the proclamation of a Soviet Republic in Budapest that March. But relief unfolded as a US directed initiative. It was founded on the principle of what Wilson himself termed "American control over American resources."[111] The other members of the SEC, which was weaker than the wartime bodies, argued for its powers to be extended. They sought to use the SEC to mitigate an unfolding crisis of hunger, inflation, and unemployment across Europe, as well as the outbreak of uprisings in their own countries or the stirrings of Bolshevism.[112] According to one left-leaning British representative on the SEC, the fact that the British public now saw Allied purchasing and price fixing as necessary to prevent the cost of living from rising further made it dangerous to abandon these arrangements as food riots and strikes were breaking out across the empire.[113] Doing so would turn the left and Labour against the League of Nations, which was already being criticized as an "instrument by which Governments may defend the interests of capital and commerce against the insistent demands of new democratic opinion."[114] Preventing the League from losing working-class support at the moment of its birth meant endowing it with the same powers as the wartime councils: to control surging prices for food, clothing, and other daily necessities. This inflation was not limited to the United Kingdom, Italy, France, and Belgium, but was global in its reach. It was felt across the British Empire—from Trinidad to Egypt to Australia—and from the Dutch East Indies to South America.[115]

At the same time, businesses were demanding a removal of wartime controls in Britain and France and winning official support—even among former members of the Allied bodies like Loucheur.[116] Some of the French members of the bodies had sought to keep them in place at war's end for precisely this reason: to fasten control over private industry indefinitely. As one official told Layton just before the armistice, Allied economic agreements could be used to neutralize the demands of private businesses "to free themselves from the very absolute power . . . which controls distribution and production."[117] But these efforts to turn the SEC into a more powerful organization failed. So did French and Italian attempts at the Paris Peace Conference to write some version of the Paris Resolutions into the treaty or to clarify in the League's Covenant that the League would be empowered to redistribute raw materials among member states.[118]

The SEC was fatally weakened when US members were removed that summer. British members weighed quitting shortly thereafter, anxious not to alienate the Americans. Suggestions for the League to control the purchasing, pricing, and distribution of raw materials appeared to be threatening US membership in it altogether. Eric Drummond, a career Foreign Office member appointed the first secretary-general of the League in May,

warned Salter shortly after the Paris Peace Conference that any suggestion of "international control" would lead to a "violent reaction" around
the world.[119] When the US Senate rejected the Treaty of Versailles a few
months later, Drummond again told Salter that "American opinion is not
enthusiastic for continuance of Supreme Economic Council especially if
it is to control buying selling and price of food and raw materials in international transactions."[120] Rumors were swirling in the United States
that the SEC would be attached to the League to work as a combine of
European purchasers that could dictate the terms on which the Americans sold to them, just as the Nitrate of Soda Executive had done in
Chile.[121] Salter agreed that it was crucial to stress publicly that the League's
economic functions would not include purchasing or price fixing. But he
also pleaded with the British Treasury not to remove support for the SEC
until the League was operational.[122]

By the end of 1919, the problem of international raw material controls was not yet fully resolved. Support for the idea had moved beyond
the realms of diplomacy and strategic planning. It was now being widely
advocated by women's, socialist, labor, and miners' groups in various
countries, largely for the sake of preventing unemployment. That year saw
a global wave of excitement about the possibility of repurposing war-
making powers for the sake of economic planning and redistribution,
whether on the international or national level—an excitement shared by
socialists and capitalist technocrats alike.[123] Alfred Zimmern, a classicist
scholar who worked during the war in the British Foreign Office (before
taking up the first academic position in international relations at the University of Aberystwyth in 1919), articulated this fashionable view when
he called for "Governments to organise what resources they can lay their
hands on with at least the same thoroughness as they have devoted to the
business of mobilisation or making war." This required national governments to do something radical: "delegate powers to purchase, allocate,
and convey supplies on their behalf to an international Commission."
While he thought this was not logistically difficult, given existing inter-
Allied bodies, Zimmern doubted such institutions were popular enough
to keep in place for long.[124]

Up through 1920, proposals for the League of Nations to redistribute
raw materials remained popular among civil society groups and political
parties in various countries. In late 1919, for example, the Industrial
Women's Organisation made a characteristic plea for the League to keep
international controls of important commodities like wheat and wool in

place.[125] At the first meeting of the International Congress of Working Women, similar proposals were made for a more equitable global distribution of raw materials and the maintenance of international shipping controls to ameliorate rising costs.[126] These calls came as part of broader efforts by women's associations to protest the continued Allied blockade of the Central Powers.[127] Humanitarian groups like the Fight the Famine Council in London also lobbied the League to implement such policies, which were key to the peace terms drafted by the British Labour Party as well.[128] Attempts to revive the Second International at an early 1919 meeting of socialist parties in Berne similarly involved the promulgation of plans for a league that oversaw a return to freer trade while wielding controls over the global production and distribution of raw materials and foodstuffs.[129] Despite their popularity with an array of public and private actors, these suggestions faced much tougher resistance now that the war was over. There were widespread demands for a return to conditions of market competition, the abandonment of price fixing arrangements and state controls, and the prevention of external involvement in domestic questions concerning resources, business, and private property.

When the League of Nations was inaugurated in early 1920, it received many requests by international worker and humanitarian groups to oversee a system of resource controls. Among official representatives to the League, it was the Italians (who during the war had made the most desperate pleas for help with coal, shipping, and food) who now pushed the idea.[130] But they were alone among the Allied governments in demanding the realization of wartime visions. When the Italian diplomat and former foreign minister Tommaso Tittoni proposed the idea at an October 1920 meeting of the Council (the League's executive body), the British delegate Arthur Balfour, a former Conservative prime minister and foreign secretary, rejected it. The League could not "limit the control which every nation at present possesses over its own products," Balfour insisted.[131] The next month, discussion at a meeting of the first Assembly (the League's deliberative body) turned to the issue of whether the organization could develop any economic powers at all. Tittoni again asked whether the Covenant empowered the League to take control of raw materials. But delegates from Britain, the Dominions, and India waged an all-out attack on the proposal. The Canadian delegate H. N. Rowell insisted that the very limited economic powers outlined in the Covenant did not authorize the League to get involved in resource questions. No country, he added, would ever agree in this way to "losing control of their own internal affairs." Commitment to the idea of non-interference was fiercely held in the "New World," Rowell warned, which meant the Italian demands were further imperiling the likelihood of the United States ever joining the League.[132] Tittoni fulminated against Rowell's retreat behind the barrier of "domestic politics" and "internal legislation," claiming this jurisdictional extremism threatened the entire League project. After all, Tittoni insisted, economic policy on the national level still had worldwide effects.[133] The Italians attempted to reassure their colleagues that they had "no intention of interfering with the internal affairs of other countries" or of laying claim to their property. But the precedent of domestic jurisdiction over questions of resources and the regulation of imports and exports was successfully mobilized to block their efforts.[134] The fact that the US government had insisted on a domestic jurisdiction clause in the League's Covenant, to ensure US tariff and immigration policies were not opened to the reach of outsiders, could now be cited by representatives of the United Kingdom and British Dominions to reject pleas to open their own natural resources to external control. Raw materials, private property, and tariffs were to be matters for domestic administration alone—though, of course, only in countries powerful enough to translate this ideal of economic sovereignty into reality.

The Italian government was granted a small compromise: the appointment of the Italian statistician, Corrado Gini—later famous for his eponymous measure of income inequality, and infamous for his role as fascist technocrat—to conduct a survey on the global distribution of raw materials and foodstuffs.[135] In his report, Gini expressed sympathy for the "Socialist" idea of international raw material controls so popular during the war. It was an error to think states could not delegate powers over their resources and policies to an international organization, he claimed. This was fully within their competence as sovereign entities.[136] But Gini also recognized the powerful opposition to this idea—as well as the fact that the much feared postwar shortages were giving way to an even more dangerous situation of financial crisis.[137]

While the window of opportunity for equipping the League of Nations with an ambitious system of resource control had closed, the inter-Allied institutions themselves provided a corps of personnel for the League's technical agencies. When the Paris Peace Conference ended in the summer of 1919, Salter and Monnet had worked to link the SEC to the League. Just before Wilson left Europe, Lloyd George had called for transforming the

SEC into an international economic council that could function until the League was operational.[138] This transitional council would lay the foundations for the League's work on the one economic task assigned to it by the Covenant: facilitating the "equitable treatment of commerce" between member states.[139] While this council was never created, Salter and Monnet themselves moved into new offices in Geneva, where they worked to ensure that the League embodied the principles of inter-Allied cooperation. Salter was made the director of the Economic and Financial Section in the League's Secretariat, the sprawling technical bureaucracy of the organization that supported the Assembly and the Council.[140] Other former inter-Allied officials joined them in Geneva or influenced the development of the League's work from afar, including Loucheur, Cecil, and the US investment banker Dwight Morrow.

What remained of these principles of international cooperation in 1920 was the idea of coordinating national policies in ways that avoided imposing external authority on them. But some of the architects of the League's economic functions also suggested more ambitious proposals. One was E. M. H. Lloyd, a former member of the British Ministry of Food and War Office, who had also worked with the SEC in 1919 and as assistant to Salter. Lloyd became one of the most important early designers of the League's economic work, alongside Layton, Churchill's deputy at the inter-Allied Munitions Council, and Alexander Loveday, a Scottish statistician at the Ministry of Munitions, who worked in the League's Economic and Financial Organization until its end in 1946.[141] In blueprints for the League's technical organizations, Lloyd described their foundational principle: avoiding the "dictation of an international authority" for the sake of "agreement between national authorities."[142] But his vision of the League's powers went beyond this. Alongside other left and Labour supporting members of the inter-Allied councils, Lloyd was committed to the idea that the economic bodies of the League would not just coordinate national policies but also ration goods among member states.[143] He indicated in blueprints for an economic wing of the League that this rationing was, alongside financial policies, a function that went well beyond the limited regulatory powers of prewar international public unions—a suggestion he knew was opposed by contemporary business opinion.[144] When a private transport association in Britain pitched the League to oversee arrangements for controlling the price of petroleum, Lloyd excitedly told Drummond that this demand showed that some representatives of capital might be interested in measures otherwise generally associated with labor.[145] But Drummond demurred. These were powers that were now clearly outside the realm of possibility.

The League's rejection of powers of resource control for the lighter touch of bureaucratic coordination was formalized in an influential theory of international organization developed by Salter himself. In a 1921 book on Allied shipping control, Salter argued that the lesson of wartime cooperation was that an international institution could be effective and legitimate only if it avoided dictating to national decision-makers. Like the Allied shipping council, the League was a "medium," not "an original source of power." It was not an "external organization based on delegated authority," but "national organizations linked together for international work and themselves forming the instrument of that work."[146] Salter further justified this arrangement with a critique of economic planning that was then becoming more common. He claimed it was impossible to create a single locus of control over the infinite individual interactions that made up the economic life of a nation. It was even harder to delegate this power beyond the bounds of a legitimate government. Unlike military decisions, which could be concentrated under a single authority like Foch, the Allied supreme commander, economic decisions taken on the international level reverberated down to the most local levels of the individual shopkeeper and consumer through the interactions of supply and demand. Salter articulated a traditionally liberal justification for giving the League such weak economic powers: the further away control was delegated from the individual economic actor, the more ineffective and coercive it would be.

This liberal conception of the bounds of legitimate international authority nonetheless represented a dramatic departure from prewar practices. Before the war, national governments had agreed only to the constitution of international public unions that handled problems "limited in character, in scope, and importance," and that avoided questions involving the vital interests of nations. Now they were joining an organization with functions that went beyond the standardization of scientific measures or the collection of statistics. Perhaps the League could someday evolve into an organization that wielded enough legitimate authority to "override the powers of national Governments"—just as, over many generations, provinces were united into kingdoms, and kingdoms into empires. But Salter claimed that this future was far off.[147]

In the following years, this conception of an international economic institution eschewing external directives for the sake of coordinating national bureaucracies proved to be highly influential, not only among the architects of the League's technical functions but also for a generation of internationalists.[148] Salter was praised for having demonstrated how wartime Allied cooperation laid the foundations for a form of technical administration that was neither external to national governments nor demanded delegation to it. The League, built on this philosophy, could not be considered a "super state."[149] Among the accolades Salter received after the war—in addition to having made Allied victory possible through the shipping organization he had helped design and run—was that he had killed off the nineteenth-century utopian fantasy of a "world-government" or a "Parliament of Man."[150] On this model, the League's economic role was clear: It was to be a coordinator of self-governing polities, not an authority external to them that meddled in their affairs.

Salter's philosophy of international governance, however, was based on sanitized myths of the wartime experience. The inter-Allied system had not been an experiment in international administration for its own sake; it was an experiment in inter-imperial economic collusion for the sake of industrialized slaughter. It offered a way of overriding the disorganization of global markets to ensure cheap and reliable sources of goods for building explosives, tanks, and chemical weapons. It was a system of inter-imperial cooperation for the sake of war against a shared enemy that was created at a moment of profound jeopardy for some European members of the alliance. This explained why it had not proven easily adaptable to the peace after these conditions of emergency were gone. Nor was this system easily compatible with the liberal orthodoxies that so many after the war, including Salter, sought to return to. Wartime Allied cooperation was made possible by the extension of state control over national economies. As these controls were lifted, there was little left to coordinate, since most governments had not yet developed significant peacetime powers over their national economies. For supporters of schemes of nationalization, this point was obvious: unlike the inter-Allied bodies, the League as coordinator would remain weak, they claimed, without institutions of national economic control that rivaled those of the war years.[151]

Although the inter-Allied system had been designed to be as little taxing on the national sovereignty of its leading members as possible, it was immediately abandoned by its most powerful member, the United States, which also rejected the League, its apparently inoffensive progeny. The League appeared to risk wielding powers over US policy of the kind that US officials and businesses were accustomed to wielding over the governments of subordinate countries like Chile, which had rarely enjoyed the practical benefits of the right to non-interference. The idea that the League was to be based on a universal principle of this right reified the fiction that all states enjoyed full sovereign equality in practice. Several of its member states, including China, Greece, Siam, Haiti, and Liberia, continued to face restrictions on their sovereignty at the hands of others. They enjoyed "burdened membership" in the organization.[152] From its earliest days, moreover, the League was facilitating the extension of the British and French empires to their zenith through its mandates system.

Salter was right to think that endowing the League with powers to interfere would make it less popular and doom its chances in the United States. The United States was, after all, a hegemon-in-waiting that was nearly self-sufficient in natural resources, which the war had transformed into the world's leading financial power. But Salter did not tell the full story of what happened when the organization he had helped design began to make more interventionist demands on some of its members. Over the 1920s, as the League developed new methods of economic policy-making, these went well beyond any stylized depictions of its commitment to non-interference. It was not only the US government that resisted a meddling League. The governments of states with partial or weakened sovereignty also pushed back against the organization for allowing rival foreign powers to get involved in their domestic affairs. It was during the catastrophic financial crises of the 1920s that these political stakes first became clear.

CHAPTER 2

Enforcing Austerity in Postwar Europe

A FTER THE FIRST WORLD WAR, Europe's economic problems were different from what many had expected while it was raging—and in some cases, much worse. As the Paris Peace Conference opened in January 1919, food and raw material shortages were developing into full-blown crises of famine and unemployment, particularly in Central and Eastern Europe. A sharp economic boom that began early that year accelerated a dizzying inflation of the prices of many goods, culminating in a wave of uprisings around the world, from the Caribbean to North Africa, where costs of living had risen more quickly than wages. Just a year later, however, the boom was over. As a devastating global influenza pandemic wound down, interest rate hikes by several of the world's most powerful central banks in 1920 led to a sudden economic contraction. Millions were thrown out of work in industrialized countries, while plummeting commodity prices battered the producers of agricultural goods and raw materials around the world. When recovery from this recession began, various European countries marched to the edge of a hyperinflationary abyss.[1] In many places, new barriers to trade were erected and existing ones solidified. The collapse of the Austro-Hungarian Empire caused a formerly vast region of free exchange in Europe to shatter into competing national units. Assumptions that a return to prewar normalcy would be straightforward once wartime controls were removed were proven false.[2] As the magnitude of the economic challenges became clear, they presented opportunities for the architects of new international economic institutions. They inaugurated a series of controversial experiments in adapting old techniques of financial imperialism to the conditions of postwar Europe.

Beyond immediate relief measures, the comprehensive reconstruction and economic stabilization of postwar Europe was never seriously considered by the one government that could have afforded it: the United States. Some bankers and entrepreneurial technocrats, like a young John Maynard Keynes at the British Treasury, drew up ambitious schemes for channeling US capital to the rebuilding of Europe.[3] But Washington was reluctant to commit to any intergovernmental scheme for financing European reconstruction. Private efforts also faced strong headwinds. One of the principal stumbling blocks was that the countries most in need of financial assistance were also the most politically unstable, particularly the new countries created out of the remnants of the Russian and Austro-Hungarian empires. Many were stuck in a vicious circle: needing foreign capital for their economic and political stabilization, but needing stable politics to attract capital in the first place: "The more prostrate a country is and the nearer to Bolshevism the more presumably it requires assistance," as Robert Cecil put this point in early 1919. "But the less likely is private enterprise to give it."[4]

The League of Nations, inaugurated in January 1920, initially could do little in the face of Europe's instability. The institution's powers were too constrained. As we have seen, when the economic functions of the League were first delineated over 1919–1920, it quickly became clear that it would not take up the task that so many had imagined for it during the war: rationing raw materials between member states. The League's Covenant, moreover, appeared to set a firm limit on its ability to influence the economic policies of a member country. That the Covenant did not mention finance explicitly at first seemed to rule out any role at all for the League in this domain.[5] The organization was also prohibited from adjudicating any problems said to reside in the "domestic jurisdiction" of member states—a clause that was included in the Covenant to appease Republican lawmakers worried about US trade and immigration policies being opened to the League's reach. The domestic jurisdiction clause had wide but uncertain implications. Some legal experts thought it made it impossible for the League to deal with commercial issues at all.[6] Even when it was not explicitly invoked, this clause provided a standard for determining what was legitimate business for the League.[7] The League's Covenant assigned it only one economic function: Article 23(e) called for it to ensure the "equitable treatment for the commerce" of its member states.[8] In late 1920, when the Assembly agreed to establish an Economic Committee to oversee the implementation of this ambiguous article, it was given a strictly limited remit.[9]

Yet within a few years, its twin body, the Financial Committee, developed extensive powers to reach into the domestic economic realms of a select number of member states—despite the limits that the Covenant had placed on its ability to do so. This unexpected turn of events took place as the League facilitated financial stabilization loans to a handful of countries. These loans were made conditional on domestic schemes of fiscal austerity, the establishment of independent central banks, and the international oversight of sources of public revenue. Unlike later institutions, such as the World Bank or the International Monetary Fund (IMF), the League did not have direct access to capital it could lend. But what it could do was mediate the relationship of foreign lenders and member states, particularly newly democratic and sovereign ones, by appointing advisers to their government to control their budgets. This discipline was supposed to improve their credit and make them less likely to default by ensuring that they committed to the policies almost universally deemed necessary for their financial stabilization: slashing public spending, raising taxes, ending the printing of money, removing central banks from political control, and returning to the gold standard. This was to be a new regime of austerity—and the very first to be overseen by an international institution.

These reforms involved extremely sensitive political questions. Balancing budgets required the mass dismissal of government employees and the neutralization of demands from both left and right for spending: on veterans, the unemployed, and the hungry, as well as on armaments to defend Europe's new borders and manage the violent aftermath of a war that, in many places, had not yet come to an end.[10] The global wave of labor unrest, strikes, and revolts of 1919, moreover, had raised the specter of Bolshevism spreading beyond Russia's borders. In many countries, political parties were locked in fierce struggle over questions of spending and distribution. Public discontent about spending cuts and rising costs of living was widespread and could be easily channeled by parliamentary opponents to a sitting government.[11]

Already by late 1919, however, it was also clear that unstable postwar governments in search of loans would have to demonstrate a real commitment to far-reaching currency reforms and balanced budgets if they expected to receive any aid. How could this be done? The League came to be seen as providing a way of enforcing these policies. When Arthur

Salter was planning an economic role for the League, he had assumed that one of its first tasks would be to oversee such financial stabilization loans, which would have to come with strict conditions and "external control" over the borrower's domestic policies concerning currency, imports, exports, and taxation.[12] But it was obvious that having an external organization get so deeply involved in such domestic issues was an explosive proposition. Such interventionist powers went far beyond Salter's own vision of the League as simply a coordinator of national policies. These ideas encountered immediate pushback. At a meeting of leading British internationalists, economists, and former members of the inter-Allied bodies in late 1919—including Salter, Walter Layton, E. M. H. Lloyd, and Keynes—there had been fraught debate about whether this was possible at all. While attendees broadly agreed that any reconstruction loans to "weaker" European countries had to come with "strict conditions," they also insisted that these plans avoid an "international body . . . controlling internal economic policy in detail."[13]

That the League of Nations soon did develop powers to reach into these internal spaces marked a truly radical innovation. Several reasons explain why it happened with finance and not in other domains. First, financial instability, more so than any issues of trade, posed a real strategic liability to some of the League's most powerful countries. A string of failed states throughout Central and Eastern Europe and the Balkans threatened renewed territorial competition, war, and the collapse of the fragile peace settlement. A second reason was that only in a limited number of places would this intervention be necessary, and they were unique cases. The League's role could be justified as a form of emergency intervention in the vanquished former Central Powers, like Austria and Hungary; in Balkan states with long histories of partial sovereignty, like Albania, Bulgaria, and Greece; and in territories already placed under international administration, like Danzig.[14] There was also a clear set of prewar precedents for institutions staffed by "outsiders" being empowered to control the assets and budgets of sovereign countries in exchange for loans. Bankers had long demanded risky borrowers in the Middle East, North Africa, Latin America, East Asia, the Caribbean, and the Balkans relinquish autonomy to ensure debts were serviced. From the vantage point of Wall Street and the City of London, this model was clearly adaptable to postwar Europe. A new problem of the postwar—hyperinflation—could thus be reframed in terms of a more familiar one—sovereign debt—which had a traditional solution: foreign control.

But the prospect of establishing public debt commissions in Vienna or Berlin like those set up decades before in China, Egypt, and the Ottoman Empire was extremely controversial. It unsettled imagined boundaries separating the so-called "civilized" world of Europe from the non-European world. By exposing European countries to a form of foreign interference long visited by Europe's bankers (and the empires that protected their interests) on regions of the world coded as "backward," the sovereignty of European countries was thrown into confusion. So was their perceived standing in the postwar international order. The aim of the League of Nations was to make such practices more tolerable for sovereign and "developed" countries by providing an intermediary between them and the foreign banks that insisted that their financial stabilization come at a real cost to their autonomy. But critics saw this as little more than an attempt to launder old-fashioned imperial practices: "When England and France restored the finances of the Khedive, seventy years ago, they did it without any League, to their economic and political advantage," as the Austrian Marxist Franz Borkenau later wrote. "The only difference between earlier reconstructions and those effected under the auspices of the League was that Geneva provided convenient machinery. No new thing was ever achieved through the League."[15] Borkenau was wrong, though, to think that the machinery did not matter: It was designed to legitimate what were otherwise certain to be seen as coercive attempts to erode the economic sovereignty of member states.

The success and failure of the League financial stabilization loans from the 1920s—pioneered by former members of the wartime Allied economic bodies, such as Jean Monnet and Salter, who were joined by central bankers, treasury officials, experts, and financiers in the League's home in Geneva—have long been debated. Some scholars have pointed out how many of these loans were in default by the 1930s; others that the League's role in arranging them gave rise to international practices of conditional lending, which before then had only been done by private commercial banks.[16] This provided an "antecedent" to the later work of the IMF.[17] But the implementation of these loans was also interpreted around the world in light of a much larger and longer-term struggle to define the legitimate bounds of external involvement in the domestic economies of sovereign states. It was a widely acknowledged maxim in a hierarchical international order that allowing foreign actors any say over domestic economic questions, regardless of whether they were appointed by a disinterested international organization or a rival foreign government, threatened the sovereignty, power, and civilizational standing of any country that agreed to such discipline. The crises of the 1920s put this maxim to the test in novel ways, as semi-colonial practices were internationalized and brought to the center of Europe.

These political stakes become clear when the best-known case of League intervention—postwar Austria—is put into the context of other attempted and realized projects of financial reconstruction, including in Albania, Bulgaria, Liberia, Portugal, and Yugoslavia. The League loans were not limited to addressing problems related to the breakup of the Habsburg Empire; instead, they generated controversies around the world—from Latin America to West Africa to India and China. Whether a sovereign state could or should consent to League interference for the sake of stabilization became a vexed question throughout the decade. Even those governments that saw the political value of inviting an outsider to do their dirty work—by insulating them from domestic opposition as budgets were cut and civil servants dismissed—recognized the dangers that such interference posed to their legitimacy. But it also threatened the legitimacy of economic internationalism itself. By the end of the 1920s, the first attempt by an international institution to shape domestic economic policies led to a crisis for the future of international economic governance. The practices innovated in the early 1920s, however, would not be abandoned for long.

Foreign Advising and Self-Determination

When members of the provisional economic and financial bodies of the League of Nations began to work in the early 1920s, they attempted to carve out roles for themselves that were powerful enough to respond to the economic instability of postwar Europe while also avoiding charges of illegitimately meddling in the affairs of member states. This was a difficult balancing act to achieve; even the prospect of providing the assistance of League-appointed financial and technical experts was highly controversial. This was unsurprising. The practice of sending economic experts or "money doctors" from one country to another had long been used as a strategy for extending the informal reach of empires.[18] But the assistance of the League of Nations was supposed to be different. As an institution that ostensibly represented the interests of all its members, its backers claimed it could provide apolitical help without advancing the claims of one state over another. More than ever, though, allowing foreign advisers with real powers to reach beyond the protective membrane of sovereignty was seen to be an insult to national pride and even a threat to security. Because the League was made up of rivals of widely different powers, the principle of its detachment from politics was shown to be a myth whenever it was tested.

These political stakes became clear as soon as the Provisional Economic and Financial Committees first considered the prospects of appointing financial advisers to member states in 1921. This idea was proposed by the Italian statistician Corrado Gini. As we have seen, Gini had been hired to produce a report on the global distribution of raw materials and foodstuffs in order to appease unrealistic Italian demands for the League to ration resources between members. While Gini had professed some sympathy for what he called the "socialist" idea of redistributing commodities, he admitted that the crisis of scarcity had now mostly been overtaken by problems of financial instability. Unlike the global allocation of raw materials and foodstuffs, this problem was something that the League could, at least in principle, address. It could appoint advisers to governments that lacked the administrative capacity to undertake controversial programs of austerity needed to stabilize the value of their currencies. But Gini acknowledged that few European governments would welcome the idea. While Britain had "by means of technical advisers . . . been able to direct the economic policy of several Asiatic States with advantageous results to their economy and to her prestige," he wrote, doing so now would exacerbate international rivalries, as other countries saw this as a British attempt to bring unstable countries under British control.[19] And while various countries outside Europe, like China and the Ottoman Empire, had allowed "foreign Commissions" to "administer their revenue," Gini doubted "any other European people would submit to such interference." The only exception was the anomalous—and, as we shall see, important—case of Austria.[20]

In August 1921, Gini nonetheless wrote to Secretary-General Eric Drummond about inaugurating a League program of technical advising, particularly for successor states of the Russian Empire that were building up their government administrations nearly from scratch.[21] There was a ready audience for the proposal. In September, the Council resolved to task the Economic and Financial Committees with preparing a list of experts and drafting a contract establishing the terms of their service, modeled on a contract between the imperial Persian government and a group of Belgians it had hired to reform its customs service.[22] Several of the people involved with the initiative worried about its optics. Since it was likely that most governments, "on the grounds of prestige," would reject the offer of help from a foreign government directly, the success of the League's initiative depended on making a convincing case for its absolute impartiality.[23] Offering the assistance of League-appointed experts was a "question of extreme delicacy," as one member of the Financial Committee put it. Few governments, "from the point of view of amour propre," would accept the help of "foreigners."[24] When a letter was sent to member states in March 1922 offering the services of League-appointed experts, most rejected the offer or ignored it.[25] Devawongse Varoprakar, the Siamese minister of foreign affairs, responded by insisting that Siam, even with its "administration in the process of reorganisation on modern and western lines," and already employing numerous western advisers, had no need for the League's help.[26]

One of the reasons this outreach was unsuccessful was because of the perceived risks of admitting to a form of assistance traditionally provided by the powerful to the weak. In a dangerous and uncertain early postwar international order, a cry for help—even one addressed to an ostensibly impartial body—was likely to be interpreted as an invitation to meddling or an admission of low standing or "damaged" sovereignty. When it came to financial questions, moreover, the precedents were yet more troubling. European and US bankers and governments had long used various methods for attenuating the sovereignty of states that received foreign loans. For a risky sovereign debtor, relinquishing control over policy-making and sources of revenue was a tried-and-true method for making itself an attractive borrower. This was why colonies tended to enjoy lower borrowing costs: They were not seen as independent political entities that set their own policies and controlled their own assets. Instead, they enjoyed the credit of the metropolitan government that subjected them to alien rule. If a risky sovereign borrower acted as if it had become a colony, this could have similar results.[27]

Before 1914, one way that sovereign borrowers had been made to relinquish autonomy in exchange for loans was by agreeing to the establishment of a foreign-run commission to take control over public revenues and, in some cases, supervise fiscal policies to ensure foreign bondholders were repaid and loans did not go into default. The first such commission was created in 1869 in Tunis, but the most notorious was the Franco-British *Caisse de la Dette Publique* set up in Egypt in 1876. It was followed by a similar commission in the Ottoman Empire in 1881, and in the 1890s in Serbia, Greece, Bulgaria, and other Balkan states. Similar institutions under US control were created throughout Latin America and the Caribbean.[28] They provoked fierce resistance wherever they appeared. In Egypt, which in the late nineteenth century remained formally part of the Ottoman Empire but in practice enjoyed a large degree of autonomy, the siphoning off of revenues to foreign creditors played a role in the outbreak of a nationalist uprising led by the military officer Ahmed 'Urabi. This uprising sparked a British military intervention in 1882, and led the British colonial administrator Evelyn Baring (later, Lord Cromer) to be appointed the de facto ruler of an Egyptian protectorate.[29] Egypt's experience was widely seen as the worst-case scenario for a sovereign debtor: default, loss of assets and policy autonomy, and then invasion. The fear of such interference even loomed over debtors like China that had already ceded considerable control over its domestic policies and assets to foreign powers, and frightened others like Brazil and Argentina into reaching unfavorable settlements with their creditors. From the perspective of lenders, the system worked as intended: Countries put under such "house arrest" or faced with military intervention are estimated to have been more than 60 percent less likely to default than those that retained their full sovereignty.[30] After the First World War, these precedents were on the mind of anyone considering the idea of the League providing economic advisers to member states or helping them undertake the domestic reforms needed to attract foreign loans.

A Difficult Start in Albania

The first country that agreed to the appointment of a League financial adviser was one that had already been under international control: Albania. When its formal independence from the Ottoman Empire was recognized in late 1913 after the Second Balkan War, Albania's civil and financial administration had been placed under the control of an international commission of European countries to prevent competition among various regional powers over its territory, which included an extensive Adriatic coastline.[31] In the wake of the First World War, the government sought Albania's admission to the League as an independent state and requested that the organization help settle its national borders and protect its territorial integrity from the threats of Greece and Yugoslavia.[32] In May 1922, the government made another request for help attracting foreign capital and developing the country's natural resources.

Albania was a unique member state. It was a recently independent and politically and territorially unstable country. Its population was religiously divided, largely between Sunni Muslims, Catholics, and Orthodox Christians. It had been occupied during the war and was reinvaded in late 1921 by Yugoslav forces. And it was now developing institutions of parliamentary government. League officials feared Albania's financial collapse would be exploited by Yugoslavia, Italy, and Greece, which eyed its territory hungrily—even more so now that its significant oil reserves were widely known. The prospect of stabilizing this small, resource-rich country in the region of southeastern Europe that had recently plunged the world into war was, to them, an attractive one—not least because it provided an opportunity for them to show that the League's assistance was neither humiliating nor a vehicle for foreign domination.[33]

But Albania was a special case. While it was a member state, it was generally regarded by members of the Provisional Economic and Financial Section as an underdeveloped "Oriental" one—a "mountainous, primitive, agricultural, sparsely populated, and until recently rather barbarous country," as Salter described it, which was now "trying, with the aid of the League of Nations, to civilize itself."[34] It also had a special status as a ward of the League, which made the application of semi-colonial forms of economic interference there less likely to harm the League's reputation than if they were brought elsewhere. At the same time, there were high stakes to this project: Because Albania was the first sovereign member state to ask the League for a financial adviser, failure risked it being the last.[35]

The financial stabilization of Albania required a large foreign loan. The Albanian government was unlikely to win the confidence of potential creditors, however, unless it agreed to being brought further under foreign control. Having this control wielded by a League-appointed adviser would represent a new departure for the organization, endowing it with powers that went far beyond the coordination of national policies that Salter and others had insisted were the limits of its economic reach. How challenging this undertaking would be became clear during the search for a financial adviser for Albania from the summer of 1922 through the spring of 1923. Only applicants with considerable experience in colonial administration were considered. This adviser was said to have to start from the basics. Albania was only now "in the process of creating that machinery of government which economists tend almost to take for granted in civilised communities," wrote Frank H. Nixon, a British Treasury official who served as director of the Provisional Economic and Financial Section after Salter left for a short stint on the Reparation Commission.[36] From Nixon's vantage point, the best candidate was someone with "an experience and character similar to those which are required by the best men in the Colonial Services of the British Empire."[37] It was for this reason that suggestions for the Belgian national Paul van Zeeland (later prime minister of Belgium) were rejected, since he was "not the type of man who makes a pioneer or colonial administrator" and lacked the necessary experience for building up "the Albanian administration in a colonial manner."[38] Many British nationals leaving positions in colonial governments were available, however, as well as former US colonial authorities from the Philippines.[39]

One candidate given serious consideration was the British official John Campbell, just then leaving a long career in the Indian Civil Service.[40] Although he was not chosen for this job, Campbell would later play a major role in the League's work in Greece, as we shall see, and then as a powerful financial adviser in the Colonial Office. Another candidate was Reginald Patterson, a longtime British financial adviser in the Egyptian Civil Service, who after the outbreak of the First World War had overseen drastic cuts to the government's public expenditure.[41] But the French government rejected a British adviser on the grounds that he would give British companies an advantage in tapping Albania's oil. The new fascist government in Italy, just weeks after the March on Rome, also objected to empowering a British national, as well as a French or US one, in an oil-rich neighboring country of particular strategic interest.[42] Such disputes quickly gave the lie to the myth that the League's formal impartiality would by itself depoliticize its work.[43]

The prospect that a League adviser in Albania would exacerbate geopolitical tensions in the Adriatic led to a search for someone from a country that had been neutral during the war—but also one with colonies and thus a pool of civil servants with the experience deemed necessary for the job.[44] The obvious choice was a Dutch national (despite the clear interest Dutch companies also had in Albania's oil).[45] An official who had worked in the Dutch East Indies was thought to have the additional advantage of experience governing Muslim populations and potentially a knowledge of Islamic finance.[46] In his application, J. G. Moojen, a longtime official in the Dutch East Indian Service, drew attention to his experience governing Muslims and suppressing uprisings, most notably among the Ampat Lawang people of Tebing Tinggi in South Sumatra: "the most troublesome people of whole Palembang," he wrote, "independent and fond of liberty by nature, which makes one think of the description of the Albanian mountain inhabitants. They were those who offered the longest resistance against our weapons."[47] Moojen's application was rejected due to his lack of financial expertise. But Nixon was impressed with his experience "governing rather wild people."[48] He saw Albania as a country where "a certain amount of financial wisdom may have to be instilled by means of a revolver."[49] These colonial assumptions about the necessity of potentially violent intervention, expressed in the vocabularies of civilizational hierarchy, were key to how these League officials understood their work in this unique Balkan member state.

The Albania job was eventually given to a former colonial administrator in the Dutch East Indies, Jan Hunger, who had the experience of overseeing the reorganization of Java from a "feudal sultanate," as one of his Dutch referees put it, to "an indigenous state administered according to more Western principles." In that case, however, Hunger had been backed by the full coercive force of the Dutch colonial government, an advantage he would lack in Albania.[50] In May 1923, Hunger took up a post in Tirana with a set of difficult tasks: to help the Albanian state create an independent central bank free from government control, to assess applications from foreign and domestic companies for concessions, and to oversee an ambitious program of austerity in order to win the confidence of foreign lenders. Despite his invitation from Albanian political elites, and assumptions that the reorganization of a "primitive" and "Oriental" country was relatively simple—one that was certainly within the capacities of a former colonial administrator, even one without much financial expertise—Hunger's work in Albania would not be easy.[51] Recreating semi-colonial forms of financial control in a sovereign state would, despite Albania's shaky claims to full autonomy, be very difficult to pull off.[52]

Hunger's tenure began with an error of judgment that showed how fraught the entire endeavor was. Shortly after he arrived in Tirana, Hunger published a report that revealed sensitive information about Albania's domestic economic and political conditions. The report also made clear Hunger's frustration with the wide powers enjoyed by the Albanian Parliament and the relative weakness of government ministers, which he claimed made it difficult to implement the reforms he demanded. The country was rich in resources—not only oil, but also metals and timber. Huge tracts of land lay fallow. Forests went unexplored. But Hunger claimed that the Albanian government was mismanaging its finances and granting unwise concessions to foreign capitalists in a desperate search for revenue.[53] Drawing attention to these details in a publication for the League, however—one that would be read by potential investors and government officials around the world—set him on a collision course with the Albanian government.

Despite their views about the civilizational standing of a Muslim-majority and newly independent Balkan state, several League officials conceded the validity of the complaints they received from Tirana: that putting this report on the agenda of the Council amounted to a form of interference in Albania's internal affairs. The aim of such reports was to increase the confidence of foreign lenders in the government's ability to service new debt by making the country's conditions known to them. These reports would also strengthen the government's hand against its domestic opponents, since their obstruction would now be reported abroad.[54] But Hunger's publication raised a serious problem: It exposed Albania's "interior affairs" to the gaze of outsiders. Those affairs were clearly not in the "sphere of action" of the League's Council and thus not legitimate business for it, as Article 4 of the Covenant clarified.[55] The Albanian League representative Benoit Blinishti furiously insisted to Drummond that putting Hunger's report on the agenda of Council was itself an act of interference, particularly since the report dealt not only with economic matters but also with sensitive questions about minority populations in the south.[56] Since Albania's first outreach to Geneva, Blinishti had insisted this request for assistance was not a request for its control: Albania, he told the Council, "would do the controlling itself."[57]

Drummond recognized the importance of avoiding any impression that the League was interfering in Albania's domestic matters, particularly as this was one of the principal charges made by the political opposition against the sitting government in Tirana.[58] Paul Mantoux, head of the Political Section, agreed that the "awakening" of Albanian "amour propre and spirit of independence" made it imperative to clarify that the League was not attempting to impose "tutelage" on the country. Mantoux used very specific language: "tutelage" was the term used in the Treaty of Versailles to describe the powers exercised by the League over a mandated colonial territory—a status that a semi-sovereign country like Albania naturally sought to avoid.[59] The director of the League's Legal Section, Joost Adriaan van Hamel, agreed. Even discussing Albania's domestic financial affairs, he insisted, could be interpreted as an act of interference if the initiative for doing so did not come directly from Tirana.[60] Blinisthi's protest was successful. The topic was taken off the Council's agenda.[61] Hunger had put the League in a difficult position. It was heading a program of financial assistance clearly modeled on colonial precedents while defending itself from charges that it was violating its own Covenant by meddling in the domestic affairs of a member state.[62]

Hunger's work in Albania soon came to an end. As the country's financial situation deteriorated, his advice was resisted. The government did not follow his advice for radically austere reforms to balance the budget. His proposals included abolishing the army completely, dismissing huge numbers of public employees, and raising taxes on lightly taxed rich landowners, since the rest of the population was too poor or already too heavily taxed.[63] Officials ceased inviting him to cabinet meetings, as called for by his contract. Laws were passed and concessions granted without his approval. In early 1924, the government canceled Hunger's contract. He left the country, having failed to subject the government to his discipline.[64]

The very first attempt at an international program of financial stabilization and economic development had failed. As the League retreated, fascist Italy pulled Albania further into its sphere of influence.[65] Hunger was widely blamed in Albania for the country's poor financial conditions. That summer, an uprising brought to power a new prime minister, the Harvard-educated Orthodox bishop of Durrës, Fan Noli. A common charge against the prior regime of King Ahmed Bey Zogu was his willingness to employ foreign advisers like Hunger. The League's intervention had, as feared, contributed to a legitimacy crisis for a sitting government and even to the outbreak of revolt against it.[66] That summer, Noli traveled to Geneva to attack the League for its errors in Albania: "take my application for a loan to the dead files of the Secretariat and lock it up there tightly," Noli told representatives in a long-winded and poorly received speech at the Assembly, "but be sure to choke it before you bury it in your necropolis, because it is likely to rise from the dead."[67]

The Turn to Vienna

Just before Noli made his speech in early September 1924, the League's Assembly gave a rousing ovation to the Austrian Chancellor Ignaz Seipel, a Catholic prelate and conservative Christian Social politician who just weeks before had been seriously wounded in an assassination attempt.

Seipel was applauded for his role in facilitating the League's program of financial reconstruction in Austria, which had begun not long after he came to power in May 1922. The League's role in stabilizing the Austrian currency was already being hailed as one of the organization's first major achievements, and Seipel had the dubious distinction of being the first European head of state to allow a League-appointed adviser to exercise real powers of control over national policy-making for the sake of winning foreign loans. He was praised that day for being the "masterbuilder" of Austria's rehabilitation. What went unsaid was how difficult the process of getting him to agree to League control had been—and how much the League's actions in Austria were regarded with apprehension in and outside the country, even by those who supported them.[68]

From the vantage point of foreign lenders, the solution to the financial instability faced by the rump Austrian republic was obvious, though difficult to implement. Most assumed that Austria's hyperinflation—like that faced by its German neighbor—was caused by the printing of paper money to cover the government's massive budget deficit. Halting the collapse of the Austrian krone appeared to necessitate tough reforms: cutting food subsidies and unemployment benefits to a population suffering from dire shortages and little work; raising taxes; and dismissing large numbers of public employees, whose numbers had swollen after German-speaking civil servants from across the former empire flooded into the successor state. But no government was popular or stable enough to undertake these reforms on its own. The country was highly polarized, with frequent strikes and public unrest. The two leading parties, the Christian Social and Social Democratic, were at loggerheads. The hope was that a foreign loan could help the government cover its expenses as it enacted these reforms, while a new and independent central bank could remove monetary policy from the quicksand of party conflict. Austria was stuck in the same vicious circle as other new states in Central and Eastern Europe: it needed foreign loans to facilitate economic and political stabilization but was too unstable to be an attractive borrower in the first place. The solution that many advocated was stability imposed from the outside. The stakes were high: Austria's collapse threatened to plunge the region back into war as neighboring countries like Italy, Czechoslovakia, and Yugoslavia contemplated military occupation. After the experiences of revolutionary Budapest and Munich, Vienna also appeared to be vulnerable to Bolshevism. Most worrying from the vantage point of the Allies, particularly the French, was the prospect of German annexation, an idea that was popular across Austria's ideological divides. Nearly every major European power had a stake in preventing the collapse of this strategically significant country at the crossroads of Central Europe and the Balkans—a country that many in Austria thought simply might not be viable at all.[69]

The program of financial reconstruction implemented by the League of Nations in postwar Austria has long divided opinion. It was once common to see the republic as having been victimized by a bullying League, and with disastrous economic effects.[70] The Austrian social theorist Karl Polanyi famously described the League's intervention as a "brilliantly successful operation on Austria's krone which the patient, unfortunately, did not survive."[71] Others have shown how the Austrian government and business elites invited the League's control to circumvent parliamentary opposition to the reforms they claimed were needed to forestall the country's collapse, but also how, once control was implemented, they skirted it as much as possible while sloughing off blame for unpopular decisions on to the League.[72] Looking over the track record of the League, it was later common for internationalists to claim that Austria's financial reconstruction, despite the subsequent descent of the country into far-right authoritarianism and annexation by Nazi Germany, was one of the League's few great achievements.[73] Already in the 1930s, some argued that it was the first and most convincing demonstration of the effectiveness of the new international economic institutions created after the First World War.[74]

But the financial reconstruction schemes in Austria and elsewhere also involved protracted political struggles about opening domestic spaces to the involvement of actors external to the sovereign carapace of states—not only in places where League loans were provided, like Austria, but also even where they were just offered.[75] While the vanquished Central Powers had lost power and status, there was nonetheless widespread apprehension among political and economic elites in the former Entente countries that subjecting them blithely to the kind of foreign controls used before the war in places like Egypt and China threatened to open a Pandora's box: Doing so would efface a clear border between what was acceptable in Europe and what was not. In the case of Austria, it was true that its membership in the League, which it had joined in December 1920, offered protections unavailable to these other countries. Nor was Vienna bullied into accepting League "tutelage" under threats of outright violence. That this control was to be exercised by an international institution and not directly by foreign governments or banks did mark an important development—but the obvious reality that the Financial Committee was dominated by the British did not make appeals to this fact very reassuring.[76]

The League's involvement in Austria was seen by many contemporaries to be setting a troubling precedent: asking a "developed" European republic to allow far-reaching external involvement in its domestic affairs. The political power of the charges of "financial colonialism" made against the League that were so common in Austria should thus not be seen exclusively as the conspiratorial ravings of an anti-Semitic right—though they were also this—or the exaggerated rhetoric of left opponents to a sitting conservative government. Instead, these charges were characteristic of a debate taking place in many countries about what the Austrian case implied for the meaning of sovereignty and status in a world order transformed by the war. Even the supporters and designers of the scheme readily admitted it was an adaptation of prewar semi-colonial practices. The question was whether these practices could be detached from their roots in empire and turned into a legitimate practice for a sovereign European republic that claimed the status of one of Europe's oldest and most "advanced" civilizations.

Designing Austria's Control

In the first few years after the war, the Austrian republic depended heavily on food aid from the Allies and frequent injections of foreign capital to prevent the country from collapse.[77] But its financial reconstruction necessitated much more interventionist measures. During 1920–1922, as Austria's rescue was debated by a range of public and private actors beyond its borders, most assumed that the stabilization of the krone required the Austrian government to relinquish full autonomy over its domestic fiscal and monetary policies.[78] Austria was in such dire straits that it appeared that the state's priceless collection of Gobelin tapestries would need to be pledged as securities for foreign loans—a prospect that was widely considered a humiliating affront to the cultural standing of the former seat of the Habsburg Empire. Before the League became involved, early proposals called for the Reparation Commission to take charge of the problem. This idea was promoted by the French, particularly Louis Loucheur, who had served during the war on the Allied Maritime Transport Council before joining Aristide Briand's government as minister with responsibility for reincorporating the regions of Alsace and Lorraine. He suggested using this commission to oversee a kind of a debt commission in Austria, modeled on the International Financial Commission set up in Greece by its foreign creditors in 1898.[79] While some British members of the Reparation Commission made similar suggestions, British and US bankers were skeptical of plans that connected Austria's loans in any way to the politics of reparations or to French efforts to isolate postwar Germany. In London, there was also a reluctance to link reparations to prewar practices of financial imperialism. In Germany, the terms "Ottomanization" and "Tunisization" were already being used to describe the humiliations of reparations and the Allies' supposed betrayal of the racial and civilizational bonds that linked Western European Christendom together, despite the rupture of the war.[80] This charge resonated with observers outside Germany. David Lloyd George himself rejected proposals made by Loucheur to create a debt commission in Germany to enforce the payment of the indemnity, since it was scandalous to treat a major European power, even a former enemy, like Turkey or China.[81] In the case of Austria, Lloyd George wanted nothing to do with the idea of the Reparation Commission handling a loan.[82]

Gobelin tapestries in the War Ministry in Vienna, 1918. *© SZ Photo / Scherl / Bridgeman Images.*

Alternative proposals involved plans for a small board of advisers, appointed by Vienna but approved by the Allied governments, to veto the further issuance of money but without any further "coercive powers."[83] But even in this milder form, there was little disputing that some kind of external control over the government was needed to arrest the collapse of the currency. The question was who would wield it—bankers or governments. Both ideas were perilous: the former, because it would be rejected by the Austrian left as the imposition of a kind of foreign capitalist autocracy; the latter, because it would draw the Allies, as the British Chancellor Austen Chamberlain put it, "into the internal politics of Austria," as well as pledge taxpayers' money for the reconstruction of another country at a moment of postwar rebuilding and belt-tightening in Britain. For British officials, the most attractive idea was control exercised by the League of Nations, since this was an institution that could claim impartiality but still remain under considerable British influence.[84]

The first plans for the League of Nations to oversee a loan to Austria involved adapting proposals made at a 1920 financial conference in Brussels for a commission of bankers and businesspeople working under the auspices of the League to oversee assets designated as securities for European reconstruction loans. The so-called "Ter Meulen" scheme, named for the Dutch banker who proposed it, required a borrowing country to relinquish full control over valuable national property; for this reason, it was attacked from the moment of its suggestion for applying the "Turkish system" or "Chinese system" to Europe.[85] This analogy was not inappropriate: The Ottoman and Greek debt commissions did, in fact, provide the models for legally authorizing the League-appointed Commission to work in the domestic jurisdiction of the borrowing country.[86] Getting Europe's new states to agree to the same treatment would only be possible, as one League report put it, if "it is brought home to them that it is on these conditions and on these conditions only that their countries will get the necessary loans or credits."[87] The first proposed League scheme faltered in part due to the refusal of the Austrian government to agree to any such foreign controls. There were also conflicts between various governments about releasing liens with respect to the costs of military occupation, the payment of reparations, and temporary relief credits.

Support for the involvement of the League of Nations in the Austrian crisis, and for delinking it from the problem of reparations, found other backers. The most powerful was the Bank of England, whose new governor, Montagu Norman, was approached by Salter, Monnet, and other

League officials for help. For Norman, the Austrian crisis provided an opportunity for realizing his broader goals for reshaping postwar Europe by creating independent central banks, insulated from mass politics and linked closely to the Bank of England, to facilitate a return to the gold standard. As a theoretically impartial body, the League's Financial Committee offered a way to legitimate the Bank of England's involvement in the domestic reforms of other countries. The goal was to cement the pound's centrality to the fate of Europe in a world in which British financial hegemony was ceding place to that of the United States.[88] When it came to Austria, Norman articulated a strong vision of depoliticization: anything attached to geopolitical aims was "political," whether this concerned reparations, territorial revisionism, Franco-German rivalries, or Italian designs on Austria.[89] He contrasted this unfavorably with what he called a purely "Economic" or "Financial" system of control. But Norman was not shy about the powers that a League-appointed adviser had to wield in Vienna to protect the interests of bondholders. This was a job, he said, for a person of "high standing, great authority and autocratic powers."[90]

The Bank of England's efforts were closely linked to the interests of the City and Wall Street. From the autumn of 1921 through the summer of 1922, representatives from major US and British banks, like J. P. Morgan and Barings, examined the feasibility of a loan to Austria, as well as a private form of control in Vienna that avoided the foreign policy questions that they claimed would jeopardize the project. Something like this was briefly attempted when the British Treasury made an emergency loan of £2 million to Austria in February 1922 and placed its spending under the supervision of the British banker G. M. Young. This had put Young into the unusual position of playing an important role in Austrian "internal politics," as one contemporary observer wrote in *The Economist,* and temporarily taking up the "position of dictatorship" in Vienna. This innovation was dangerous, the author warned: Putting financial control directly in the hands of one foreign national, rather than spreading it among several different ones, was likely to lead to international rivalries, particularly if this person were British.[91]

League officials similarly worried about placing the powers of control into the hands of bankers. Nixon claimed that an adviser working under the authority of J. P. Morgan would be dismissed as a stooge of foreign capital, which would stoke further conflict in a country with one of Europe's strongest left-wing parties: "To invite [workers] to accept additional financial burdens to satisfy the requirements of a representative of international capitalism is to take the surest means of provoking serious trouble, and this trouble would not be confined to the internal politics of Austria." While bankers sought to avoid "politics" by exercising their own power over Vienna, and thereby sidestepping the designs of the French and Italian governments, Nixon claimed that this risked stirring up even greater political trouble, since empowering a banker over the government threatened the outbreak of a left uprising that could spill over into the rest of southeastern Europe.[92] Nixon was adamant that the Austrian public had to be convinced that the country had not been taken over by foreign bankers.[93] It was "extremely difficult to believe that the Austrian people, however down-trodden, would accept, for instance, to have the price of bread increased at the behest of English or American capitalists," Nixon claimed. The left would see this as "capitalist tyranny."[94]

The form of control that was ultimately developed for Austria over the summer of 1922 was designed to mark a contrast to the direct involvement of a single foreign power or private banks in Austria's domestic affairs. Instead of allowing foreign bondholders or governments to themselves tell the state what to do, the League would act as an intermediary between the state and its creditors. The League would play the role of a "political buffer," Nixon wrote, "to absorb the political shocks and to allow the lenders to secure the efficient administration of their assets with as little meddling in politics as possible."[95] Without placing responsibility for the foreign controls in the hands of an ostensibly neutral organization, he added, it would be impossible to resolve the conflict at the heart of the matter: between a national government reluctant to give up its autonomy and the bankers that insisted it do so if it wanted their money. The bankers naturally saw the Austrian case in the terms of the Chinese Maritime Customs Service or the Egyptian and Ottoman debt commissions. But "Austria is not an Asiatic or African Community," Nixon wrote; instead, it was one of the "oldest civilizations in Europe."[96] Its reform could thus not be "carried out at the simple behest of foreign capitalists:"

> some kind of screen is necessary both to make this control acceptable to the borrowers and to protect the lenders against being drawn into political conflicts. The bankers who are refusing to accept the League of Nations scheme for fear of getting involved in politics have got the thing the wrong way up. Our League Commission of control would bear the brunt of political trouble.[97]

Placing the League as an intermediary between the bondholders and the Austrian government was supposed to distinguish this form of control from that exercised by the debt administrations in Cairo and Istanbul. "It would be absolutely impossible to have a modern enlightened European state controlled by a capitalistic controller," as Monnet put it. "His mission would be a complete failure."[98] They justified this idea in explicitly racist terms. "The City and Wall Street prefer to lend money to Austria direct, partly because they distrust the League (i.e., they distrust France), but more because they do not want any intervention between lenders and borrowers," Nixon told Keynes in April 1922:

> Our scheme is based on the belief that such an intermediary is necessary because of the inter relation of finance and politics. The City thinks of loans to Austria in terms of Egypt or Turkey or the Chinese customs, but they ignore the fact that Austria is not a nigger country and the currency reform is a more complicated and political question than the control of an external debt.[99]

Nixon's casual use of this racist slur showed how he, like many of his colleagues, viewed the symbolism of asking Austria to allow a foreign controller into its internal realms. Unlike in Egypt or China, Nixon insisted, this controller would have a more difficult job in a "complex" society like Austria: not only controlling assets to service the foreign debt, but also intervening deeply in the domestic politics of distribution.[100] The promise of the League was that it could function as a "shock absorber." Its multilateral nature would allow it to get around the "anomaly inherent in the control by private groups of the finances of a civilized European country."[101] The bankers involved had to come to grips with the fact that "neither Austria nor her neighbours," as Nixon told J. P. Morgan partner Dwight Morrow, "will allow Austria to be humiliated by being handed over, as they would say, to the mercy of western capitalists."[102]

In practice, however, the system of control designed for Austria was directly modeled on the debt commissions that had been set up in Tunis, Egypt, the Ottoman Empire, Santo Domingo, and China. Members of the Financial Committee studied these precedents, and, behind closed doors, they formed common, though fraught, points of reference.[103] In a debate about the coercive power that the controller could wield, one Czechoslovak member asked his British counterpart how foreign control in Egypt had worked. "This was very simple," he responded. "The powers of Lord Cromer were purely advisory, but he was supported by a strong 'gendarmerie.'"[104] Members of the Financial Committee knew a Lord Cromer figure for Vienna had to be found. But unlike Cromer, he could not appear to be such an obvious tool of foreign domination that he provoked an uprising. Nixon once again laid out the powers this person needed: the ability to control and manage pledged assets, to approve or disapprove any note issue or law and regulation concerning currency and exchange, and to have the final say over the budget and methods used to raise money. He needed to be satisfied that adequate increases in revenues were being made, but was "so far as possible to abstain from interfering in internal politics."[105] The controller had to break the deadlock of parliamentary conflict without being pulled into it. But if he did not wield enough leverage over the government, bankers would not do business with it. His principal power was to veto spending and refuse to release funds if the government violated its commitment to the reforms.

Nixon claimed that the League's Financial Committee was a nonpolitical entity, since it was formally nongovernmental. But at the same time, he admitted that the work of this controller was, in the end, bound to become as "political as it is possible to be." It was to be far more difficult, he thought, than simply siphoning off revenue to service a foreign debt, as had been done in Egypt, the Ottoman Empire, and China. Instead, it would involve overseeing the dismissal of vast numbers of civil servants, the removal of subsidies to industry and for food, and decisions on basic distributional conflicts:

> The dismissal of railway employees in Austria means a conflict between the Government and the best organised Trade union in a country where social democracy has more power than anywhere else in Europe. The abolition of food subsidies means increasing the cost of living, the choice between fundamental methods of raising revenue is the fundamental question of class legislation. There is no avoiding the fact that the restoration of sound finances in Austria will necessarily entail considerable hardship on certain sections of the population. The responsibility for deciding which those sections shall be is the responsibility which the Controller is asked to assume.[106]

For members of the League's Financial Committee, the reforms Austria needed were obvious. That their implementation would be "very painful" was also clear.[107] The more challenging question was how to legally authorize the powers of the controller. One issue was whether this person was to simply tell the Austrian government in detail what to do, or whether he would outline general benchmarks and then leave it to the government to design its own policies. In Austria, there was support in some elite circles for the former idea, on the grounds that party struggle would prevent the stabilization of the krone unless precise policies were prescribed. Another concern was how to win full parliamentary authorization of his powers, while preventing parliament from interfering with his work. Josef Avenol—a French member of the Financial Committee and later secretary-general of the League—insisted that the government needed a "blank cheque" from parliament that authorized him to undertake reforms without any party interference at all. (Whether it was intended ironically or not, this was a rather loaded metaphor to use in reference to Austria.) Czechoslovak member Vilém Pospíšil suggested that the controller be given the "complete right of sanction" over all Austrian financial policy.[108] There was also the question of whether a single controller or multiple ones were preferable. One member of the committee argued for the former with a criticism of parliamentary democracy then becoming popular on the far right: "one bad cook [is] better than an infinite number of good ones," he argued, "what was wanted was a single Controller who would not be afraid of taking decisions."[109]

In late summer 1922, the Austrian government agreed to the appointment of a League controller in Vienna. Until then, this prospect had proven on multiple occasions to be a red line. But it was clear that Seipel's own efforts to oversee a scheme of austerity thorough enough to win the confidence of foreign lenders had failed. Various political, business, and financial elites in Austria agreed that nothing short of foreign control was needed to rescue the republic from collapse.[110] Opinion in Austria had never been uniformly opposed to it. Seipel had come around in part due to recognition that foreign control was useful for defanging his Social Democratic opponents, who would no longer be able to mobilize parliamentary opposition to austerity.[111] But the prospect was not accepted lightly. Foreign control would continue to be fiercely denounced in Austria and viewed with apprehension in many other countries. Newspapers were full of warnings about the "Tunisification" or "Macedonification" of Austria. One article after another described the dangers of the republic being reduced to the level of a China, Egypt, Turkey, Serbia, or Greece.[112] The charge of "Ottomanization" was so common that it was reported abroad as evidence of anxiety in Austria about the civilizational stakes of

Ignaz Seipel, front right, at a meeting of the League's Council in Paris. *Bibliothèque nationale de France.*

relinquishing sovereignty and pledging state assets, like the Gobelin tapestries, as securities.[113] It was common on both the Austrian right and left to accuse the League of turning the country into a colony and reducing Austria's status to that "of a Madagascar."[114]

Yet Seipel announced at the League's Council that adopting "humiliating" foreign controls was now recognized as the necessary price of relief.[115] On October 4, 1922, the League scheme was inaugurated with the signing of the loan protocols, which detailed the nature of control and set a timeline for reforms to be completed. They were attacked bitterly by the Social Democrats for empowering a foreign dictatorship over the republic and for allowing Seipel to call on outside help to consolidate his counterrevolution.[116] After fierce debate, the Austrian Parliament ratified the protocols the following month, empowering the controller to act outside the bounds of its authority. The person who filled the position was the former mayor of Rotterdam, Alfred Zimmerman, a member of the Dutch Liberal Party with little financial expertise, but who had the advantage of being unlikely to be seen by the Austrian left as overtly capitalist in orientation.[117] He did, however, have another piece of relevant experience: "combating socialists" in Rotterdam, but doing so, as one League official approvingly noted, with "tact."[118]

The International Law of Debt Collection

The novelty of a European state like Austria agreeing to controls by an international institution posed complicated questions about sovereignty for observers at the League, in Vienna, and among government officials in the Allied countries. These questions were also addressed by European and US international lawyers and economic experts, who considered the Austrian case in the context of long-standing debates about foreign financial control. From their vantage point, what was so striking about this case was not the financial control itself, but that it was being implemented by an international institution in a member state in the middle of Europe.[119] But the nature of control was no less onerous as a result. In fact, some legal experts thought it was much more severe in Austria than it had been in places like China, since it was not limited to controlling certain pledged revenues but extended surveillance over all public spending.[120]

The case of Austria fit into a long tradition of debate about the legality of sanctioning debtor states, and more broadly, about the enforcement of contracts between sovereign states and the foreign individuals who lent them money. At the end of the nineteenth century, when more foreign investment was being made than ever before, it was unclear what international legal recourse there was for creditors when foreign governments defaulted on their loans. This became a vibrant topic of legal debate—one that fit into wider discussions about the legality of intervention and interference that had grown so fraught since the Napoleonic Wars.[121] Opinions were generally divided between those interested in protecting the capital of creditors and those interested in defending the sovereignty of states that became debtors. Two programmatic statements were taken to represent these competing views. The first was the 1848 Foreign Office circular of Lord Palmerston, then British foreign secretary, which insisted that it was a matter of discretion, not law, whether a state used diplomatic means to retrieve capital that its citizens lent abroad. The British government was to avoid intervening on behalf of citizens who made risky loans, but it would not rule out doing so if necessary. The second view was most influentially defended in the 1860s in the writings of the Argentinian jurist Carlos Calvo, who claimed that a state could never legally use diplomatic or military force to redress injuries caused to its citizens. The debate came to a head when European gunboats blockaded and bombarded Caracas in 1902 after the Venezuelan government refused to service its foreign debts. At the 1907 Hague Peace Conference, an agreement was reached to denounce the European intervention in Venezuela and set up safeguards against future acts of gunboat diplomacy. It was based on arguments by the Argentinian jurist and foreign minister Luis Drago, who claimed that military interventions were an illegitimate means of recovering debts owed to foreigners. Lenders were aware of the risks they ran when they made loans, and debtors already faced an effective sanction in the reputational injury that default brought.[122] Although it never achieved universal support, the decision at The Hague instantiated a strong legal taboo against the violent recovery of sovereign debts.

But could a state ever legally interfere in the domestic affairs of another to ensure repayment to its citizens? Many legal experts agreed that the modern system of international law was premised on the idea that this would violate the strict independence and legal equality of sovereign states.[123] As we have seen, debates about the legitimacy of interference had earlier focused on whether insurrection or civil wars in one state could be quelled by outside forces, especially during the period of conservative restoration across Europe after the Napoleonic Wars, when the priority of sovereignty took a backseat to that of counterrevolution.[124] The debate moved into financial questions later in the century. For some legal experts, the case was clear: Interference by one state in the domestic affairs of another was justified when the latter became indebted to the citizens of the former. The nineteenth century was full of instances of this kind of meddling. The refusal of Benito Juárez to make interest payments on Mexico's debt in 1861, for example, led to the occupation of Veracruz by several European powers and the ill-fated French attempt to put the Austrian archduke Maximilian on an imperial Mexican throne.[125] The debt commissions established in Istanbul and Athens were among the clearest instances of foreigners reaching into the domestic administrations of other sovereign states. Such meddling was made possible only by a dramatic abdication of these countries' status and powers.[126] For critics, it was no wonder that the creation of these institutions laid the groundwork for further violations of sovereignty. The Egyptian debt commission, one US economist wrote, was the first step to Britain becoming the "practical dictator of Egypt."[127]

The standard liberal justifications for such institutions often relied on claims of civilizational hierarchy and developmental status that were difficult for defenders of these institutions to invoke in the case of Austria. According to these ideas, the Austrian administration was already highly developed, and Vienna was the capital of a former Christian empire that had never, unlike the Ottoman, agreed to foreign controls. If a long history of interference had made the sovereignty of Muslim-majority states more a myth than a reality, the same could not be said of a European state like Austria. Here, different legitimation strategies were needed. Foreign control in Austria was thus justified in two ways. The first justification invoked the supposedly good intentions of the League, which aimed to stabilize the country and not line the pockets of foreign bankers. The second pointed to Austria's membership in the organization itself. The curtailment of sovereignty that the League demanded was acceptable, because the country under control had accepted it freely. The fact that it was exercised by an organization in which the government was a member was key. Illegal interference, in this view, was transformed into legitimate policy delegation by the fact of membership alone.[128]

Such legalistic arguments, however, obscured the fact that a new precedent was being set. Before the 1890s, foreign financial control had only been used in Muslim-majority countries that were, as the Greek economist and League delegate André Andréadès argued, already "accustomed to certain restrictions of their sovereignty." At this point, the doctrine of "non-intervention" remained the rule in Christendom. But beginning in 1896, these controls were brought to Orthodox Christian states in the Balkans, and then to other Christian countries in Latin America and the Caribbean. A line was said to be crossed. Thirty years later, another was. It was not until the 1920s, Andréadès wrote, that such controls were erected in European states that could claim to have once been great powers, even after defeat and dismemberment in the war.[129]

After Seipel's government agreed to the League's intervention in late 1922, the Austrian republic was added to a list of countries that shared the status of a small Balkan country like Serbia—the same upstart that Austria-Hungary had attempted to humiliate and cripple in 1914. Austria's diminished status was made clear in the choice of legal precedents used to write the loan protocols, particularly the clauses protecting Austria's independence and territorial integrity. These clauses were based primarily on early twentieth-century agreements between European empires concerning non-European countries like China and Ethiopia, which were designed to prevent competition over the territory of the latter from leading to war between the former. One of these was the 1907 Anglo-Russian Convention, which was supposed to reduce tensions in Central Asia by confirming Persia's formal sovereignty as well as Russian and British spheres of influence, Tibet's right to non-interference in its internal affairs, and British predominance in Afghanistan. There was some irony that this agreement, which provided a direct model for the Austrian loan protocol, had solidified the Triple Entente that went to war with Austria-Hungary just a few years later.[130]

The Specter of Foreign Control across Europe

It took more than two years of austerity and the sacking of nearly 100,000 government workers, in the face of fierce Social Democratic resistance, for Austria to be declared stabilized.[131] The loans that the League arranged proved popular with investors, and by the early summer of 1923, foreign capital was flowing into Austria. The collapse of the krone was halted. In the summer of 1925, Zimmerman was decommissioned. From the point of view of Geneva, the whole program was a great success. It inspired similar schemes elsewhere, most notably in Hungary.[132] In Greece, a League loan was also made in 1924 to settle more than a million Greek Orthodox refugees from Turkey, though, as we shall see, this marked a new departure into a form of international development lending. In 1926–1928, Bulgaria underwent a similar program of refugee resettlement and financial stabilization.

The reconstruction of Austria also provided a direct model for important provisions of the Dawes Plan, the 1924 agreement reached by Germany with its former enemies for a settlement of the reparations problem and the stabilization of the German currency. The Dawes Plan, also a brainchild of Salter, involved the implementation of foreign controls over the German central bank and various public assets and state railways in exchange for a loan of 800 million marks. Fully aware of the optics, its drafters clarified that, beyond specified functions, it was to avoid all "foreign economic control or interference."[133] But such claims were not convincing to the factions in Germany that exploited public outrage at these controls for their political aims. Just as in Austria, outrage at the foreign interference brought by the Dawes Plan was articulated in racist terms: "If we except the one possible case of Greece," the influential German economist Max Sering wrote in 1929, "no parallel to this situation can

Campaign poster of the Austrian Social Democratic party attacking Seipel's austerity program, which was referred to in German as "die Sanierung." *Austrian National Library/Vienna Picture Archive PLA16333101.*

be found in countries inhabited by the white race, outside Egypt, the Central and South American republics and a few other tropical and sub-tropical places." The implementation of these controls by the Allies in all of the defeated Central Powers showed how much the Versailles Treaty had "debased" Germany "to the level of the subjugated coloured peoples."[134] These criticisms of foreign controls were by no means confined to the far right. By this point, German liberals were also attacking the controls associated with the Allied reparations regime, which came to be seen as one of the principal weaknesses of the Dawes Plan in Britain, the United States, and France as well. The Young Plan that replaced it in 1929, as we shall see, was designed to offer an alternative to what were widely recognized as increasingly untenable practices of foreign control.[135]

Financial controls were not only implemented in the former Central Powers, but also in countries that had already faced the interference of foreign banks in their affairs. Bulgaria was both: It had joined the war on the side of Germany and Austria-Hungary in late 1915 and had since the 1890s had its economic sovereignty chipped away at by its lenders. When Bulgarian politicians and the press fought against a League-appointed adviser in Sofia with veto powers over the budget in the late 1920s, which they claimed violated the country's right to non-interference, they were rehashing an old conflict in a new form.[136] The situation was even more challenging in Balkan states that had fought alongside the Allies but that had faced financial controls before the war. In 1930, King Alexander I of Yugoslavia considered the possibility of a League-controlled loan as an alternative to having French banks continue to bring the country further under French influence.[137] But his finance minister, Stanko Švrljuga, insisted that this would be a tough sell, given Yugoslav "amour propre" and unwillingness to put the country into the same category as former Central Powers or semi-sovereign states like Greece that had long faced foreign controls. Serbia had, after all, fought on the victorious Allied side. And it had been Austria-Hungary's threat to interfere in Serbia's affairs in 1914 that had led to the outbreak of war in the first place. In private, Švrljuga admitted the political and financial advantages of League control. But he doubted other members of the government would allow it. There would be no League loan for Yugoslavia or Romania, a former Balkan member of the Entente.[138]

Other European governments rejected the offer of League loans with controls on similar grounds: for violating their self-determination, insulting their national prestige, associating them with the vanquished Central Powers, and providing a vehicle for rival League member countries to use to their strategic advantage. In Poland, which also experienced hyperinflation in the 1920s, one government after another rejected the idea. They played foreign banks off one another until a loan with the weakest control provisions was found. This opposition was so intense, in part, because Germany, which joined the League in 1926, sought to use a Polish loan to retrieve territory lost during the war. After a coup led by military officer Jósef Piłsudski, Polish officials rejected all plans for international control. In 1927, Piłsudski's government signed the protocols of a foreign loan to be supervised by a single US adviser, Assistant Secretary of the Treasury Charles S. Dewey. His powers were to be strictly limited: potential alignments with political parties or efforts to influence government ministers were prohibited.[139] Opposition from the Polish right and left to such interference resulted in a higher interest rate than what the government would have been offered otherwise. Sovereignty came at a price—but one that even a relatively poor country like Poland was willing to pay.[140]

In the case of European powers with overseas colonial empires, foreign control had other implications. That same year, the Portuguese government rejected a League reconstruction program because of the humiliation that such control was said to bring both to national pride and to the standing of the empire. After the May 1926 coup put the National Dictatorship in power, Portugal's deteriorating financial position led representatives of the new government to turn to Geneva for a £12 million loan to stabilize the escudo, reform Portugal's central bank, and oversee a limited program of economic development. A League group was sent to study Portugal's financial conditions. They recommended a loan managed by a relatively weak foreign controller, who would hold access to the funds but otherwise avoid criticizing the government.[141] But republican exiles furiously lobbied against the idea. They insisted that the 1911 constitution prohibited the government from taking out a loan or allowing any audit of its finances without parliamentary approval. They pleaded with the League to avoid interfering in Portugal's internal affairs for the sake of bailing out the dictatorship.[142] "I must protest against a demand for tutelage that would superimpose external dictatorship onto the internal," the former president Bernardino Machado told Drummond.[143] While League control was appropriate for the vanquished, Machado added, Portugal had chosen the right side of the war alongside its fellow Allied democracies.[144] Other critics of the plans claimed it was impossible to place one of the largest colonial empires in the world under foreign control like the rump states of Austria and Hungary. Doing so would reduce Portugal's status to that of a protectorate.[145] If "a nation confesses that it needs the economic tutelage of the League of Nations," as one contemporary argued, "what moral right . . . can justify its possession of extensive colonies[?]"[146]

The public backlash against League control in Portugal pressured members of the dictatorship to refuse the offer. For the bankers in London involved behind the scenes, control was always the sine qua non for a Portuguese loan, no matter the obstacles posed by national pride.[147] "Control in some form or another is nowadays a market necessity," the Financial Committee chairman Otto Niemeyer told Portuguese diplomat Júlio Dantas in March 1928. This had nothing to do with whether a country had won or lost the war or whether it was new or old, he claimed. Niemeyer, until recently a fast-rising star at the British Treasury, had been hired to the Bank of England by Norman, and became one of the most influential advocates of League controls. While he described them in the neutral language of markets, Niemeyer always insisted they were necessary. Once Geneva was involved with a loan, it had strict responsibility to the bondholders.[148]

Yet in the late 1920s, these arguments were losing their force among possible borrowers. Niemeyer told Dantas that it was better for Portugal's controls to be implemented "by an international body, on which Portugal herself is actually a member, acting impartially in the interests of Portugal, than by a syndicate of private bankers who, with the best intentions, are bound to have regard primarily to the interests of the lenders." Niemeyer reassured him that a foreign expert would not interfere in the country's administration, unlike in Austria or Hungary. But the offer was formally rejected. No loan was seen as worth the risk to Portugal's autonomy.[149] Elsewhere, critics of the League and its methods of financial assistance took heart. Just after Portugal refused the loan's conditions, a short poem published in a right-nationalist German satirical weekly, for example, depicted an impoverished Portuguese peasant proudly rejecting a large sterling loan that came with financial controls. The implication was clear: If such controls were incompatible with the national pride of a poor country like Portugal, why would they be tolerated elsewhere?[150]

In Portugal, the outcome of these events had dramatic effects. The minister of finance who had first approached the League, Sinel de Cordes, was removed from office after supporters turned against him for inviting external supervision of Portugal's affairs. He was replaced by the young University of Coimbra economist, and future leader of the dictatorship, António de Oliveira Salazar. The scheme of austerity that Salazar immediately imposed impressed bankers in London and members of the Financial Committee. They described his iron rule over the budget as an "act of considerable courage," given Portugal's unproductive colonies (such as Angola), a weak balance of payments, the falling value of émigré remittances from Brazil, and the growing risk of communism in Spain.[151] What Salazar demonstrated was that national dictatorship could be used to enforce austerity in a politically and financially unstable country without the need for external controls. Portugal's stabilization won him the support of rich landowners and capitalists and helped to vault him to the head of the state, which he ruled with autocratic authority until 1968.[152] One of the longest-ruling dictators of twentieth-century Europe rose to power in part due to outrage at the prospect of League meddling.

Members of the League of Nations and the Bank of England recognized how unpopular these methods had become. One government after another rejected offers of help.[153] Salter acknowledged the poor reputation of the model he had helped to design. The Austrian case had given the Financial Committee's methods a bad name among other countries looking for loans, particularly those that did not face such dire straits as Austria and that were unlikely to tolerate what he admitted were the drastic measures applied to the former Central Powers.[154] As far off as Mexico, China, and India, observers saw these controls as humiliating affronts to self-determination—or, at best, tools used by victors on their vanquished enemies. They anxiously compared different categories of polities: those that could expect their formal sovereignty to be taken seriously, those that could not, and those that did not have any sovereignty to begin with. As the Indian social scientist Benoy Kumar Sarkar wrote in 1926, Austria and Hungary were now to be listed alongside the South American and Asian states that had shown the political difficulties that came from foreign lending. Although India desperately needed capital for its industrialization, Sarkar wrote, it was clear that foreign loans were "no unmixed blessing"—though India, already under British control, he added, had "nothing new to lose."[155]

In countries that were already suffering under more outright forms of imperialism, there was occasionally support among political and economic elites for the opposite argument: that controls exercised by a multilateral organization were meaningfully different from the direct control of a foreign government or business. In the case of Albania, as we have seen, it was true that League membership brought some benefits: The government was able to protest the terms of control in Geneva in ways that had not been possible in the case of, say, the Egyptian government. This fact had not made it any more popular in Tirana. But the adviser could be sent away when his presence was no longer welcome, though not without risking the country's credit in the process. In China, a few lone voices in the Nationalist government would make similar claims for the advantages of multilateralism over unmediated empire. In the case of a semi-sovereign African member country like Liberia, Nnamdi Azikiwe—a Nigerian nationalist intellectual and later first president of postcolonial Nigeria—claimed that the experiences of Albania, Austria, and Greece had shown how much League control was preferable to direct US or European domination.[156]

But the Liberian case was a difficult one. As the League attempted to define its technical role in a sovereign African member state that faced extensive US official and private forms of interference, there was broad recognition that any League control there had to be in the hands of a Black adviser and avoid overreaching into Liberian internal affairs. But as everywhere, this person would have to wield real powers over the government.[157] For some observers, the attenuation of Liberian sovereignty this entailed was seen as the League, again, being used to launder empire. W. E. B. Du Bois described US attempts to use the League to control the West African country as so far-reaching that even European members of the organization recoiled at their brazenness.[158] African American and anti-imperialist political associations lobbied the US government not to use the League to weaken Liberia's sovereignty. In early 1932, Liberian representatives to the League made it clear that they objected to any proposals that empowered large numbers of foreigners to interfere with Liberia's domestic administration. Continued deadlock between the League, the Liberian and US governments, and the Firestone rubber company threw the prospects for a League program of technical assistance into jeopardy. Ultimately, Monrovia's continued resistance to foreign control forced the project to be abandoned in 1934.[159]

As controversial as they had proven to be, however, the League loans represented a major innovation: An intergovernmental organization had, for the first time ever, actually reached into domestic spaces of policy during times of peace in ways that were supposed to be formally compatible with sovereign equality, de jure if not de facto. As such, these schemes, despite their unpopularity, provided an adaptable model that inspired others for years to come. Postwar planners in the 1940s looked to them as a model for financing development projects and restarting the flow of private capital to devastated countries.[160] Later, the League loans were seen as a precedent for the IMF's conditional loans to Global South countries and successor states of the Soviet Union.[161] But it needs to be emphasized that these ideas did not return out of the blue a half-century later. As we shall see, the conditional form of lending pioneered by the League in the 1920s was already being used by the IMF in related forms as early as the late 1940s, and more during the 1950s, when access to the organization's funds was linked to anti-inflationary and austere fiscal and monetary policies in some member countries. The League did not simply "prefigure" a practice that reappeared at the end of the twentieth century.[162] It developed a practice that, after a hiatus of twenty or so years, became a nearly constant feature of international economic governance.

The League had managed to do the impossible. It had empowered "outsiders" to adjudicate conflicts over domestic economies outside the context of total war. But doing so led to a backlash that temporarily jeopardized the viability of such projects. In the wake of the First World War, the prospects for these attempts to legitimate interference were profoundly uncertain. The extremity of distributional struggles on the national level and the parliamentary deadlock they created, the proliferation of national self-determination claims, and the fierce strategic competition between small and large powers alike made these practices of interference difficult to sustain. Implementing such loans required accommodating European governments to derogations of their sovereignty that amounted to admissions of lower status and diminished power. Doing so also threatened imagined racial hierarchies and challenged a supposed civilizational boundary between non-Orthodox Christian Europe and the rest of the world—one that was assumed to be as inviolable as that of the sovereignty of the Great Powers itself.[163] In the early 1920s, Salter defended the methods that the League developed for Austria as giving "just so much control as, at any moment, is essential to secure the desired object and no more; a method which automatically means less interference as the need is less."[164] But he did not mention how much this marked a departure from the vision of international cooperation he had developed, on the basis of the wartime experience, to legitimate the League's economic powers at its birth. Nor did he mention another fact: the extent to which the organization had come to provide a vehicle for realizing the political visions of the bankers who influenced its work. It is to their visions, as they looked away from Geneva, that we now turn.

CHAPTER 3

An Independent International Bank

A T THE END OF THE 1920s, the search for a solution to the vexing problem of German reparations presented an opportunity to establish another economic institution new to the international scene: what many contemporaries referred to as a "world bank." While the original purpose of this bank was to facilitate the transfer of reparations from Germany to its former enemies, it also provided a vehicle for broader aims. Internationalists had long sought to create an international bank to finance development and international public works, institutionalize a system of economic sanctions, and perform various financial functions to grease the wheels of commerce. In the aftermath of the First World War, groups as politically disparate as Wall Street bankers and French socialists developed plans for an international bank to mobilize resources for Europe's reconstruction.[1] On the eve of the Depression, a new approach to the German reparations issue was seized on by Europe's leading central bankers, who sought to place ad hoc practices of central bank cooperation on firmer institutional footing. Their vision of a politically independent international bank entailed the prospect of a striking new kind of authority and with it the possibility of new forms of interference in domestic realms of banking and monetary policy.

The establishment of the Bank for International Settlements (BIS) over 1929–1930 took place against the backdrop of the postwar rise of these central bankers into new roles as arbiters of international affairs. Led by Montagu Norman of the Bank of England and Benjamin Strong of the New York Federal Reserve, these "lords of finance" attempted during the 1920s to restore the gold standard and oversee a return to what they claimed were the sound financial practices required for a capitalist world economy.[2] The Bank of England, as we have seen, was heavily involved in Europe's postwar financial reconstruction, as were the Banque de France and the New York Federal Reserve Bank, which alongside US investment banks like J. P. Morgan, played an important role in interwar European affairs—despite Washington's official aloofness. The League of Nations' Financial Committee was instrumental in this process. Norman saw it as an "outside body" that could "exercise a wide and impartial authority," as he put it, "behind anything the Central Banks may do."[3] The implementation of the League's stabilization loans in the 1920s was tied to his aim of establishing new, politically independent central banks across Europe to facilitate a return to gold and maintain stable currencies. The multilateral nature of the League was useful for this task, since it provided a way of legitimating what otherwise would have been seen as the unwanted direct involvement of foreign bankers in the painful domestic reforms required for financial stabilization.

Critics often saw the relationship of the League of Nations and Bank of England in sinister terms. In countries where financial stabilization programs were implemented, these programs were routinely criticized for the encroachments on sovereignty they involved. In addition to the appointment of a controller to oversee the balancing of a government budget, another condition of these stabilization loans was the placement of a foreign adviser on the governing board of a central bank to ensure its decision-making was insulated from party conflict and the prerogatives of sitting governments. This demand for externally enforced central bank independence was widely attacked for necessitating an embarrassing abdication to foreign capitalists and for opening the door to the reach of rival powers. This was particularly true in countries that already faced foreign financial controls. In Bulgaria, for instance, critics of the League's reconstruction scheme attacked Bulgarian elites for putting the central bank, the "regulatory node" of the national economy, into foreign hands for the sake of their own narrow interests. This was a serious insult to the national pride of an "ancient" Bulgarian people that had no need for foreign "tutelage."[4] Such charges were not limited to interstate European rivalries. The attempts of US financial experts to create new banks of issue in "underdeveloped" and new countries, and to staff them with foreign experts or bankers, were criticized for similar reasons. When the US financial expert Edwin Kemmerer proposed appointing foreign bankers to the board of directors of the Chilean central bank in 1925, for example, the idea was fiercely denounced in the Chilean press and by domestic bankers as unsuitable to Chile's sovereign status. The only countries that had been forced to allow foreign actors to shape their monetary policy, these critics claimed, were those that had lost the war, including Germany and Austria. Why would a sovereign neutral like Chile accept such an insult to its autonomy and national pride?[5] In a world in which formal sovereignty did not offer guarantees of independence, the question of which countries allowed an "outsider" to shape their domestic policies was always a question of their status and power.

Yet by the late 1920s, the alliance of the League of Nations and these central bankers had proven to be unstable. Due in part to resistance to its programs of financial stabilization, the Financial Committee came to be seen by Norman as less useful to his project of remaking Europe's economies.[6] The establishment of the BIS promised a different approach. Its creation represented a new departure in efforts to compel governments to grant extensive powers to an independent international institution.[7]

The BIS was designed to be a fully nongovernmental institution, run exclusively by representatives of national central banks—and in the case of the United States, private investment banks. On the national level, many of these central bankers were at this time engaged in fierce struggles to defend their autonomy from political control. It was in the wake of the First World War, in fact, that the first international movements to formalize the independence of central banks took off, long before the global push for central bank independence of the late twentieth-century neoliberal era.[8] The creation of the BIS involved these bankers making two demands: first, that governments confirm the independence of their national central banks; and second, that they be allowed to act in concert with foreign counterparts free from any political influence. This strict independence was also supposed to reduce tensions arising from the collection and distribution of German reparations and allow for the removal of the foreign controls placed on Germany by the Treaty of Versailles and the Dawes Plan. By the end of the 1920s, as we have seen, these controls had become widely unpopular both in Germany and beyond it.

But creating a fully independent "world bank" raised the possibility that it, too, could develop powers to interfere in domestic arenas—not only in Germany, but also in its former enemies. During 1929–1930, the fierce contests over the institutional design of the BIS among government officials, bankers, and political parties and activists in many countries put new pressure on postwar conceptions of economic sovereignty.

From J. P. Morgan to the French Chamber of Deputies to the central bank of fascist Italy, debates about whether the BIS would take on governmental or private form, and whether it would be attached to the League, involved clarifying whether banks or governments had the final say over important financial policies—whether on the national or international levels. Who, in the end, was sovereign? As disputes about the foundation of the BIS intensified, it became clear that key assumptions about central bank independence and its meaning as a norm of international governance were more unstable than the defenders of the ideal of "depoliticized" banking were willing to admit. Once the BIS was set up, national governments would have no way of checking its decisions—a power that was to be entrusted to autonomous central banks alone. While the international bank was designed to be fully "nonpolitical," however, not all of its member banks, in practice, enjoyed the same degree of independence from government control. Thus the bank could potentially become a vehicle for some countries to indirectly influence the domestic monetary conditions and policies of others. What had emerged as an elegant solution to one form of interference—that implicated in the German reparations problem—now posed a broader challenge to the sovereignty of postwar states.

Reparations and Foreign Control

The immediate reason for the establishment of the BIS was to facilitate a final settlement of the German reparations problem and to remove the many foreign controls placed on Germany by the Allies after the war. Its creation was to be the final step in a series of efforts to depoliticize this problem, which was an extraordinarily destabilizing force in interwar European politics.[9] Repeated attempts to reduce tensions over reparations in the 1920s either failed outright or generated other problems. The original Allied reparations regime had placed significant burdens on German sovereignty. This was one of the reasons why it was so controversial and unpopular. Article 231 of the Treaty of Versailles, which assigned Germany exclusive blame for the outbreak of the First World War, provided a legal basis for far-reaching measures to collect the indemnity in Germany. The Allies also established an intergovernmental body, the Reparation Commission, to extract sensitive economic and military information from the German government, collect payments, and demand adjustments to its domestic policies. The Reparation Commission was one of several temporary international bodies created at the Paris Peace Conference that was endowed with extensive administrative powers, far more than the League of Nations itself.[10] As we have seen, the French originally suggested that the Reparation Commission take charge of Austria's finanical reconstruction before the League was chosen as a less "political" alternative. In Germany, the Reparation Commission also functioned as a kind of tribunal. When it determined that Germany was in default of required deliveries of timber and coal, French and Belgian forces occupied the Ruhr Valley in early 1923, which threw the entire postwar settlement into jeopardy.

In the wake of the occupation of the Ruhr, the Dawes Plan was implemented in 1924. A major revision to the reparation regime, it was designed by US bankers and businesspeople in consultation with European governments to reschedule German reparation payments while effecting a broader stabilization of German finances. The Dawes Plan involved balancing the government budget, improving the collection of taxes, arranging a foreign loan of 800 million marks, and establishing a new independent gold bank to help stabilize the value of the currency.[11] Directly modeled on the Austrian financial stabilization scheme, the Dawes Plan involved several new forms of foreign control: the empowerment of a foreign adviser to arrange the transfer of payments without destabilizing currency markets; the appointment of foreign members to the new gold bank; the foreign administration of certain controlled revenues, which, if necessary, could be extended to other controls over the German budget; and foreign supervision of the state railways.[12] This arrangement was highly intrusive. When visiting Germany in 1925, Strong described his amazement at the "interference and inquiries and controls" imposed on Germany, which he doubted people in the United States would tolerate. "The extensive character of these controls in Germany is really unbelievable," Strong noted:

> A large part of the western frontier is in possession of a foreign army, extending right into the vitals of German industrial districts; foreign directors in the Reichsbank; a commissioner for supervising their note issue and accounts; and the entire railroad system in the hands of a French commissioner; all of the industrial establishments mortgaged to foreign nations, and in general under the supervision of a foreigner; government financing, the budget, and the whole scheme of central banking and foreign finance subject more or less to inquisitorial supervision by the Transfer Committee; they are called upon

to make endless reports and statistics; to have matters of policy and specific transactions questioned.[13]

Over time, these foreign controls became a serious political liability. While the Dawes Plan was celebrated then and later as an elegant response to a profoundly dangerous situation—one that brought Europe some stability in the mid-1920s and allowed US capital to flood into Germany—it was undeniably linked in the eyes of many contemporaries to controversial prewar practices of financial imperialism.[14] In Germany, these control provisions were attacked by right-wing movements and parties as insulting to German sovereignty and national pride.[15]

One of the reasons for renegotiating German reparation payments at the end of the 1920s was to replace these foreign controls with arrangements that did not involve the same derogations of German sovereignty. The Young Plan agreed to in 1929, after long negotiations in Paris, reduced the total sum of reparations, arranged another loan for Germany, removed all occupying military forces and foreign economic controls, and set into motion the establishment of the BIS. It won support from influential German liberals, who claimed it had overturned the troubling impositions of the reparations regime—which for "the first time in history," the economist Moritz Julius Bonn wrote, had put the "financial management of a fully developed country" under foreign control. The Young Plan was to return European civilizational balance to equilibrium, Bonn implied, which had been unsettled when the Reparation Commission had attempted to rule over Germany like European debt commissions in "backwards" or "distressed" countries, such as Turkey, Egypt, and China. Unlike the "benevolent supervision" of these commissions, Bonn wrote—which had set unstable countries on a path of development and progress—the Reparation Commission simply existed to siphon off the wealth of an already developed European country. The Young Plan did away with all of this: "The internal contradiction, that Germany was a sovereign democracy, but that its administration and legislation were determined by other powers, has been overcome," Bonn insisted. "Responsible freedom takes the place of irresponsible servitude."[16]

The removal of foreign controls over Germany also appealed to the British, French, and US designers of the Young Plan. In London, as we have seen, there had long been apprehension about subjecting Germany to an excessive degree of interference for the sake of collecting reparations and doing so in ways that were reminiscent of prewar practices of

Anglo-French financial imperialism in North Africa, the Middle East, and China.[17] While the Dawes Plan had been designed to alleviate political tensions concerning reparations, it had not gone far enough. Before the Dawes Plan, as the French central banker Pierre Quesnay put it, the German government had paid its former enemies directly, as the "tribute of one people to another." This had made the process political to the point of deadlock. The innovation of the Dawes Plan had been to empower an intermediary between the German government and the Allied powers—the supposedly neutral US agent general, Seymour Parker Gilbert, a former undersecretary of the Treasury. Gilbert acted as a "filter" through which the reparation payments lost some of their political character.[18] But, like the League advisers in Vienna and Tirana, Gilbert came to be seen as the stooge of a foreign government. In 1927, as he began to openly criticize German government spending and was loudly attacked in Germany,

"Save with Gilbert!" An image of Seymour Parker Gilbert on the cover of the satirical German weekly *Simplicissimus* from November 1927, depicting him enforcing spending cuts on Germany. Simplicissimus.

Gilbert himself increasingly recognized that the drama of reparations would never be resolved as long as Germany was under his supervision.[19] Other economic and legal experts outside of Germany similarly criticized the "international receivership" that Gilbert led over the German state.[20] The designers of the Young Plan justified it on the grounds that it removed Gilbert from Germany and thereby provided the country with "welcome freedom from interference and supervision."[21]

The experts involved with the crafting of the Young Plan called for the creation of an international bank as part of the process of restoring German sovereignty and removing the reparations problem even further from political considerations. By acting as a trustee for the indemnity payments and managing their distribution, the bank would obviate the need for any interference in German domestic affairs. It would transform the entire problem from a "political" one into a financial one. The German central bankers involved in the bank's foundation supported it for this reason: It removed controls that were "irreconcilable with the dignity of a sovereign State."[22] The authority of Gilbert, the US "king" in Germany, as he was called, was to give way to the disciplinary—though impersonal and nonpolitical—forces of international markets.[23] A disinterested institution, in which Germany was an equal member—unlike in the Reparation Commission—was to oversee the collection and distribution of payments. This new kind of intermediary was needed because the problem, if it were to be solved, had to be "depoliticized," argued Josiah Stamp, a director of the Bank of England, using what was then an uncommon term. The issue of reparations was to be handed over to bankers, who were said to see the world in terms of balance sheets, not questions of national prestige or strategic competition.[24] These bankers were meant to exercise a more legitimate form of power than the personal authority of Gilbert, who was closely tied to the US government. But they would exercise their own discretionary judgments on financial matters that could not, by their very nature, ever be fully detached from political considerations.

Central Bank Independence as an International Norm

While there was broad support in 1929 for establishing an international bank to remove existing forms of interference in Germany's domestic affairs, it quickly became apparent that this bank might be able to develop powers of interference itself—not only in Germany, but also more widely. As the details of the powers and legal basis of the BIS were worked out among government officials, bankers, and economic experts from Europe, the United States, and Japan, its precise relationship to national governments was at the center of debate. This process unfolded over a roughly twelve-month period, beginning in early 1929 at the international conference in Paris where the Young Plan was designed. The next stage in the bank's creation came in August at a conference at The Hague, where the Young Plan was ratified and a committee designated to finalize the bank's technical and legal details. This committee met in Baden-Baden that autumn. Its plans were ratified at another conference at The Hague in January 1930. The BIS opened its doors shortly thereafter.

Throughout this process, leading the charge for the international bank were the world's leading monetary authorities, who sought to use it to facilitate and formalize central bank cooperation. Since the war, central bank cooperation had mostly been orchestrated by the outsized personalities of Norman and Strong. The latter's death in 1928 added urgency to the task of replacing these personal links with more durable institutional arrangements. These central bankers also provided another source of support for ensuring that the international bank was removed from all "politics," which they claimed was the archenemy of sound money. Its establishment unfolded against the backdrop of their efforts to formalize their own freedom from governmental control on the national level.

In the wake of the First World War, a powerful movement for central bank independence had taken off in various different countries, as many banks attempted to regain the autonomy they had lost during the war, when they had been corralled by governments into financing its costs. The supporters of central bank independence claimed it was necessary to prevent inflation, as the march of democracy threatened to turn these banks into tools of political patronage—a "political octopus, a national Tammany Hall," as Paul Warburg, one of the founders and vice chair of the US Federal Reserve, put it in 1922.[25] By this point, it had become a staple of financial orthodoxy on both sides of the Atlantic that there existed a rigid firewall between the realms of "politics" and "finance." The language of "interference" was also used in this case to describe the dangers of effacing the clear border between them. Above all else, central bankers were said to need protection from the "day-to-day interference" of politicians.

Europe's major central banks had always had a complex relationship with the governments of their country of domicile. When the Bank of England was founded in 1694, for example, it was a joint-stock company that was authorized to perform a variety of functions, including issuing notes and discounting bills. In practice, it made most of its business by lending to the Crown. Over the following century, as the British state accumulated vast debts to the Bank of England from the costs of waging nearly ceaseless war with France, the Bank's privileges were expanded when its charter was renewed. During the second half of the nineteenth century, it took on a greater role in promoting domestic financial stability: playing the role of lender of last resort during crises by adjusting the rate at which it made loans to other banks and protecting the convertibility of the pound to gold at a fixed rate. But it was still a private institution, free from direct government control.[26] At this time, as Otto Niemeyer put it, a "change in bank rate was no more regarded as the business of the Treasury than the colour which the Bank painted its front door."[27] While Niemeyer's later recollections exaggerated the extent to which a clear doctrine of independence existed from time immemorial, it was true that over the second half of the nineteenth century, and certainly by the eve of the First World War, there was an increasingly formalized notion of the need to keep the Bank free from political control.[28] During the First World War, this idea was unsettled. In its wake, Norman, who became governor in 1920, asserted the Bank's autonomy and put himself at the head of a transnational movement to remove central banks from the supposedly corrupting influences of elected politicians and authoritarian demagogues alike, who were said to make a mockery of sound money in their appeals to the masses.

In practice, each major central bank enjoyed a different degree and kind of independence after the war.[29] The Bank of England's status was widely seen as the ideal. But even though Norman was fiercely antagonistic to politicians, the Bank of England had extensive contacts with the Treasury. There remained a large degree of consensus on policy among central bankers and government officials—as there had been in the nineteenth century—even when the latter did not formally dictate to the former. When Churchill as chancellor made the decision to return to the gold standard at the prewar parity in 1925, it was true that he was pushed do so by the Bank of England, famously over the advice of John Maynard Keynes, who published a critical pamphlet on the folly of this decision.[30] But Churchill was also encouraged to do so by members of the Treasury, led by Niemeyer, who left the government to join the Bank two years later.[31] Overlapping official and financial circles in London were in broad agreement that this was the right course of action. While the Treasury had the final say, however, the Bank of England would be widely blamed for the disastrous effects that the return to gold had on British employment. This set the stage for the years of the Depression, when the Bank's failure to rescue the economy led to its further fall from influence, leading to its nationalization in 1946.[32]

By contrast, the Banque de France, founded under Napoleon in 1800, had traditionally enjoyed less autonomy than its British counterpart, though it, too, straddled an awkward middle ground between the public and private. Its governor and some of its regents were appointed by the Ministry of Finance, but most of its regents represented the interests of shareholders. In the 1920s, French central bankers loudly defended their independence, particularly after the moderate left-wing coalition government of the Radical Socialist Édouard Herriot, the Cartel des Gauches, came to power in the elections of May 1924. During the period of financial and political instability that followed, marked by inflation, budget deficits, capital flight, and frequent government turnover, the Banque de France refused at key moments to cooperate with the government to stabilize the currency. Shortly after the appointment of Émile Moreau to the governorship of the bank in 1926, the cartel government fell and was replaced by the right-wing government of Raymond Poincaré. Although the franc was finally stabilized, suspicions of the bank deepened, on account of its power to decide the fate of an elected government.[33] In the United States, the Federal Reserve System, established only in 1913, also sought greater independence from the Treasury after the war. In the 1920s, the Federal Reserve Bank of New York became a powerful actor on the international stage under the leadership of Strong.[34]

The push to create an international bank over 1929–1930 became closely intertwined with these national contests for central bank independence. One of the reasons the European central bankers involved in the establishment of the BIS insisted so strongly that it be detached from government control was to affirm the autonomy of the banks they ran on the national level, leading to suspicions that their efforts were in the service of a transnational "'hands off central banks' movement."[35] Since the war, insisting on independence on the international stage to protect it on the national front was a common strategy for central bankers and other defenders of financial orthodoxy. At international conferences in Brussels in 1920 and Genoa in 1922, for example, attendees had called for creating new and autonomous banks in countries that lacked them and for existing banks to be insulated from political interference. The League of Nations' financial reconstruction schemes had attempted to put these ideas into practice, as had the Dawes Plan, through the appointment of foreign advisers to central banks to prevent their policies from being controlled by governments.[36] While such international efforts to institute and affirm the independence of national central banks were common after the war, they were most successful in countries that already faced other forms of foreign interference. The new or reformed independent central banks of the postwar were almost without exception established in countries that did not, in practice, enjoy full economic sovereignty: the former Central Powers; new countries in the Baltics, Balkans, and Eastern Europe; countries like Greece already under foreign control; or Latin American countries that had long been sites of US and European informal imperialism. The others were established in colonies, including India, Madagascar, and Angola.[37]

Contemporaries frequently remarked on the unusually far-reaching degree of independence enjoyed by these postwar banks. Some claimed that the one set up in Vienna under League supervision was the first, in fact, to enjoy true political autonomy.[38] In early 1922, the Allies also successfully compelled the German government to legally grant the Reichsbank an extensive degree of political independence in exchange for a reparations payment moratorium. While the autonomy of the German Reichsbank was celebrated as being rivaled only by that of the Bank of England, it was also attacked, even by the German bankers who supported this autonomy in principle, as an imposition by the Allies on a defeated enemy. Its legal independence, in any case, did little to prevent the Reichsbank from discounting government bills in ways that accelerated the inflation already under way.[39] But financial instability, the political and administrative chaos of many postwar states, and the leverage wielded by the Allies over postwar reconstruction and reparations made possible the first experiments in externally instituting central bank independence across Europe.

Insisting on the complete independence of the BIS, however, was a more audacious demand than creating independent banks in new, unstable, or defeated countries like Austria or Albania. While these new banks of issue were established in countries with already damaged sovereignty, the BIS could potentially exercise interventionist powers in states that were not accustomed to such interference. In wealthy and powerful countries like the United Kingdom, the politics of central bank independence, as controversial as they could be, did not involve the same questions about foreign meddling. Even in countries where central bankers were granted autonomy, they were still nationals who worked within the legal bounds set by governments. In Britain, extensive informal links existed between civil servants and central bankers, even when the latter's independence was respected. But asking governments to allow these bankers to make decisions in concert with their foreign counterparts, without a way to check these decisions, had different, and potentially more significant, stakes. Would a powerful government, like that of Britain, allow questions about the pound to be put into foreign hands in an institution that it would not be able to control directly? For other countries, the bank was threatening for other reasons. Unlike the League, it was not an institution theoretically open to the membership of any sovereign state, but was controlled by a small handful of the world's most powerful financial institutions.

Debating the Independence of the International Bank

The struggle over the creation of the BIS in 1929–1930 involved a variety of political actors, bankers, and experts from different countries. Over the summer of 1929, it was the British government that posed the greatest resistance to granting it a significant degree of political autonomy. This reluctance was due, in part, to general apprehension about the Young Plan among members of the Labour government of Ramsay MacDonald that had come to power that June. The new chancellor, Philip Snowden, a longtime Labour politician and former chancellor in the first MacDonald government, sought to square the circle of attacking lingering British unemployment without further unbalancing the budget. He opposed reducing the total sum of reparations for this reason. In the first Labour government of 1924, Snowden had undertaken cautious and orthodox policies and had enjoyed good relations with the Bank of England as a result. But now, the Bank of England was being widely blamed for having thrust the country into unemployment after insisting on returning to gold in 1925, and it was criticized for its detachment from democratic politics.[40] Allowing an international bank to enjoy a wide degree of autonomy was an even more alarming prospect: It threatened to create a "financial autocracy," Snowden claimed, "without parallel and quite outside Governmental control."[41] In agreeing to its creation, there was a risk that the government would be admitting its powerlessness to deal with the pressing political problem of domestic unemployment by conceding to the deflationary rules of gold enforced by the bank with its foreign partners.

In the British Treasury, one solution that was proposed to this problem was to attach the international bank to the League of Nations, where the British government still exercised significant influence.[42] Some officials opposed this idea, since it would prevent the United States from joining the bank and thus jeopardize the Fed's further involvement in Europe. It would also put the problem of reparations back into the sphere of "politics," which would violate the whole purpose of the bank in the first place, and would encourage poorer League member countries to ask it for handouts.[43] But other members of the government worried about the bank exercising unaccountable powers.[44] Attaching the bank to the League provided at least some way of checking it. Arthur Salter was a major proponent of this idea. As the League's Assembly convened in September 1929, he met with MacDonald to remind him that Article 24 of the Covenant specified that all future "international bureaux" were to come under League direction.[45] Salter agreed that central banks should be free from the daily reach of politicians, but he insisted that the Treasury was never as powerless to direct Bank policy as some claimed. Giving an international bank "world powers entirely independent of any control whatever," however, would prevent any government from being able to influence its decisions.[46]

The idea that the League of Nations could be brought into a direct relationship with the BIS was not only advocated as a way for the British Treasury to ensure a back-channel route of control over it. This idea was also supported by representatives from countries that were not involved in the bank's foundation. At the League's Assembly, delegates from Denmark, Norway, and Poland called for allowing the League to have some relationship to the BIS, certainly if its work was not to be limited to German reparations but was to include policies that affected economic conditions around the world.[47] A fully nongovernmental bank would provide no recourse for these countries if it were "exerting a preponderating and undesirable influence" on their economic interests, as one Norwegian delegate put it. He spoke to an obvious problem of an international financial organization with a narrow membership: Although its decisions would have widespread effects across an interdependent global financial system, only a few countries would have a say in how these decisions were made. While delegates to the Assembly called for the bank to have a closer relationship with the League to prevent it from becoming a tyrant, others sought to link them so that the League could direct the bank's resources to productive purposes, including the economic development of non-

European countries. The Austrian delegate Max Hoffinger suggested that the bank be used to finance the League's liberal aims by providing credits that governments could use to help protected industries adapt to international competition, thus encouraging timid politicians to lower barriers to trade.[48] But French delegates opposed these ideas, as did their British counterparts, as Snowden had grown nervous about the League becoming involved with the bank's organization at this late stage.[49]

One of the leading architects of plans for a highly autonomous international bank was also French. This was Pierre Quesnay, a young financial expert who in 1926 had been hired by the Banque de France away from the League's Financial Committee, where he had played an important role in Austria's financial reconstruction.[50] Quesnay was sensitive to the charge that a private international institution could provide a vehicle for the forces of international finance to subordinate national governments. But he claimed that such fears were exaggerated. The relationship of the international bank to governments would be no different from that between these governments and the autonomous central banks already within their borders, to which these governments already "delegated responsibilities for the general interest."[51] Quesnay knew firsthand, however, that this principle was not as uncontroversial as he made it out to be. He had himself only just recently waged a struggle to preserve the autonomy of the Banque de France from the reach of the French Ministry of Finance—an autonomy that had always been less secure than that of the Bank of England. Despite public protestations about the nonpolitical nature of their institutions, moreover, Norman and Moreau, governor of the Banque de France, competed over the stabilization of Europe. Their banks were never divorced from national strategic aims and seldom as insulated from governments in defining these aims as they claimed.

Yet Quesnay insisted that the Banque de France and the Bank of England could productively cooperate in the founding of the BIS. And he was confident that Norman would not seek to dominate it as he had the League's Financial Committee. Quesnay insisted that both banks shared a similar conception of the new international institution: completely nonpolitical and detached from the League, rigidly anti-inflationary in its aims, and not limited to dealing with reparations. But Quesnay also recognized the anxiety in the Bank of England that the French would attempt to seize control of the BIS to compensate for their relative lack of power in the League's Financial Committee. Norman had, after all, long refused to believe that the Banque de France was truly independent of the French

Pierre Quesnay. *Bibliothèque nationale de France.*

government. At the same time, Moreau also worried that the BIS could evolve into a "super bank" that controlled national markets and interfered "in the affairs of each country." To make the plans successful, each side had to be convinced of the other's political disinterest in this new institution.[52]

When Quesnay traveled around Europe in September 1929 to win support from other central bankers for his vision of a fully autonomous international bank, he found that there was no consensus on this question. Despite Norman's commitment to central bank independence, the Bank of England was anxious not to alienate the new Labour government in power. For this reason, Norman decided to appoint Walter Layton to the organizational committee set to meet in Baden-Baden the following month. After leaving the League's Economic and Financial Organization, which he had played a role in designing after his wartime stint as Churchill's deputy at the inter-Allied Munitions Council, Layton had returned to *The Economist* as editor-in-chief, where he advocated Treasury control of the international bank. While Layton's publication opposed currency and banking questions from being "dragged into the cockpit of party politics," the magazine was also skeptical of the idea that a central bank should act as a "sovereign power within the State."[53] When Norman first contacted Layton about ensuring a fully independent international bank, Layton apparently told him that this idea violated basic principles of democratic self-governance.[54] But for Norman, appointing Layton, who was clearly antagonistic to his views, was a useful strategy for preventing the project from being blown up by the Labour government.[55] Norman told Moreau that his appointee would not be suspected of "speaking for any of us Central Bankers," which would help dispel suspicions they were creating an international financial "autocracy"—exactly what Snowden told Layton to prevent.[56]

What was striking was that one of the most vocal supporters for Quesnay's highly autonomous vision of the BIS was not Norman, but instead the Italian financial expert Alberto Beneduce, one of Mussolini's closest advisers. Beneduce agreed with Quesnay that the international bank should be completely free from any government control, detached from the League, and run according to a constitution written by central bankers alone. He was deeply opposed to Layton's attempts to involve treasuries in its functions.[57] Beneduce, one of the single most influential individuals in interwar Italy, was a close associate of the long-time director general of the Bank of Italy, Bonaldo Stringher, who had fought to protect his bank's autonomy after Mussolini's attacks on it during the early years of the fascist regime. For many strict adherents to the ideal of central bank independence outside of Italy, the Bank of Italy appeared to be little more than the appendage of an illegitimate dictatorship. But in the second half of the 1920s, as the US Federal Reserve and J. P. Morgan became more involved in the stabilization of the Italian lira, guarantees of the bank's independence were made a condition of their assistance. Italy's dependence on external aid thus provided a real constraint on Mussolini's encroachments on the bank. After the lira's return to gold in 1926, the Bank of Italy was granted a greater degree of autonomy, according to Beneduce's and Stringher's designs.[58] Throughout his role in the creation of the BIS, Beneduce occupied a unique position: the financial "eminence grise" of fascist Italy was claiming this new international institution be given full insulation not only from the corrupting influences of democracy, but also from the highly antidemocratic strain of nonetheless mass-based politics being pioneered in Rome.[59] His efforts to establish a nongovernmental BIS were in line with this strategy of cementing the independence of the Bank of Italy on the international stage while affirming it at home.

In the case of the United States, it was the same J. P. Morgan bankers who had played a role in bailing out Mussolini's regime who took charge of US involvement in the establishment of the BIS.[60] As the Young Conference met in Paris in 1929, the Hoover administration had clarified that the US Federal Reserve would not participate in any international institution, even though the president was not legally authorized to issue this decree, as contemporary observers like the US economist Eleanor Dulles eagerly pointed out.[61] Hoover's decision reflected abiding worries about Republican senators rejecting any such foreign entanglements as well as the unwillingness of the US government to get directly involved in the reparations problem or risk touching a third rail of US politics: connecting reparations in any way to the issue of Allied war debts, which, as business transactions, were defined officially as matters of domestic policy that could not be opened to diplomatic negotiation.[62] At the US Treasury, the idea of depoliticizing the reparations problem by turning it into an investment opportunity was also unconvincing. Reparations would always be "political," officials claimed, meaning that the Federal Reserve could have no jurisdiction over this issue.[63] US participation in the BIS was thus to remain in the hands of the investment banks that had already played a role in financing Europe's reconstruction.

These bankers agreed that the international bank needed to be protected from any government interference. And they held deep apprehensions about the designs of the British Labour government.[64] It was Thomas Lamont, in fact, an influential partner at J. P. Morgan—and one of the principal private architects of US financial diplomacy in Europe—who became one of the most influential propagandists for a nongovernmental international bank. Lamont worked to convince MacDonald and Snowden to drop their insistence on the involvement of the British Treasury, which he claimed would turn the BIS into little more than "a new and glorified Reparation Commission."[65] But Snowden held his ground. He insisted that governments would not tolerate a bank they could not prevent from deleteriously affecting "the national economic interests for which they are responsible" and that could be harnessed for "reactionary policy."[66] Lamont and other J. P. Morgan bankers thought Snowden's obstinance was threatening to torpedo the whole plan, and they worried about rumors that Layton sought to link the BIS to the League. This was "probably the worst thing that could happen to" it, wrote Gilbert, who after leaving his position as agent general in Germany had become a partner at J. P. Morgan.[67] As we have seen, US investment banks like J. P. Morgan had not avoided working through the League on other occasions. In fact, Jeremiah Smith Jr., a legal adviser to the Morgan bank, and also involved with BIS planning, had served as the commissioner-general for the League's financial reconstruction program in Hungary, where he, like Alfred Zimmerman in Vienna and Jan Hunger in Tirana, had fought with a national parliament over the interference he posed in Hungarian domestic affairs.[68] But in this case, the League, by dint of its connection to foreign offices and treasuries, was considered by these bankers to be far too political for the job of handling reparations and central banking issues, whatever League officials claimed about their strict impartiality in matters of finance and politics.

Creating the Independent International Bank

The disputes about the nongovernmental character of the BIS between the winter and late summer of 1929 set the terms for negotiations over its institutional and legal details that autumn, when a committee of organizers—mostly bankers from Germany's reparations creditors and from Germany and the United States—met in the Black Forrest spa town of Baden-Baden. Punctuated by the announcement of the Wall Street crash in late October, their highly secretive work focused on technical questions about the bank's legal status and its financial powers. Many of the seemingly arcane matters they discussed, however, were framed in light of the bank's relationship to "politics" and governments. When the question was raised of whether a member of the British House of Lords could serve on its board, for example, there was protracted debate about whether an unelected hereditary peer could be said to be speaking for an elected government, which would disqualify this person from the job.[69]

Much of the organizational work in Baden-Baden focused on establishing the relationship of the BIS to national governments in its founding legal documents. Various agendas were in play. The British delegation was led by Layton and Charles Addis, a longtime member of the Hongkong and Shanghai Bank and architect of British financial diplomacy in China, who had joined the court of the Bank of England in 1918 and served as a foreign member of the German Reichsbank under the Dawes Plan.[70] While Addis was close to Norman, Layton ensured they operated with an eye to the Treasury's demand that the bank be brought under some governmental control.[71] They proposed a dual legal structure for it. Its constitution would be submitted to governments for approval and could be periodically revised by them, while the statutes laying out its functions would be written and modified by bankers alone.[72] The separation of the "legislation" governing the bank from its day-to-day "administrative control" would preserve the "ultimate right of a State to intervene" while creating "as many barriers as possible between the administration of currency or credit and political influences."[73]

The analogy they had in mind was the relationship of the British Treasury to the Bank of England. While tradition granted the Bank of England a large degree of autonomy from political direction, the government never relinquished the right to write the rules determining the nature of this relationship. The Bank's privileges were outlined in its charter, which had been periodically renewed by the government since the late seventeenth century, until the 1844 Bank Charter Act by Parliament granted it a new set of powers over the currency. In the case of the international bank, more autonomy than this was unlikely to be tolerated by national governments that insisted on their sovereign right to prescribe the national currency and credit institutions; these governments regarded any institution handling "large sums of public money" with suspicion. If a government chose to exercise its sovereign powers by delegating responsibility to a central bank, Lamont and Addis claimed, it did so only by clarifying the terms of this delegation—and by reserving the right to withdraw or alter it at any time. The same had to be true for the international bank.[74] The power to establish the bank, determine its activities, and fix and later revise its constitution should all belong to governments. But the actual activities of the bank would be removed from politics. This meant that the bank was to be kept from acts like granting credits to one country over another on the basis of political or strategic considerations.[75]

Beneduce and Quesnay fought for a much stronger version of the bank's autonomy. In their view, not only were governments to have no ability to interfere with its work, but its statues were to be written and modified by central bankers alone, without any government involvement at all.[76] The BIS was to be external to the sovereignty of any state. But it was to be prevented from encroaching on this sovereignty and interfering in a country's internal affairs by veto powers given to national central banks.[77] Quesnay acknowledged fears that a bank completely beyond the reach of governments might create credit at will, make political loans to states, and weaken national sovereignty.[78] But he and Beneduce insisted that the relationship of governments to the international bank would be no different from their relationship to the national central banks to which they already delegated significant powers.[79] The BIS would bring administrative efficiency to the informal contacts that existed between these banks without entailing any dramatic transformation of the international order whatsoever.[80]

But this ideal of universal central bank independence was a myth. The robust vision of it that Quesnay and Beneduce claimed was a settled matter was not even guaranteed in their own countries. It was also already clear that demand for the BIS to use its resources to develop poorer and rebuilding countries was immense. This, by itself, showed that central banking orthodoxy was for many contemporaries far less important than the mobilization of capital for particular strategic aims or profit-making opportunities. While in Baden-Baden, for instance, Quesnay wrote to French diplomat Robert Coulondre to tell him to deny a Lithuanian government request for using the BIS to finance the country's reconstruction, despite any interest the Quai d'Orsay might have in doing so. Allowing the BIS to become involved in such projects would give it the appearance of a "political organism and confer on it powers that governments and public opinion are justly frightened of."[81] But Quesnay had less to say about the opposite fear: that removing the bank completely from government control was also dangerous—a fear that would soon be expressed by critics in the French government itself.

As the details of the bank's design were worked out in the last weeks of 1929, some of the most difficult questions its architects faced concerned how to delimit its powers while at the same time preventing governments from being able to do so themselves. There were various anxieties about the bank's potential powers, including its ability to make direct loans to governments, become involved in international political intrigues, or create credit at will and risk inflation. One of the compromises they reached was to give national central banks the ability to veto any decision that affected its domestic market or currency. Quesnay referred to this as writing into the rules of the BIS a clear rule about "non-intervention." But this was a novel twist on an old ideal. For the right to non-intervention was, in this case, not to be guaranteed by governments but by politically independent central banks alone.[82] To the critics of the BIS, this implied a dramatic cession of sovereignty from the public realm to the private.

One particular source of controversy was the bank's powers as lender. Some of its architects had quite far-reaching visions. The most ambitious proposals came from Hjalmar Schacht, president of the German Reichs-bank, who called for using the BIS to finance the infrastructural develop-ment of non-European countries and colonies. Since becoming the head of the German central bank in 1923, on the basis of his role in tackling Germany's hyperinflation, Schacht oversaw a period of real de facto au-tonomy for the bank from government control, quarreling on multiple occasions with the Weimar government.[83] He also became a fixture of German financial diplomacy and a close associate of Norman, as well as a nationalist advocate of German expansionism. At the Young Confer-ence in Paris earlier that year, Schacht had suggested using the bank to finance investments in "backwards countries" to increase external demand for German exports, provide a stimulus to the German economy, and thereby make reparations easier to pay off.[84] His vision for the interna-tional bank as development financier was linked to broader plans to se-cure overseas markets for what he considered a German empire that had been unjustly stripped of its African and Pacific colonies at war's end.[85] Schacht was an idiosyncratic and extreme figure, whose behavior at the Paris Conference nearly threw it into jeopardy.[86] His demands for the return of German colonies and his subsequent highly publicized denun-ciation of the Young Plan, leading to his dramatic departure from the Reichsbank in early 1930, was seen at the time by critics of central bank independence as proof of their case, including by German officials them-selves. Independence only guaranteed stability, they claimed, if it was granted to a stable caretaker.[87]

But Schacht was not alone in linking the infrastructural development of non-European countries and colonies to the resolution of the repara-tions problem. Other experts and bankers had also argued for using de-velopment projects in the colonial territories of Germany's creditors, like French Morocco or the Belgian Congo, to similar ends.[88] At the Paris Con-ference, the Belgian businessman and former diplomat, Émile Francqui, made similar proposals.[89] Despite the credit he later took for prefiguring the idea of the World Bank and Truman's Point Four Program of global development years before their appearance at the end of the Second World War, Schacht was thus joined by others in advocating the BIS as a devel-opment bank.[90] More than anyone else, though, it was Schacht who brought wide attention to the still controversial prospect of using an inter-national institution to channel capital to the development of non-European countries and dependent territories—even though such plans were in his mind linked to ambitions to recreate a German colonial empire.[91] But the idea of endowing an untried international bank with such "artificial" powers to create credit was opposed at the Paris Conference by French delegates for threatening a global inflation.[92] While the vague wording of the final report of the Young Plan held out some possibility that the bank could take on development functions—an idea that became more popular after the outbreak of the Depression—few of the central bankers involved imagined this was appropriate business for it.

The disputes about the powers and activities of the bank over 1929, however, showed that assumptions about central banking on the eve of the Depression were in flux. Despite protestations by Quesnay and others that the international bank would simply make it easier for bankers to do the work they already did, there was no real consensus about their rights, powers, and purpose. Allowing national central banks to be the last line of defense against the international bank, moreover, implied a universal orthodoxy about their aims and character that did not exist. How much could these private institutions be expected to act in line with public interests, and were they free to define these interests as they saw fit, without the input of parliaments or executive government agencies? Different central banks also enjoyed varying degrees of autonomy in practice. Thus, some member banks of the international bank were more likely than others to fall under the sway of treasuries.[93] This posed an asymmetric risk: Some governments could harness the BIS for policies that affected the domestic markets of other countries, while governments with less influence over their national central bank would have no way to stop this. In countries where central bank independence was a reality, in other words, government officials were left potentially defenseless against an institution they could not be sure had not been captured by their foreign rivals.

Reactions to the Independent International Bank

When the founding legal documents of the BIS were ratified in January 1930 at the Second Hague Conference, a radically novel institution was born. The final version of the bank's statutes clarified its functions: It could not issue notes, accept bills of exchange, make loans to governments or open accounts in their names, acquire a "predominant interest" in any private business, or own property beyond what was needed for its basic functions. These statutes could not be modified by anyone but members of the BIS themselves. The BIS was authorized to perform various banking functions. While anything the BIS did that affected a national market or currency could be vetoed by the national central bank concerned, the latter could not veto the removal of funds from its national market or the granting of funds to another central bank. A constituent charter for the BIS was approved and ratified through a convention signed by the governments of the countries concerned and the government of Switzerland, where it would be domiciled.[94]

Legally speaking, the international bank was an anomalous organization. It had a "dual personality," wrote the British international lawyer John Fischer Williams, who worked on drafts of its founding documents. It was designed to "move in the world of States and regulate the financial relations of governments," while at the same time remain a completely private institution.[95] One thing was settled: The bank was to be detached from mass politics and run by capitalists, whose judgments, Williams claimed, were "superior to the passions of the crowd and independent of rulers who are dependent on the crowd."[96] Its directors would be *ex officio* heads of member central banks and their delegates, and in the US case, members of J. P. Morgan and the First National Banks of New York and Chicago. Its directorship was given to the US banker Gates McGarrah, who was also a former foreign member of the Reichsbank's council, and who left the New York Fed to take up his new job in Basel.

In certain respects, the international bank had been designed according to the model of international cooperation that Salter and others had advocated at war's end. It was not authorized to impose any external authority on its member central banks but instead only to provide a means of coordinating their work. This limitation was supposed to allay fears of it becoming what critics claimed was a dangerous "super bank."[97] But for obvious reasons, these analogies were strained. Most of all, the BIS was not an intergovernmental organization, but one that linked national banks of varying public-private characters. Its constitution was premised on the idea that governments had already delegated significant powers to these national central banks, which were entrusted to act in concert with foreign institutions that were also assumed to be nonpolitical entities—an assumption that at the time strained credulity.

This two-pronged demand for delegation came under attack in many countries as the bank was being established. Some of these attacks reflected common anxieties about international economic institutions becoming involved illegitimately in domestic affairs; others evidenced more specific concerns about foreign bankers doing so—charges that were sometimes obviously anti-Semitic. But they were not always: The German Jewish journalist Leo Stahl, for example, writing in a liberal German newspaper, offered a characteristic account of early 1929 plans for the BIS as a plot of Wall Street, the City, and Burgstrasse to wrest powers away from national parliaments to create an "unprecedented dictatorship."[98] Others argued that the bank's nongovernmental nature would prevent it from using its resources for the sake of internationalist aims. One popular idea was to bring the bank under League control to provide financial firepower to the League's system of economic sanctions. By giving it the power to cut enemies off from access to global finance, the BIS could be turned into a "temporary dictator of the world," as one supporter of this idea approvingly noted. "There would be no need of soldiers nor of ships of war. The world bank, and the world's banking system alone, could keep the peace."[99]

The most vitriolic attacks on the BIS came from the German far right, which framed it as another scheme for weakening Germany and strengthening its enemies. These criticisms were made against the backdrop of a major public campaign against the Young Plan orchestrated by conservative nationalists and the rising Nazi party. Although a national referendum held on the Young Plan in December 1929 failed to achieve mass support, the campaign left a deep mark on right-wing politics in Germany, which Hitler and Goebbels used to their advantage.[100] The bank was not universally condemned in Germany, however. There was support for it as an alternative to the Dawes Plan and the foreign controls it had involved. For many Germans, though, the fact that the bank had been created to handle the indemnity meant it was tarnished from the outset as little more than a "reparations bank." These fears seemed to be confirmed when Quesnay was named its first general manager, leading to predictable denunciations of the BIS as a French tool to subordinate Germany.[101]

In the United States, opposition to the bank was led by one of the country's own far right: Louis McFadden, a Republican representative from Pennsylvania and head of the House Committee on Banking and Currency, who had earlier spearheaded attacks on the creation of the Federal Reserve. While the conspiracy-minded and anti-Semitic lawmaker was soon ostracized from his own party, his loud attacks on what he called a "financial League of Nations" were considered serious enough to merit anxious rebuttals from Lamont.[102] McFadden's claims reflected basic misunderstandings of how the bank worked. But he articulated a criticism shared by observers in many countries, on both the right and left, about

Members of the far-right paramilitary Stahlhelm group in Germany, 1929. Their banner reads "Down with the Young Plan." © *SZ Photo/Scherl/Bridgeman Images.*

the dangers of a powerful international financial institution being kept in private hands. After the conclusion of the Second Hague Conference in January 1930, for example, Snowden, the original British advocate of a government-controlled bank, found himself defending its private character when members of Parliament queried him about the risks of allowing such a powerful international body to be free from "public control." Snowden suggested the possibility of "friendly contact" someday being made between the "non-political business institution" and the League of Nations. But he insisted that the British Treasury could not yet exercise any influence over it.[103]

In France, there was also widespread criticism of the private nature of the BIS, which opponents claimed would allow foreign bankers to override the policies of the French government and provide a Trojan Horse for US financial imperialism in Europe.[104] One important precedent for such worries was the response of the Banque de France to the financial instability faced by the Third Republic in 1925–1926, when the bank had refused to use its gold reserves to support the franc, leading to a fissure between the bank and the government and accusations that the former had effectively starved out the left coalition in power. Central bank independence was said in this case to have been mobilized as a barricade against the French left—or, as critics called it, a "wall of money" (*mur d'argent*). For the French left, the episode was a symbol of the dangers of central bank independence, just as the Bank of England's pressure to return to gold the year before was for the left in Britain.[105]

Shortly before the Second Hague Conference met in January 1930, the center-right government of André Tardieu faced similar criticisms from members of various parties in the French Chamber of Deputies, who demanded an explanation of how a private international bank would be prevented from becoming a tyrant, creating inflation, attenuating the independence of sovereign states, and facilitating the rise of US hegemony in Europe. Tardieu and Finance Minister Henry Chéron repeated a line that Quesnay had used to defend the bank: Its powers would be modest, since it would be run by orthodox central bankers alone. And it could not be used by the US government for political aims. Since financial issues were now highly internationalized, Chéron added, it was better to entrust their management to an institution of central banks than to leave them to private banking syndicates alone.[106]

But critics insisted that the private nature of the BIS was itself a problem, since it would allow bankers to use the institution and the capital it controlled to pursue their own political objectives. Even though a national central bank could veto BIS operations in its own domestic market, this national bank had little recourse if it was refused BIS credits. The appointment of the governor of the Banque de France to the BIS was cold comfort, argued the center-left Radical Georges Bonnet, given the Banque de France's recent track record in starving out the Cartel des Gauches government—an event with which Bonnet had had direct experience as budget minister in 1926. What would happen in future conflicts between the government and the Banque de France, which alone represented French interests in the BIS? The obvious problem of leaving veto power over the BIS's decisions in the hands of central bankers was that it was possible they shared more in common with their counterparts in other countries than with an elected government in their own. Once the BIS made capital available to a national central bank, moreover, it could withdraw it at will, without needing to seek permission or worry about a veto. This gave the BIS incredible leverage over the policies of sovereign states. Governments would cower in fear of an international capital strike being orchestrated against them whenever they fell afoul of the bankers' wishes. The BIS would possess a mighty tool for enforcing its decrees, much more so than the League of Nations. And it could shelter central bankers looking to evade the grip of their own national governments. Like the Banque de France, the BIS was thus attacked by its French critics, particularly on the left, as a new kind of *mur d'argent*.[107]

These critics also worried that the private nature of the international bank would prevent the realization of various internationalist aims. The idea of a "world bank" had for years been popular on the French left. When Léon Blum first heard of plans for the BIS, for example, he claimed they were merely a belated embrace of ideas he had advocated nearly a decade before at a meeting of the Second International.[108] In legislative debates, left-wing members of the Chamber claimed the international bank should have its powers expanded so that it could facilitate Aristide Briand's designs for a European union.[109] But this would only be possible if the bank were put under public control. Outside of the Chamber, one of the most articulate French backers of the idea of transforming the international bank into a public institution was the young left-wing lawyer and activist, Pierre Mendès France—later prime minister of France and, before that, French delegate to the Bretton Woods Conference and executive director at the World Bank and International Monetary Fund (IMF).[110] Around the time of the second Hague Conference, Mendès France wrote a long book chronicling the squandered political promise of the international bank. He admitted the irony that a plutocratic project had become a focus of left mobilization. But he insisted that taking control of the BIS away from "oligarchs" and putting it into the hands of the League, with a board of directors broadened to include government officials and representatives of labor and other sectoral interests, would allow the bank to help realize true internationalist aims: development projects in Europe's colonies and non-European countries, humanitarian and financial stabilization projects like the League's rescue of Austria and the settlement of Greek refugees, and European integration. But for now, in its private form, it was a "federal bank," Mendès France lamented, "of a federation that does not exist."[111]

The Future of the International Bank

When the BIS opened its doors in the spring of 1930, it was a nongovernmental central banking institution that was detached from the League. Its private nature had two major political consequences. First, it left some governments powerless to prevent the bank from making decisions with potentially important consequences on their domestic economies; and second, the bank was unlikely to be used to realize the internationalist aims of channeling capital into public investment or development projects. The financial powers and legal character of the BIS had been shaped by common assumptions about the aims and limits of central banking, particularly the idea that central banks were to be fully nonpolitical actors. But these assumptions were thrown further into uncertainty with the worsening of the global crisis that had begun while the BIS was being designed.

The events of the dark year of 1931 further clarified that the ideal of depoliticized central banking was a myth, as some of the member central banks of the BIS demonstrated their continued links to the political and strategic aims of the governments from which they claimed autonomy. This became clear when the BIS was enlisted to help rescue banks from crisis in early 1931 in the former Central Powers. In Austria, the collapse of the Creditanstalt bank in May was the beginning of the European banking crisis that augured the dramatic worsening of the global economic downturn. When the BIS was called to lead the international rescue of Austria, it had insufficient capital at its disposal to play the role of lender of last resort. The credits it arranged, only $14 million in total, were used up quickly. The issuance of a subsequent loan, however, was obstructed by the political conditions placed by the French on any loan to Austria. They called for Austria to abandon recently announced plans for a customs union with Germany, which appeared to be a violation of the protocol of the League of Nations loan from late 1922 and a step toward the long-held French fear of Austro-German unification. When the crisis arrived in Germany that summer, a similar script was followed, though it was made even more complex by explosive controversies over reparations and a US proposal that June for a moratorium on payments. As credits arranged by the BIS were depleted, Germany's worsening financial instability was seized on by the French to provide leverage for concessions, complicating the issuance of any further loans. Finance Minister Pierre-Étienne Flandin and Clément Moret, who had moved from a long career in the Ministry of Finance to replace Moreau as governor of the Banque de France in 1930, told the president of the Reichsbank, Hans Luther, that credits would be granted to Germany only on the condition of naval disarmament, territorial concessions, and the abandonment of the customs union project with Austria. These were not conditions that the German Chancellor Heinrich Brüning, who operated against the backdrop of a rising Nazi party, could easily meet. The BIS was sidelined as responsibility for rescuing Germany was shunted from central banks to governments. No foreign loans were forthcoming. The German government attempted to achieve financial stabilization on its own. Within a year and a half, the Nazis were in power.[112]

Regardless of whether a more robust coordinated international response to the 1931 banking crises of Central Europe might have slowed the collapse into the political abyss, and whether blame lies more in French or German hands, what this and the Austrian episode clearly confirmed was that central banks were paralyzed by these extreme geopolitical tensions and that they were not as apolitical as they claimed.[113] Quesnay, the architect of the most robust vision of the BIS's autonomy, was closely involved in the drama of negotiations over loans to Germany and Austria. Despite his protestations to the contrary, it became clear that he was not only closely tied to every member of the cabinet of French Prime Minister Pierre Laval, but was also attempting to directly influence the British Foreign Office as well.[114]

Another attempt to use the international bank to slow the contagion of the Depression collapsed in the face of other problems. At the beginning of 1931, the Bank of England director Robert Kindersley, backed by Norman, suggested the creation of an international corporation to help prevent the complete breakdown of global finance by issuing bonds and raising money that could be lent to governments, municipalities, mortgage banks, and utility companies. The aim was to restore credit, channel gold out of the United States and France to where it was needed, and revive general confidence at a moment when "the capitalist system" was "under the microscope" and being "attacked from many sides."[115] This corporation would be authorized to do things that the BIS could not. Kindersley recognized that few central bankers would see this kind of lending as their business.[116] Norman pushed for the BIS to act as trustee and financial backer of this corporation, which was designed, as he put it, to "start the wheels going round again." He found some sympathy for the idea on certain conditions: that this corporation avoid any kind of political lending, that it was kept a strictly commercial affair, and that it was not structurally linked to the BIS.[117] But Moret opposed the plan, claiming it would result in an indirect violation of the bank's statues, and that it was impossible to put French financial resources into the hands of an institution not under close French control.[118] Leon Fraser, US vice president of the BIS, bluntly described French opposition to the Kindersley proposals as a refusal to cede control of French capital to an institution run by "non-French personalities."[119] Yet bankers at J. P. Morgan opposed the idea on similar grounds: for putting US capital in the hands of an international institution making risky loans to public authorities abroad. The US market would not "be willing to surrender its own judgment in these matters to any International Institution," they wrote, certainly not to one that, by making loans to public institutions, would be uniquely opened to political influence.[120] Francqui, one of the original proponents of using the bank to finance development projects, made an alternative proposal: having the bank indirectly support the financing of public works to provide a reflationary stimulus to the world economy.[121] But these ideas were also rejected. Not only would they tie up the bank's limited liquidity, but they also would violate the bank's prohibition of government lending and revive ideas of long-term lending that had already been rejected.[122] These proposals went beyond contemporary central banking orthodoxies, but Norman worried that the failure of such ambitious measures would destroy the foundations of the world economy, as countries abandoned the gold standard and even capitalism itself.[123]

Some historians have argued that the failures of the BIS and central banks to coordinate a response to the Depression in 1931, whether from the political nature of Franco-German relations, the limited liquidity of the BIS, or US isolationism, accelerated their fall from the pinnacle of power and influence.[124] During the following years, particularly after the gold standard collapsed, these banks were sidelined by governments from the center of policy-making.[125] As we shall see, they played little role in the next wave of international economic institution-building in the 1940s. At the end of the Second World War, many were nationalized. The central bankers who had insisted on their strict independence overplayed their hands. During the 1930s, the BIS mostly functioned as a meeting place for central bankers, a data collector, and a means of exchanging information. Its larger policy goals were put on ice. The BIS appeared to be unlikely to survive the war.

There was one particularly important reason for the near demise of the BIS: The "depoliticized" bank became implicated in the strategic aims of the Third Reich. One episode, in particular, the most scandalous in the history of the BIS, showed how its incomplete political autonomy and the unevenly maintained norm of central bank independence created strategic vulnerabilities for some states. After the Nazi invasion of Czechoslovakia in March 1939, bankers in Prague were forced, under threats of violence,

Montagu Norman returning to London from Basel, 1931. *AP Photo/Len Puttnam.*

to direct the BIS to move about £6 million worth of Czechoslovak gold held in the Bank of England in the name of the BIS to accounts held for the German Reichsbank. When questions were raised of why an international institution was facilitating the looting of Czechoslovak gold, Niemeyer, now chairman of the board of the BIS, justified the decision on the grounds of the bank's neutrality and the fact that it could not decline a commercial transaction on the basis of political criteria if asked to do so by governments that did not exercise any legal powers over it. When the French government and Pierre Fournier, governor of the Banque de France, sought to halt the transaction, Norman, fully aware of what was happening, refused to consider any government involvement in an interaction between the BIS and the Bank of England at all. Although many in the Treasury accepted Norman's views about the legal limits of their influence over the BIS, this episode demonstrated to other members of the government, particularly at the Foreign Office, the risks posed by central bank independence at a moment of extreme danger to British security. This turn of events also appeared to confirm the fears that many had expressed about the BIS at its founding: that central banks captured by one government and working for its strategic aims (in this case, Hitler's) could use the BIS in ways that jeopardized the interest of other governments (in this case, Britain's) that were formally powerless to intervene because of rules about central bank independence. This episode, which came in the midst of acrimonious disputes about the economic and diplomatic appeasement of Nazi Germany on the eve of war, kicked off renewed debate in Britain about whether the autonomy of the Bank of England could allow it to act in ways detrimental to British security and the national interest, and whether British membership in the BIS should be cancelled. But throughout the controversy, Norman held the line. He claimed that the BIS was a completely nonpolitical institution that had never even been required to tell the government about its role in the German looting of Czechoslovak gold in the first place.[126]

This dark episode profoundly damaged the reputation of the institution. That most of the member banks of the BIS were soon either domiciled in Axis countries or in countries under Axis occupation did not help matters. The bank's formal neutrality allowed representatives from Allied countries to continue to attend its meetings, and its location in Switzerland prevented it from coming under direct Nazi control. But its wartime history appeared to confirm the risks posed by asymmetric commitments to central bank independence. The BIS's association with the Third Reich and sour memories of the Czechoslovak affair led to concerted efforts in the United States to dissolve it at war's end. But this never happened. In the years after the Second World War, in fact, it became more powerful, as central banks gradually regained some of their earlier clout and autonomy. By the turn of the twenty-first century, the BIS had returned to its former position as guardian of central bank independence, which had once again become a central guiding norm of global economic governance.

The struggles over the foundation of the BIS in the late 1920s and early 1930s cast the innovations of the 1940s in stark relief. At the end of the Second World War, two intergovernmental agencies were established to perform functions that the BIS could not. The first was the IMF, which was designed to direct resources to countries experiencing financial instability on a scale that private efforts alone had been unable to shoulder.[127] In fact, Keynes, one of the architects of the Bretton Woods agreements, suggested in his 1930 *Treatise on Money,* which went to print just as the BIS opened its doors, that the international bank could, with some tweaks, evolve into the kind of supranational agency that he thought was necessary to manage a reformed international monetary standard.[128] But in debates about the foundation of the IMF in the 1940s, the BIS was seen as both a model to avoid and one to emulate. The mobilization of Wall Street bankers against the IMF (including many former designers and staff members of the BIS) was founded on the idea that an intergovernmental financial institution, unlike an independent private one, could not be trusted to handle large sums of capital. Other critics of the Bretton Woods agreements saw the precedent of an independent central banking institution in different terms: They worried that the IMF would allow foreign banks to meddle in domestic issues and prevent the execution of expansive government policies by neutralizing parliaments, just as an independent Bank of England was said to have done when sterling was returned to gold in 1925.

The second innovation of the 1940s, international development and reconstruction lending, also unfolded against the backdrop of the experience of the BIS. After the failures of Schacht's quixotic efforts to endow the international bank with development lending powers in 1929, the idea was kicked around for several years, particularly in connection with plans popular on the French left to finance massive public works programs—in Europe and abroad—to put hundreds of thousands back to work and provide an infrastructural foundation for a future European union and a stimulus to a world economy in depression.[129] Just before his unexpected death in 1932, for example, the director-general of the International Labour Organization (ILO), the moderate French socialist Albert Thomas, called for what was effectively a European New Deal of continent-wide infrastructure building, headlined by a massive roadbuilding initiative. The promulgation of the Kindersley and Francqui plans for long-term lending appeared to backers of such plans at the ILO and the League to indicate a role for the BIS in securing financing for them.[130] Similar plans were considered at the League of Nations. They were promoted by Keynesian-minded experts, like the young British economist James Meade, who proposed even more ambitious global infrastructure projects, including new rail lines from Spain to Senegal via Gibraltar, or the linking of Russian and Indian railways through Afghanistan to make Delhi accessible from Paris in nine days.[131] The BIS joining forces with the League was widely suggested as a way to coordinate the financing of such projects. These ideas for international reflationary public works, while unrealized in the 1930s, directly shaped the elaboration of international development plans in the 1940s. The continued interest in the BIS arranging their financing spoke to the urgency of finding more feasible ways of doing so.

Before the 1940s changed how international development was understood in theory and in practice, however, there were a few experiments with using multilateral institutions for such projects. These experiments also led to fierce disputes about the kinds of interference—by bankers, businesses, and governments—that international development might entail.

CHAPTER 4

The Origins of International Development

O NE OF THE MOST consequential innovations of international economic institution-building after the First World War was in policies of international development. Development was once understood as a US-led Cold War initiative. But its roots have been increasingly traced to earlier practices of European empire.[1] Between these two contexts, there were a few attempts by international institutions to implement development programs.[2] The League of Nations embarked on a small number of ambitious schemes as it weighed the question of what kind of economic powers it could wield. These provided important precursors to the work of later institutions like the World Bank. While unsuccessful US–Latin American efforts to establish an international development bank in 1939 also provided blueprints for later development organizations, the League was alone in actually putting these ideas into practice. It did so with two quite different projects. The first was its assistance to the Greek government to settle more than a million Greek Orthodox refugees from Turkey in 1923–1930; the second was the provision of technical experts to the Chinese Nationalist government in 1931–1935 for a scheme of infrastructural, industrial, and agricultural development as war with Japan approached. These two very different political settings raised new questions of sovereignty and international cooperation.

During the 1920s and 1930s, the idea of using an international institution to finance development projects was extremely controversial, as debates about the foundation of the Bank for International Settlements (BIS) had shown. Development aid was something that most central bankers wanted little to do with; the League's Financial Committee sought to avoid it as well.[3] While the League's financial reconstruction schemes had relied on controls over countries like Austria and Hungary, doing so in conjunction with a development loan was far more difficult. Ensuring that loans were spent on "productive" projects that would, over time, facilitate their repayment involved a more extensive degree of interference in a country's affairs than overseeing a scheme of austerity. "From the point of view of the League, development loans involve many difficulties," as Otto Niemeyer put it in 1928, just after taking charge of the Financial Committee. "They are much more difficult to control than ordinary budget loans, and are nearly always mixed up with international rivalries among industrial firms seeking orders."[4] Putting a country under control to make it an attractive borrower would make it more difficult for countries that did not agree to such controls to win the confidence of lenders. For this reason, banks were to be left to make decisions about financing a railway project or port improvements according to market conditions, as they always had. The risk for the League would be too high if it got involved with such loans without being able to guarantee their repayment.

Moreover, although only a limited number of countries needed to curtail hyperinflation, there was no limit to those seeking foreign capital for their development. Agreeing to their requests for assistance thus risked pulling the League into endless controversies.[5] In December 1925, when Albanian delegates again turned to Geneva for development aid, British Foreign Secretary Austen Chamberlain rejected their demands because of the dangerous precedent he claimed would be set. Despite sympathy for the country's plight, arranging a League loan for Albania would ruin the credit of other "smaller countries" attempting to borrow without League supervision. Taken to its extreme, this view implied that inaugurating a development program for Albania would entail making the League the final arbiter of the creditworthiness of all other poorer countries looking for such aid.[6]

Occasionally, a small amount of funds was earmarked for an infrastructure project, such as when the League arranged a municipal loan for Danzig in early 1925. But Danzig, already under League administration, was an exception.[7] Outside such "peculiar circumstances," development lending was not supposed to become a common practice.[8] While sometimes there could be "a little jam with the powder," as Niemeyer described this policy, the League was never to offer "a loan consisting solely of jam."[9] This position was further clarified in 1928, when the Zionist leader Chaim Weizmann attempted to secure a League loan to finance the Jewish settlement of Palestine. His proposal was rejected, in part, due to fears it would invite endless requests for handouts from "minor countries" for development funds and because it was impossible to place a British mandated territory under international financial control.[10]

In interwar Greece and China, however, the League did become involved in two unique projects of development. While there were countless differences between the two countries, both projects raised new questions about the bounds of legitimate interference in countries that already faced extensive foreign economic controls. Would a sovereign state allow an external body to control not only its budget and revenues, but also policies concerning the productive capacities of its citizenry and the management of its infrastructure? Could foreign investors agree to entrust capital to an international institution that did not become deeply involved in sensitive internal problems? And could the provision of technical advisers without powers of control be offered as an alternative?

The League's role in settling Greek refugees was the first time that an international institution successfully channeled capital into a national program of development. The Greek scheme involved an enormous effort to create a population of smallholding agriculturalists as well as infrastructure-building and support for small-scale urban manufacturing. Because it did not focus on major industrial projects, it is rarely considered in histories of development. But the similarities to later development projects become obvious when considering its aims and details. This was the first instance of an international institution attempting to finance the agricultural development of a sovereign member state and enhance the productivity of a vast labor force through private loans that it controlled. At the time, the Greek scheme was certainly seen by those involved as a unique case of the League acting as development financier. For this reason, members of the Financial Committee worried that this scheme set a troubling precedent for the organization's involvement in other development programs. Indeed, it was the Greek case that Weizmann and the Albanian League representative Mehdi Frasheri referred to in their requests for League assistance—seemingly confirming fears that overseeing one development loan would open the floodgates to more.[11]

In many respects, the Greek project was an exceptional experiment for the League, one that would have been very difficult to replicate elsewhere. It was made possible by the emergency conditions of the enormous refugee crisis Greece faced in the aftermath of its 1919–1922 war with Turkey and the population exchange that followed in 1923—a crisis that threatened to bankrupt Greece and destabilize the region. The response to this crisis, as is well chronicled, involved lasting innovations in the international management of refugees and the inauguration of new, brutal practices of population transfer, later brought to other parts of the world, such as during the partition of India and Pakistan in 1947.[12] But it also involved nothing less than a dramatic innovation in how international institutions controlled and supervised investments in the domestic economy of a member state.[13] The aim of the 1924 Refugee Loan was not to shrink the Greek state for the sake of austerity, but to expand its powers while removing them from the control of elected governments, in order to place the lives of a large population of new Greek citizens under the watchful eye of investors who placed a bet on their future productivity. This was possible only because Greek public finances were already under the control of the International Financial Commission (IFC), established in 1898—one of the remaining prewar foreign debt commissions. Members of the Financial Committee insisted that the Greek case was entirely unique in order to reject requests for such assistance from other countries (though a similar project, on a smaller scale, was implemented in Bulgaria).[14] While he was still at the British Treasury, Niemeyer described the risk that the "wholly abnormal" project in Greece would become a model for others: The League could not afford to be viewed "in the eyes of the world" as the "agents of capitalist foreign bondholders."[15] But in many places, as we have seen, it already was.

In the aftermath of the Greek refugee settlement, the apparent stabilization of the Chinese government under Nationalist rule in the late 1920s presented another opportunity for innovating practices of development. The British government saw the League as offering a way of breaking the deadlock between the Chinese state and its foreign creditors, as demands for China to accept new controls and pay back old loans were resisted by a Nationalist government that wagered its legitimacy on resisting such interference. The League's economic work there began by considering the possibility of arranging loans for Chiang Kai-shek's government to jump-start China's development and facilitate the repayment of foreign debts in arrears. While the League oversaw a novel program of technical assistance to the Nationalist state, these larger aims proved out of reach. This was due in part to the deteriorating security situation and impending conflict with Japan, but also to the political challenges that came with inaugurating a development program in a country with a long and painful history of foreign interference and that was now ruled by an increasingly powerful nationalist government. Squaring development loans with real economic self-determination, it turned out, would be difficult to do without a broader transformation of the role of private bankers on the international stage.

Creating a "State within a State" in Greece

Just as the League's financial reconstruction programs in Austria and Hungary were getting under way, the organization undertook a very different economic challenge in Greece, which had been thrown into turmoil by the conclusion of its war with Turkey in late 1922. More than a million Greek Orthodox refugees fled Turkey for Greece in the wake of the war and the compulsory population exchange instituted in 1923. Their settlement into housing and productive work was beyond the financial capacities of the postwar Greek state. The League's involvement in the Greek refugee problem began in the autumn of 1922, largely due to the efforts of Fridtjof Nansen, high commissioner for refugees.[16] It quickly evolved from a humanitarian task into an experiment in mediating international investments in Greece's economic transformation. The League oversaw the spending of a huge foreign loan on the settlement of the refugees. This project involved the construction of tens of thousands of houses and the provision of the means of livelihood for a huge new population of citizens, mostly in agricultural areas in Macedonia and Thrace, though also in Crete and a string of urban settlements around Athens, Piraeus, and Salonika. Unfolding over 1923–1930, the refugee resettlement scheme was designed to turn a humanitarian catastrophe into a boon for the Greek economy. By enhancing the productivity of a new source of rural labor and providing agricultural machinery and livestock, it was supposed to help solve Greece's endemic balance of trade problems by reducing the country's dependence on imported cereals and providing a fillip to the production of crops like tobacco.[17] It also aimed to bring stability to southeastern Europe by transforming sparsely populated border areas in the north of Greece, only recently annexed, into productive regions that met a new and troubling postwar benchmark for stability: ethnic and religious homogeneity. The Greek refugee resettlement program provided a lasting model for handling economic challenges of mass migration and was studied by experts from around the world dealing with uprooted rural populations.[18] On the League's terms, it was a major success.

Just as in Austria and Hungary, the League's work in Greece began by arranging a major loan for the government. Greece was already heavily indebted and subject to foreign controls exercised by the IFC, which had been set up in the wake of Greece's defeat in a short war with the Ottoman Empire in 1897, when a Greek state already deep in debt was forced to pay an indemnity far beyond its financial capacities in exchange for the evacuation of occupying Ottoman forces from Thessaly. To service both a new indemnity loan and existing debt obligations, the IFC, staffed by government representatives of several leading European powers, had taken control of sources of public revenue, including customs duties from ports like Piraeus and Volos and state monopolies on kerosene, salt, and matches. It also exercised veto powers over domestic policies like taxation and the issuance of currency and treasury bonds. To avoid enflaming opposition to its interference, the IFC empowered a Greek-run corporation under its direction to do the actual work of collecting payments. But the IFC continued to be attacked by Greek political and economic elites into the 1920s for its infringements of Greek sovereignty. At the same time, it played an important role as gatekeeper to foreign capital.[19] The prior existence of the IFC, dominated by the British, was one of the reasons the League became involved in the refugee loan project in the first place, since the IFC could itself assure the servicing of the new loan. That Greece was already under foreign control saved the League from having to put the government under its own "tutelage," as it had in Austria and Hungary.[20]

Another distinctive feature of the refugee loan to Greece was that, unlike in those states, it was not designed for the sake of austerity, but instead for the construction of houses, bridges, water infrastructure, roads, schools, and medical facilities. It was used to provide livestock, fodder, seeds, ploughs, threshing machines, and fishing boats, as well as advances for domestic industries like carpet-making that employed thousands of refugee women. This scheme also unfolded alongside a significant program of land reform.[21] Unlike the financial assistance to Austria and Hungary, the loan to Greece was to be used to create a productive population from which surplus could be extracted to repay it. The idea of turning the refugees into "self-supporting" workers to end their dependence on foreign humanitarian aid had been a standard strategy since the first US and British efforts to deal with the refugee crisis.[22] For nearly a year after the end of the war in late summer 1922, temporary relief was led by US and British humanitarian groups, which in addition to providing food and medicine also created workshops to employ women in small-scale crafts work. The intention was to end the "demoralizing effects" of charity on a population vulnerable to thieves, sex traffickers, and corrupt military officers, as the Indian doctor, Alice Sorabji Pennell, director of the Stringos camp outside Athens, described her task.[23] Creating a productive labor force out of people facing dire situations of dependency was a traditional humanitarian goal. When US relief organizations ended their work in the summer of 1923, the League was enlisted to facilitate this transformation on a much larger scale: moving an entire population from one side of an imagined balance sheet to another by turning hungry mouths into hands that could feed. While it resonated with other practices of biopolitical humanitarianism, this project was distinguished by its remarkable feat of financial engineering: It placed the everyday lives of the recipients of aid under international financial control.

As with all of the League's other financial reconstruction schemes, the work of the League in Greece unfolded according to the demands of foreign bankers and the Financial Committee that protected their interests. When the Bank of England and investment banks like Hambros turned to the Greek question, they set conditions for their involvement. These included the demobilization of the Greek military and the establishment of a constitutional regime that was recognized as legitimate both at home and abroad.[24] Their most consequential demand was that any loan money be handled exclusively by an autonomous League of Nations body, the Refugee Settlement Commission (RSC), which would not allow the government to touch the funds it controlled. The aim was to keep the money from being spent on the military and to prevent party struggle and the domestic politics of refugee issues from derailing the foreign investment in their future productivity.

Like the independence of a central bank, the autonomy of this commission was designed to insulate its work from Greek mass politics. In the wake of the First World War, Greek politics were characterized by continued struggle between the forces of Venizelism, roughly committed to Greek republicanism and named for the liberal leader Eleftherios Venizelos, who had pushed Greece to join the First World War with the Allies for the sake of expansion into Asia Minor, and a conservative and broadly royalist anti-Venizelist opposition. After the defeat of Greek forces in Turkey in the summer of 1922, returning military officers forced King Constantine I to abdicate and executed several leading royalist politicians and officers, widening the schism between these factions. After the failure of a counterrevolutionary coup by anti-Venizelists in late 1923, a national plebiscite the following April showed support for the proclamation of a republic, and the monarchy was abolished. In June 1925, the Venizelist military officer Theodoros Pangalos led a successful coup d'état and attempted to rule Greece as a self-styled Mussolini until his own dictatorship was overthrown a year later. It was against the backdrop of these developments in Greek politics, particularly from 1923–1926, that the first refugee loan was made and the League's scheme of development was put into action.

The bankers who arranged the loan distrusted what they saw as a particularly unstable form of mass politics in Greece. When the Bank of England offered a £1 million advance in July 1923, it insisted this money be managed exclusively by the autonomous RSC established that September. As we have seen, there was nothing new about an international lending scheme being designed in ways that removed control of the funds from the borrower. One thing that was unique in the Greek case was the role played by the refugees in electoral politics: They formed a powerful swing constituency overwhelmingly committed to Venizelism that on its own could decide elections. This made the courting of refugee support crucial to any would-be Venizelist leader and, indeed, to the continued existence of the republic under Venizelist rule itself. [25] For the bankers, this situation appeared to pose a distinct threat. They worried that Greek politicians would threaten to take the RSC's money and give it to the refugees in exchange for their political support. For this reason, keeping the commission free of government control was of the highest priority. After the first advance and a subsequent one were spent, a £12.3 million loan was issued in December 1924 in London, New York, and Athens at the high interest rate of 7 percent. This was a major loan for the Greek state—and a significant additional burden on its already heavy debt load. But it was popular with investors, particularly in London, where it was oversubscribed.[26]

Legally speaking, the League refugee commission was an anomalous institution. It worked by taking over ordinary functions of the Greek state and removing them from parliamentary oversight and the executive and administrative control of the government. It was a "new type of organism," as one contemporary legal expert described it, which was "responsible for solving internationally a problem that, a few years ago, could only have been the responsibility of national organisms with the aid of charity and private finance."[27] The RSC possessed international legal personality, meaning it could own property, including the land on which the refugees were to be settled;[28] 500,000 hectares, most of it formerly owned by the exchanged Muslim and earlier Bulgarian populations, was given free of charge from the government to the RSC. Its first directors were Henry Morgenthau, a former US ambassador to the Ottoman Empire and Democratic Party figure, who had led US relief efforts in northeastern Greece; and John Campbell, a former member of the Indian Civil Service, who had been considered for the League's 1923 work in Albania, and who after leaving Greece became an influential expert in the British Colonial Office, overseeing the implementation of commodity policies throughout the empire.[29] Both were granted legal extraterritoriality. They answered only to the League and the holders of Greek sovereign debt, and they worked alongside two Greek members appointed by the government. The rest of the RSC's staff were existing employees of the government, growing in number to 2,000 by 1929. Much of its daily work was handled by government offices placed under RSC control, such as the directorates of colonization for Macedonia and Thrace. Working through these state agencies, the League oversaw what was explicitly described as a vast program of internal "colonization" in Greece.[30] Employees of the Greek government worked in a "separate sphere" for the RSC, which exercised special powers over them. When they did work approved by the RSC, it was not subject to any government authority. They only came under the jurisdiction of the government if criminal charges of corruption or fraud were brought against them. But as long as they did not violate criminal law, these employees were only responsible to the League commission.[31]

The autonomy of the RSC was designed to protect the capital it controlled from being spent on anything besides the economic development of the refugees and their transformation, as Morgenthau put it, from a "liability and a burden" into "one of the greatest assets of the country."[32] None of the money could be used for the military, humanitarian relief, or anything considered "unproductive." Supplemental humanitarian aid was needed to make up for these strict rules against any spending on clothing, food, medicine, or relief designated for "women and children."[33] An explicit logic lay behind this earmarking of the loan for exclusively "productive purposes:" It was the refugees themselves who had to repay it. Once they were settled into productive work, they would pay rent to the RSC for the houses that were built for them or make installments on

Workshop built by the RSC for the manufacture of carpets in Athens.
United Nations Archives at Geneva.

their purchase, and reimburse the commission for any agricultural machinery, livestock, or supplies they were given.[34] In this way, the interests
of the foreign bondholders were to be made theoretically coterminous
with those of the refugees themselves: the transformation of their needi-
ness into productivity. The rules guiding this arrangement were enshrined
in the protocols of the loan, which were consulted, like holy writ, whenever members of the RSC claimed the government threatened their autonomy. Far from being a "scrap of paper," as the disappointing treaties
of this era were often called, the loan document allowed the representatives of Greece's creditors to wield real force within the country. Guided
by the protocols, the RSC set and enforced the legal bounds of the government's involvement in the economic livelihood of this large new population of Greek citizens.[35]

Making the League commission the sole guardians of the economic
development of the refugees, however, appeared to its foreign directors

to set them on a collision course with the Greek government. In the months following its establishment in late 1923, the RSC was attacked by politicians and the press for violating Greece's sovereignty. It was often referred to in the National Assembly as a "state within a state" or an "imperium in imperio."[36] "Imperium in imperio" was a commonly used expression at the time, often pejoratively, to refer to a quasi-sovereign authority operating in a formally sovereign territory, such as independent central banks, the Catholic Church, Native American nations, the British and Dutch East India companies, and foreign-run debt commissions like the IFC in Athens. The foreign directors of the commission took these charges seriously. They were convinced that the RSC was attacked as a way for various political actors to gain support from the new refugee constituency in Greek politics, which wielded an influential political machine, tightly integrated into local Venizelist political organizations that were vibrant in areas of refugee settlement. They assumed that the refugee political leaders, the so-called "refugee fathers," sought to exchange the votes of their constituencies for policies designed to give them greater control over the RSC's funds. This was a redline for the bondholders whose interests the League had been enlisted to represent in Greece.[37] As one observer of this political situation described it to Morgenthau, the greatest difficulty faced by the RSC was "the patient we try to cure": the refugees and their parliamentary representatives, who could put real pressure on the government. Campbell warned refugee representatives that the RSC could never become involved in party politics.[38] While he celebrated the popularity of the refugee loan with investors and the progress made on the settlement work, Campbell worried about working in a country that he claimed was "cursed" by politics: "everything here," he told Morgenthau in December 1924, "becomes 'political' sooner or later."[39]

Behind closed doors, the foreign directors of the RSC warned leading Greek political figures that any attacks on the RSC's autonomy would jeopardize the likelihood of Greece getting future loans. In May 1924, just weeks after the left Venizelist Alexandros Papanastasiou became the first prime minister of the new republic, Morgenthau reminded him that he was bound by the decision of the prior government to sign the protocols of the loan, an agreement with a quasi-international character. By agreeing to these protocols, the Greek state had agreed to a "complete delegation of authority" to a League commission removed from "all connexion with party politics in Greece." Morgenthau warned Papanastasiou that any attempt to violate the terms of the protocol by bringing the RSC under parliamentary control, curtailing its autonomy, or subverting the "admittedly onerous" terms of the loan would damage Greece's credit.[40] Morgenthau worried that Papanastasiou was promising the refugee leaders to bring the commission under government control: "Inside, for its own work, it was autonomous," Papanastasiou told the RSC, but otherwise "in all respects subject to the Greek Govt., which could exercise any control which the sovereign powers of a State implied." Campbell warned Papanastasiou that if he brought any disputes to the League's Council for arbitration, which was within his rights, it was likely to have negative repercussions on Greece's ability to access future sources of foreign capital.[41]

After the successful conclusion of the £12.3 million refugee loan in December 1924, the relationship of the government and the RSC remained tense. In Macedonia, the work of the RSC was subjected to frequent attacks in the press. League officials thought these attacks were encouraged by refugee leaders and were egged on at the highest level of government. They worried this was creating an atmosphere of hostility to the RSC.[42] In December 1924, a law was passed allowing for the imprisonment of anyone suspected of misusing government money—not only for fraud, but even for signing contracts considered "disadvantageous" to the public fisc. This law appeared to pose an existential threat to the RSC's autonomy.[43] In a formal sense, the League commission could not be said to be handling government money, since the protocols specified that the RSC alone controlled the loan's proceeds. But its directors worried that this legal distinction was unlikely to prevent its 1,200 employees in Macedonia from working under the constant fear of imprisonment.[44] Since this new law prohibited not only corruption but also wasteful spending, it in principle allowed any contract written by the RSC to be subject to the scrutiny of Greek courts. Campbell warned the right Venizelist Prime Minister Andreas Michalakopoulos, who had come to power in October 1924, that this law violated the loan protocol, since it constrained the RSC's autonomy and was inapplicable to the loan funds that the government had no claim to. But Michalakopoulos insisted that no government could agree to removing the jurisdiction of Greek courts over Greek citizens.[45] Fears that the law could be used as a pretext to arrest Greek employees of the RSC and erode its autonomy came to pass shortly after it was promulgated. In April 1925, the chief of transport in Macedonia was imprisoned on an unspecified charge and held for seven weeks.[46]

The situation deteriorated dramatically that summer, when Michala-kopoulos was overthrown in the coup that empowered General Theod-oros Pangalos, whose antipathy to the RSC was well known. The De-cember 1924 law, Campbell lamented, would allow Pangalos to "put a crowbar any day into the moving parts of our engine." Pangalos called its new director, the US attorney Charles Howland (Morgenthau had re-signed in late 1924), an "enemy of Greece." He justified his attacks on the RSC as restoring Greek sovereignty and uprooting an "imperium in imperio." Campbell feared this was likely to win Pangalos popular sup-port. The tensions between the RSC and the government were threatening to turn into a major crisis. Shortly after the coup, the foreign directors of the RSC attempted to understand the risks they faced from the new re-gime. Campbell was confident that Pangalos was unlikely to destroy the RSC and jeopardize Greece's credit. But he worried that Pangalos would attack the commission to win the support of refugee deputies in order to gain a slight parliamentary advantage. For this reason, Campbell was most worried about the refugee deputies. The greatest threats faced by the RSC, he claimed, were the constant small obstacles the Pangalos gov-ernment would put in its way to win refugee support—a series of "coups d'épingle" that could prove to be more dangerous, in the end, than the coup d'état itself.[47]

Shortly after the June 1925 coup, the relationship of the RSC and the government was profoundly damaged when the director general of colo-nization in Macedonia, Ioannis Karamanos, was arrested along with his two chief engineers. Karamanos was accused of granting a "disadvanta-geous" contract of 13 million drachmas to a construction company for the completion of 4,000 refugee houses in Salonika.[48] Just as Campbell and Howland had feared, the December 1924 law had provided a pre-text for Greek authorities to grind the work of the commission to a halt. It appeared that Greek officials were attempting to show that they wielded final authority over the funds the RSC controlled and the Greek citizens it employed.[49] The situation deteriorated when the government issued a decree stating that misuse of government funds was a crime that could be tried by court martial and punished by death by hanging or life imprisonment with hard labor.[50] The government warned the League of Nations to stay out of the Karamanos affair and that a "free and sover-eign State cannot tolerate any interference in matters affecting Justice."[51]

Formal legal provisions about the nature of the RSC's autonomy, and the agreement the government had made with its creditors, became questions of life or death. That summer, the court martial began. The RSC was on trial and with it potentially the League as well. The prosecution and defense quarreled over the two questions that would decide Karamanos's fate and that could only be answered by appeal to the loan protocols: first, whether the League commission or the government owned the proceeds of the foreign loans; and second, whether the Greek employees of the RSC could face criminal charges for enacting a contract approved by the commission itself—not for fraud, in other words, but for wasteful spending alone. The prosecution claimed that the RSC, while owning the lands and homes of the exchanged Muslim population, did not own the proceeds of the loan, which it merely administered as a "mandatory of the Government." They also claimed that Greek employees of the commission could be tried under domestic criminal law. The defense made the opposite case: that the protocols specified that none of the loan funds came under the control of the Greek state, and that the RSC was the mandatory of the League of Nations, not the state. In executing a contract approved by the RSC, Karamanos had committed no act of corruption or theft and could not be tried for a criminal offense in any Greek court.[52]

The courtroom proceedings reflected in miniature the broader conflict between the League and the sovereignty of a member state: the fact that by controlling the loan funds, the League effectively had responsibility for the economic livelihoods of a large minority of Greek citizens. The proceeds of the loan, as Howland told Pangalos, "did not, at any time, come into the fisc of the Greek State;" instead, they passed directly from the bankers to the RSC. This meant these funds were "subject only to the rights which, under the Protocol, the League of Nations possesses in respect of this matter. The Greek Government cannot control the expenditure of that money; it exercises no powers in respect of it."[53] All the Greek state could do was refer the issue to Geneva for arbitration. Any Greek employee of the RSC suspected of theft, bribery, or fraud would be handed over to Greek authorities for criminal prosecution. But bringing charges against a contract approved by the RSC would be considered an attempt to destroy it.[54] Members of the government reassured Howland that the protocols would be respected. Emmanouil Tsoudéros, deputy governor of the National Bank of Greece, claimed that they would be complied with "even up to the smallest detail."[55] But even if Karamanos were pardoned, Howland feared his engineers would be executed or face long prison sentences.[56] He saw Pangalos's brand of authoritarianism as closely wedded to public opinion and the theatrics of mass politics. The Pangalos government had forgotten "its international obligations," Howland told Salter, "in favour of domestic affairs."[57]

Whatever the verdict, moreover, these attacks on the RSC would have real consequences in international capital markets. They were "exceedingly short-sighted from the Greek point of view," Niemeyer insisted, "particularly if [the Greeks] ever hope to raise more money for refugees."[58] To the heads of the RSC, the arrest of Karamanos appeared to be an act of pure demagogy. The government, as one of the RSC's former Greek directors wrote in a newspaper article that summer, had understood the political advantage of relinquishing Greece's sovereign rights when it had signed the loan protocols. Doing so had removed controversial questions about the settlement of the refugees from a "million party and political interferences," even as it wounded "national prestige." But now, the government was sloughing off blame for any refugee grievance onto the RSC, which was also attacked by disgruntled former employees, contractors that failed to win bids for work, journalists searching for scandals, and most of all, the refugee leaders themselves.[59]

The way out of the impasse was to refer the matter to Geneva. But doing so threaten to turn a local drama into a global spectacle with an uncertain outcome. In September 1925, members of the League's Financial Committee mounted a maximalist defense of the RSC's powers and autonomy. Continued violation of that autonomy, they claimed, would make it impossible for Greece to get further loans.[60] Members of the commission had warned the government that bringing complaints to Geneva was unlikely to deliver the results they sought. As predicted, the matter was settled decisively in favor of Greece's foreign bondholders. It was unclear, though, whether the decision taken by the League's Council would have any effect in Greek courtrooms or whether magistrates would even be aware of it. Members of the RSC hoped that the backing of the League might help to swing the opinion of Greek elites against the government's alleged flouting of its international obligations. Bringing attention to the matter in the next report of the RSC's work could also damage Greece's credit. Eventually, after members of the RSC further demanded that the government take the decisions of the League's Council seriously and bring the prosecution to an end, Pangalos relented.[61] After weeks of delay, the case was dismissed. Karamanos was reinstated for work in Macedonia in early 1926.[62] The RSC had survived the greatest threat to its existence.

Greek Sovereignty and the Search for a New Loan

But Greece was still a questionable borrower. The government was spending large sums on the military, its budget was unbalanced, and the value of the drachma was falling. War debts to the Allies went unpaid.[63] Making matters worse was the outbreak of a brief war with Bulgaria in October 1925 over a border dispute and Pangalos's increasingly erratic rule, which included the promulgation of a much despised law that December dictating the length of women's skirts.[64] Fears of political instability were exacerbated by the government's search for loans not under League control, its threats to the RSC's autonomy, its efforts to weaken the protocol's rules, and its refusal to give up certain valuable property promised to the RSC, such as tobacco lands, olive groves, and vineyards left by exchanged Muslim landowners in Mytilene and Crete.[65]

Another serious issue arose in the spring of 1926, when the Pangalos government, desperate for revenue, implemented a new 7 percent national tax on crop sales.[66] The tax did not discriminate between native and refugee. As such, its implementation put the government in violation of the loan protocols, which stated that the League had first dibs on any revenue from the refugees—a status analogized to the priority of claims in a bankruptcy proceeding.[67] The added financial burden of this new tax also threatened to jeopardize the refugees' progress toward economic self-sufficiency and thereby drag out repayment of the loan.[68] Since the future revenues of the refugees had been guaranteed to the bondholders, whose interests the RSC was obligated to protect, the government had to either pay over the share of the tithe collected from the refugees to the RSC or drop the tax altogether.

But preventing the government from implementing the tithe, particularly given its desperate need for revenue, was an intrusive demand. Salter warned the heads of the RSC to proceed gently, since they were claiming the right to interfere with one of the most fundamental internal expression of sovereignty: the ability of a state to tax its citizens. While the RSC had a right to the money it was owed, and could put pressure on the government to receive it, the League could not "determine the Greek fiscal system."[69] In private, however, Campbell warned Finance Minister Demetre Tantalidès that taking money belonging to the RSC would have "disastrous consequences to the credit of Greece."[70] But Tantalidès refused to relent.[71] At every turn, the government worked under the unforgiving loan protocols. Even the members of the RSC admitted these protocols were severe, while they interpreted them with exacting contractual textualism to protect the interests of Greece's creditors.[72] While there was some discussion of amending the protocols to allow the Greek state to levy the tithe and thereby exercise its sovereign powers of taxation, Howland insisted this was impossible "without the consent of every bondholder—which is of course impracticable."[73]

That the economic lives of the refugees had been made an object of surveillance by officials, bankers, and investors thousands of miles away generated other quixotic legal problems with real material consequences. In the spring of 1926, after the National Bank of Greece made crop loans to refugees, regional officers enforced their repayment harshly, forcing some refugees to sell off cattle provided to them by the RSC. But these animals were technically the property of the RSC until the refugees paid for them, putting the bank in violation of the rules of the loan as well.[74] Once again, the RSC ended up in a position of far-reaching involvement in the daily lives of the refugees. It warned Greece's largest bank not to separate any of them from the specially branded cattle they had, in effect, been leased by Wall Street and the City of London.

There was nothing new about the representatives of foreign bondholders eroding the autonomy of sovereign states for the sake of pro-

Agricultural work in Macedonia. *United Nations Archives at Geneva.*

Workshop for carpet manufacture outside Athens. *United Nations Archives at Geneva.*

tecting their investments. What was so radical about the 1924 Refugee Loan was the degree and nature of this interference: It did not aim at the enforcement of austerity like in Austria and Hungary, but at the expansion of state powers and their simultaneous removal from the control of a sitting government. When and whether refugees could sell their livestock, the productivity of individual women weavers, the contracts of domestic construction firms, and local disputes about rent and evictions—all this and more had become objects of international intervention. Each time any rules of the loan protocol were threatened, Greece's credit was put at risk. This fact was frequently emphasized as discussion picked up in 1926 about the possibility of another loan to finish the settlement work. Niemeyer put this point bluntly to Salter that August: the Financial Committee was unlikely to support a new loan to Greece to finish the work of the refugee settlement "when the provisions governing the last loan had been broken by the Greeks."[75]

The League of Nations as a Debt Collector

The most controversial and complex responsibility that the commission undertook was as debt collector. Over the seven years of the RSC's existence in Greece, the question of how to ensure refugee families paid back what they technically owed proved to be so difficult that its directors doubted it would ever be successful. The problem could not be given full attention, moreover, while conflict raged with the Pangalos government, culminating in the Karamanos affair. In Macedonia and Thrace, responsibility for collecting payments was given to regional colonization services. After the refugees' economic "self-sufficiency" had been reached, officials would collect money from local cooperatives, to which individual families paid their dues.[76] This decentralized process was designed to avoid the "chaos" of the RSC directly collecting money from countless individual families.[77] Given the coercion needed to ensure payments—the threat of eviction and imprisonment—this arrangement would also prevent the commission from directly intervening like a despotic foreign landlord. A "frictionless eviction of a lazy cultivator by his own fellows," as one member of the RSC told the British banker Eric Hambro, was better than "an eviction of a refugee by a centralised organisation," which "might in fact be oppressive in an individual case, and might in many cases, and perhaps all, lead to a consolidation of refugee feeling against the debt collection organisation."[78] The legitimacy of this process of extracting revenue to pay off the lenders depended on it appearing as the demand of one Greek citizen on another, not that of an outsider.

As the process of debt collection began, it faced an additional stumbling block. The 1923 convention concerning the population exchange with Turkey guaranteed that refugees who left property in Turkey would be compensated in Greece according to its value. But these same refugees were now being asked by the RSC to pay for the houses they were settled in. The heads of the League commission recognized that this contradiction made the collection of the debt extremely difficult: The refugees' legitimate claims for reimbursement, ratified in a treaty, were pitted against the League's demands that they repay the bondholders for the costs of their settlement. Shortly after the 1924 loan was made, the foreign directors of the RSC began to worry that the Greek government would attempt to win refugee support by preventing the commission from forcing them to pay for what they had been promised for free: "One cannot coerce a whole mass of people," Campbell warned Salter:

> The practical point is—: can we in fact recover our money from the peasants? I am extremely doubtful as to this. The question is—like everything else in Greece—assuming a political character; and once the idea spreads and takes root, we may easily find ourselves up

against an organised refusal to pay, that refusal being supported by a body of political opinion which it will be impossible for any Government to disregard.[79]

These tensions boiled over in the summer of 1925, on the eve of the Pangalos coup, when a string of protests and riots broke out in impoverished and squalid urban settlements around Athens. Thousands of refugees moved into unoccupied and unfinished RSC houses, insisting that they would not pay the exorbitant rents demanded of them by the RSC, particularly for the poorly built houses to which they were assigned.[80] Communist groups further encouraged them not to pay for what they were already supposed to own.[81] To the heads of the RSC, the threat from the left was less worrying, though, than the plot they thought existed in the government: to win refugee support by allowing them to squat in these houses. General Georgios Kondylis, then minister of the interior, was suspected of telling the police not to interfere with the occupation of the houses to shore up support from the refugees he was cultivating as a source of backing for his own coup attempt.[82] From the vantage point of the League, Kondylis appeared to be buying refugee support for the sake of his own political ambitions—and risking Greece's credit in the process.[83] The RSC warned Prime Minister Michalakopoulos to suppress the "anarchy" in these settlements so the RSC could return to its work safeguarding the financial interests of the bondholders to whom it had fiduciary responsibility.[84] If the government did not comply, Greece's credit would be destroyed: "The Government understands clearly what will happen to its credit and prestige," Howland told Salter, "if the refugees are allowed to occupy properties and refuse either to pay rent or to buy on an instalment basis according to the plan we have been maturing."[85] After taking power a few days later, Pangalos sent troops to evict the refugees, as he had promised the directors of the RSC. This ignited an uprising that was violently suppressed.[86] Even as "order" was restored, the larger issue went unresolved. If the government solicited refugee support in exchange for leniency in debt collection, the RSC would struggle to extract payment from them.[87] As long as the refugees claimed they were owed reimbursement as compensation for their displacement, there was no way they could be forced to pay the RSC without leading back to this political conflict.

After the fall of the Pangalos government in the summer of 1926, and the return of some normalcy to Greek politics, relations with the RSC

improved. But finding a way to get the refugees to pay continued to occupy the attention of the directors of the RSC. They devised various strategies for extracting themselves from the business of debt collection and es-
caping the political quicksand they felt themselves sinking into. Their
hope was to reach an arrangement mutually beneficial to the Greek government and its creditors—the two parties whose relationship the League
had been enlisted to mediate. The aim was to remove a "foreign body"
from Greece while giving the government an incentive to collect the
money and repay the bondholders, instead of promising leniency to the
refugees in exchange for their political support.[88] Niemeyer wanted to get
the RSC out of the business of dealing with the refugees altogether, who
he claimed wielded their political influence to "blackmail" the government.[89] One suggestion was for the IFC to take on the job of debt collector. But this was rejected by the foreign debt commission. In view of
the "delicate position of the Commission as a foreign element in the Administration," as one member of the IFC wrote, it was not suited to the
work of debt collection from individual families:

> The difficulties already experienced in the collection of debts by the
> Refugee Settlement Commission, a body working under the League
> of Nations for the benefit of the refugees and partly administered by
> Greeks, will be greatly enhanced in the case of a body under exclu-
> sively foreign direction and acting solely in the interest of the bond-
> holders. The [International Financial] Commission will find itself
> continually assailed by appeals from refugees for the postponement
> or remission of debts. If it gives way, the collections will be gradu-
> ally whittled down to insignificance.[90]

If the IFC attempted to force the refugee families to pay, they would rally
parliament and the press against it, use the IFC's name as a "symbol for
oppression on behalf of foreign creditors," and throw into jeopardy the
work it had been doing since 1898 to extract revenue for Greece's lenders,
well guarded from public scrutiny.[91] The foreign members of the IFC, well
aware of the risk of instigating further resistance to their work, turned a
common argument in favor of the League's role in sovereign lending
against it: because the international institution was a more legitimate med-
dler than a foreign debt commission, it had to do its own dirty work.

Until the RSC was dissolved in 1930, it struggled to collect the money
it was due.[92] A large percentage of urban refugees were unable or unwilling to pay. By early 1929, only 40 percent of the families settled in

Athens and Piraeus had paid installments on their habitations; the rest had paid nothing or their payments were in arrears.[93] The conditions of these urban settlements, which had been given less priority than their agricultural counterparts, remained impoverished. The degree of foreign interference that the entire project of debt collection involved was becoming increasingly untenable. "This duty is an unpleasant duty," as the last British head of the RSC, John Hope Simpson, a former colleague of Campbell in the Indian Civil Service, put it coolly that February. "The RSC would be just as glad to escape from the necessity of collecting debts from the refugees as the refugees themselves would be if the debts were excused."[94] There was continued uncertainty about what combination of coercion and leniency was needed to complete this work.[95] The RSC gave mixed instructions to the bureaus charged with collecting the payments: to avoid the exertion of pressure if this forced the refugees into further debt, while impressing on them the importance of paying what they could.[96] Threats of eviction and imprisonment were used sparingly, due to fears of resistance from the refugees. When members of the RSC met with leading Greek government figures in early 1929 to discuss these problems, after the return of Venizelos to power, Simpson warned them that mass evictions would "probably lead to revolution." Evictions were particularly likely to generate resistance. As such, it was better to incarcerate the head of a family, government officials agreed, than to throw the whole family into the street and thereby spark an uprising.[97]

In the end, however, the Greek refugee resettlement scheme—coming to a conclusion just on the eve of the Depression—was celebrated by the League of Nations as a resounding success.[98] By 1930, most of the refugee families had been settled, and the RSC was dissolved. Early threats about the inability of Greece to raise another loan had not prevented one from being made—though now for broader aims. In late 1926, as progress on the lingering issue of Allied war debts was made and the unpopular Pangalos was ousted, plans for another loan had taken off. After visiting Greece in 1927, the League's Deputy Secretary General Josef Avenol suggested a £9 million loan to finish the refugee resettlement and stabilize Greek finances, on the condition of fiscal reforms and the creation of a politically independent central bank. After unsuccessful attempts by the Greek government and National Bank to ensure another League loan did not come with foreign controls, an agreement was reached in September 1927 for a £9 million loan that did.[99] This loan was closer in its aims to the financial reconstruction schemes in Austria and Hungary than the 1924 Greek refugee loan. It also involved another project of central bank independence being imposed externally on a postwar republic in the face of resistance across the country's ideological and party divides to the creation of an additional "state within a state."[100]

But before this point, the League had managed to do something new in Greece. It had taken over powers of the state, removed them from government control, and used them to oversee a major foreign investment in the transformation of a large group of Greek citizens, all with the aim of protecting the postwar settlement in a region where it was continually tested by the wars and near wars that followed the conclusion of the First World War. In public, League officials celebrated the project as a great humanitarian and peacekeeping achievement. Behind closed doors, the RSC, a League organ, was described in other terms: as "a trustee for the bondholders in the sense that it owes them a duty to manage its affairs and assets for their benefit as its fiduciaries, and to do all it can for their protection," as Howland put it. "This kind of trusteeship requires the RSC on every point to look to the interests of the bondholders."[101] There had been few more explicit descriptions of the League acting as a guardian of foreign investors—ones who in this case had staked their money on an extraordinary experiment in the rural development of a region that had plunged the world into war just a few years before.

The far-reaching degree of interference in Greek affairs that came with the 1924 loan was difficult to universalize as a practice of development lending. When new requests for development loans came to the Financial Committee, Niemeyer was forced to attack the "utterly and absolutely untrue" idea that the "League financial activities have been humanitarian."[102] But what the Greek refugee loan had shown was that humanitarian, nation-building, and developmental practices could be paired with older forms of bondholder diplomacy. The League had undertaken a dramatic experiment in "peasant recolonisation," as one contemporary put it, carried out on "Lombard Street principles."[103] It was unique as an institution in attempting to reconcile these tensions. But such a reconciliation would prove almost impossible to reproduce.

The International Development of China

Soon after the League's refugee resettlement work in Greece came to an end in 1930, a very different scheme of development was attempted thousands of miles to the east. At the beginning of 1931, the Chinese Nationalist

Government of Chiang Kai-shek (Jiang Jieshi) enlisted the League's help as it consolidated power in Nanjing and attempted to bring China under unified control after years of instability. During the decade between the seizure of power by the Nationalist Party (Guomindang) in Nanjing in 1927 and the outbreak of war with Japan in 1937, the government oversaw a major project of national industrial and infrastructural development. This project was complementary to, and sometimes in conflict with, the government's contemporaneous efforts at military build-up. The League played a small but important role in this process. Its economic involvement in China began not with the Financial Committee, as it had in Europe, but with its Health Section, under the initiative of its entrepreneurial head, the Polish bacteriologist Ludwik Rajchman.[104] Rajchman's public health work in China in the 1920s laid the foundations for the League's ties to the Nationalist government and marked a new phase of economic collaboration with a member state at the outset of the Depression.

The League's involvement in the Nationalist project of state-building has been described both as an incomplete effort that collapsed in the face of China's conflict with Japan and as setting an important precedent for the work of international development bodies like the World Bank just a few years later.[105] Both descriptions are true. Yet the League's China project also unfolded in the context of broader experiments in transforming how external private and public actors attempted to legitimize their involvement, via multilateral institutions, in the domestic affairs of a range of formally sovereign states. This context is key for understanding the larger stakes of this project. China was not the only non-European League member state with constrained sovereignty that sought the League's technical assistance. Siam engaged the organization on a variety of projects in public health, opium control, and human trafficking.[106] Liberia, as we have seen, was a site for an attempted though ultimately unrealized League-controlled project of technical assistance.[107] Ethiopia, by contrast, did not receive such assistance.[108] China was unique in being the only member state to become a site of development assistance that targeted not only infrastructure and agriculture but also industry. Like Greece, it occupied a distinctive position in the eyes of possible creditors. It was a borrower that already faced various restrictions on its autonomy and a sovereign state whose domestic affairs were already the object of external surveillance and diplomatic negotiation.[109] While its constrained sovereignty made China a possible site for a controlled development loan, the long history of semi-colonial interference there also made the politics of any further derogations of its sovereignty that much more explosive. The prospect of channeling foreign capital into China's railways and industry involved squaring an extraordinarily complex circle: reaching a working relationship with the Nationalist government by avoiding anything like the kind of interference China had long faced at foreign hands, appeasing the foreign lenders accustomed to violating China's sovereignty, and re-assuring a Japanese government attempting to further subject China to its control that its efforts would not be overtly thwarted in the process.

China was a founding member of the League of Nations, but its rela-tionship to the organization was tenuous. China had joined the Allied war against the Central Powers in the summer of 1917, sending around 140,000 workers to Europe to build shells and dig trenches, and had ex-pected real gains in return.[110] But expectations that the Allies would hand back the territory of Shandong to Chinese sovereignty at war's end were disappointed at the Paris Peace Conference when it was given to Japan, which had seized it from Germany early in the war.[111] This deci-sion led to mass student demonstrations in Beijing that May, which spread throughout the country in the form of the broad-based May Fourth Move-ment, which provided a fillip to the growth of the Guomindang and the establishment of the Chinese Communist Party in 1921. Suspicions in China ran deep of an organization dominated by the European powers that continued to exercise controls over its domestic policies and sources of wealth. When Rajchman first visited China in 1925, he reported that the very term "International" had "a sinister meaning" there. Any hope for the League's outreach to China, he added, depended on the League's technical assistance appearing completely impartial.[112] As we have seen, the Chinese diplomat V. K. Wellington Koo (Gu Weijun) had attempted at the 1919 Paris Peace Conference to ensure that the "domestic jurisdic-tion" clause in the League's Covenant, pushed for by US lawmakers anx-ious about foreign interference in US trade and immigration policy, did not preclude Chinese attempts to remove foreign controls.[113] But some also hoped that membership in the League of Nations would augment China's prestige on the international stage and win the assistance of tech-nical experts.[114] In his 1921 *International Development of China,* the Na-tionalist leader Sun Yat-sen had called for an international institution like the League to provide expertise and capital for China's development without further derogations of its sovereignty. Sun's book provided a guide for Nationalist leaders attempting to redefine China's economic relationship with foreign powers and was later widely credited as the first blueprint for international development (as it would come to be commonly understood).[115]

For nearly a century, China had faced numerous foreign controls over its sources of revenue and policy-making. It was a textbook case of a "semi-colonialized" country, whose domestic spaces had been wrenched open to the reach of external powers, despite no formal loss of independence.[116] After the First World War, most existing forms of foreign control remained in place. Even after the Guomindang took Nanjing in 1927, extraterritoriality continued to allow foreigners to operate beyond the reach of domestic authorities, and the Maritime Customs Service and Salt Administration controlled sources of revenue to service China's foreign debt. (Like the Greek Refugee Settlement Commission, the Maritime Customs Service was referred to in China as an "imperio in imperium.")[117] While Britain's trade with China made up a small percentage of total British exports, Britain was still a leading foreign power there. British capitalists played a significant role as financiers and providers of commercial services, and the prospect of a politically stabilized and infrastructurally developed China turning into a major destination for British exports remained a tantalizing foreign policy goal in London.[118]

During the 1920s, the Chinese government wrested further control over domestic policies and assets, and the Nationalists demonstrated the power of mass mobilization to resist further erosions of Chinese sovereignty. This process was accelerated after an uprising in late 1925, sparked by the shooting of Shanghai students by the British-led Shanghai Municipal Police. The May Thirtieth Movement that followed involved a major campaign of strikes and anti-British boycotts targeting Hong Kong and Canton, which the rising Guomindang used to its advantage. This movement so spooked Whitehall that it led to a formal reconsideration of British China policy.[119] From the British vantage point, not only did the Guomindang appear to be backed by the Soviets, who could mobilize Chinese nationalism to destabilize the empire in Asia, but the power of the "anti-foreign feeling" the uprising had exacerbated was forcing a decision about the future of British economic and imperial power in the region. Foreign communities in China were calling for a swift and violent suppression of the movement, but the British government and bankers worried that such action was no longer a realistic response to the power of Chinese nationalism: "The old gunboat policy," as one put it, "is as dead as the dodo."[120] After the opening of the Nationalists' Northern

Expedition, a new policy was formalized in a December 1926 Foreign Office memorandum, which stated that the British Empire would no longer attempt to bring China under foreign tutelage. It was at this moment that a decision was taken to grant the Chinese some right "to be masters in their own house," as John Pratt, a leading China hand in the Foreign Office, described a shift in policy that he played a central role in shaping.[121] Shortly after this decision, negotiations were opened for China to regain the ability to set its own tariffs, though extraterritoriality and the Customs Service remained in place into the 1940s.[122]

There is debate about the significance of the recalibration of British imperial strategy in China in the wake of the 1925 May Thirtieth Movement. Some have claimed it was emblematic of a broader strategy of British "imperial retreat," as London reconsidered the future of informal empire in places it could no longer afford to dominate outright.[123] Others have cautioned against exaggerating the claim. They point out that by the late 1930s, British financial influence in China had not been significantly weakened, and that British imperialism in China was in the process of being transformed, not abandoned, when the Second World War began.[124] What was clearly true was that after the May Thirtieth Movement, leading members of the Foreign Office reconsidered the future of British economic imperialism in China, in the face of strong resistance from foreign merchant communities that insisted their privileges be defended, with violent force if necessary. Making some concessions to Chinese nationalism increasingly appeared to be necessary to protect the empire's long-term interests in a region where its military power was on the wane.[125]

The consolidation of Nationalist rule in Nanjing in 1928, and Chiang's violent purging of the party's communist elements, provided a fillip to forces in London that supported the move away from further foreign controls. Putting a friendlier face on British interference in China could be used to facilitate a working relationship with the moderate elements of what was set to be the first stable post-Qing government. That might make possible the repayment of China's foreign debts in arrears and jumpstart the long-anticipated development of its railways. These were seen as the two keys to China's development, which if successfully managed could unleash a seemingly limitless source of external demand for British exports, and thereby fuel the growth of British trade and ameliorate lingering unemployment at home.[126] It was against the backdrop of this changing British policy in the late 1920s that the League emerged as a candidate

for playing a mediating role between the Chinese state and its foreign creditors. The challenge was to legitimate old tools of financial imperialism
in a new world of self-determination and mass politics.

A League Loan for China

The League's economic involvement in China began with consideration
of China's eligibility for loans to stabilize its finances and kickstart its development. This almost completely forgotten episode took shape after
Avenol traveled to China in the winter of 1928–1929, not long after he
had gone to Greece to arrange the second League loan. Avenol's trip
roughly coincided with the visit to China of the Princeton economist and
famed US money doctor Edwin Kemmerer, who had been unofficially invited to advise the Nationalist government on a program of financial reform.[127] Avenol sought to prevent the Kemmerer mission from leading
to a US loan instead of a League loan, as had recently happened in Poland. The timing of his visit was auspicious, since it coincided with a debate in London about the possibility of using the League to oversee a
new kind of financial engagement with China.

However, any League involvement would necessitate either replacing
or working alongside the China Banking Consortium—a public-private
cartel-like grouping of British, US, Japanese, and French banks that had
for years controlled any loans to China with public issue abroad. Like
other inter-imperial arrangements from this era, this multinational banking
cartel had been developed to mitigate competition among foreign powers
over spheres of influence by dividing up investment opportunities.[128] After
the 1894–1895 Sino-Japanese War, an earlier syndicate of foreign banks
had emerged to ameliorate conflict over railway investments, which in
China had real geopolitical stakes. After the 1911 Revolution, this first
consortium expanded its activities into making a £25 million loan to the
republican government of Yuan Shikai to consolidate his conservative
rule. It was made conditional on sources of revenue being put under foreign control and the placement of foreign advisers into the government
administration. The so-called Reorganization Loan of 1913 was a fiasco.
It was profoundly unpopular in China for the controls it involved, and it
helped spark the outbreak of a Nationalist revolution led by Sun Yat-sen.
(It also provided Yuan with the funds to violently suppress this uprising.)[129]
Before the loan was completed, Woodrow Wilson, only two weeks after
coming to power in 1913, announced that the United States would not

participate in it due to the degree of interference in Chinese affairs it entailed, which he claimed threatened the "administrative independence of China itself."[130] The Consortium went into hiatus during the First World War but was reorganized in 1920 as a four-power group, including the United Kingdom, France, Japan, and the United States. Each national banking group was led by a single bank, represented by one person, and was backed by its respective government. In the United States, the banking group was headed by J. P. Morgan, led by Thomas Lamont; in Britain, it was the Hongkong and Shanghai Bank, represented by its London manager Charles Addis.[131]

The principal justification for this arrangement was to freeze a geopolitical status quo in place by ensuring that none of the powers, particularly Japan and the United States, got a head start on financing China's railways and development. The Consortium thus aimed to keep any single foreign power from bringing the country further under its political sway and to ensure the Chinese government did not receive any new loans until it agreed to the terms of its creditors. Of particular importance to the United States was preventing Japan from making further uniliteral loans to China, as it had done in 1917–1918 with the so-called "Nishihara" loans. The establishment of the second Consortium was thus linked to broader strategies for containing conflict between the former wartime allies in the Pacific, embodied in the treaties signed at the Washington Conference of 1921–1922 for naval disarmament, the promotion of the Open Door in China, and the return of Shandong to Chinese sovereignty. In practice, though, the Consortium amounted to a collective effort in China's underdevelopment.[132]

Because it was genuinely seen outside of China as preventing great power competition from leading to war, the Consortium acquired a kind of perverse reputation as an international institution. Both Lamont and Addis, its two most powerful members until the 1930s, were, as we have seen, influential representatives of a transatlantic club of internationalist bankers, who played critical roles in establishing the BIS in 1929–1930. It was thus perhaps unsurprising that they described the Consortium in internationalist terms—as a "little league of Nations" or a "far-eastern League of Nations."[133] But the Consortium also acquired a reputation in the 1920s as an anachronistic inter-imperial cartel, which the Chinese government would never work with until it was granted membership in it, thereby transforming it from a semi-colonial debt commission into a real international body. At key moments, its member banks did not see eye-to-eye with their government backers on the future of financial imperialism in China.

Since the Reorganization Loan of 1913, no Chinese government had agreed to work with the Consortium, in large part because its member banks continued to insist that any loans come with further foreign controls over the administration of railways and sources of revenue. Because the member banks of the Consortium could pressure their respective governments to prevent banks outside the Consortium from lending to China, it was, in effect, able to exercise a stranglehold over the Chinese government's access to foreign capital. Far from channeling capital into China's development, by the 1920s, the Consortium was functioning more as a financial blockade than anything else (though the political instability of China and the government's poor credit did not help make it an attractive borrower). For the backers of the Consortium, this inefficient institution was nonetheless said to be useful for preventing any one power from beating others to securing the hypothetical future China market for themselves. Remove the Consortium, Addis claimed, and foreign powers would race to subject China to further-reaching forms of "foreign interference," bringing it under their tutelage and effectively ending its status "as a Sovereign power."[134] The claim that the Consortium protected Chinese sovereignty instead of constraining it, was, of course, not convincing in China.

Over the 1920s, the stranglehold that the Consortium exercised over loans to the Republican government became increasingly frustrating to foreign capitalists and some government officials, who saw it as drying up profit-making opportunities.[135] "The Ch. Govt never have and probably never will recognise the Consortium as far as railway construction is concerned," as one Foreign Office minute put it in 1924; "(they are too afraid of foreign international control), a fact to which the [banking] Groups have hitherto seemed to make a point of closing their eyes, ever since they brought the Consortium into being with sublime disregard of the existence of the Ch. Govt. with which they proposed to do business."[136] The Chinese were now more than ever seeking to "emancipate themselves from all forms of foreign control," as another observer put it. They saw the Consortium "as a political instrument designed to limit their sovereignty by creating an international control over their finances and revenues of their State railways."[137] British capitalists appealed directly to the Consortium to loosen its iron grip over industrial and development loans, so that money could start flowing into the railway work that would redound to the benefit of exporters.[138]

After the consolidation of Chiang Kai-shek's government in 1927–1928, the Foreign Office reconsidered the future of the Consortium as part of its broader reorientation of China policy. As long as the Chinese saw it as a "sinister instrument of international finance designed for the financial enslavement of their country," the influential British Minister Miles Lampson wrote to Foreign Secretary Austen Chamberlain in April 1929, they would never work with it.[139] The Nationalist government refused to countenance any foreign controls or cooperate with an institution representing Japanese interests. It was also attempting to bring the Maritime Customs Service and Salt Administration further under its control. Since the December 1926 demarche, London agreed to stop pressuring Nanjing to accept any new controls. But bankers would not risk their money without such controls, which created a high-stakes impasse.[140] As Lampson admitted to Chamberlain's successor, Arthur Henderson, there was some validity to complaints that the Consortium was impeding the activities of British firms looking to profit from industrial and railway development projects, though he maintained that it was risky and impractical to remove it now.[141] Other members of the Foreign Office took a firmer line against it. During 1929, they attempted to abolish the Consortium once and for all and to replace it with another form of international financial cooperation that was less insulting to China's sovereign rights.[142]

This task was theoretically well suited to the League of Nations. By mediating the relationship of the Chinese state to foreign governments and banks and offering a more legitimate way of guaranteeing the use of foreign loans for "productive" purposes and not the military, the League could ensure that revenues were collected and old debts repaid—all without subjecting China to "tutelage." Two visions were in play. One was that the League would help to arrange loans; the other that it would only send advisers, without any powers of control, to increase China's credit. Some even suggested the recently founded BIS could also take on this role—though, as we have seen, this form of development financing was ruled out for the bank from the beginning by its designers, which included Addis himself.[143]

At the Bank of England, the proposal was a welcome one. Despite his reluctance to have the League get involved in development loans, Niemeyer was intrigued by the prospect of using it to help China put its financial house in order, so that old debts could be repaid and infrastructural development could be stimulated. He continued to make the old argument in support of League loans: The League "could be presented as an entirely different kind of control from that hitherto identified in China with the foreign devil."[144] Unlike the Consortium, after all, China was a member of the League. Membership in an institution was, by itself, again framed as sufficient to make this institution's potentially interventionist powers more legitimate. Other bankers also considered plans to have the League develop a more politically acceptable form of control in China than that of the Consortium.[145] Addis himself, a defender of the Consortium to the end, had for several years entertained the possibility of a Dawes Plan for China and would continue into the 1930s to suggest that the League oversee an Austrian- or Hungarian-style financial reconstruction program for the Nationalist government.[146]

The prospects for a League loan to China were bolstered by Avenol's visit to China in late 1928–1929 and his efforts to win the support of British and Japanese diplomatic officials and member banks of the Consortium.[147] Avenol similarly claimed that the assistance of the League was the only hope, given Chinese opposition to the Consortium.[148] In April 1929, he met with George Harrison, head of the New York Federal Reserve Bank, to argue that the League was better equipped to reorganize Chinese finances than the United States or Britain acting alone.[149] Around this time, some Nationalists, like the financier and official Wu Ding-Chang, began to advocate similar ideas, though on certain conditions: that they were compatible with Sun Yat-sen's vision of an institution financing China's development without any further derogation of its sovereign rights and that they broke from the practices of the Consortium. Postwar Germany, Austria, and Greece were clear precedents. But if Nanjing sought help, it would reject being treated as a "bankrupt or embarrassed government" like these European states.[150] These comparisons between China's sovereign status and that of other postwar states were mobilized to set firm limits to what the League could demand of the Chinese government.

During 1930 and early 1931, as the global Depression worsened, Ramsay MacDonald's government turned again to the idea of encouraging China to work with foreign experts that did not wield powers of control to increase the confidence of foreign lenders without "derogatory stipulations." Officials analogized the role of these experts to the British members of an increasingly Chinese-controlled Maritime Customs Service and Salt

Administration.[151] These experts would work as "servant of the Chinese," one member of the Foreign Office wrote, and "not as the agent of a foreign debtor, with the diplomatic support of that debtor's government looming in the background."[152] For some, the League appeared to offer the obvious way of helping the government to increase its credit without losing "face."[153]

But these optimistic visions of the League's financial role in China either misunderstood or misrepresented what this role had involved elsewhere. Anything that looked like the kinds of controls established in Austria and Hungary—modeled as they had been on the Chinese Maritime Customs Service in the first place—was bound to be rejected in China, where the politics of resisting such interference were arguably more developed than anywhere else in the world. Still, the Austrian model was widely discussed in 1930–1931, as the Nationalist government cast about for sources of foreign capital. Pressure was coming from some US diplomatic officials and experts, including Howland, to use the League to oversee a large silver loan to China to finance road and railway development projects, even though the United States was not a member of the institution. But these ideas never moved past the level of wishful thinking. President Herbert Hoover apparently remarked when he heard of such plans that "if anyone was so foolish to try to put the finances of China on a satisfactory footing, [Salter] was welcome to do so, and had his (Hoover's) best wishes!"[154] Similar sentiments were expressed by some British officials. According to the Indian Office official Cecil Kisch, the only reason that the Austrian scheme had worked was because the republic had agreed to "put itself under tutelage"—a prospect that was impossible, he claimed, in a country as vast and as politically unstable as China.[155]

The prospect of a League program of economic reconstruction in China got new legs, however, when Salter was extended a personal invitation from the Nationalist government to visit China.[156] From the vantage point of the British Foreign Office, the League appeared to be the ideal and possibly only way to navigate the political challenge of laying the groundwork for new loans. This had to be done carefully, avoiding any risk that Salter be seen as an agent of the British state: "Chinese confidence in the League is a plant of very tender growth," Pratt wrote, "and any attempt to <u>force</u> it may cause it to wither up."[157] But there was potentially a huge payoff to replacing the Consortium with the League and using it to achieve the Consortium's ends.[158] While members of the Treasury regarded the idea as "utopian," they agreed that a foreign adviser that the Chinese government trusted was better than the impositions of the Consortium. Still, they could not accept the idea of any future loans coming without foreign supervision.[159] At the Bank of England, Norman, a supporter of the Consortium, nonetheless recognized that the only way to get the Chinese government to deal with the Consortium was to offer the League as intermediary. This would have the added benefit of softening the Labour government's reluctance to work with the Consortium as well. But some kind of "outside" supervision and advice was necessary if China wanted any more money.[160]

Salter himself had more modest ambitions. He supported the Foreign Office view that the time had arrived to abolish the Consortium. But he rejected the analogy of Austria and Hungary, and he thought it was unlikely that conditions were ripe for a large international loan to China in any case. In recent years, Salter had become convinced that the poor reputation of the League's financial stabilization projects in Austria and Hungary meant that they no longer provided tenable models for the League's economic activities elsewhere. He thought that financial control had to give way to advising.[161] If the Nationalist government invited foreign experts on its own initiative for schemes of development, the League

Arthur Salter, 1930. © *National Portrait Gallery, London.*

could send them. This might increase the government's credit. But these experts could no longer have the status of a "master disguised as a servant."[162]

Advice without Control

When Salter arrived in Shanghai in the spring of 1931, he aimed to involve the League in the domestic economic affairs of a member state in new ways: not only by providing the services of experts without controls, but also by attempting to help the Nationalist government innovate an altogether new form of national economic administration. His immediate task was to help Finance Minister T. V. Soong (Song Ziwen), a US-educated Nationalist technocrat and brother-in-law of Chiang, set up an economic council to execute what was effectively a capitalist version of the Soviet Five Year Plan.[163] This council was to have Chinese officials and capitalists on staff and draw on foreign experts to design a massive project of economic and infrastructural development.[164] Unlike the RSC in Greece, the Chinese National Economic Council (NEC) would not be removed from government control. Its members would have only advisory, not executive, powers. Soong hoped that centralizing economic policy-making in this council would ameliorate the bureaucratic fragmentation of the state and win the support of powerful domestic capitalists for the development plans that he and Nationalist leader Wang Jingwei sought to prioritize over Chiang's drive for rearmament. Soong's belief that China's economic development was necessary to strengthen the state against foreign incursion put him in a protracted struggle with Chiang over devoting resources to civilian reconstruction.[165] Soong was close to Rajchman, who arranged the invitation to Salter to help Soong with these plans, at the same time that the broader reconsideration of China policy in London was taking place.

The proposals for an economic governing body that Salter developed with Soong combined elements from councils that had emerged across Europe since the war. These councils combined representative functions— they were widely referred to as "economic parliaments"—with the provision of expert advice. In Europe, these councils were promoted by fascists, communists, Catholics, and syndicalists alike, and were seen as part of a shared postwar trend toward the centralization of government economic decision-making.[166] Salter had come to support the idea of a limited form of capitalist planning, and was becoming an influential pro-

Headquarters of the National Economic Council, Nanjing. *Annual Report of the National Economic Council for the Year Ending December 31, 1935.*

ponent of the idea in Britain. He saw Europe's councils as promising a way to make economic decision-making more democratic.[167] Salter also thought that linking these councils together through the medium of the League, leading ultimately to the creation of a "world economic council," would make international governance more responsive to the demands of different national interest groups and parties.[168] The other major constituency for these ideas were Italian fascist internationalists, who promoted similar ideas of corporativist international institution-building at the League as well.[169] In 1932, the League published a report on these new councils by the German scholar Elli Lindner, who claimed in other writings that their emergence across Europe, led by what she saw as the vanguard of the Italian Council of Corporations, was accelerating the process of European economic unification.[170]

Before Salter arrived in China, he had also been invited to India—the only non-self-governing member of the League—to advise the colonial government on the establishment of a national economic council. This had been the idea of George Schuster, the unorthodox finance member of the viceroy's council in Delhi, who sought to offer a token concession to Indian nationalists by fulfilling demands for some kind of economic planning body as the Depression stoked discontent. Schuster sought to enlist the League with the project of building this Indian council, modeled on the one recently established in London, to give "the impression that Indians are consulted on things that matter," as Walter Layton, whom Schuster asked for help, put it.[171] For his part, Salter saw Schuster's outreach as an opportunity to improve the reputation of the League in India and to broaden the organization's reach into Asia.[172] But their designs were opposed by other members of the colonial government, who claimed that an Indian council would further politicize policy-making and create "unnecessary difficulties for ourselves," given controversies about the sterling-rupee exchange rate and the growing appeal of ideas of Indian economic self-sufficiency.[173] Schuster and Salter's failed initiative was not ignored completely: It was held up by an array of Indian nationalists, economists, and supporters of planning, some of who claimed that its rejection represented an exemplary moment of colonial hypocrisy, when the government could have adopted a more representative and rational system for governing the Indian economy and chose not to.[174]

The prospects for a national economic planning council were much better in a sovereign country ruled by a nationalist government, however, than in a colony controlled by a regime that was committed to preventing the idea of a national economy from taking root and to keeping domestic interest groups from having a real say in its governance.[175] The inauguration of the NEC was interrupted by the Japanese invasion of Manchuria in September 1931, but its doors opened shortly afterward, and it was filled with leading Chinese bankers and industrialists. Its work focused on developing the cotton and silk industries and cementing the government's ties to domestic capitalists, from whom Soong sought to raise revenue to finance his state-building endeavors and who, in turn, looked to the state for protection.[176] The council also hosted a series of foreign experts sent by the League to work with the government in a new kind of Sino-foreign joint venture that was distinct from institutions like the Customs Service, because it involved no derogation of Chinese sovereignty.[177] Over the following four years, nearly thirty experts were sent by the League to work with the regime on industrial, agricultural, and infrastructural development schemes. These experts included one of the last heads of the Greek Refugee Settlement Commission, John Hope Simpson, who arrived in China to work on water infrastructure schemes in the aftermath

A bridge on the Weipei canal constructed by the NEC in Shaanxi Province. *Annual Report of the National Economic Council for the Year Ending December 31, 1935.*

of late 1931 floods—one of the deadliest natural disasters in history. The most successful initiative of these experts was advising on the construction of thousands of miles of new roads.[178] This was the first time that an international institution had ever attempted to provide technical assistance for a development project of this scope.

Accounts of the short-lived League experiment in China, and the work of these experts, tend to emphasize how the Japanese invasion of Manchuria, one of the very worst crises that the League ever faced, made these broader efforts impossible to realize. Although the League issued only a mild rebuke to Japan, it still prompted the Japanese government to quit the organization in early 1933 and to intensify its opposition to the work of foreign experts in China. In 1934, Avenol, now secretary-general, ended Rajchman's contract for work in China, to bring Japan back into the organization's fold.[179] This effectively brought the League's economic work in China to a close. Yet up to this point, the initiative had represented a new departure in how the League related to a member state with uncertain and partial sovereignty but that had nonetheless demonstrated its power to resist further foreign interference. Unlike the experts sent to Albania or Austria, those sent to China were given no powers of control.[180] This became a source of frustration for them. René Charron, for

Members of the NEC researching cotton cultivation methods. *Annual Report of the National Economic Council for the Year Ending December 31, 1935.*

example, who had previously worked in Sofia as controller of the League loan to Bulgaria, found that in China, by contrast, he was powerless to tell the government how to manage its affairs.[181]

Another obstacle to their work was that the Consortium continued to exercise a stranglehold over the government's access to foreign capital. The government had little chance of winning the necessary foreign capital to pay for the NEC's development work unless it paid back old debts and agreed to whatever terms the Consortium imposed. This deadlock was very difficult to break. The Japanese government insisted that no other powers take the lead in financing China's reconstruction without their direct involvement. They had backers among the other banking groups. Lamont, for example, became an apologist for and even supporter of Japanese designs on China.[182] There was no chance that the Chinese government would work with an institution representing Japanese interests, certainly not without being offered membership in it. Soong looked for new ways to get around the Consortium, including by seeking loans beyond its control. In the summer of 1933, while in London for the World Economic Conference, Soong attempted to drum up British support for new credits. Then, in the United States, he successfully arranged a loan from the US Reconstruction Finance Corporation to purchase wheat and cotton to resell in China to provide funds for the NEC. This loan evaded the Consortium's control.[183] In addition, Soong also inaugurated a new domestic institution, the China Development Finance Corporation (CDFC), in 1934, with the help of Jean Monnet and David Drummond, son of the former League secretary-general. It was headed by Soong and his brother-in-law H. H. Kung (Kong Xiangxi), governor of the Central Bank of China and a leading Nationalist economic official. Capitalized at $10 million, the CDFC was to be staffed by both Chinese and foreign experts to manage a pool of domestic and foreign capital, examine development projects, arrange financing for those it approved, and oversee the use of funds.[184] It was a Sino-foreign joint venture that was supposed to replace the Consortium without needing to formally dissolve it. Most of all, it provided a way to channel foreign capital to the underfunded NEC without any need for new foreign controls.[185]

Opponents of the Consortium enthusiastically greeted the inauguration of this new banking institution. It appeared to offer a way of lending

T. V. Soong and Ramsay MacDonald at the 1933 World Economic Conference in London. *Photographic News Agency Ltd, United Nations Archives at Geneva.*

to the Chinese state without onerous new forms of interference. The CDFC provided a "channel and façade through and behind which a considerable amount of foreign interest could work without it any way lessening the Chinese 'face,'" the British commercial counselor in Shanghai Louis Beale wrote, and "not only in regard to railways but in almost every development of industry in China."[186] It would allow foreign financiers to work behind a Chinese "façade" to get old debts repaid and development jumpstarted without foreign countries needing to "police and virtually colonize the whole of the country," as Drummond put it bluntly—which was impossible, in any case, in a country the size of China. It was only by "her helping herself," Drummond added, that China could be reconstructed.[187] The way the CDFC would provide a safe vehicle for investment without violating Chinese sovereignty was by putting the money of Chinese capitalists on the line, so that they would lose just as much as foreign bondholders did if the government defaulted. This provided a more reliable security for foreign investors than controls that led to antiforeign uprisings and could be used to prevent foreign loans for industrial projects from being diverted to military or "political" use.[188] "The best basis for the investment of foreign capital in China," as Salter put it, was "the association on equal conditions (not necessarily in equal proportions) with Chinese capital. The best security for the foreign investor will be the close association with Chinese investors whose fortunes are linked with his and who will bear the controlling share of responsibility."[189]

But the fact that the CDFC was designed to replace the Consortium was also why it was opposed by those who backed the Consortium, whether British bankers like Norman or, more importantly, Japanese officials, who were deeply suspicious of Monnet and any plans even indirectly related to the League. Cutting out the Japanese from a share in loans to China was seen by critics of this arrangement as a dangerous proposition, one that threatened the entire British strategy of avoiding direct confrontation with Japan.[190] If the League's technical assistance were to continue, Pratt now argued, the Japanese government had to be reassured that it was not connected in any way to "political" schemes for channeling capital into China.[191] The plans for the CDFC's creation, along with the US wheat and cotton loan from the year before and the League's technical assistance work, played an important role in prompting the issuance of a statement by the Japanese Foreign Office in April 1934 that claimed Japan would resist any foreign financial or military assistance to China.[192]

Like the Monroe Doctrine it emulated, the so-called Amau Statement posited a right to non-interference in a zone demarcated by one imperial power as its exclusive sphere of influence. It was another manifestation of the old idea of non-interference being weaponized in the 1930s for new projects of militarized regionalism.[193]

But by this point, deteriorating economic conditions in China—which had for several years managed to escape the worst of the Depression—combined with increasingly dangerous tensions with Japan to foil these schemes. Soon, the League was gone from China altogether. The Nationalists continued to seek out sources of foreign capital and expertise, not only from Britain and the United States, but also from Nazi Germany.[194] In 1935, the British economic expert and official Frederick Leith-Ross (also a member of the League's Economic Committee) travelled to China to advise the government on a major program of monetary reform. After the currency was removed from the silver standard, optimistic plans were developed for further railway and currency loans. But ongoing conflicts over foreign controls and the Consortium (which survived until 1946), along with the accelerating conflict with Japan, continued to complicate these issues. The window for ambitious efforts to redesign China's relations with foreign powers and banks via the international institutions that mediated these ties was closed. By the summer of 1937, China was at war.[195]

The Future of Development

These two League projects represented a vanguard moment in the longer history of international development. In neither case was the institution attempting to innovate a universalizable practice but was instead responding to specific crises and seizing on the opportunities they presented for expanding its powers, reputation, and reach. In the case of China, some factions in the British government, particularly in the Foreign Office, saw the League as offering a tool for redesigning informal empire at a moment of declining British global power. But competition in China among many foreign and domestic actors complicated the intervention of an external organization like the League—as well as ad hoc efforts like the CDFC that unfolded on its periphery. In Greece, the League was also responding to a very specific crisis, in a member state with constrained sovereignty, and at a moment of significant danger. However, taken together, these two different projects shared the distinction of being the first halting attempts to implement practices that would soon be generalized: the channeling of long-term loans to development projects and the provision of technical assistance to oversee them. In the 1940s, the experiences of the League in China and Greece were seen as models for future projects of international development, technical assistance, and foreign investment.[196] Their relative success and failure showed the political limits for such projects at a moment when the nature of economic sovereignty was in profound flux.

These two experiences showed that making risky loans on productive projects would, as long as private investment banks and central banks were involved, continue to come at the cost of derogations of sovereignty and far-reaching forms of interference. Such interference included not only the empowerment of foreign advisers to veto budgets or control assets, but also to oversee infrastructure projects, approve contracts, and even collect debts from individual families. When planning for a new international development institution began a few years later in the United States and Britain, there was growing conviction among its architects that development had to be less taxing on national sovereignty. Plans for the Inter-American Bank (a direct predecessor to the World Bank) in the United States, for example, were developed against the backdrop of the Roosevelt administration's formal commitment to the so-called Good Neighbor Policy of 1933, which held that Washington would avoid interfering in Latin American countries. This policy, which was analogous to the British Foreign Office's new approach to China from late 1926, was the product of concerted efforts by Latin American officials, drawing on a long tradition of Latin American diplomacy and law, to translate their countries' political sovereignty into real economic autonomy vis-à-vis the United States.[197] During postwar planning in London, officials also recognized that a new international development body faced real political constraints, as disparate movements against old practices of debt diplomacy took off around the world. Any development body had to avoid an "unnecessary amount of interference and supervisions over the detailed affairs of the borrowing countries," as one member of the government stated, which would lead their populations to think their "private lives" were "being handed over to a dictatorship of high banking capitalism."[198]

As we shall see, the World Bank was designed in ways that were supposed to obviate the need for such far-reaching forms of interference, though without directly challenging the continued existence of colonial empire: namely, by making loans less risky without forcing governments to relinquish their autonomy or pledge their revenues. But this problem was not decisively solved at the Bretton Woods Conference. There, new practices of development continued to be advocated by members of the Chinese Nationalist government, who made up the second-largest delegation at the conference. Indeed, Chinese Nationalists, including Soong, formed one of the leading wartime constituencies for the idea of putting international development at the center of postwar economic planning.[199] But China's experience in the 1920s and 1930s had shown that using an international institution to develop China—and thus strengthen its sovereignty, not weaken it—was, despite its appeal to various actors, extremely difficult to realize in practice. In the years to come, such affronts to sovereignty would remain common as long as the bankers providing the capital continued to demand control of its use.

CHAPTER 5

Controlling Commodities

BEFORE THE OUTBREAK of the Second World War, there was one final area of policy in which international institutions came to exercise real powers over the domestic economies of a range of sovereign states and colonies: the governance of commodity prices during the Depression. In addition to throwing millions of people out of work and sending global financial markets into turmoil, the outbreak of the crisis led to a dramatic collapse in the prices of many primary commodities, which had devastating consequences around the world. During the interwar period, agricultural products and raw materials like cotton, wheat, copper, and rubber constituted a large percentage of the total volume of goods traded on global markets. Their production employed a majority of the world's population. For countries and colonial territories that relied on the production and export of primary products, the Depression—coming on the heels of a period of wide fluctuations in commodity prices since the global crisis of 1920–1921—was catastrophic. While the mid-1920s saw a recovery of world trade, prices for many commodities began to fall well before the Wall Street crash of 1929 as supply outstripped demand. These deflationary pressures were due in part to the expanded production of many goods, made possible by innovations in mining and agricultural technologies, including the mechanization of grain production and use of new seed varietals. It was also due to the emergence of new producers around the world, the cultivation of previously fallow land, and the implementation of protectionist policies and subsidies for producers in many places. The outbreak of the Depression accelerated these deflationary trends as global demand for most goods collapsed.[1] This crisis threatened to destabilize colonial empires, depress external demand for manufactured exports, and throw imperial finances into disarray. But it also presented another opportunity for innovating the architecture of international governance. This, in turn, led to disputes about how insulated the economic affairs of colonies that relied on the production of such goods could expect to be from the scrutiny and influence of other states and empires.

Before the Depression, there had been various governmental attempts to stabilize the prices of the major commodities traded on world markets, whether through national or imperial regulation schemes targeting goods like rubber, sugar, and copper. Private international cartels, which had begun to emerge before the First World War to control the marketing of some primary and finished goods, such as zinc and steel rails, proliferated during the interwar period. Sometimes these cartels involved state-owned firms or were backed and promoted directly by governments. But they were generally private arrangements.[2] What was new during the Depression were the intergovernmental institutions that mobilized the combined powers of sovereign and colonial governments to control the production and trade of goods in order to stabilize their prices. These were the first peacetime experiments in international economic planning, which were inaugurated just as other Depression-era multilateral efforts to stabilize global trade and finance were failing.[3] The establishment of these intergovernmental bodies led to controversies about the involvement of external actors in internal regimes of raw material and agricultural production, particularly in British colonies. These new institutions did not limit their focus to regulating international exchange or dividing up markets among firms; they also shaped domestic policies concerning production and trade. Their demands were far more intrusive than those of an ordinary commercial treaty, since they opened up internal questions about labor, resource management, and the regulation of businesses to the supervision and intervention of external authorities.[4]

After the abandonment of wartime commodity controls in the aftermath of the First World War, political debates about the powers wielded by international economic institutions had centered mainly on financial issues, involving currency stabilization, central bank cooperation, and development lending. These powers were shaped in light of assumptions about sovereignty and mass politics shared by European and US bankers, many of whom saw democracy as a risk to sound money and formal sovereign equality as a fiction to be dispensed with when it jeopardized the servicing of loans. But the Depression threw international efforts in the

domains of finance into disarray: It froze international lending, exacerbated interstate rivalries, and accelerated a turn to nationalist policies that
made the sacrifices demanded by international cooperation more politically costly. As many histories of the interwar have described, it was at
the moment when multilateral efforts in the financial realm were most
needed that the political will for them was the hardest to find.[5]

But not all international responses to the Depression were failures.
Intergovernmental commodity controls were an important exception.
Beginning in 1931, an array of new intergovernmental institutions were
established to control the global production and exchange of goods like
tin, rubber, tea, wheat, and coffee.[6] After the Second World War, most of
these arrangements were reinvigorated and expanded. In 1960, they were
joined by the most powerful intergovernmental commodity institution
ever created: the Organization of the Petroleum Exporting Countries
(OPEC).[7] These Depression-era institutions were widely seen as providing
a model for stabilizing global capitalism and as part of a broader trend
toward increasing intergovernmental control over the world economy.
They were promoted by the League's Economic and Financial Organization
as tools of economic stabilization. And in the 1940s, they were considered vanguards of international governance by British and US postwar
planners, though the fact that they were pushed for by private interests
meant that some also criticized them as monopolist arrangements. While
the 1930s saw the promulgation of various international plans for governing the world economy and provided clear lessons about the dangers
of economic nationalism, these commodity bodies were alone in exercising
real international influence on domestic policy-making during the years
of the Depression, when so many other internationalist economic schemes
were suspended.[8]

These institutions shared a basic aim with the many international cartels that had emerged since the late nineteenth century: replacing competition with collusion in order to raise the price of a particular good, usually by reducing its supply. But because they were government bodies,
which could enforce their dictates through law and executive fiat, they
tended to be more powerful, durable, and globally encompassing than the
secretive "gentlemen's agreements" reached by private firms to collude
across national borders. They were also designed to achieve broader aims
than profit maximization. The interwar period saw a move away from
private international cartels toward commodity agreements managed by
governments—a phenomenon that some Marxists diagnosed as a sign of

increasing "state capitalism," but that was also part of the crucially related move toward the growing international bureaucratization of economic policy-making.[9] For both the British and Dutch empires, agreements to control the production of tin and rubber—the major export
goods of their Southeast Asian colonies—were used for various ends: increasing revenue for colonial governance, augmenting US dollar earnings,
paying off war debts, and preventing worker uprisings from erupting into
anti-colonial resistance.[10] These institutions were widely advocated during
the 1930s and 1940s as a way for governments to collaborate in breaking
the disastrous deflationary circuits that linked primary production and
manufacturing around the world. E. M. H. Lloyd, one of the original designers of the League's economic bodies, described them as applying
"man's collective intelligence to the elimination of the harsh and often
wasteful ruthlessness of *laissez faire*," and as a tool for ameliorating the
dramatic fluctuations of the business cycle.[11] The creation of these international commodity bodies represented the last round of intergovernmental economic institution-building before the Bretton Woods Conference of 1944.

The first major and successful intergovernmental commodity institution was set up to control the global production and exchange of tin, a
valuable strategic mineral produced overwhelmingly within the bounds
of the British and, to a lesser extent, Dutch empires.[12] This new kind of
international economic body was led by an alumnus of a major League
of Nations' economic project, John Campbell, who left the Greek Refugee Settlement Commission in 1929 to join the British Colonial Office.
An important innovation of the scheme he oversaw was to empower an
international economic institution to shape policies concerning the production of resources inside European colonial territories. Its enforcement
involved opening up the interior of one of the most economically valuable colonies of the entire British Empire, Malaya, to outside intervention—a prospect that during the First World War, as we have seen, had
been rejected by London.

The politics of this new style of governance can be seen most clearly
in the struggles that came from its enforcement in Malaya, the world's
largest producer of tin, where it generated a powerful backlash among
European and Chinese businesses and risked creating mass unemployment
and political unrest, jeopardizing Malaya's political stability.[13] The British
opponents of this new arrangement attacked its supposed violation of legal,
diplomatic, and cultural norms about the insulation of colonial economic

spaces from the reach of outside actors besides those of the colonial authorities and foreign businesses that expropriated the colony's natural wealth. That this innovation was possible at all shows how seriously metropolitan authorities took the crisis of commodity prices during the Depression—and how much the crisis challenged key assumptions about imperial sovereignty.

The Origins of the International Tin Control Scheme

The political conflicts over sovereignty and interference sparked by international efforts to stabilize commodity prices during the Depression were as complex and fraught as those that came from other forms of international economic cooperation and control. On the surface, however, the logic of their implementation was simpler than the financial or contractual complexities involved with sovereign lending or central bank cooperation. In the abstract, all that raising the price of a commodity required was reducing the amount of it that was exchanged on international markets. But in practice, this was extraordinarily difficult to achieve. It required enforcing restrictions on the production or export of the good in question in as many places as possible. Doing so in only one or a few sites of production would fail to raise prices for long, since producers elsewhere would expand their activities to capitalize on higher prices as their competitors cut back. This happened with one unsuccessful effort to stabilize rubber prices after the global slump of 1920–1921, when lobbyists for producers in Malaya convinced the British government to restrict exports from Malaya and Ceylon. Competitors in the Dutch East Indies responded by expanding production, however, while smallholding Malay planters waged fierce resistance against these restrictions, threatening what appeared to the colonial government to be the real possibility of mass uprisings.[14] Before this act, the so-called Stevenson Plan, was repealed in 1928, sending rubber prices tumbling, it also led to furious denunciations in the United States, where it was seen as a British strategy to raise prices for a strategic raw material that could not be produced in significant quantities on US soil. The short-lived rubber restriction scheme, widely considered a failure of international commodity controls, encouraged two extreme manifestations of privatized US imperialism, both aiming to secure exclusive US sources of rubber: the expansion of Firestone's political and economic penetration of Liberia, and the efforts by Henry Ford to establish a private company town, Fordlandia, in the Brazilian Amazon.[15]

However, the obvious solution to the shortcomings of the Stevenson Plan—implementing restrictions in many places at once—was a challenging global collective action problem. While international cooperation to reduce supply of the good in question would eventually lead to higher prices for all, getting to this point required sacrifices from many individual producers in many places, some of whom would be driven out of business in the process. This problem was theoretically well suited to an international institution that could facilitate negotiation between stakeholders from different countries and empires and compel governments to enforce certain policies. But doing so required this institution becoming the arbiter of domestic issues of major distributional, political, and strategic significance, involving the production of raw materials and agricultural goods that many countries and colonies relied on to pay for government and employ a large percentage of their populations.

These schemes also necessitated relinquishing any strict conception of full resource sovereignty—a right that was rarely accorded to primary producing countries in Latin America and Asia, as we have seen. In the case of Europe's empires, however, it was still a widely accepted legal and diplomatic norm that metropolitan authorities could declare affairs in the colonies—as well as the relations between the constituent units of the empire—to enjoy a right to non-interference from other powers. At the time, some referred to this as a kind of imperial "Monroe Doctrine," which the British Empire, for example, could use to prevent institutions like the League of Nations from interfering in colonial policy.[16] The League's mandates system was a clear exception to this rule. Yet even though it involved colonies taken from the Ottoman and German empires being put under the League's oversight, it did not unsettle the broader international legal norm of non-mandated dependent territories being subject only to the domestic jurisdiction of the empire that controlled them.[17] While the Permanent Mandates Commission was unique in overseeing a limited set of economic issues in these specific territories and in attempting to establish standards and principles applying to trade and labor (which were unevenly realized in practice), it did not exercise powers to set economic policies.[18] The minority rights regime guaranteed by the League, which involved similar disputes over foreign interference, also never applied to non-mandated colonial territories. In the 1930s, the British Foreign Office shot down efforts to generalize its reach.[19]

During the interwar period, and particularly during the Depression, the stakes of stabilizing commodity prices became high enough to weaken the grip of this otherwise bedrock assumption of imperial sovereignty. Collapsing prices threatened uprisings across Europe's colonial empires, as government revenue from customs duties shrank and millions of farmers and workers were thrown out of work. But they were also damaging to wealthier primary producers like the United States, Australia, and Canada, and jeopardized industrialized economies by reducing the global demand for manufactured exports. Falling coffee prices in Brazil, for example, meant lower Brazilian demand for British manufactures, depressing production in Britain, leading to lower demand for coffee imports from Brazil, and so on, in a deflationary global cycle. This dangerous interdependence of primary production and manufacturing was widely seen by contemporaries as one of the reasons that the Depression spread around the world so quickly.[20]

The first site for legally enforcing an international agreement over many domestic producers was in British Malaya. By the 1920s, Malaya had become one of Britain's most economically valuable colonies on the basis of its vast wealth in tin and rubber. These two raw materials were unique in being almost completely unavailable in Europe and North America and were crucial to the important new global industry of automobile manufacture.[21] A successful approach to managing tin and rubber prices was seen by members of the British Colonial Office to offer a model for other commodities. Of these two goods, it was tin that was first placed under the control of an international organization in 1931. Three years later, a similar agreement was reached for rubber. Tin was in high demand for the manufacture of motor vehicles and food canning, but was also used for electrical technologies and various other finished goods, many with military applications. This made it a key strategic raw material. Most of the world's supply of tin was found in a belt extending from China's Yunnan Province, Lower Burma, and Western Siam down along each side of the Malay Peninsula and through the islands of Singkep, Bangka, and Billiton in the Dutch East Indies.[22] Outside this region, it was also mined in Nigeria and Bolivia, and to a lesser extent, in Australia, South Africa, the Belgian Congo, and Portugal. But by the 1880s, most tin came from Malaya, after deposits in Cornwall, until then Europe's largest source, were depleted. The explosion of demand for tin in the late nineteenth century coincided with the discovery of the world's richest deposits in Malaya, which accelerated the British penetration of the peninsula and efforts by British capitalists to displace the Chinese firms that had dominated Malayan mining for decades.[23]

The collapse of tin and rubber prices at the beginning of the 1930s presented an acute economic and political challenge to the British Empire. Export duties on these goods provided the main source of revenue for the Malayan colonial government. And tin mines and rubber plantations were the largest employers of the many thousands of Chinese and Indian migrant workers that constituted a large percentage of Malaya's population. Unemployment concentrated among these groups raised worries about uprisings and the spread of Bolshevism in Asia. The closure of mines if the Depression was left to run its course was predicted to result in the unemployment of 100,000 migrant workers in Malaya and, in Nigeria, up to 40,000: "What this would mean in the way of unrest in these colonies," as one memorandum supporting government intervention put it, "is best left to the imagination."[24] If the collapse of tin prices was not arrested, another British journalist in Ipoh wrote after the outbreak of the Depression, this would produce an "army" of unemployed Chinese workers who had been led by communist agitators to believe low tin prices had been "engineered by European capitalists."[25] The threat of a left uprising in early 1930s Malaya was exaggerated, as it was in many places.[26] But the social and economic dislocations caused by collapsing tin and rubber prices were enormous. In the state of Perak alone, the mining workforce fell by more than 66 percent before the first three years of the Depression had ended.[27] Between 1928 and 1930, the total mining workforce in the Federated Malay States was reduced by nearly 23 percent, with the crisis falling most heavily on Chinese firms and workers.[28] In addition to preventing anti-colonial resistance, stabilizing tin and rubber prices was seen as crucial to the financial stability of the empire as a whole. The export of these goods provided a major source of dollars earnings, which could be used to pay off war debts.[29]

The tin control scheme was first inaugurated with a push not from colonial authorities, however, but from producers, who recognized that an international means of addressing the slump was necessary to protect their bottom lines. Negotiations began in the summer of 1929, just before the Wall Street crash, when representatives of hundreds of tin companies established a lobbying group in London—the Tin Producers' Association—to call for production cuts in Malaya through a voluntary suspension of mining activities over the weekend. But the weakness of a plan that relied on self-policing soon became evident. In Malaya, where many individual firms worked countless mines, it was clearly not sufficient. Representatives from the lobbying group pushed the British Colonial Office to

Chinese workers in a tin mine in Gopeng, Perak, in the Federated Malay States, 1927. *The National Archives, UK, ref. CO1069 / 499 (3).*

enforce a more coercive regime. Some argued that Chinese producers, in particular, could not be trusted to obey a scheme that was not backed by "legal compulsion."[30] In early 1931, the colonial governments of Malaya, Nigeria, the Dutch East Indies, and the government of the sovereign Bolivian state signed an agreement to mandate production restrictions within their borders. They were joined that summer by the Kingdom of Siam. This was an ambitious arrangement. It involved collectively setting strict production restrictions to reduce the global supply of a strategic mineral, on the basis of statistics about worldwide demand, and for governments to enforce these restrictions on the ground.[31]

Enforcing Production Restrictions

Reducing the global supply of tin required a distinctive form of external intervention in the domestic affairs of producing countries and colonies that implicated a range of business and financial interests, workers, and government authorities. First, as part of the tin agreement, an intergovernmental institution was established to decide how much supply needed to be manipulated globally to raise tin's price. This institution, the International Tin Committee (ITC), was staffed by delegates from signatory governments and by representatives of the private industry group in London. It was a hybrid public-private body that met on a rotating schedule in London, Paris, and The Hague. It shared features in common with other international institutions, including a working budget, secretariat, and research wing. In certain respects, it was similar to the inter-Allied commodity bodies created during the First World War—though it was designed to solve the problem of glut, not shortage. Its head, Campbell, had become a powerful civil servant in the Colonial Office after leaving his work in Greece.

The tasks of the institution that Campbell led were to set a global production target on the basis of statistics received from official and private sources around the world and to assign quotas to member governments. For 1931, total production was set at 145,000 tons, of which Malaya was assigned a maximum quota of 52,000.[32] It remained a "domestic matter" to ensure producers did not exceed these limits.[33] In the case of the Malayan and Nigerian delegates to the ITC, they were also members of the British Colonial Office (Campbell represented both colonies), which meant they were authorized to set policy directly for the colonial governments they represented—though the precise nature of this authority came into question as the production cuts took effect. This was another similarity to some of the wartime inter-Allied bodies. While the Allied Maritime Transport Council was allowed only to make recommendations, the officials who led it wielded executive power in their respective countries, meaning they could easily translate international decisions into domestic policies.[34] Since most signatories to the tin agreement were colonial governments, their delegates to the ITC could act much more decisively than if they had faced democratic pressures—though in Malaya, as we shall see, the work of this body raised difficult questions about the relationship of the Colonial Office to the colonial government.

Enforcement of the tin restriction plan was particularly challenging in Malaya, where many individual mining companies were working more than 1,000 mines, and where the industry was split along ethnic lines between Chinese- and European-led companies. In the Dutch East Indies, by contrast, tin production was either entirely in government hands or in the hands of a private firm, Billiton, of which the government was the largest shareholder.[35] British Malaya was also a complex and divided territory. It was split into three administrative units: the Federated Malay States (FMS), made up of the states of Pahang, Selangor, Negri Sembilan, and Perak; the Unfederated Malay States, which included Johore, Kelantan, Trengganu, Kedah, and Perlis; and the Straits Settlements of Singapore, Malacca, Dinding, and Penang. Governance in the Federated and Unfederated States of Malaya was shared between colonial authorities and Malay sultans. The population was divided between Malays, Chinese, Indians, and a smaller number of European administrators and capitalists. As Crown Colonies, the Straits Settlements were ruled directly by British authorities, whereas the Federated Malay States were governed as a protectorate. Both were headed by the same person: the high commissioner of the Malay States and the governor of the Straits Settlements, who stood at the head of a Federal Council made up of colonial authorities, representatives of British (and to a lesser extent Chinese) businesses, and Malay sultans.[36]

When the tin agreement was translated into law in April 1931 by the Federal Council of the FMS government, it was brought to the sultans of each state to rubber stamp. The law formally authorized the FMS government to control the production, sale, possession, and export of tin; to appoint agents to carry out these rules; to punish violators; and to enjoy legal immunity from any challenges to it.[37] Enforcement involved the issuance of new government certificates to producers across Malaya, which they required to legally make sales. Granting these certificates was extremely complex. It necessitated the creation of new government bureaus to estimate the production capacity of around 1,200 individual mines and to make binding decisions about how much could be extracted from them.[38] This entailed a strict legal regime. Companies that exceeded their quota could lose their mining license, and individuals caught counterfeiting their licenses, withholding information, or misrepresenting data could be charged exorbitant fines and, if in default of payment, imprisoned for up to two years. The powers of colonial police and mining and customs officials were expanded to allow the arrest of suspected violators without warrant and to seize their product.[39]

Enforcement required a system of domestic surveillance that extended not only to more than a thousand mines, but also to the countless women workers, the majority of whom were Chinese, who hand-sifted alluvial deposits with wooden pans, a physically demanding form of work, often done with a child strapped on the back. The *dulang* washers were given documents authorizing their own production quotas, which they had to carry to avoid fines and the loss of panning rights, and which they exchanged on a vibrant secondary market. Taken together, they put significant quantities of tin onto the market, and had long been seen by colonial authorities as particularly difficult to control.[40] Now, like the Greek refugees in the 1920s, their labor became the object of surveillance for an international bureaucracy—though one that sought to constrain their productivity, not to enhance it.[41]

What was so novel about the International Tin Agreement was that the British Empire, through the intermediation of a new intergovernmental agency, was setting rules for a coordinated expansion of government intervention in colonial economies alongside representatives of other empires, sovereign countries, and private businesses. Even during the First World War, as we have seen, the British Colonial Office refused to allow decisions about Malayan tin production and export to be shaped by the demands of Britain's allies. But the disastrous commodity price slumps of the years after the war led to a gradual weakening of this barrier. Although the tin control scheme was first pushed for by private firms, as a form of government protection from the turbulence of the Depression, it was seen in the government (particularly in the Colonial Office) as a tool of stabilization for an empire that relied heavily on the production and export of many primary goods, including coffee, sugar, and rubber.[42] Private backers of the scheme encouraged the Colonial Office to think in these imperial terms and not to focus on possible opposition in Malaya itself.[43] "All over the world governments, business men, and economists are trying to bring about the rational production of primary products," as Philip Cunliffe-Lister, head of the Tin Producers Association (and soon head of the Colonial Office), put it. "In tin we have found a solution."[44] The British Empire had long used various quotas, duties, and licenses to direct imperial trade, and temporary wartime export controls had been set up during the First World War to prevent German traders from acquiring Malaya's strategically valuable raw materials. But this arrangement went much further.[45] It was referred to explicitly by the head of the Colonial Office as a scheme of "deliberate planning of production in correspondence with the world's demand" that represented a "legitimate substitution of order for anarchy."[46] But putting this novel regime of economic planning into action involved relinquishing assumptions about domestic questions concerning the production of a strategically sensitive mineral being fully insulated from external actors.

When the International Tin Agreement was translated into policies in Malaya, it encountered immediate opposition. Its encroachment on imperial sovereignty collided with competition among private interests in a divided polity. As soon as it became law in early 1931, the tin agreement sparked a clash between the international institution in Europe that set its rules, the colonial government in Malaya told to enforce them, and the producers whose profits and autonomy it jeopardized. While this clash took place in a colonial setting, the FMS government nonetheless found itself on the backfoot, struggling to legitimate the decisions it was pushed into by London, Amsterdam, La Paz, and Bangkok.

The Private Backlash to Restriction

Opposition to the international tin restriction agreement gathered force among mining companies in Malaya before the ink on the law had dried. This opposition reinforced divisions in the Malayan tin mining industry, both between firms employing different mining technologies and between European and Chinese producers. At the outbreak of the Depression, the industry was divided between smaller Chinese- and British-led companies and a sprawling multinational mining conglomerate, Anglo-Oriental. This arrangement was relatively new. Until the middle of the nineteenth century, tin extraction in Malaya had mostly been done on a small scale by Malays as a complement to farming. After Chinese mining companies gained a foothold in the second half of the century, an influx of Chinese labor and capital followed. With the further intervention of British power on the peninsula beginning in the 1870s, property rights and mining regulations were formalized under British rule, and tin mining expanded dramatically, still largely under the control of Chinese companies. Chinese mining was generally less capital-intensive than British. It relied on privileged access to large numbers of workers from China, both before and after the abolition of the indenture system in 1914. The introduction of expensive new dredging technology in the early twentieth century gave British firms, with access to City financing, the power to mine untouched deposits. This environmentally disastrous work allowed British firms to gradually overtake their Chinese competitors—though by the beginning of the 1930s, around half of Malaya's tin was still produced by Chinese miners.[47]

In the 1920s, many of these British firms were merged under the control of the global conglomerate Anglo-Oriental, headed by the British merchant and financier John Howeson and the Bolivian tin magnate

Simón Patiño. Anglo-Oriental controlled numerous companies in Malaya, Burma, Nigeria, and Siam, as well as one of the companies that smelted Malaya's tin. By the end of the 1920s, it had assumed a dominant position in Malaya's tin mining industry.[48] But several smaller British- and Chinese-led firms remained outside its control. They employed less capital-intensive technologies, which allowed them to operate with lower overhead costs. This made them natural rivals with Anglo-Oriental. The heads of these lower-cost firms argued that the restriction scheme was a tool for propping up their inefficient rivals, which would be driven to bankruptcy in the battle of the "survival of the fittest" to which falling prices would lead if the government did not intervene. They opposed Anglo-Oriental's attempts to buy them up and pushed the government to pass legislation preventing foreign businesses from acquiring any British companies in Malaya—a move that was clearly targeted at Patiño.[49] While Anglo-Oriental's operations were too expensive to continue for long with low prices, production restrictions would give them a lease on life. It would allow them to close some mines or shut down some dredges, while leaving others open until prices rose. This strategy was a luxury that smaller companies could not afford. For them, production cuts meant bankruptcy. The fact that restriction had originally been called for by the heads of Anglo-Oriental through the lobbying group they controlled, and that Howeson and Patiño themselves sat on the International Tin Committee, was evidence of how much the scheme had been designed to serve their interests. Their inefficient companies, which were created when tin prices were high, so critics claimed, should be left to wither now. The alternative was the colonial government keeping them alive for the sake of speculators and the investors looking to profit from rising prices.[50]

The private critics of the restriction scheme defended their interests by attacking the foreign interference it invited in a British colony. This criticism was grounded in a commitment to pre-existing colonial hierarchies: members of the lower-cost British firms themselves already benefited from colonial laws and regulations that expropriated Malaya's natural resources and protected their property with the threat of violence. But these British capitalists nonetheless raged at the prospects of other "foreigners" jeopardizing their position in the Malayan tin industry. Their opposition to restriction was a conflict of regionally focused companies with a global conglomerate, and of well-established businesses with incumbent moguls, but it was also a political conflict involving racially coded claims about sovereignty and the illegitimacy of government intervention in markets.[51]

British opponents of the restriction law in Malaya insisted that the colonial regime should not prop up the inefficient producers of the Anglo-Oriental group that the natural laws of the market had destined for failure. Production restrictions, they claimed, went against the supposed traditions of colonial laissez faire and amounted to violations of British property rights that bordered on Bolshevism.

A common charge was that the Colonial Office had, in effect, sold out the interests of the British to the non-British. Speculators outside the empire were said to be conspiring against British firms in Malaya in order to profit from rising tin prices as these firms were driven to bankruptcy. The restriction act handed them a victory. "Why should British output be sacrificed, for the sake of keeping uneconomic properties in operation in Bolivia and elsewhere?" one critic of the scheme wrote in the *Straits Times,* a publication owned by the Straits Trading smelting company that opposed restriction. This was an idea, it added, that was "Alice-in-Wonderland-like."[52] The restriction act was criticized as a gross violation of a long-held norm of colonial government: jealousy "of the possibility of domination by outside interests." The act did not only restrict the autonomy of producers. It also took the final say out of the hands of the government that regulated their business and gave it to an "unknown body."[53] When the restriction bill was brought to the Federal Council, Archibald Glenister, head of the Osborne & Chappel mining company, claimed it violated the spirit of British imperial cooperation, since it involved Nigeria giving up a percentage of its quota to the Dutch East Indies, instead of to Malaya.[54] "We are exhorted on every hand to think Imperially, to buy Imperially and to act Imperially," he insisted. "And yet Nigeria, willing and able to give up some of its allowance, gives up a portion of its quota to a foreign country [the Dutch East Indies] in preference to Malaya which so badly needs every picul which it can get."[55] Coming as it did just months before the 1932 Ottawa Agreement for imperial preference—an agreement that encouraged trade between the constituent units of the British Empire—this was a stinging charge. The tin agreement appeared to violate the norm reaffirmed by the Ottawa Agreement: that the relations between the units of the British Empire were insulated from the involvement of outside actors.

Opposition to the International Tin Agreement was also framed in racial and civilizational terms. British opponents to it in Malaya claimed they were being forced to sacrifice because the colonial government had forged a partnership not only with the Dutch, "who have always been capable of looking after themselves," as one member of the FMS Federal Council put it, but also with a "somewhat irresponsible Latin Republic in South America."[56] These critics insisted that the FMS government was fanning the flames of Chinese resistance, since Chinese miners were bound to see the restriction act as a European plot designed to drive them out of business. While Chinese mining firms were destined to go under sooner rather than later, they claimed, the restriction scheme was accelerating this process and providing an obvious culprit to blame for it. This would be exploited by the propaganda of communists and used to kindle riots. Without restriction, the "Chinese miner" would "tighten his belt till he could tighten it no more," they claimed, "and then he would say it was the operation of world causes, which he must just accept." With the restriction law, however, he would no longer blame the natural laws of global capitalism for his fate, but instead blame rules set to benefit European competitors. This would create a major political liability.[57]

The possibility that production cuts would generate mass Chinese unemployment and political resistance gave pause to the FMS government. In the run-up to the passage of the restriction act in April 1931, colonial authorities gauged support for it among European and Chinese producers, though not among the broader Malayan population or the tens of thousands of workers whose livelihoods it would directly affect.[58] At this point, the opinion of Chinese producers in Malaya was generally in favor of restriction. But members of the FMS government worried that enforcing a scheme that forced many of their mines to close at once would lead to a change of heart. Campbell agreed. Although uneconomic Chinese mines were destined to close, he claimed, the fact that these closures would effectively be mandated by the government, while European firms survived these measures, was likely to create unnecessary political risk. Other members of the Colonial Office nervously admitted that a close watch needed to be kept on Malaya, to see whether "political or racial feeling on the subject is growing up."[59] For the FMS government, there were thus two major threats to the restriction scheme: first, the mobilization of a powerful minority of British capitalists against it; and second, the unemployment of Chinese workers generating unrest.

The opposition of British firms led to one of the most serious challenges to the act—one that was shaped by a set of long-standing legal claims about property rights and colonial governance in Malaya. In March 1931, the Pahang Consolidated mining company brought a suit against the colonial government on the grounds that the restriction act violated the

A tin mine near Kuala Lumpur in the 1930s. *Lee Kip Lin Collection, courtesy of the National Archives of Singapore.*

terms of a lease granted by the British resident in 1898 on behalf of Sultan Ahmad al-Muadzam Shah. This lease had given the company rights to mine a 300 square-mile plot of land in the central Malayan state of Pahang, as well as exemption from taxes and a covenant for "quiet enjoyment" for 77 years. When the restriction act came into force, the firm's lawyers claimed it represented an unlawful abrogation of the lease, which the Federal Council—formally only an advisory body to the sultans—was not authorized to do. But the Court of Appeal in Kuala Lumpur ruled against them, arguing that the Federal Council exercised full legal sovereignty over the entire colonial federation through treaties with the sultans. Just like Parliament in England, it could pass laws that annulled private contracts.[60] In practice, the Federal Council only devolved powers to the sultans over religious and civil matters; the British colonial government had the final say over property matters. When the case ended up in the Privy Council in London, the highest court of appeal in the British Empire, the decision of the Malayan appellate court was affirmed.[61]

Although unsuccessful, the Pahang Consolidated lawsuit showed the strength of opposition among some British firms to the expansion of the colonial government's economic powers, which the international agreement had facilitated. British capitalists benefited from Malaya's administrative fragmentation and from a regime of limited government intervention in the Malayan economy, which was generally restricted to the setting of property rights and regulations to their advantage.[62] This made some of these firms willing to support the legal paramountcy of Malayan rulers over the colonial regime, at least in this case. The head of Pahang Consolidated claimed the Privy Council's ruling against it was a sign that the British government was wading into dangerous waters. On what grounds, he wrote, could Whitehall complain about violations of British property at the hands of foreign governments if a colonial government was allowed to abrogate contracts at whim? "We stand to the Sultan of Pahang and the FMS Government . . . in exactly the same position as the Anglo-Persian Oil Co. stands to the Persian Government." He used a metaphor he knew would strike a nerve: London was then preparing to lodge a formal complaint about Reza Shah's revocation of Anglo-Persian's oil concession at the League of Nations. "I should think the position is unique," he continued, "the breakers of a contract [the British government] are appealing against another nation for using the same privilege—namely, autocratic power to over-ride contractual obligations."[63] The foreign secretary recognized the power of the analogy and the urgency of preventing Persian

League delegates from using the precedent of Pahang Consolidated to justify the Shah's seizure of British property.[64]

Other critics similarly built a case against the restriction act, and its apparent violation of contracts and property rights, in terms later used to oppose the nationalization of natural resources: Foreign investors would flee, they claimed, if property rights were not guaranteed against government violation.[65] The charge was prescient, though not in ways these critics fully anticipated. In both Malaya and Bolivia, the enforcement of the tin restriction act set into motion the growth of government powers over the industry. In Bolivia, this laid the foundations for the nationalization of the industry two decades later, including, in an ironic twist of fate, the vast properties of Patiño himself.[66] What was so extraordinary about this expansion of government powers during the Depression, however, was its political organization: It was demanded by an international institution for the sake of a price stabilization project with global implications.

The Colonial Government Backlash

Not only private companies opposed the implementation of the international tin restriction act. Members of the colonial government in Malaya also came to see it as jeopardizing the legitimacy and stability of their rule. The high commissioner of the FMS government and governor of the Straits Settlements, Cecil Clementi, supported the restriction scheme when it was proposed, because falling tin prices were drying up government revenues and threatening political uprisings. But he also recognized that restriction would be impossible to enforce without the support of British and Chinese business interests.[67] Clementi insisted on canvassing their opinion before agreeing to it and on delaying its implementation until after the Chinese New Year, when Chinese firms sold off their stocks.[68] Clementi, a longtime colonial administrator, had been governor of Hong Kong during the height of the May Thirtieth Movement—which led, as we have seen, to a reorientation of British China policy away from earlier practices of gunboat diplomacy. During the uprising, Clementi, who spoke both Mandarin and Cantonese, opened talks with Chinese authorities, and helped to eventually bring the boycott of Hong Kong to an end.[69] Clementi was thus acutely aware of the risks of alienating the Chinese population of Malaya. For their part, members of the Colonial Office were wary of forcing the policy on Clementi and further unsettling an already difficult relationship between London and the FMS government. While the latter had traditionally exercised autonomy from the Colonial Office, the balance of power had shifted in London's favor since the war.[70] Clementi realized that the colonial government would be stabilized over the long term from rising tin prices. But he worried that enforcing restriction would also create new problems for it, leading not only to attacks from British businesses but also potentially violent resistance to polices that pushed thousands of Chinese workers out of employment at once.

The political difficulties involved with enforcing the restriction act in Malaya became apparent as soon as the law was promulgated. During the first months of restriction, the FMS government was unable to bring production under the quota it had been assigned by the ITC. There were enormous logistical challenges to assessing the production capacity of more than 1,200 mines across Malaya and assigning certificates accordingly. This necessitated the creation of new administrative powers and offices from scratch. Assessment errors led to the granting of licenses well over Malaya's quota.[71] To the British critics of the restriction scheme, this was no surprise: "The idea of the Bolivian Government, for instance, appointing an army of officials to spy on all the tin-mines, big and small, within its territory, is merely a joke," one railed. "A lot of jobs could, of course, be found for people out of employment in doing detective work at the mines in Malaya. It would cost money, but Governments never worry about that."[72] Efforts to assign certificates were alienating miners across Malaya, who complained about their handling by autocratic local administrators and warned that enforcing the cuts "at the ukase of Government" was politically dangerous. But these efforts were also failing to bring production under the quota.[73] This put Malaya in violation of the agreement that the Colonial Office had reached with the Dutch and Bolivians, whose representatives on the ITC angrily criticized Malaya's failure to obey its rules.[74] Sentiment in the markets was dropping, and prices continued to fall, as speculators sold off stocks. They had little confidence in Clementi's ability to discipline producers in the face of the political instability to which further cuts might lead. Brokers and other members of the ITC were anxious to reassure markets that Malaya's breach of international obligations would be rectified.[75]

The failure of the FMS government to enforce the scheme angered the Colonial Office. To the latter, there appeared to be two ways of addressing this situation: first, compelling the colonial government to temporarily enforce larger cuts; and second, having it buy up excess tin. Both involved further political risks. Implementing a larger cut would force many mines to close at once, particularly Chinese ones. Clementi shared the common belief among the British in Malaya that Chinese-owned mines were eventually going to be forced under by the crisis. But he insisted that it would be a "political blunder" to demand their closure at the same time. He estimated that this would require the deportation of about 30,000 Chinese migrant workers at government expense, as well as the implementation of new internal security measures.[76] The FMS government relied on the repatriation of Chinese and Indian migrant workers as a way of dealing with unemployment, since it was cheaper than public works programs or maintaining relief camps. Between 1930 and 1932, more than 75,000 unemployed Chinese workers were repatriated; between 1930 and 1933, almost 250,000 Indians were.[77] Over the first three years of the Depression, such policies resulted in a huge reduction in Malaya's total population, by roughly 14 percent—a higher figure than other comparable instances of mass flight from severe economic hardship, such as during the famine that began in Ireland in 1845.[78] While repatriation was a tool of colonial governance designed to prevent political and social pressure from boiling over during times of high unemployment, it was a costly one, since it was extremely unpopular with the firms that relied on these sources of cheap labor and led to opposition among the communities it affected.[79]

The danger of the restriction act leading to uprisings was seen by the colonial government as heightened by ethnic divisions in Malaya. Any tin policies that disproportionately affected Chinese miners were considered a possible source of instability. By contrast, colonial administrators paid little attention to the effects of the scheme on the Malay population, whom they generally regarded as producers of agricultural goods for domestic consumption, not commodities for export.[80] The Depression would have a devastating impact on the Malay population, particularly smallholders of rubber-growing lands and government employees, though less so on food cultivators.[81] But Colonial Office records are silent about the effects of the tin restriction scheme on them, likely because the number of Malays involved in tin mining was lower than those of other groups. There were greater numbers of Indian migrant laborers involved in this work, though fewer than Chinese.[82] It was unemployment among the Chinese population that members of the FMS government saw as a major threat to their rule. They claimed that the Colonial Office was, in effect, demanding policies that exacerbated local unemployment for the sake of stabilizing global commodity markets. At the same time, the colonial government did little to alleviate the profound economic distress of the non-European subjects of Malaya, which intensified hostility to it.[83]

The other response to the excess production of Malayan tin in late 1931 was having the FMS government buy up surplus stocks. This action posed other risks. It necessitated asking the Federal Council to authorize spending at a moment of austerity. This authorization was unlikely to be granted. Forcing the Federal Council to approve it, however, threatened to fan the flames of resistance to the restriction act—not least because opponents of the act themselves sat on the Federal Council, including Glenister of Osborne & Chappel and Frank Mair of Tekka and Gopeng Consolidated, the two ringleaders of the faction of lower-cost producers that sought to prevent the act from being realized.[84] While members of the Colonial Office recognized the dilemma they were pushing Clementi into, they insisted that he force the hand of the Federal Council. Malaya's surplus was depressing prices and threatening the viability of the international agreement altogether.[85] The Bolivian and Dutch governments could not be asked to shoulder the costs of Malaya's failure to uphold its end of the bargain, which was hurting "British prestige internationally."[86] Dutch and Bolivian delegations on the international committee were, in turn, pushing the Colonial Office to ensure Malaya was fulfilling its international obligations.[87] For London, ensuring the success of this scheme had real stakes, since Malaya's failure to enforce the tin agreement would jeopardize the likelihood of the Dutch committing to a rubber control scheme. Malaya's violation of its quota was thus considered a serious problem. The FMS government seemed unable or unwilling to follow the lead from London in adhering to an agreement that was supposed to be the first act in a broader strategy of stabilizing colonial Southeast Asia and, by extension, the British Empire itself.[88]

All these tensions contributed to a larger quarrel between the FMS government and the Colonial Office. Clementi was already at loggerheads with London over his plans to reform the complex government of Malaya and, for him, bungling the tin restriction act would jeopardize this project. In September 1931, James Henry Thomas, secretary of state for the colonies, told Clementi to force the spending through the Federal Council, regardless of any political difficulties or embarrassment this caused.[89] Clementi warned him that bullying the council would have deleterious political consequences. The sultan of Perak was calling for the abolition of the Council, and the Pahang Consolidated lawsuit was bringing unwanted attention to the government's unsettled relationship to the sultans. Clementi worried that dictating to the council would make it impossible to oversee the creation of a looser federative structure in Malaya, with greater devolved powers to the sultans (to weaken non-Malay demands for representation and thereby strengthen British rule). This project was already being resisted by members of the Colonial Office, with whom Clementi was increasingly at odds.[90] The demand from London to ram the purchase of tin through the Federal Council, he insisted, was all the more galling, because this involved submission to the "dictate" of the Bolivians and the Dutch instead of acting to protect British interests.[91] Clementi thus mobilized the ideal of non-interference to get the Colonial Office off his back.

A fundamental conflict had been created by the tin restriction act: While the Colonial Office saw the importance of this regulation in imperial and international terms, it was only viable if the Malayan government implemented it in the face of the threats this caused to its own stability. In the FMS Federal Council, European, Chinese, and Malay members threatened to create new alliances of convenience against it, while the prospect of mass unemployment among Chinese workers raised worries of riots and the spread of Bolshevism. It was risky enough for such policies to be enforced by a colonial government in a divided territory. But now it was threatening to turn a powerful minority of European business elites against an agreement they claimed had been designed for the sake of their foreign competitors. This all exacerbated a conflict between the combined interests of City banks and the Colonial Office against the FMS government, which saw their demands as posing real risks to its rule and which had traditionally exercised some autonomy from metropolitan authorities. Asking the FMS government to buy up excess tin stocks was yet more controversial, because it would lead to a further bifurcation of interests between the government and the lower-cost British producers in Malaya. Once it began to buy stocks, the government would profit from the closure of mines, because doing so would help raise the price of an asset it now owned. If that happened, the government would effectively be speculating on the collapse of British businesses.[92]

There was a similar problem when members of the ITC explored the possibility, on the prompting of the Anglo-Oriental group, of creating an international "pool" to buy tin stocks and store them until prices rose, when they would be sold off at a profit. This strategy would help stabilize prices in the short term, since restriction on its own could take years to have the desired effect.[93] However, when it was established in August 1931, the obvious political danger of the tin pool was that it would be controlled by Dutch and British financial syndicates, not by members of the industry themselves. This would confirm fears that the scheme had been designed for the sake of bankers that profited from the closure of mines. The pool was to work closely with the ITC, and Campbell was made its ex-officio chairman. But it was effectively controlled by Reginald McKenna, chairman of the Midland Bank and a former Liberal MP and chancellor of the exchequer.[94] The creation of the pool led to a direct conflict between the interests of the European bankers who funded it and the British and Chinese producers in Malaya hurt by the restrictions they demanded. Every additional worker unemployed and every additional company driven to bankruptcy meant less tin on global markets, which meant profits for those who bought and held stocks. Malayan mining companies demanded to know who was funding the pool and whether it had pushed for major new cuts in production.[95]

While the supporters of the pool claimed it would ease opposition to restriction if it helped raise prices quickly, its proponents on the ITC insisted that its success necessitated the complete delegation of policy-making authority away from member governments. It was risky to speculate on tin prices if governments enforcing the restriction act could abandon it on a whim. They insisted that the Colonial Office commit the FMS government to restriction for several years and enforce any demands for further cuts made by the ITC.[96] What this meant, in practice, was forcing Clementi to give up all "power of veto" over the decisions of the international institution in order to allow its delegates to become full plenipotentiaries.[97] Members of the British Colonial Office and the ITC recognized the controversial nature of this demand for the FMS government to relinquish control over its internal policies. Doing so meant accepting any request for an alteration of Malaya's quota based on what statistics revealed about global supply and demand, and according to the interests of the British and Dutch syndicates that funded the pool, without any "consideration being given to political and administrative difficulties which such cuts may entail" at the domestic level.[98] In effect, the interests of these British and Dutch financial syndicates were to take priority over those of the FMS government.

Clementi acquiesced to this demand to relinquish his control over policy. But a similar delegation of powers was opposed by the Nigerian colonial government.[99] There, colonial authorities recognized that the pool worked by pitting the interests of speculators who profited from production cuts against the mining companies in Nigeria they forced out of business.[100] Howeson mobilized many larger mining companies in Nigeria to lobby the colonial government to give up veto power over the decision for future cuts, but his efforts were resisted.[101] The Nigerian colonial government recognized the short-term dangers of the restriction act, which in the coming months led to the closure of nearly 80 percent of the mines in Northern Nigeria, causing enormous labor dislocations across the region and a mounting economic and food crisis that exacerbated an already perilous situation for the mining workforce in the Jos Plateau region.[102]

The lower-cost British producers in Malaya that opposed the restriction scheme also mobilized against the pool. Mair attacked it as an even more offensive form of external interference in Malaya's economy, since it handed final decision-making power over domestic policies to "a group of unknown financiers whose motives and impulses, whatever they may be, certainly cannot be assumed as being altruistic," as he put it. "Quite apart from a business standpoint," this marked "a regrettable departure from the procedure of British Colonial administration," since it was "absolutely wrong in principle to allow countries—countries moreover without the British Empire—over-producing unwanted tin to harass and interfere with countries within the British Empire."[103] Mair and his fellow lost-cost producers complained that they had been "disregarded and ignored" for the sake of an arrangement that operated with "super-secrecy." They pushed for the appointment of a representative of their interests to the ITC.[104] But the government demurred, and the British and Dutch banking syndicates pushed the Colonial Office to bring Clementi to heel.[105] The City had a long history of making speculative investments in mining operations across the British Empire, which at times pushed investors into opposition with the colonial officials and firms that were directly affected by volatile boom and bust cycles.[106] In this case, it turned out that the Colonial Office was more responsive to the demands of the British and Dutch financial syndicates, and to those of the multinational tin-lobbying group in London to which they were tied, than to the FMS government.[107] It was no coincidence that the new secretary of state for the colonies, Cunliffe-Lister, had moved into his government position in November 1931 directly from the Tin Producers Association.

This situation reached a fever pitch of controversy in early 1932, when at a meeting of the ITC, the Malayan delegates agreed to demands from other governments to further drastic cuts of an additional 20,000 tons to Malaya's quota. Clementi, who had not been consulted, angrily claimed that the Colonial Office had allowed these delegates to assume illegitimate plenipotentiary powers.[108] Many Chinese firms in Malaya had turned against restriction, fearful that new cuts would force them under and exacerbate a perilous crisis among Malaya's Chinese population. Lowering Malaya's quota would have serious "political repercussions," Clementi warned, requiring the repatriation of about another 2,000 migrant laborers.[109] Chinese mining associations, led by powerful industry representatives, such as Lee Hau Shik (later, the first finance minister of postcolonial Malaya), were rallying against the cuts, which they claimed fell disproportionately on Chinese mines.[110] The year before, representatives of Chinese business interests in the Federal Council, like the Selangor miner and banker San Ah Wing, had unsuccessfully pushed for quotas to be assigned to firms on the basis of their mining methods.[111] Now, a suggestion for European firms to shut while Chinese ones remained open was rejected by Glenister for "raising difficult racial questions."[112] Clementi was willing to suffer the criticisms of the local industry, but he was furious that he had been forced into doing so by an international institution without his input. By acting ultra vires, he claimed, the ITC had put his government "into a position so invidious as to jeopardise the public confidence hitherto enjoyed by the administration."[113]

The financial backers of the pool were themselves irate, however, that the colonial government was even consulted at all in decisions about Malaya's quota.[114] Since member governments were at risk of being pressured by domestic interest groups to abandon the controversial measures required by the restriction act, these governments had to be cut out of decision-making altogether. McKenna went so far as to claim that no local conditions in the colonies were relevant to the policy at all. Decisions were to be made exclusively on the basis of global statistics of supply and demand. He insisted that Cunliffe-Lister simply dictate to the Malayan and Nigerian governments.[115] Clementi warned that prioritizing global markets while ignoring local conditions was dangerous in a colony where the political economy of mining was far more complex than in Bolivia or the Dutch East Indies, given the ethnic divisions that ran through it and the "large number of small producers of alien nationality." Setting domestic policy thousands of miles away, without regard to "political operability," and solely on the basis of data about global supply and demand, was a risky error, one that removed the rights and powers of colonial government.[116]

But the financial interests that influenced the Colonial Office insisted that the FMS government had already given up the final say over internal policy to an institution whose agenda they shaped. The Colonial Office was to act in concert with its Dutch and Bolivian counterparts, without allowing their decisions to be influenced by any political consequences they had in Malaya.[117] Stabilizing global markets took priority over stabilizing the politics of this particular colony.

Commodity Controls as International Governance

From the vantage point of the Colonial Office, the tin scheme was a success. Prices were gradually stabilized, and a model was found for dealing with other commodities. Yet the political challenges involved in enforcing this scheme in Malaya jeopardized the success of controls for other goods. The Colonial Office remained committed to the expansion of these control schemes during the 1930s and drew encouragement from the fact that League of Nations was now promoting them. But officials recognized that the unresolved difficulties presented by the tin scheme in Malaya threatened the generalizability of this form of governance.[118]

Whether national, international, or imperial in scope, restriction schemes always had uneven distributional consequences. This was true for capital, since some firms benefited from restriction and others did not, as well as for labor. These problems were exacerbated when these controversial measures were demanded by an institution external to the domestic jurisdiction of the polity where they were enforced. It was for this reason that British opponents of the scheme in Malaya framed their criticisms in terms that were similar to other attacks on international economic institutions, arguing that they empowered outsiders to interfere in the internal affairs of a colony. This charge was loaded with assumptions about standing, prestige, and race in a hierarchical global order. In the case of tin, the fact that British producers were forced to sacrifice for the sake of competitors in Bolivia made it that much harder for them to accept. The enforcement of the scheme in Malaya involved a full delegation of powers from the colonial government to an international institution to prevent the government from endangering the restriction act in the face of pressure from domestic interest groups. The controversies this entailed were tangled up in debates about the nature of sovereignty and authority in the British Empire, as well as the stability of a multiethnic polity that was considered vulnerable to mass mobilization against colonial rule.

But tin control, in one form or another, continued for more than fifty years—long after the establishment of the postcolonial Malayan state in 1957. As the tin control regime was renewed and expanded over the 1930s, Campbell reflected on how difficult the politics of ensuring its success had been, especially in the face of opposition from a powerful minority of British capitalists, who amplified their opposition through propaganda outlets like the *Straits Times* and whose intransigence antagonized the Dutch and Bolivian partners to the scheme. Relations between the Malayan government and the ITC were further strained due to the continued opposition of this faction of British producers in Malaya, who pressured the colonial government to appoint representatives of their interests to the ITC.[119] Just enough was done, however, to keep tin control in place for years to come. The final tin agreement collapsed only in 1985.[120]

There was an obvious advantage to experimenting with this kind of intergovernmental commodity control scheme in an authoritarian colonial state, where fewer avenues were available for political opposition and where violent coercion could be deployed more easily than elsewhere. Here, authorities could "rule by decree" and "act legally with much greater freedom and speed" than if they had faced the opposition of democratic institutions, as the US scholar and political adviser William Yandell Elliott described as the reason for the unusual power of the tin restriction act.[121] In Malaya, as mines were forced shut, the prospect of labor actions could be handled by repatriation. As much as members of the colonial government in Malaya quarreled with the Colonial Office, moreover, these were power struggles in the ruling apparatus of the British Empire. While they might have jeopardized the viability of the tin restriction policy, they did not jeopardize the empire itself. The most powerful opponents of the scheme were themselves British, who worked under a colonial government designed to promote their interests over the Chinese, Indian, and Malay populations, and to legally and administratively ensure British dominion over Malaya's resources. This made the conflict less threatening than it would have been had it taken an anti-colonial turn.

But the resistance faced by the tin agreement still showed how difficult generalizing this form of governance would be. During the height of enthusiasm for using intergovernmental commodity controls as a tool for stabilizing the world economy in the early 1940s, the Colonial Office cautioned against enthusiasm for these controls on the basis of the Malayan experience. One of the reasons that tin and rubber had been amenable to control was because they were goods produced by firms that exercised tight control over their workers and in colonies where unemployment was concentrated among immigrant communities. As global tin and rubber supplies were manipulated, the labor problems that were caused could be dealt with simply by adjusting the quotas for migrant workers into Malaya. It was impossible to imagine exercising the same discipline over workers in the United States or England, for example, or of asking "millions of farmers" in a democratic country to hand over control of production to "a sort of embryonic world government," as Sidney Caine, head of the Economic Department of the Colonial Office, put it in early 1941.[122]

The international tin control scheme did prove to be a vanguard, however, just as its proponents had hoped it would be. In the coming years, similar controls were implemented for various other commodities, including rubber, tea, coffee, wheat, and oil. Many of these schemes generated similar backlashes. In the case of rubber, an international restriction agreement reached in 1934 led to conflict between signatory governments and the businesses it affected in Malaya and the Dutch East Indies, as well as between Campbell and Clementi over forcing the FMS government to pay the political costs of enforcing restriction.[123] Even so, the many internationalist backers of these schemes, including those at the League of Nations, saw them as providing a ray of hope during the Depression, as efforts to craft international trade and monetary policies appeared out of reach, particularly after the ignominious failure of the 1933 World Economic Conference.[124] In the 1940s, this institutional form, which was created largely for the sake of securing British and Dutch colonial rule in Southeast Asia, was to be put to use for the Keynesian and New Deal ends of mitigating the instabilities of global capitalism.

During the Second World War, the US and British governments considered similar measures for joint Anglo-American controls over various primary goods. While the tin and rubber schemes were unpopular in Washington, since they effectively locked the United States into paying higher prices for strategically significant imports, there was nonetheless a deep well of support in the Roosevelt administration for using intergovernmental commodity agreements to stabilize major US export goods. As we shall see, the first postwar planning initiative that the US government opened with London during the Second World War was to reach a new agreement to protect US wheat and cotton growers. Even the diehard free trader Cordell Hull, US secretary of state from 1933, was grudgingly won over to the idea.[125] "Any of the great international control schemes in rubber, tin, tea, and the like," the influential US postwar planner Eugene Staley wrote in 1939, "might be managed in the social interest with results better in some cases than could be obtained by free competition." Such schemes of "world-wide effect," which already played a central role in "world economics," could be used to combine market capitalism and economic planning on a global scale—provided that the membership of these bodies was broadened to include representatives of other interest groups, such as labor.[126]

For some left-leaning internationalists, there were several reasons to celebrate the emergence of institutions like the ITC. Its establishment appeared to signal the end to an era of absolute sovereignty over natural resources, a move away from laissez faire, and a return to the plans for international resource control that had been abandoned at the end of the First World War, when the Allies had prematurely dismantled their temporary world economic government.[127] While this sovereignty had never been respected in the many non-European countries whose resources were expropriated by foreign businesses, the innovation of the Depression-era schemes was to open up primary commodities in Europe's colonial territories to the possibility of international control. During the 1930s, however, these ideas took a different turn, as the governments of Germany, Italy, and Japan fought against the restrictions and controls maintained by other empires over their colonial resources. In a major 1935 speech before the Assembly of the League of Nations, the British Foreign Secretary Samuel Hoare indicated the receptiveness of the British government to appeasing some of these worries by ensuring the free distribution of raw materials from colonial areas.[128] The following year, an ad hoc committee of members of the Economic and Financial Committees studied similar proposals, including suggestions for international raw material controls and new mechanisms of colonial oversight to appease concerns of the revisionist powers. These efforts resulted in a major report in 1937. But in the face of the unwillingness of Germany and Italy to cooperate in efforts ostensibly aimed to appease them, the proposals had little chance of realization, particularly as they came on the eve of Italy's invasion of Ethiopia.[129]

The very different kind of intergovernmental commodity control arrangements that emerged during the Depression, however, would continue to expand during and well after the 1940s. The first successful ones were developed for the sake of protecting empire in Southeast Asia, but later they were also advocated by the governments of many developing countries to ameliorate their poor terms of trade and stabilize employment. The pinnacle of this form of governance was reached with the creation of OPEC. The movement for a New International Economic Order in the 1970s made the expansion of commodity price stabilization schemes one of its central demands as well.[130]

But the innovation of this form of governance continued to pose difficult questions of sovereignty. The tin scheme had opened up the interior of a colony to international economic institutions in ways that London had explicitly rejected just over a decade before. In this case, it was not that a country with partial or damaged sovereignty was being meddled with; instead, an empire was inviting a partial erosion of its sovereignty for the sake of its prosperity and stability. This would not be the last time that the British Empire would weigh the costs of interference, though the fact that it did so was taken to be a sign of its declining power. In the 1940s, when the US government began to push for new intergovernmental agreements for agricultural goods like wheat, crafted in light of US producer interests, Washington demanded a further-reaching form of involvement in the domestic economy of metropolitan Britain itself—effectively placing the production of English farmers under the watch of an international institution designed to promote the interests of US producers.[131] This led to controversy among electorally significant interest groups and members of the wartime government in London, who worried about what this kind of US interference meant to the British war economy and to the power and prestige of the empire itself. As we shall see, the debate triggered by the proposed wheat agreement nearly derailed Lend-Lease and Anglo-American cooperation altogether in 1941.

As wartime planning for these new primary production regimes unfolded, there was a sense that these international measures, as important as they were, had not cracked the hard problem of non-interference. "If you are to have a limitation of the primary products of the world," as one Liberal MP put the matter bluntly in a debate in the House of Commons, "if you are to dictate to a country how much primary production it should go in for, you are seriously interfering with national sovereignty."[132] John Maynard Keynes, a prominent backer of intergovernmental commodity price stabilization schemes, saw these stakes clearly.[133] As he drew up plans for commodity controls in the 1940s, Keynes pointed to the danger of intergovernmental arrangements that demanded countries "accept arrangements by which the amount they are entitled to produce, of not merely a particular crop which has got into trouble, but of

<u>all</u> their crops, is up to regulation and restriction by an outside body." There was no way the United States would agree to "hand over the whole of her internal agriculture to an international body," he insisted, or allow any arrangement that involved "every farmer being told some years beforehand what he is to grow."[134]

Part of this problem of sovereignty was that what counted as the internal realm of an empire was still widely seen to include colonies as much as the metropole. Despite the innovation of the tin scheme, this jurisdictional ideal—that the colony and metropole enjoyed the same right to non-interference from the reach of those outside the empire—persisted. The domestic jurisdiction clause of the Charter of the United Nations, for example, designated the affairs of non-self-governing territories not directly under UN Trusteeship as domestic issues beyond the organization's reach.[135] But in a striking example of the continuing indeterminacy of this idea, this same clause would also be used in the years to come by the governments of postcolonial countries to assert sovereign rights over natural resources in their borders and to wrest control from the private foreign companies that laid claim to them.[136] Non-interference, a right long claimed by the powerful, would be forcefully asserted by postcolonial and semi-sovereign states as well. When the Second World War began, the question of who, in practice, could enjoy this right was again thrown into profound flux.

CHAPTER 6

Sovereignty and the IMF

THE SECOND WAVE OF twentieth-century international economic institution-building began during the early phases of the Second World War, which confirmed the status of Britain as an empire in decline and that of the United States as guardian of global capitalism. By the summer of 1940, after Nazi Germany's invasion of much of Western and Northern Europe and the opening of the Battle of Britain, the costs of the war mounted for Britain. Assets were sold off, exchange reserves dwindled, and instability loomed for primary producers around the world, threatening political uprisings and economic crisis throughout the empire.[1] It is a myth that Britain truly "stood alone" at any point in the Second World War.[2] But when US assistance came, it had real strings attached. This first became apparent in September 1940, when fifty US destroyers were exchanged for 99-year leases on British naval bases in Canada and the Caribbean. After the decision was made at the end of 1940 to continue US aid, London was told it would come at the cost of something else: a transformation of the empire itself. Beginning in the summer of 1941, the US government insisted that Lend-Lease, its program of wartime aid, was conditional on Britain's commitment to nondiscrimination in trade. In practice, this appeared to mean an end to the imperial economic bloc established in 1932—the system of imperial preference that allowed the constituent units of the empire to trade preferentially with one another, while imposing costs on outsiders. This arrangement was antithetical to the commitments of powerful US free traders like Secretary of State Cordell Hull, who saw it as one of the first obstacles to overcome in the return to multilateral exchange. But many in London saw imperial preference as the last thing protecting Britain from economic catastrophe. Members of the wartime government invoked the biblical story of Jacob, who asked his starving brother Esau to trade his birthright for a bowl of stew, to describe what US demands represented: a new hegemon forcing an old one to relinquish power and prosperity for the sake of rescue from defeat.[3]

It was at this moment, when the scale of US demands on Britain first became apparent, that new institutions to govern the world economy were designed—in ways that both departed from and built upon the earlier innovations charted in this book. The architects of these institutions navigated familiar questions about what kinds of demands they could legitimately make on domestic policies—concerning trade, commodities, budgets, currencies, and social welfare. These discussions culminated in the Bretton Woods agreements of 1944. Most accounts of Bretton Woods open with the efforts of John Maynard Keynes, who joined the wartime government in the summer of 1940, to find a way out of the dilemmas that Lend-Lease posed for Britain. Beginning the following summer, Keynes designed an international monetary institution to stabilize currencies and prevent a return to freer exchange from leading to a balance of payments disaster, while guaranteeing that Britain was freed from the constraints of the gold standard. This led to negotiations with his US counterpart, the Treasury economist Harry Dexter White, and ultimately to the compromise reached at Bretton Woods, which was designed to reconcile the aims of international monetary stabilization with national full employment and welfare policies. The Bretton Woods agreements also established two new international institutions, the International Monetary Fund (IMF) and International Bank for Reconstruction and Development (later known as the World Bank). It is now standard to date the birth of global economic governance to this moment.[4]

But postwar planning did not involve a full leap into the unknown. Instead, it opened a new chapter in an ongoing saga. In the realm of various policies, not only concerning monetary issues, Anglo-American negotiations involved continued disputes about how international institutions could walk the tightrope of exercising legitimate powers over sovereign states without subjecting them to the meddling of foreign governments and private interests. These disputes also drew in a familiar cast of Wall Street bankers, who attempted to preserve their powers to use these institutions to shape the domestic policies of borrowers, despite their temporarily diminished influence over the Democratic administration in Washington. What had changed since 1918 was the strength of many countries' claims to self-determination and the relative power and standing of the British Empire and the United States. When talks with Washington began, members of the wartime British government sought to prevent the empire from being weakened and full employment policies from being jeopardized, and to reaffirm borders between the domestic and the international. Removing the gold standard was just the first step to guaranteeing autonomy. Doing so would not prevent an international institution from pushing policy adjustments on the British, just as they had done elsewhere. It was in negotiations over the foundation of the IMF that these issues were confronted most consequentially.

Histories of the IMF that consider the origins and development of its conditional lending practices have shown how wartime disputes, and unresolved disagreements between US and British negotiators, resulted in ambiguities in the IMF's Articles of Agreement. These ambiguities allowed the IMF, within a few years of its founding, to link access to its resources with demands on the fiscal and monetary policies of borrowers.[5] After the war, the promise of access to capital came to provide the IMF with enormous leverage over the policies of some of its member states, long before the rise of neoliberalism.

But the promulgation of formal rules at the IMF was only one part of a larger and longer-term process of clarifying whether—and whose—domestic economic policies could be opened to external scrutiny. The reality of unrivaled US power in the 1940s meant that the United Kingdom itself could no longer assume that it would enjoy the degree of insulation to which it was accustomed. A problem of internationalism born out of the First World War was not conclusively resolved during the Second. While both British and US policymakers agreed that a reformed international monetary order should allow states to experiment with new national policies, it is a mistake to see the powers that the IMF developed in light of this ideal. As the institution was being established, powerful US bankers—including some who had played central roles in the foundation and early work of the Bank for International Settlements (BIS) or who had worked alongside the League of Nations—sought to ensure that the IMF would, like the League before it, be able link its assistance to demands on the policies of members. In fact, two League alumni, the Dutch economist Jacques Polak and Swedish economist Per Jacobsson, played major roles in providing theoretical and institutional support for this practice as it emerged after the war. The early years of the IMF showed that an older bankers' vision of using an international institution to control the purse strings of borrowers would find a home in a postwar settlement supposedly designed to allow states to escape such pressures.[6]

This tension that characterized postwar planning, between a new right to non-interference and old practices of meddling, became clear at the very beginning of wartime discussions in 1941. Well before Bretton Woods, this tension emerged in negotiations concerning an entirely different set of issues: wartime aid and commodity controls.

The Second Wave of International Economic Institution-Building

During the ten years between the Wall Street Crash of October 1929 and the outbreak of the Second World War, the prospects for economic internationalism dwindled as Europe rearmed, trade and exchange controls proliferated, and imperial economic blocs were established. The economic nationalism of the 1930s has long provided a set of lessons about how quickly a globalized world economy can fall apart when states fail to make collective sacrifices to maintain it.[7] But while the first wave of international economic institution-building slowed to a halt, economic diplomacy was not completely moribund. In 1936, the French, British, and US governments reached a major agreement for a coordinated devaluation of the franc, which offered a prelude to the 1940s transatlantic cooperation of treasuries and a demonstration of how much governments had wrested control of policy from central banks during the preceding half decade.[8] But the Tripartite Agreement did not result in any new institutions.[9] Between 1931 and the Bretton Woods Conference in 1944, the only new intergovernmental economic institutions of significant power, as we have seen, were established to govern the production and exchange of commodities like tin and rubber. Internationalists celebrated the emergence of these controversial cartel-like arrangements, given the broader difficulties of reaching multilateral trade and financial agreements. But the international tin and rubber committees, which did not give the United States any representation as a consuming country, were fiercely attacked in Washington, even as the US government pushed for similar arrangements for wheat and cotton.[10]

As is now well known, enthusiasm for international economic institution-building did not fade in the 1930s, even during the darkest years of economic nationalism. The League of Nations continued to conduct economic research, collect data, and plan for a future world economy, even after it went into exile in the United States in September 1940.[11] The BIS, widely discredited for having fallen under Nazi influence, weathered existential threats and emerged from the war in a position to become stronger than ever. Most importantly, as soon as the war broke out, the governments of the world's two most powerful capitalist empires began to plan, separately and together, new institutions to manage currencies, commodities, trade, relief, development, and even the coordination of full employment policies. Already in December 1939, the US State Department began working on these issues. It was soon joined by the Treasury, Federal Reserve, Department of Agriculture, and later ad hoc wartime agencies like the Board of Economic Warfare. In London, similar efforts began in early 1940 across the government and at the Bank of England.[12]

In Britain and the United States, rival factions were committed to different visions of the postwar. In Britain, there was competition among groups advocating for varying degrees of multilateralism, protectionism, and imperialism. The United States was riven by struggles over New Deal–like arrangements and the future of US foreign policy as well as by squabbles between political parties and different branches of the federal government. At the center of all postwar planning disputes were familiar questions from other moments of international economic institution-building since 1918: What counted as exclusively domestic questions, and what distinguished legitimate sacrifices of autonomy for the sake of international cooperation from the unwanted interference of foreign rivals? These matters took on new urgency in light of ever-stronger demands for national self-determination and as a new consensus solidified about the role of states in guaranteeing employment, mitigating the consequences of crisis, and providing new forms of welfare. All the while, the dramatic reality of US global primacy was put on full display.

Disputes over the terms of Lend-Lease involved wrestling with these issues. When members of the Roosevelt administration informed their British counterparts in July 1941 that US assistance would come at the cost of a commitment to nondiscrimination in trade, many in London fumed at the extravagant nature of this demand to reshape the economics of the empire for the sake of what they considered an outdated vision of free trade. Conservative imperialists saw Article VII of the Lend-Lease Agreement as a humiliating attempt to undo the bounds of the empire altogether; the left saw it as ringing the death knell for expansive postwar national policies. The Roosevelt administration had already made clear on several occasions that imperial preference was on the chopping block.

This had been the case during early 1941 talks about the governance of dependent territories in the Caribbean, for example, which resulted in the creation of an Anglo-American Caribbean Commission but also raised fears among British negotiators that any agreement with the Americans would open the door to US involvement in the internal economic affairs of the colonial empire.[13]

As negotiations on the terms of Lend-Lease dragged on in 1941, members of the wartime government in London worried that acquiescing to Washington's demands would represent a watershed moment. It was a staple of British imperial ideologies that the entire empire was to be afforded the same insulation from external actors as the domestic affairs of metropolitan Britain itself, certainly concerning issues of imperial trade.[14] As we have seen, there was broad agreement in international law that preferential intra-imperial trade relations were a question of domestic jurisdiction alone.[15] When the Ottawa Conference met in the summer of 1932 to reach an agreement on imperial preference, its attendees favorably contrasted its chances for success with the ineffective international conferences of Geneva and Lausanne—since it was, unlike an unwieldy international summit, a purely "domestic affair."[16] The year before, the Statute of Westminster had granted the self-governing Dominions full legislative independence. And the myths of imperial bonds were far more fraught than such statements let on, particularly as the Dominions became increasingly independent members of the Commonwealth. But the ideology of the intra-imperial realm as a purely domestic one continued to exercise a hold on how sovereignty within the empire was understood and defended. Similar ideas were also now being echoed by the revisionist powers, Japan and Germany, which declared their own regional spheres of influence to be domestic spaces that were to be shielded from outside interference.[17] As London's efforts to oppose the more onerous aspects of Lend-Lease intensified, members of the government doubled-down on their insistence that trade relations in the empire could not be put on the negotiating table.[18] Just days before the Lend-Lease Agreement was signed in February 1942, Churchill personally warned Roosevelt that his cabinet viewed its terms as threatening "intervention in the domestic affairs of the British Empire." Accepting these terms would lead to "dangerous debates" in Parliament and confirm Nazi propaganda that the wartime alliance had been designed to reduce Britain's status to that of a dependent US territory.[19]

Wartime negotiations over Lend-Lease made concrete the material realities of US primacy and shattered the myth that the British Empire could naturally expect to enjoy the kind of insulation it once had. But Lend-Lease did not result in any new international institutions. The first consideration of plans to do so concerned a different problem—one that became so contentious that it nearly derailed subsequent Anglo-American economic cooperation altogether.

Just as debate over Lend-Lease was beginning in early 1941, London and Washington also began to discuss ambitious plans to reshape the global production and exchange of primary commodities, beginning with the major US export crop of wheat. After the Nazi invasions of Western and Northern Europe in the spring and summer of 1940 and the entrance of Italy into the war, the extension of the British blockade to occupied countries and the closure of the Mediterranean removed major continental European export markets for many primary producers. This led to disruptions in trade that were exacerbated by shipping problems. As a glut of commodities like oilseeds, bananas, coconuts, groundnuts, sisal, and cotton piled up among producers in British colonies and in Latin America, London turned to Washington to map out a cooperative approach to alleviating this problem of surplus, which was destabilizing the peripheries of the world economy, jeopardizing the blockade, and threatening the spread of Nazi influence.[20] In early 1941, the Department of Agriculture seized on this initiative to push for a new international agreement to regulate the production and trade of wheat and cotton, which had undergone dramatic price fluctuations throughout the 1930s, to the detriment of US farmers.

When Henry Wallace, a Midwestern internationalist New Dealer and head of the Department of Agriculture from 1933 to 1940, became vice president in January 1941, he led the charge for an ambitious new wheat agreement, upheld by an international institution and far-reaching domestic laws and regulations in signatory countries.[21] This multilateralism did not sit comfortably with Hull, who at first regarded such regulated commodity arrangements with skepticism. But he was won over to their value by advisers—at least enough to allow the United States to join an international coffee agreement in 1940 and to push for wheat and cotton control schemes.[22] In early 1941, members of the British government interpreted the US government to be offering wheat as a "test case" for a broader commodity policy—even though the plan was designed for the sake of electorally significant economic groups and not for stabilizing global trade for its own sake.[23] Nevertheless, this sparked the earliest talks in the spring and summer of 1941 about creating new international means of regulating primary commodities—and, by extension, about reshaping the governance of the postwar world economy. Keynes, working with Frederick Leith-Ross at the Board of Economic Warfare, saw this overture as reason to be optimistic about the possibility of other talks, and as "promising a move to postwar cooperation."[24]

But before these commodity talks could be used as a springboard to other postwar issues, the two governments first had to agree on the troublesome good of wheat. And this would not be easy. While the United States, alongside Australia, Canada, and Argentina, was one of the world's largest exporters of wheat, the United Kingdom was its largest importer. Any agreement that raised the price of wheat was thus bound to further damage Britain's postwar balance of payments and push up the price of food for consumers. The US Department of Agriculture was, in effect, calling for an international arrangement that forced London to halt subsidies to domestic producers and reduce the acreage dedicated to the cultivation of this staple grain. Although British wheat production was low by global standards, the government had been subsidizing production for the sake of food security and defense preparations. Members of the Conservative government also had close ties to agricultural interest groups that could mobilize fears of blockade to defend their preferential treatment. The idea of putting their fate into the hands of an International Wheat Council, dominated by representatives of the world's four largest producers, was not a welcome one.[25] There was also an infuriating irony that Hull was pushing for free trade while also insisting that US producers be protected with "a degree of control of a kind and on a scale, which has never before been attempted internationally in regard to an agricultural product," as one report by the Ministry of Agriculture and Fisheries put it.[26]

Perhaps the most galling aspect of the proposed international wheat agreement was that the US government was attempting to open sensitive realms of domestic British production to the reach of an international institution that Washington would dominate alongside other major wheat-producing countries, two of which were members of the British Commonwealth. This was a double affront. One of the principal challenges of any intergovernmental commodity institution that enforced production restrictions, as we have seen, was convincing governments to allow internal questions about businesses, prices, and labor to be scrutinized by an international board. Even though many of the first such agreements had been designed for application in British colonies, and were dominated by British producers and colonial officials, they nonetheless generated a backlash for the interference their British opponents claimed they entailed. Internationalist proposals for governing the global wheat trade, which had been attempted with little success throughout the 1930s, faced the same problem: how to compel a government to adjust its internal agricultural policy for the sake of international cooperation without browbeating it into doing so.[27] In the 1930s, the British Empire had tolerated a partial erosion of its sovereignty for the sake of international agreements to regulate the production of goods like tin, rubber, and tea. But what Washington was proposing in the summer of 1941 went much further than this: an international council to subject metropolitan British agricultural interests to strict rules about the production, export, and pricing of wheat at a moment of profound danger—just as the Nazi invasion of the Soviet Union was under way. The idea of allowing British food production to be put into the hands of an international institution designed to promote the interests of more efficient foreign cultivators was astounding. But Anglo-American cooperation was hanging in the balance, which provided Washington with enormous leverage.

This demand was met with outrage in the wartime British government, not only at the Ministry of Agriculture but also more widely. Keynes described the proposed international agreement with characteristic color: "We are asked to lead the way in allowing our domestic policy to be settled by the Americans as a quid pro quo for all they are and will be doing for us."[28] Some greeted the plans with resigned acceptance, given the extraordinary power that the war had put in US hands: "we are no longer the most powerful (or richest) nation," one Treasury official wrote. This meant accepting the same trade-off that Britain had long compelled other countries to make: assistance in exchange for the relinquishment of full sovereignty.[29] Others were nervous that these plans would force the UK government to continue rigid wartime controls into the peace and eliminate the normal relations of supply and demand in the grain trade. E. M. H. Lloyd, one of the original designers of the League's Economic and Financial Organization and now in the Ministry of Food, where he was reprising his role from the First World War, claimed that, taken to its extreme, this "revolutionary" design for a "world monopoly" would destroy any semblance of free markets for wheat.[30] Lloyd was much less sanguine about international commodity controls than he had been at the end of the last war. Arthur Salter joined his former assistant in attempting to prevent the worst-case scenario. After leaving the League in 1930 and moving to the University of Oxford, where he was elected to Parliament, Salter had been appointed to the Ministry of Shipping in 1939, working again with Jean Monnet on wartime shipping problems. Now he was tasked with negotiating a way out of Britain being pressured to join an international wheat institution that fixed prices globally and interfered with British domestic agricultural policy—but without jeopardizing Anglo-American cooperation in the process.[31]

By late 1941, US material assistance in the war against the Axis powers had come to hinge on the British allowing US involvement in two realms long defined as strictly domestic: preferential intra-imperial trading relationships and agricultural production.[32] For all signatories, the latter threatened to involve the prospect of an external body "[dictating] the details of domestic economic policy."[33] An International Wheat Council was successfully established in the spring of 1942, though it was more a relief planning body than an enforcer of a global restriction regime. It was the first new international economic institution created after the United States joined the war. The attack on Pearl Harbor in December 1941 encouraged Washington to give way on some of its more onerous demands, but the negotiations about wheat had grown so controversial that they had put a damper on Anglo-American cooperation.[34] These talks also clarified that the internal realms of metropolitan Britain and the empire were no longer as safe from external encroachment as they once had been. From the official US point of view, the wheat agreement was only the "first effort to establish some international economic order in our post-war dealings."[35] The US commitment to postwar planning was, from London's vantage point, a welcome development. But the second wave of international economic institution-building was off to a rocky start.

An International Monetary Institution

Around the time that the wheat talks reached their highest pitch of controversy in late 1941, the British Treasury also began to consider broader postwar economic measures. These plans were led by Keynes, who turned his focus to monetary issues, followed closely by broader commodity policy. His plans were developed in light of growing British anxieties about US intentions.[36] In September 1941, Keynes finished his first sketch for a new international monetary institution to stabilize currencies and prevent competitive devaluations—his famous idea for an "International Clearing

Union." It was designed to allow Britain to return to a more open system of trade, as demanded by Article VII of Lend-Lease, without leading to a balance of payments catastrophe. It would also remove the need to face the external disciplinary pressures of the gold standard. Keynes called for what was essentially an international bank, holding accounts for national central banks denominated in the artificial currency of bancor, which members could use to settle balances between them. The system would provide credits automatically to deficit countries to help them keep their balance of payments in equilibrium while allowing them greater autonomy to pursue expansive national policies. One of the most remarkable aspects of Keynes's plans concerned the issue of who could be asked to adjust. In the early drafts of the proposal, he clarified that the Clearing Union would exercise a minimal form of discipline over a country in deficit. What was so ambitious about his plans were the demands it made of surplus countries— namely, the United States—which could be asked to adjust their policies to return international balances to equilibrium. This idea was celebrated then and later as a truly internationalist vision of burden-sharing between creditor and debtor alike.[37] It also implied, as we shall see, a controversial inversion of hierarchies: empowering the debtor to sit in judgment on the domestic policies of the creditor, or so its critics claimed.

When the first drafts of Keynes's plans were circulated in the government—which was generally split between factions of imperialist protectionists, free traders, and those who straddled the two—they were criticized for making unrealistic demands on sovereignty. The prospect of allowing any external authority to have a say in currency issues gave members of the government pause. According to the economist Hubert D. Henderson at the Treasury, it was unlikely that any government would agree to give "large, though doubtfully effective, powers of interfering with the domestic policies of member-States to an international body, whether or not this is subject to effective Anglo-American control," despite the appeal of this idea to the "Geneva-minded."[38] Others criticized the plans for their lack of clarity on whether the institution could compel member countries to enact deflationary policies, thereby sneaking in through the back door the "evils of the old automatic gold standard."[39] Keynes agreed that neither Washington nor London would agree to a system of rules that required "surrender by legislation of discretion normally inherent in a government, with the result that in certain circumstances sovereign rights would be infringed." But an institution that functioned according to the discretionary judgment of its management presented other problems.[40] Keynes insisted that the Clearing Union demanded no more sacrifice of sovereignty than an ordinary commercial treaty—and far less than the measures of military disarmament likely to be implemented at war's end.[41] This was an old distinction, and one that would prove central to the drawing of battle lines over the powers of the new international institution: between a relinquishment of some freedom for the sake of international cooperation and an unwanted opening of questions over budgets and monetary policy to external inspection. Even those who sought to prevent a return to the gold standard worried about an international institution with discretionary powers becoming embroiled in unpredictable ways in the domestic affairs of its members. They insisted that Keynes was downplaying the radical nature of his proposal by drawing false analogies to other international agreements.[42]

Negotiations between London and Washington over the plans began slowly in 1942 before accelerating the following year, after London received US plans for an International Stabilization Fund, drafted by Treasury economist Harry Dexter White. By this point, the US Treasury, led by Henry Morgenthau, Jr., had overtaken the State Department as the locus of US postwar planning. Monetary problems, more than commodity or commercial policy, became the priority. White's plans shared with Keynes's the aim of stabilizing exchanges and preventing competitive devaluations, while allowing governments more leeway to enact expansionary policies than had been possible under the interwar gold standard. But White's plans involved a more traditional vision of the creditor-debtor relationship and did not impose any demands on surplus countries to adjust.[43]

The many technical differences and similarities between the White and Keynes plans, and the attempt to find a synthesis of them, have long taken center stage in histories of the road to Bretton Woods.[44] These negotiations did not only result in a shaky compromise about the postwar international monetary system; they also involved fraught and ultimately unresolved disputes about competing conceptions of sovereignty. Underlying all these discussions was the obvious reality that US participation in any new institution was possible only if Washington dominated it. This was apparent in White's early plans for an International Stabilization Fund, which clarified that member states would be allowed to alter their exchange rates only when this was approved by a four-fifths majority. Since voting power was to be weighted according to a country's contribution to the Fund, this meant that its richest member would have the largest voting share. In other words, the United States would hold the power of veto. Member states could draw on the Fund's resources when they faced short-term financial problems. But the questions of how much they could draw and on what terms would soon become extremely controversial. That this institution was to be overwhelmingly controlled by its US representatives raised the stakes of this controversy, since it ensured that the United States could both push for the Fund to scrutinize the policies of other countries and prevent the same scrutiny from being applied to itself.[45]

These issues were at the center of the public controversies that these plans generated when they were leaked in early 1943. They were attacked in both countries on the basis of their implications for questions of hierarchy, status, and sovereignty in a postwar world order—criticisms that heightened the challenge for both governments of selling the plans at home, whether to lawmakers or to the "man in the street."[46] In the United States, public opposition to both plans, led by New York bankers and articulated in leading US newspapers, was fierce.[47] Keynes's idea of a Clearing Union was attacked for allowing debtors to exercise powers over the policies of creditors, which was said to go against all precedent of the traditional hierarchies of this relationship. "Under the [Keynes] plan, the governing board will have the right to interfere in the internal affairs of the United States as a creditor nation," as one editorial in the *San Francisco Examiner* put it: "[as] fantastic as it may appear, the theory underlying this delegation of authority would be that the US might become too successful and amass too great a credit balance."[48] More threatening were criticisms of White's plan, which had a greater chance of success. White's error was said to have been his substitution of the knaveproof gold standard with the fallible decision-making of officious foreign bureaucrats. The editorial board of *The New York Times,* one of the most influential promoters of Wall Street criticisms of the plans, defended the gold standard as an internationalist solution for a world in which international agreements were seldom obeyed—one that avoided putting national currencies at the "constant mercy of a group of international bureaucrats."[49]

This contrast between the fixed rules of the gold standard and the discretionary decision-making of administrators not only reflected a commitment to anti-planning and pro-market views, but also to the idea that asking a country to relinquish autonomy to human decision-makers could, in practice, result in a greater affront to its sovereignty than asking it to adopt the fetters of a metallic standard. US economists and bankers attacked the Keynes and White plans for precisely this reason. They claimed that these plans involved unrealistic expectations about governments submitting to "outside jurisdiction" on full employment policies.[50] Early neoliberals, like the Princeton economist Frank Graham, similarly contrasted the light burden of the gold standard on sovereignty with the plans of Keynes and White. Fixing the value of a currency to gold required giving up some freedom of action, Graham wrote, but it did not demand submission to any external authority. By contrast, the inclusion of possible sanctions against rule-breaking countries in these plans ensured that no "important capitalistic country would enter the plan except under misapprehension of its nature or a conviction that it can dominate its management."[51] Yet Graham failed to grasp the unique genius of the Keynes scheme, which sought to recapture the best aspects of the gold standard— its supposed automaticity—without returning to its obvious weakness: the constricting and deflationary effects it had on the national level.[52] As other supporters of the plans pointed out, the classical gold standard had also never been as automatic as its ideological backers (like Graham) made it out to be. A country adhering to the rules of gold did not surrender any sovereignty to an international institution, but it did lose some autonomy to an outside authority that made discretionary judgments: the Bank of England, which through its control of bank rate influenced the domestic monetary conditions of countries around the world.[53] But it was undeniable that these plans, certainly White's, called for an institution that wielded a significant degree of discretionary power. Neither Britain or the United States had ever before considered such power being applicable to itself as an "important capitalistic country."

In addition to calling for a return to the gold standard, Wall Street and Republican critics made alternative proposals that drew directly on interwar models of economic governance. These proposals were often voiced publicly or behind closed doors by the same bankers who had played critical roles in designing the BIS or who had worked with the League on its financial stabilization schemes. Some suggested entrusting the tasks of monetary stabilization to a "revitalized" BIS, which they said was a more reliable guarantor of US capital than an intergovernmental institution. Because it was completely detached from fiscal authorities, the BIS would not allow its resources to be wasted by profligate member governments on welfare or other political projects, they claimed.[54] In fact, it was former architects and staff members of the BIS, like Leon Fraser and Thomas Lamont, who were among the most influential US opponents of plans for an intergovernmental, as opposed to a fully private, institution. Another major proponent of this idea, J. H. Riddle, an economic adviser to the Bankers Trust Company, had been an assistant to S. Parker Gilbert during the latter's time in Germany and an attendee at the 1929 conference in Paris where the BIS was first proposed.[55] One of the most powerful opponents of the plans, the banker W. Randolph Burgess, president of the American Banking Association that led lobbying efforts against the Bretton Woods agreements, had also been a major US advocate and designer of the BIS.[56] The earlier efforts of these bankers to ensure that the BIS was completely "nonpolitical" now shaped their lobbying against an institution that would be controlled by governments.

Another alternative model was provided by the League of Nations' financial reconstruction loans of the 1920s. The idea of reviving this kind of international governance was backed by one of the most influential GOP critics of the Keynes and White plans, the Illinois congressman Charles Dewey—who, as we have seen, had exercised controls over the Polish government when it received a US stabilization loan in 1928. While Dewey's control in Warsaw had been lighter than that of a League commissioner-general, he had nonetheless performed a role similar to that of Alfred Zimmerman in Vienna and Jan Hunger in Tirana. Dewey had also been appointed to a powerful position in the Polish central bank. Now in Congress, Dewey led a faction of lawmakers that was opposed to any intergovernmental monetary body that did not wield the kinds of controls that had characterized the League's style of financial governance. Dewey counted on the support of the long-time money doctor Edwin Kemmerer, whose mission to Poland had laid the groundwork for Dewey's own work there, and who became one of the most influential intellectual antagonists of the Bretton Woods agreements.[57] From the vantage point of the British Treasury, Dewey's efforts to recreate something like the League's approach to lending—which London had itself played an important role in designing and implementing—was regarded with trepidation. For it clearly implied the possibility of Britain facing the kind of controls formerly reserved for Britain's vanquished enemies or semi-sovereign and new states.[58]

In Britain, where Keynes's plan had greater support than White's plan had in the United States, there was nonetheless anxiety about agreeing to the authority of any international institution. Keynes attempted to assuage parliamentary worries by clarifying that his plans had been shaped to impose the "least possible interference with internal national policies" and "not to wander from the international *terrain*." Internal policies could not be completely ignored when they affected international conditions. But the governing board of this institution would only be authorized to make recommendations or, at most, set some conditions on continued access to its resources. But even these points would become contentious, as it became clear that the institution's management would not be "genuinely international," as Keynes insisted, but instead dominated by its US representatives.[59] When the Conservative Chancellor of the Exchequer Kingsley Wood pitched Keynes's plans to the House of Commons in May 1943, he echoed these points. Under this plan, Wood insisted, countries abusing its rules would at most face the kind of "uncomfortable interview" that a profligate customer did with the manager of a commercial bank. Wood repeated Keynes's reassuring line that Britain would not be forced to give up any more sovereignty than that demanded by an ordinary commercial agreement. Governments would retain the right to control "their own economic life," particularly when it came to employment policies.[60]

One of the aims of these arguments was to reassure Parliament about substituting the discipline of gold for that of US technocrats, which meant empowering a "human governor, an international governor consisting of human beings, to which national sovereign bodies are prepared to delegate some of their functions," as one MP put it.[61] Replacing an "automatic regulator" with a "personal regulator" meant accepting "some judgment other than our own sole judgment as to whether a variation in our exchange rate is justified," argued George Schuster, a Labour MP and former finance member of the viceroy's council in India, where he had attempted to establish an economic planning council in the 1930s. Such a surrender of judgment might be necessary for international cooperation, but Parliament needed to "be satisfied as to the tribunal."[62] Other Labour supporters of the plans, like Arthur Woodburn, worried about the power of any institution to "interfere in domestic policy," particularly by telling the government it could not afford the Beveridge Plan.[63] These MPs drew a traditional distinction: between an international agreement that involved some concessions to sovereignty and one that involved an excessive "interference with internal affairs."[64]

The Clearing Union was sold to Parliament and other members of the wartime alliance and sterling area on the grounds that it fell on the right side of this distinction. Members of the Chinese Nationalist government, for example, including T. V. Soong and H. H. Kung, were reassured that this institution would never interfere in Chinese affairs, but instead would allow China to undertake whatever domestic experiments it wished, freed from the deflationary pressures of the world economy. The British Foreign Office also monitored Soviet opinion on the plans, but found that Moscow was unlikely to allow national monetary issues to be opened to external authorities. The Soviet Union went further than nearly any other country, they noted, in avoiding any "fetter laid upon it from outside."[65] The Clearing Union was framed as an innovation that exorcised the specter of both impersonal external pressures and political meddling:

> The aim is not to interfere with the autonomy of each country to purse its own internal policy, above all its liberty in its choice of arrangements to cure the malady of unemployment. The object is to prevent events in one country from interfering with the opportunity of other countries to pursue their own proper domestic economic policies. If more elasticity can be given to the general framework of international trade and currency, shocks can be absorbed and the interference of one country with another reduced to a minimum.[66]

This was a radical vision. But it was not one that had much chance of success, particularly as it became clear that the US plans would win the day.

The Grand Inquisitor

In late 1943, as Britain and the United States inched closer to a deal, two questions about sovereignty remained unresolved. The first concerned how the new international institution would judge the decision of a member state to change the par value of its currency. One of the principal aims of the whole project of Anglo-American monetary stabilization was to prevent the kind of competitive devaluations that had made international exchange so difficult and unpredictable in the 1930s. But how could this be done without returning to the rigidities of gold? Taken to its extreme, the US plan seemed to imply that members of the Stabilization Fund could not alter the value of their currencies without the explicit approval of Washington, since any changes required a four-fifths majority.[67] Keynes claimed that this would eliminate parliamentary sovereignty over the pound entirely and demand an embarrassing British capitulation to "dollar diplomacy."[68] In discussions later that summer, British negotiators sought two important compromises: first, guarantees that only changes in exchange rates over 10 percent required the consent of the international institution; and second, clarification that this consent would be given automatically according to an objective test, based on economic conditions, rather than according to the whims of the institution's governing board.[69]

It was over another question that even more consequential problems about the institution's powers would be wrestled with: Could it make the provision of capital to member states conditional on their domestic policies? Keynes and his colleagues clarified their strategy for resisting any onerous forms of conditionality, insisting that the only limit on members' rights to these resources could be quantitative, set in terms of their contribution to the institution and not according to any political or policy criteria. White agreed that the Stabilization Fund should limit its powers to deny resources to its members only if they were grossly abusing them—by using them to finance capital flight, for example, or rearmament. But this issue remained a sticking point. Wall Street opponents rejected any institution that made unconditional loans with the dollar, which they claimed would allow US wealth to be squandered by foreign governments on social policies, political patronage, and strategic aims. Keynes, by contrast, insisted that governments had to be confident that they could draw on the resources they were entitled to without any strings attached. He used a very specific term to describe the dangers of an international institution that did not make these resources available automatically: one that exercised "grandmotherly" powers over its members.[70] This gendered metaphor had long been used in the United Kingdom and the Dominions to criticize intrusive and moralistic laws that policed private behavior at the cost of personal liberties. Public safety rules about alcohol and tobacco consumption and the carrying of firearms, as well as workplace protections and labor laws, were commonly attacked as forms of "grandmotherly interference." As it became clear that the postwar institution would look closer to White's vision than to Keynes's, what had to be avoided was opening the door to a constant, finger-wagging US presence in Britain's affairs, forcing London to do what it was unwilling to do on its own.

When Anglo-American postwar economic planning talks were held in Washington in September and October 1943, these two issues—about monetary sovereignty and the policing of domestic policies—were central topics of debate. On the first issue, British officials sought to ensure that decisions about exchange rates would be taken only in reference to objective criteria, not according to the discretionary judgments of any "executive committee."[71] In this way, they sought to avoid having questions about exchanges being turned into matters of debate at an institution staffed by other governments.[72] But it was dispute over the institution wielding "inquisitorial" powers that proved to have the highest stakes. There was continued disagreement about whether drawings should be considered a "privilege" or a "right." The Americans never budged from the former conception and the British never did from the latter, even after an agreement was reached at Bretton Woods the following summer. This was a sticking point. US Treasury official Edward Bernstein clarified to his British counterparts that Morgenthau was unlikely, in the face of Wall Street pressure, to ever give up the idea of the Fund wielding policing powers, even though this idea went completely against the British view that the Fund had to ensure countries access to its resources without any scrutiny of their income and expenditure. According to this view, allowing the Fund to wield policing powers would mean giving up the notion that creditor countries were to bear any burden of adjustment: "If the U.S. government wish to police their own affairs," one British official put it, "by all means let them."[73]

Accounts of the evolution of the IMF's powers of conditional lending have focused on the uncertainty of these discussions in late 1943 and the vagueness of the wording of the compromises that were reached, which were eventually worked into a draft Articles of Agreement of the IMF. Such accounts are right to examine these wartime discussions and the many technical details about determining criteria for drawing rights, such as how a member "represented" its need for a drawing and how limits were fixed according to member quotas.[74] But focusing primarily on the precise language of the negotiations, the drafts of the Keynes and White plans, and the eventual Articles of Agreement risks an overly legalistic approach to understanding the powers that the IMF would develop. The fundamental reality of disproportionate US power made one thing very likely: that an institution with a vaguely worded constitution, in which the United States exercised effective veto power, would move in the direction desired by the US Treasury as it responded to public and private pressures. Moreover, the Americans never clearly agreed to abjure the kind of inquisitorial powers that Keynes so feared.

After the late 1943 Washington meetings, Keynes and other British negotiators claimed that they had won some reassurance from their US counterparts that the Fund would not be too "grandmotherly." But they also admitted that the most they had gotten were concessions in the wordings of the draft plans and an indication that their US counterparts did not imagine a role for the Fund in scrutinizing the internal policies of a "great" or a "major" country. This was clearly not a universal guarantee. Nor was the category of "greatness" itself set in stone. If anything, the Americans appeared to want to keep some conditionality in place out of fears that Latin American countries would use the Fund to drain US capital. At the Washington meetings, Keynes agreed that a three-quarters majority of the Fund's governing board could be allowed to declare a member in "flagrant abuse" of Fund resources, though without any judgment of its domestic policies. No "major countries," Keynes insisted, would "tolerate an inquisition."[75] Whatever the Fund's "discretionary rights" to challenge a drawing, Keynes added, this power "should be framed to distinguish between the case of a developed country managing its affairs prudently, so as to avoid recourse to the Fund, and that of an irresponsible small country anxious to exploit a new source of borrowing."[76] After these meetings, the British economist Albert Baster clarified to War Cabinet member Alfred Hurst that the Americans had insisted that the Fund wield some "inquisitorial" powers for the sake of preventing "improvident Latin American countries" from exploiting it.[77]

But there was a palpable sense of anxiety in these British efforts to understand US motives. Were the powers of a "grandmotherly" Fund to be limited to borrowers in Latin America, a traditional site of US financial imperialism? Or was the United Kingdom itself little different now in the eyes of Washington and Wall Street from a Latin American debtor? As Baster admitted, these questions were a source of confusion at the Washington meetings. While British officials opposed the Fund exercising "intolerably inquisitorial" powers over their own country, it was unclear if US officials imagined a meddling Fund only for Latin America or for the rest of the world.[78] Just as in Germany and Austria in the 1920s, when warnings about the dangers of foreign financial interference drew on analogies to nineteenth-century practices of Anglo-French financial imperialism in the Middle East and North Africa, understanding Britain's power and standing now involved fraught comparisons to the "irresponsible" Latin American countries that had long been targets of US dollar diplomacy. During discussions about Lend-Lease in early 1941, Keynes had used a different metaphor to describe Britain's "humiliating" loss of status: It was being treated by the US Treasury "worse than we have ever ourselves thought it proper to treat the humblest and least responsible Balkan country."[79] Informal empire was being inverted.

The reassurances that Keynes and others later claimed had been provided at these meetings had mostly come from representatives of the State Department and Federal Reserve, neither of which exercised much influence over the final shape of the plans. Emanuel Goldenweiser, director of research and statistics at the US Federal Reserve, agreed with Keynes that "large countries" like Britain and the United States would not tolerate the Fund "maintaining a constant watch on them" to ensure they were not abusing its resources.[80] Adolf Berle, assistant secretary of state for Latin American affairs, made similar points.[81] But they emphasized that these powerful countries would avoid such scrutiny on the grounds of questions of prestige and domestic legislative politics. They did not articulate any universal right to non-interference. White himself admitted the poor political optics of an "external Board sitting in judgment on a Government."[82] But he never clarified how such a scenario would be avoided. The uncertainty of these claims, as we shall see, later made it easier for the IMF's Articles of Agreement to be interpreted in ways that allowed it to develop such powers of "inquisition."[83] Although US compromises helped Keynes to sell the plans at home, other members of the British Treasury, even those who supported the plans, expressed reservations about the prospect of submitting "any part of our affairs to the inspection and to some extent to the judgment of an untried international body."[84] In early 1944, Keynes painted a comforting picture of Washington agreeing to a Fund without policing powers.[85] But as it turned out, there was little reason for this confidence.

The publication of the joint Anglo-American plans in early 1944, on the basis of compromises reached in late 1943, prompted a new round of public criticism in both countries about their implications for questions of sovereignty. In the United States, Wall Street bankers and the *New York Times* honed their criticisms of the plans in terms that would later feature in congressional debates. A Fund that did not waste its resources, they claimed, needed far-reaching powers to meddle in the domestic polices of other countries. But these powers had to be so extensive that they would make the entire arrangement politically unfeasible. When private banks loaned money to foreign governments, they had little compunction about telling a borrowing government what to do. But it would be "embarrassing for foreign Governments," as one editorial in the *New York Times* claimed, "even though acting through a general fund, to demand minimum internal financial reforms within a nation before they will lend that nation money."[86] The precedent of the League loans went unmentioned.

In Britain, Keynes again insisted to MPs that the purpose of this arrangement was to reconcile the international economy with new national economic policies. But he faced continued queries about how such autonomy would be guaranteed if Washington controlled the Fund. The Labour peer Christopher Addison, formerly minister of munitions and reconstruction during World War I, echoed worries about how this institution could be prevented from being able to "dictate policies to the different nations which contribute to its building up." While Addison supported the plans, he described his "horrid memories" of the years when the "semi-independent private corporation" of the Bank of England had controlled Britain's economic fate. Among Labour MPs, who largely backed the plans, such anxieties about an independent financial institution continued to shape opinions about any arrangement that appeared to disempower the government.[87] Labour critics in the Commons similarly worried that the Anglo-American agreement would hand "over the sovereign rights of our own people to the irresponsible control of a lot of unnamed international financiers," which would leave the Treasury as powerless as it had been in 1925, they claimed, when Churchill had been browbeaten into returning the pound to gold.[88]

Asymmetric Interference

When the United Nations Monetary and Financial Conference opened in Bretton Woods in July 1944, more than 700 delegates from forty-four countries met to reshape the rules of the international monetary system and to agree on the creation of two new international economic institutions. These institutions would be endowed with greater powers, more resources, and broader memberships than any of their predecessors. The Bretton Woods Conference has been remembered as one of the single greatest acts of international institution-building of all time, presided over by the towering figures of Keynes and White, but attended by a more globally inclusive array of participants than nearly any other international summit up to that time. It was undeniably an achievement in international cooperation. But it did not decisively resolve all of the controversies that had shaped its planning—even as the Anglo-American compromise was largely, with some modifications, formalized.

At meetings held in Atlantic City just days before the Bretton Woods Conference, British negotiators had unsuccessfully attempted to address some of these lingering issues. In particular, they sought to establish more robust guarantees about the automaticity of drawing rights and to weaken the Fund's ability to deny exchange rate adjustments on the basis of full employment policies.[89] Keynes was anxious to prevent the Fund from making specific proclamations about British domestic policies—like wages, for example—or to pose any kind of "outside interference" that made "Bevin's job impossible." Walter Gardner, member of the Board of Governors of the Federal Reserve, asked Keynes how such automaticity would work: Would the Fund simply pour its money into a country that abused its resources by misguided policies, without this country accepting the need to change them? When Keynes rhetorically asked his US counterparts whether they would allow such an institution to declare that "the New Deal was all wrong," White offered a vague reassurance that the Fund would avoid criticizing social and political policy.[90] This position had been pushed for by other members of the War Cabinet before Keynes arrived in the United States. The economist Lionel Robbins argued that if the Fund criticized the decisions of a government in power, it would effectively be allying with the domestic opposition. This was unacceptable.[91] Robbins's conception of an institution that avoided any criticism of a member state in its public proclamations was a demanding vision of non-interference. But it was not one that had been adhered to consistently in British economic diplomacy before this point.

Such questions about jurisdictional barriers were not discussed at length at the Bretton Woods Conference, though some delegates, particularly from Mexico, attempted to win stronger guarantees that the sovereign equality of all member states would be respected in the postwar order.[92] There was little doubt that making access to the Fund's resources conditional would provide a way for it to exercise leverage over the internal policies of members. But there was no definitive resolution of the conflict between the idea of drawings being a "right" or a "privilege." Ultimately, the US position was flexible enough to make it look like it was both: "We all realize that a country has a right of access to this Fund," as Edward Brown, president of the First National Bank of Chicago, and head of the Federal Advisory Council of the Board of Governors of the Federal Reserve, put it. But "if the Fund isn't inclined to go broke in short order, that right has got to be conditional."[93] Consideration of the Fund's relationship to internal policy took a brief detour down a different route when representatives of the Australian government called for the Fund to oversee and coordinate national programs of full employment while avoiding any direct interference with a member's ability to decide what its specific expansive policies would be.[94] The Australian Labor government was unique in continuing to advocate the kind of international full employment policies that had earlier been taken seriously in Anglo-American discussions but had been abandoned in Washington and London some time before. Keynes himself had come out against the feasibility of these ideas earlier that year, claiming that no government would ever agree to any external involvement in its domestic full employment policies.[95] The Australian delegation drew a traditional internationalist distinction in service of a radically new political vision: encouraging sovereign states to commit to a suite of mutually beneficial full employment policies while avoiding telling them in detail what these policies had to be.

One place in the IMF's Articles of Agreement where problems of jurisdictional barriers were mentioned was in a stipulation of Article IV, Section 5, which stated that the Fund could not object to a member's proposed change in the par value of its currency on the grounds of its "domestic social or political policies." This phrase was a concession to

John Maynard Keynes and Chinese delegate H. H. Kung at the Bretton Woods Conference. British officials attempted to solicit Chinese support for the Keynes plan on the basis of its guarantees of non-interference. *AP Photo.*

British demands in order to secure parliamentary ratification of the agreements as well as to convince the Soviets to join the arrangement.[96] But it was not clear what kind of autonomy this rule actually provided. Wall Street critics of Bretton Woods interpreted it to mean that the Fund could not judge any policies that led to balance of payments problems in the first place, such as government spending on social policies or armaments. Others saw it more as a rule of decorum than anything else. It was clear why the rule had been included, though: to ensure legislative approval. Goldenweiser described this point a few months after the conference:

> There are provisions by which the Fund cannot refuse a change of rate for domestic political or social causes. There was a lot of discussion as to what was meant, but it was put in partly because it would not do for the Fund to say "You are Communists—we cannot let you have a change" or "You are Tories, and you cannot do this." Reasons of that sort cannot be used for refusing a change. What is meant by "social" is not altogether clear, but it probably means that if a country has legislation relating to women or child labor, or social security, or safety devices, the Fund cannot say, "These things are undesirable, and therefore, we won't let you make a change." In political and social issues, countries must have the say, and must handle these things as they see fit. But if a country is pursuing a fiscal or labor policy or any kind of an economic policy which is bound to result in maladjustments the Fund can say, "We cannot let you meet that by changing your rate because that will only postpone the debacle and will further disorganize the world. You must find other ways of putting your own house in order." These points are relatively vague because anything rigid written this far in advance would probably become unworkable and we could not get agreement between the countries.[97]

Crafting an agreement that was simultaneously acceptable to the Soviets, a US Congress under the gaze of Wall Street, and a Labour party ideologically somewhere between these two meant keeping the scope of the Fund's powers deliberately unclear. But it was still widely assumed that the more restrictive aspects of these powers had been designed with "small" nations in mind, not a "first-class power" like Britain.[98]

After the Bretton Woods Conference, Wall Street bankers and GOP lawmakers attacked the plans for not endowing the Fund with enough power to scrutinize the domestic policies of member states.[99] This issue became central to congressional hearings on the plans in the spring and summer of 1945, which were pushed back to after the November 1944 presidential elections.[100] Although some of the drama of these hearings was standard political resistance of Republicans to New Deal–like policies or international "entanglements," they also involved interpretations of the Fund's Articles of Agreement that were shaped by long-standing disputes about sovereignty. On the one hand, GOP critics insisted that the Fund could not be allowed to make capital available to members without conditions; on the other, they opposed allowing US policies to be subjected to the same policing, certainly not by an institution in which the Soviet Union was a member. This vision of asymmetric interference would long undergird US global power.

Some of these worries were expressed in conspiratorial terms. One extreme, though not uncharacteristic, statement was entered into the Senate record by Agnes Waters, a representative of the National Blue Star Mothers of America, a far-right women's movement, who claimed that the Fund was a communist plot to "make of this Nation a feeding trough for the have-nots of the world."[101] Bankers, economists, and GOP lawmakers made similar, though less florid, claims about the danger of US capital being squandered by a Fund that did not control its members' purse-strings. Fraser, president of the First National Bank of New York, and former vice president of the BIS, articulated the common Wall Street view that the Fund made no financial sense if its directors could not "stick their noses into the domestic affairs of people." Allowing debtors to sit on the management of a Fund that did not check the misguided use of US capital by other governments would guarantee it was squandered.[102] Other representatives of Wall Street made similar claims. Granting automatic access to the Fund's resources would prevent it from exercising any leverage over their policies. The IMF "is given no power to interfere with or to make recommendations concerning the domestic monetary and financial policies of member nations," as one critic put it, contrasting this with the wisdom accrued at the League of Nations, whose officials recognized that loans without internal fiscal reforms were quickly wasted.[103] While reference to the League as a successful model of governance had by this point become less common, given the League's association with the failure to prevent the Second World War, these critics fondly remembered the institution's method of disciplining debtors. Other internationalists, by contrast, now routinely criticized the League for having failed to demand any real sacrifice of its members' economic sovereignty or to develop any jurisdiction over their economic policies.[104] But these were criticisms of the League's inability to weaken the economic sovereignty of its most powerful European member states. These critics did not mention the unstable countries that had been asked by the League to sacrifice a considerable degree of autonomy. That was the League that Wall Street opponents of the IMF saw as a model to be emulated. They understood just how powerful the institution had been at key moments in the 1920s.

One common argument made by opponents to the Bretton Woods agreements was that the Fund only made financial sense if it were endowed with powers of interference that were so far reaching that they made the whole arrangement politically unrealistic. Because the United States would never allow a Fund to meddle in its business, the whole thing had to be abandoned. The fiercely pro-market economist V. Orval Watts told members of the House that the IMF needed to be able to veto "every important aspect of each borrowing member's financial policy, a veto power which these nations will not grant to any foreign body." Otherwise, borrowing governments would waste its money on lavish public spending like the Beveridge Plan.[105] Jessie Sumner, a Republican Congresswoman from Illinois, insisted that allowing the Fund to even issue reports could "force us to do a great many things that we would not do." But unconditional

Cartoons by Syd Hoff depicting Wall Street opposition in a pro-Bretton Woods pamphlet. *Reproduced from Joseph Gaer,* Bretton Woods Is No Mystery *(New York: National Citizens Political Action Committee, 1945).*

lending to welfare states would lead to hyperinflation.[106] Burgess claimed that financial assistance without strings attached would put the United States into the absurd position of helping strategic rivals when they acted in ways that jeopardized US security. If the IMF had existed in the 1930s, he argued, Italy would have used it to finance the invasion of Ethiopia.[107] Similar points were made in the Senate hearings. The Republican Senator Eugene Millikin, using a common stereotype of the profligate debtor, pointed out the contradiction at the heart of the entire arrangement: "it is easy enough for us to sit here and tell Greece what to do in her internal affairs," Milliken claimed, "but the moment you say shall we allow any international body to tell us what we should do, you see at once the answer should be 'No.'"[108]

In response to these worries, White himself clarified how the IMF would establish an asymmetric right to non-interference that simultaneously protected US capital and US sovereignty: The United States would never need to draw on its resources, so the Fund would not ever wield any leverage over US policies. The same was not necessarily true for members that did turn to it.[109] Other designers of the agreements made similar points. That the United States dominated voting power in the Fund and controlled the one currency that everyone wanted made it unlikely that other members would do anything to alienate its US directors.[110] If and when the IMF did develop powers to interfere in members' policies, Washington would have no reason to fear them.

The Future of Interference

The worries about sovereignty and interference that characterized legislative debates about Bretton Woods did not, in the end, doom its chances for ratification. The agreements were passed in both US congressional chambers and in the British Parliament. This was itself remarkable. Never before had an international monetary agreement of this kind been achieved or an international financial institution been given such extensive powers. Long after the Bretton Woods system ended, these two institutions, the IMF and World Bank, would continue to exercise extraordinary global influence. The British government had agreed to a series of concessions about the nature and powers of the IMF, including its seat in Washington. Yet many in London continued to hope that it would function as a truly multilateral institution, not just an appendage of the US state.

Other wartime blueprints for new international economic institutions, by contrast, went unrealized. Although sustained efforts were made to negotiate the terms of an international organization to regulate various commodities, divisions in the US and British governments about whether it would wield production restrictions and other controversies dragged on until the end of the war, when compromise was harder to reach. After the war, new agreements for specific commodities were established or renewed. But no overarching commodity organization was ever created.[111] In the case of commercial policy, wartime discussions resulted in an agreement for a charter for an International Trade Organization, but it was never ratified by Congress. The less interventionist General Agreement on Tariffs and Trade (GATT) was established in 1947 to oversee the reduction of tariffs. Its powers were limited to consideration of outright barriers to trade but no other domestic policies.[112] While it was only supposed to be a temporary arrangement, it lasted until the creation of the World Trade Organization in 1995.

Plans for the International Bank for Reconstruction and Development were less controversial and were supported by many powerful banking opponents of the IMF. The development bank did not offer members anything like the kind of unconditional access to US capital they claimed the IMF would, and it granted a veto to any member state whose national currency was being loaned.[113] At the same time, the World Bank, wielding its own capital, did not demand the pledging of state revenues and monopolies as security for development loans. Countries in need of foreign capital no longer had to "give away some of their independence to get it," as Morgenthau put it. As we have seen, Morgenthau's father, as first US head of the League's Refugee Settlement Commission in Greece, had pioneered a form of international development that was more taxing on a borrower's sovereignty. The new international bank was supposed to protect lenders without violating the self-determination of borrowers or putting their assets under foreign control.[114] Some Republican critics, like Dewey, continued to oppose any kind of uncontrolled development lending. But the World Bank was generally seen as less risky than the IMF.

The economic powers of the new United Nations, founded in late 1945, were much more restricted. The Economic and Social Council was established as one of the UN's principal organs. But Soviet delegates had made clear at the Dumbarton Oaks Conference the year before that the organization was to restrict its activities to the realm of security and avoid getting involved in members' internal economic and social affairs.[115] The

Soviets had long been among the strongest defenders of a formal principle of non-interference. Article 2(7) of the UN Charter, modeled on the equivalent "domestic jurisdiction" clause in the League's Covenant, codified this principle. It made congressional ratification of the Charter much easier, since, in addition to keeping the UN out of most domestic economic issues, it also put discriminatory US Jim Crow laws and other human rights problems beyond the institution's reach. John Foster Dulles, US delegate to the San Francisco Conference where the UN was established, insisted that this new domestic jurisdiction clause was designed to prevent the institution from being able to "penetrate directly into the domestic life and social economy of each of the member-states."[116]

In the case of the IMF, there were no unequivocal safeguards against interference in its Articles of Agreement besides rules about the organization's neutrality concerning domestic political matters and social policy. By allowing members to adjust their exchange rates up to a certain point without any need for approval, they were freed from the external deflationary pressures that the gold standard had once imposed on them. After the Bretton Woods Conference, the British government continued to hope that Keynes's interpretation of the IMF's rejection of "inquisitorial" powers had won the day. Moving from the discipline of gold to the discretionary judgment of an international institution was praised as an achievement by some of the agreement's parliamentary supporters.[117] To win British approval, the laxity of this arrangement had been emphasized. To win US approval, the Fund's ability to restrict access to its resources had been emphasized. Squaring the circle of legislative approval in both countries meant leaving the precise nature of these powers vague.

But soon after the war ended, it turned out there had been little reason to believe that real rules against interference had been provided in the IMF's Articles of Agreement, at least if this meant preventing the fiscal and monetary policies of all member states from becoming targets of scrutiny.[118] That the benefits of vagueness went in one direction alone became clear at the first meetings of the Board of the Executive Directors of the IMF. British members of the Board reiterated their insistence at its inaugural meeting in May 1946 that they had an automatic right to the Fund's resources and that the institution was to avoid all "unnecessary interference in affairs of members."[119] After Keynes died that April, White was left as guardian of the wartime compromise, until his resignation in 1947, not long before his own death the following year. Before he left the IMF, White did not hesitate to clarify that an automatic right to drawings was not possible, but only privileged access, subject to conditions. In making such statements, White was not abandoning a clear wartime promise, despite the protestations of his British colleagues. Instead, he was clarifying what had until then been kept unclear. But by then, it no longer mattered much what had been said during the war. US representatives on the IMF's Board could interpret the ambiguous rules of an institution they dominated according to their own criteria and in light of the political constraints they faced at home.

The uncertainty of the Fund's powers worried its European representatives. In 1946, the French Executive Director Jean de Largentaye threatened to request France's maximum drawing on the first day possible, without any justification, merely to prove that France had an automatic right to do so.[120] The British Executive Director George Bolton attempted to reassure the Bank of England, where he had previously worked, that the IMF would not commit to "a policy of persistent and irresponsible interference in the domestic affairs of members."[121] But this reassurance proved to be premature. Soon the conflict over "automaticity" and "conditionality" led to a near paralysis of policy-making at the IMF, as the Board became a "battleground between the British and American points of view," as one British memo later put it.[122] By early 1947, the British Treasury recognized the battle was at risk of being lost. Countries most in need of foreign exchange were avoiding the IMF, in part to avoid having to submit to its "continuous audit of their affairs."[123] By abstaining from drawing, however, the British made it more likely that a weaker borrower would do so first and be answered with a long set of conditions. This risked setting a dangerous precedent for the IMF wielding "inquisitorial" powers.[124] Even with the departure of White, it appeared unlikely that the US government would give up its position of insisting that US dollars only be spent under US control and supervision.[125] Although Wall Street had lost the fight against the Bretton Woods agreements, its demands for an "inquisitorial" IMF were being realized. The institution gradually re-adopted international lending practices similar to those pioneered by the League over two decades before.[126]

By this time, the entire Bretton Woods arrangement was thrown into jeopardy. Britain attempted to make the pound convertible to dollars in July 1947—a condition of the large US loan that Keynes had negotiated at war's end—which led to a rapid loss of Britain's exchange reserves, necessitating the suspension of convertibility.[127] Just as after the First World War, the aftermath of the Second World War was also turning out to be quite different from what many had imagined during the war, and in certain ways, much more unstable. The IMF, endowed with limited resources, did not take charge of Europe's immediate postwar financial stabilization. But there were high stakes to determining what its powers and rules would be, given what was likely to be its future role in international affairs. By early 1948, British representatives on the Board saw the situation as having become quite serious. Bolton claimed the US insistence on conditions was in violation of the terms on which Parliament had ratified the Bretton Woods agreements in the first place. He asked the Treasury to look through government records of wartime discussions between Keynes and White to build his case.[128] The Treasury confirmed that relevant wartime documents showed that there had been a rough agreement that no "important country" would allow external scrutiny of its domestic policies. But there had been no clear confirmation that all countries, regardless of their perceived importance, were to be granted this right. Although Keynes had always pushed for unconditionality, it was apparent in hindsight that the Americans had never committed to it.[129] In any case, little hope remained that US members of the Executive Board could now be talked into a more robust commitment than Keynes had been able to secure at the height of the wartime coalition, particularly as the global dollar shortage worsened and Washington had further reason to insist that US capital be made available only with strings attached. In January 1948, Andrew Overby, a former leading member of the New York Federal Reserve Bank and US Treasury, who had replaced White as US executive director of the IMF the July before, suggested a way out of this impasse. To prevent frequent invocation of Article V, Section 5 of the Articles of Agreement (which stated that a member's access to the Fund's resources could be limited or cut off if that member was found to be using them in ways "contrary to the purposes of the Fund"), Overby proposed that the institution instead make thorough audits of a member's financial situation, including its domestic monetary and fiscal policies.[130]

This was a dramatic announcement. In effect, Overby was proclaiming that a highly controversial principle of international governance become a routine matter: making the monetary and fiscal policies of sovereign states the objects of external inspection and potentially intervention. Recognizing the thin interpretative ice on which he was walking, Overby insisted that other members of the Board avoid taking "a narrow or legalistic viewpoint towards the powers of the Fund" and the Articles of Agreement, which were full of "unresolved compromises."[131] British representatives breathed a sigh of relief when discussion of this memorandum was put aside. But they recognized that the question was likely to be raised again when countries like India made requests for accessing the Fund's resources.[132] They thus continued to insist that the IMF mind its own business, since it had no knowledge of the internal political conditions of its member states nor any right to interfere with them.[133] But in September, a Chilean request for drawings was met with the demand that it confirm it was implementing sound fiscal and monetary policies, leading to a renewed round of controversy.[134] Any assumption that the IMF would grant automatic drawing rights was buried with the promulgation of the Marshall Plan in early 1948. Overby successfully pushed the IMF to clarify that no countries in receipt of US assistance could exercise drawing rights. To the British, this policy indicated that a dramatic change to the Articles of Agreement had taken place without any formal process of amendment. There were no grounds in the IMF's Articles of Agreement for this decision, they claimed. The US violation of automatic drawings was threatening to distort the "whole machinery of the Fund."[135]

It was not in Europe where stricter policies of conditionality were developed, however, but in countries that had already long been subject to external intervention in their economies. The first was Mexico, which turned to the IMF for assistance during a serious exchange crisis in 1948–1949. The Fund clarified that Mexico would be able to draw only if it committed to the "appropriate" policies of fiscal and credit restraint.[136] In the years to come, as Mexico received further assistance from the Bretton Woods institutions, the country became an important site of experimentation. Mexican officials and central bankers came to see the value in discipline imposed from the outside. They framed IMF demands in ways that provided political cover for unpopular policies—a tactic that had been used by governments in receipt of conditional loans since the first Austrian bailout.[137] In the short-run, the 1948–1949 Mexican exchange crisis demonstrated that the IMF, just a few years after its founding, could make domestic fiscal and monetary policies criteria for drawings. This was a sign of things to come.[138] In May 1949, the new US Executive Director Frank A. Southard clarified that members drawing on Fund resources could expect to be "subject to close scrutiny." Any doubts would be resolved in favor of the IMF.[139] Furious British representatives emphasized that Parliament had only ratified the Bretton Woods agreements in 1945 on the assumption that this would not happen. The British people would never "tolerate interference by the Fund in our affairs."[140] Interpretation of the Articles of Agreement had been pushed so far that their words were losing their meaning.[141] But it was also now obvious that any reference to the Articles as "holy writ" was unlikely to convince the Americans.[142] Making matters worse was the obvious fact, as one British memo put it, that these Articles were "full of barely intelligible compromises between violently opposed points of view."[143]

Thereafter, the IMF was sidelined from a central role in Europe's reconstruction. In 1949, when Britain enacted a large unilateral devaluation of sterling, it did so without asking for permission from the IMF. Some have claimed that this decision showed that the Bretton Woods system, if it ever existed at all, was effectively dead on arrival.[144] There is some truth to this view. At the very least, the fact that Western European currencies were not made fully convertible until 1958, and the dollar's peg to gold was removed in 1971, meant that this system had a much shorter lifespan than is often acknowledged. While there were few drawings in 1950–1951, however—in part due to the conditions attached to them—the IMF was never completely put into a deepfreeze. In just a few years, its activities expanded significantly.[145] The quarrels about its powers at the dawn of the Cold War thus had real consequences for its evolution. Now that automaticity was a dead letter, the efforts of Keynes's heirs continued to focus on mitigating the dangers of the Fund "interfering extensively in general economic policies of applicants" for drawings.[146] But it was clear there would be no universal rule against this. For example, Australia had been able to draw without strings being attached, but there was little chance that the US Treasury and Congress would allow countries like Ethiopia the same unconditional access to the US dollar.[147]

Some scholars have asked how the IMF could have so quickly departed from the "embedded liberal" consensus of its origins, well before the rise of neoliberalism or the birth of the Washington Consensus.[148] But there should be little surprise that the IMF began to wield leverage over the policies of member states soon after the Second World War, particularly those in the Global South, whose claims to full sovereign equality were never as powerful as those of the North.[149] Republican members of Congress had insisted during the war that the Fund could not be allowed to grant unconditional access to US dollars. This view was never contradicted by the US Treasury. After ratification of the agreements, there was no longer as much pressure to play down its powers. The powerful US banks that had pushed for an interventionist Fund during the war would gradually see their designs incorporated into its practices.[150] It is true that the scope of conditionality was more limited at this time than it would be later. But the introduction of even this limited form of "inquisition" represented a significant departure from the arrangements that most governments thought they were signing up to in 1944–1945. The IMF was formally prevented from intervening in its members' domestic political affairs. But nowhere in the Articles of Agreement was a robust doctrine of non-interference spelled out. Nor were there were any guarantees that one of the widely shared wartime assumptions about the Fund's limits would become a general rule: that it stay away from domestic spending.[151] It turned out that little was preventing budgets from being targeted, as long as this was not done in an overtly political manner. Whatever principle of embedded liberalism existed, it did not have universal applicability, if this meant a right for all members to protection from external pressures to adjust internal policies in specific ways. During the 1950s, as the IMF further clarified how it could influence such policies, these practices were generally limited to Latin America. As we have seen, across many different states, and in many different contexts, the idea that such insulation was a natural concomitant of sovereignty had never in practice been a rule of conduct in a hierarchical international system. As the interventionist powers of the IMF evolved, the institution's US government backers defended these powers in the same terms used by the British to promote the League's financial activities in the 1920s: It was easier for a sovereign state to accept the counsel of an international institution than that of a foreign government directly.[152]

The nature of US power in the IMF ultimately ensured its US executive directors would get the interpretation of the Articles they wanted in the face of pressure from US public and private actors.[153] In the early 1950s, Burgess himself—the ringleader of wartime Wall Street opponents to Bretton Woods—became undersecretary of the US Treasury. There, he greenlit the IMF's move to the stricter policies he had advocated in the 1940s.[154] Such facts can be downplayed in efforts to understand the precise meaning of the Articles of Agreement or to find documentary proof of what the US Treasury was thinking in 1943–1944. Accounts of the IMF as being born with a "jurisdictional barrier" that separated the domestic and the international thus risk exaggerating that barrier's impermeability.[155] The exasperation of British representatives in the early years of the IMF was not due to any complexity of interpreting the legal meaning of its constitution, but because the extremity of US power did not allow for any fixed meaning of it at all. As one member of the Board of Trade wrote in early 1950:

> U.S. representatives in IMF are carrying further the process of getting "interpretations" of the Agreement which over ride or over-elaborate the actual text, and are now seeking to establish, in effect, that no-one can exercise their drawing rights without U.S. approval, which might be conditional on the member concerned adopting measures of internal financial policy which the U.S. thought desirable.[156]

In 1950, it was no longer news that this had been the strategy of US representatives. What was new at this point was that the struggle to ensure its members' enjoyed a full right to non-interference was losing steam. Soon, the evolution of new lending practices at the IMF, the so-called "stand-by arrangement"—which allowed for conditions to be placed on drawings that exceeded a certain percentage of a member's quota—would provide more leverage than ever over economic policies once considered to be exclusively domestic. It was not the first time that this had happened. Nor would it be the last.[157]

Conclusion

WHEN THE IMF BEGAN making its first conditional loans during the Cold War, it faced questions about its legitimacy similar to those asked of prior experiments in global economic governance. How could the domestic economies of formally sovereign states be opened to outside intervention in ways that were compatible with self-determination and were reproducible as tools of international cooperation? What criteria would be used to decide which countries merited full protection from this interference, and would this rule apply equally to empires and postcolonial states? What, in the end, would be considered an exclusively domestic issue—and who would get to decide?

These were questions that would persist throughout the rest of the twentieth century and into the twenty-first. But as this book has shown, they first became controversial political matters at the end of the First World War, due to the particular conditions of the conflict and its settlement. The first industrialized war on a global scale led to the creation of intergovernmental controls over global exchange that offered new ways of wielding strategic power and fulfilling various internationalist aims. But at war's end, international economic cooperation took on unexpected forms. Among the powerful Allied empires and the United States, long-standing prohibitions against the involvement of foreign actors in domestic economic policy returned with a vengeance. When the League of Nations developed an Economic and Financial Organization, it was designed only to coordinate the policies of existing government agencies. It could not impose any authority over them. The meekness of this power became evident in the realm of trade policy, as the League proved unable to compel member governments to reduce tariffs. But in other areas of economic policy, and largely in places weakened by the war or on the margins of the global capitalist economy, the League and several other international institutions were able to exercise significant powers over domestic policy-making. As European and US bankers, national officials pursuing various strategic aims, and imperial authorities attempting to stabilize colonies came to see the value of such institutions, they helped to broaden their powers. Austerity programs were enforced, an independent central banking institution was established, and experiments with development and the regulation of commodity prices were conducted. These innovations all formed the first wave of international economic institution-building that set the backdrop to the creation of an even more powerful set of institutions in the 1940s.

These first international economic institutions were designed to stabilize a world economy fractured by the Great War and its aftermath and to protect the fragile international settlement put into place in 1919. Yet they pursued distinct political aims. Some were designed to facilitate a return to liberal pre-1914 orthodoxies, whereas others involved interventionist forms of planning. Some were concerned exclusively with banking functions, others with controlling the production and exchange of raw materials. However, this book has argued that the emergence of these institutions after the First World War was part of a shared phenomenon—not least because they involved a relatively small set of actors, many sitting at the intersection of British and US public and private power. Contemporaries recognized the emergence of these institutions as part of the same trend: toward increasing international control over global exchange. Over time, these institutions collectively came to exercise a new kind of international power. By the beginning of the twenty-first century, this power had acquired a name: It became common to refer to a bundle of public and private institutions targeting diverse realms of economic policy-making—including trade, central banking, development, and financial regulation—as instruments of global economic governance.

During the interwar years, each of these new institutions faced similar challenges of implementation in a highly competitive world of empire, uneven sovereignty, mass politics, and interstate rivalries. Each innovation of their powers was met with resistance that usually took a specific form: opposition to the opening of supposedly insulated domestic spaces to "foreign interference." These anxieties about interference were mobilized by different public and private actors for different agendas—by liberals, the left, and the right, and for the sake of empire and its undoing. This charge was so resonant because it spoke to what many recognized to be underlying realities of the international order of this era: first, that the formal sovereignty of most states was an insufficient guarantor of their autonomy, status, and power; and second, that international institutions dealing with economic problems were likely to expand their powers into domestic arenas instead of restricting their focus to inter-state relations. The question was whether the sacrifices of sovereignty demanded by the governance of the world economy were like those that came from any international treaty or whether they involved more demanding forms of intervention in internal political, distributional, and strategic affairs. Many internationalists at this time recognized that political opposition to the latter prospect jeopardized the chances for international cooperation. When the IMF was established, some of its designers hoped it would allay fears of interference and set international economic governance on surer footing—not least, because the junior partner in this arrangement, the British Empire, now faced the prospect of more external involvement in its own internal affairs than ever before. But soon the IMF grew more demanding as well, damaging its legitimacy in the process.

The aftermath of the First World War has been remembered for many things: the rise of claims to self-determination around the world, the expansion and destabilization of Europe's colonial empires, the radicalization of politics on both the right and left, and the international economic and security problems that led to the outbreak of the Depression and another world war. It is less well remembered for the transformations of sovereignty inaugurated by these early forms of global economic governance. In the face of new forms of mass politics and interstate rivalries, these institutions went to great lengths to handle the political fallout of the specter of their meddling in the affairs of others—in ways that permanently reshaped the landscape of global politics.

The history told in this book about institutional design, implementation, and legitimation provides a distinctive lens for making sense of transformations in the global order wrought by the First World War and its aftermath. The degree of interference tolerated by the government of a sovereign state showed its relative standing in this new order. Sovereign countries that had suffered under foreign controls of one form or another before the war, such as Albania, China, and Greece, were expected to countenance new ones afterward. They would not do so lightly. Countries on the losing side of the war—Austria, Bulgaria, Germany, and Hungary—were forced to acquiesce to a lower standing and to restricted forms of sovereignty. These countries became laboratories for two of the great experiments of the interwar period: making loans conditional on austerity and externally imposing central bank independence. These practices tracked and reproduced ideas of racial and civilizational hierarchy. Formerly great European powers that saw their budgets and assets being opened to external intervention were said to be reduced to the level of "distressed" or "underdeveloped" states like Egypt, China, and Turkey. Sovereign countries in Latin America and the Caribbean that had not suffered under foreign financial controls or joined the Central Powers during the war—but had long faced the interference of foreign businesses, banks, and governments in their economies—similarly sought to defend themselves from new challenges to their autonomy.

On the next rung of the ladder of global hierarchies were powerful European empires and former Allies, like Britain and France. But even their claims to a right to non-interference were in flux during this period. The unique place of Britain in this history, as both enforcer and target of international governance, makes this clear. The British Empire was the key underwriter of most of these new interwar institutions. But beginning with the Second World War, Britain faced the prospect of more outside involvement in its internal political economy than ever before. Soon after the Bretton Woods agreements were reached, it became clear that the IMF would develop intrusive powers of conditional lending like the League before it. The Germans and Austrians had described the threat of being subordinated to Britain and France in the wake of the First World War with metaphors of Anglo-French financial imperialism from the nineteenth century. In the 1940s, the British confronted the prospect of their new global status by comparing the risks they faced from a rising US hegemon to those long confronted by Latin American countries subject to dollar diplomacy. It was "one thing to interfere with a country like Bolivia," as one US journalist described this inversion of hierarchies, but "quite another for our Government to set itself up as a moral judge of how France or another Power shall spend money."[1] At the apex of global power, the United States never made the same sacrifices of sovereignty outside the contexts of war, even in pursuit of internationalist aims.

For those who supported their creation, the first international economic institutions had particular appeal in an age of increasing claims to national self-determination. They were designed to replace older practices of foreign bondholder control and financial imperialism with ones said to be compatible with the ideal of sovereign equality. But this did not mean that older practices disappeared. During the interwar period, US bankers, businesses, and officials continued to exercise direct powers over Latin American and Caribbean countries. Formal and informal European empire persisted for decades. While membership in these institutions was itself said to transform coercive forms of interference into voluntary acts of delegation, the reality was seldom so straightforward. Formal sovereignty was rarely sufficient to protect weaker, poorer, and recently independent or defeated states from facing external pressures to adapt and reform in ways that were unpopular with domestic constituencies.

As a result, these institutions always became lightning rods for a particular form of oppositional politics, grounded in the defense of a polity from unwanted meddling. Because the charge of interference was typically directed at an international institution making discretionary judgments, it was distinct to the resistance posed to the disciplinary pressures of the gold standard. Unlike the gold standard, international institutions could target a broad array of policies—concerning taxation, public spending, trade, and industrial and primary production. It was not only workers, farmers, and the parties that represented their interests that resisted the reach of these institutions. Capitalists and bankers also opposed constraints on their autonomy in the powerful language of antagonism to the outsider. So did anti-democratic mass political movements, particularly on the xenophobic far right. Taken together, the political force of these charges defined political limits to international cooperation during the interwar period and well afterward.

After 1945, the power of self-determination and the role of governments in providing public goods and managing national economies made older forms of interference appear yet more anachronistic. At this point, a limited form of globalization was supposedly reconciled with national economic policies and representative government in a new and more stable synthesis. But older tensions between sovereignty and the governance of global capitalism were not decisively resolved. There was no golden age of national autonomy and sovereign equality after 1945, certainly not beyond the Global North.

Interference and Autonomy during the Era of Bretton Woods

In the wake of the Second World War, a new wave of international economic institution-building accelerated. Various new bodies were founded, wielding distinct powers and toward different ends. In addition to the

Bretton Woods institutions and the General Agreement on Tariffs and Trade (GATT) the United Nations created an Economic and Social Council, which in 1964 was complemented by the United Nations Conference on Trade and Development. In 1948, the Organisation for European Economic Co-operation was established in Paris to help implement the Marshall Plan. It was expanded in 1961 to include non-European countries and renamed the Organisation for Economic Cooperation and Development.[2] The European Coal and Steel Community was established in 1952, followed by the European Economic Community in 1957. Some of these institutions had direct links to interwar predecessors, often through specific individuals. It was no coincidence that Jean Monnet was centrally involved in early processes of European integration, designing the European Coal and Steel Community and serving as its first president. Some alumni of institutions like the League of Nations and Bank for International Settlements had long and influential careers at the IMF.

These institutions continued to wrestle with the long-standing problems of legitimation charted in this book. This struggle is evident in the evolution of IMF conditional lending. For several years after the Bretton Woods Conference, as we have seen, British and Western European representatives in the IMF continued to assume it would operate according to Keynes's vision of member states having automatic access to its resources, without any scrutiny of their domestic policies. Avoiding the prospect of such a "grand-motherly" Fund had been a US concession to the British to facilitate passage of the Bretton Woods agreements in Parliament. But once they were passed, there were fewer repercussions to linking access to the IMF's resources to demands on members' monetary and fiscal policies. Partly to break out of the deadlock caused by disputes over this question, the IMF developed a new approach to lending in 1952, the so-called "stand-by arrangement." This provided a legal mechanism to attach policy conditions to a member's access to funds beyond a certain amount. It is unsurprising that these conditions were, at first, more demanding in traditional sites of US and European informal empire, particularly in Latin America. For these countries, austere fiscal policy and contractionary monetary policies, designed to balance budgets and arrest inflation, were the strings attached to assistance. Pushing these policies was the IMF's Managing Director Per Jacobsson, a Swedish economist who had begun his long international career in the Economic and Financial Section of the League of Nations in 1920, before joining the Bank for International Settlements in 1931, where he remained until 1956.[3] In 1958, a stand-by arrangement with Paraguay involved the IMF's first set of binding conditions, which included demands on Paraguayan monetary and fiscal policies and public works programs.[4] In 1959, another interventionist stand-by arrangement was reached with Haiti, the second oldest sovereign republic in the Western Hemisphere, but one that had been subject since its founding to extensive European and US meddling. European representatives worried that the IMF was setting a dangerous precedent and feared similar powers could be brought to bear on their own countries. But for the time being, such powers were generally limited in their greatest extent to the so-called "developing world," even as Western European countries like Britain, France, and Italy made use of Fund resources. Outside Europe, further fiscal and monetary conditions were placed on drawings for countries from Honduras to Chile.[5] The World Bank also gradually linked its aid to specific policies: trade liberalization, financial stabilization, the passage of laws encouraging private investment, and the repayment of foreign debts.[6]

It is true that the Bretton Woods system allowed some countries greater autonomy to pursue Keynesian and welfarist national policies than had been possible under the classical gold standard. These institutions also moved away from the more overtly imperialistic practices of earlier eras. They only worked, after all, at the invitation of a member state.[7] This fact was frequently invoked to defend the interventionist policies of the Bretton Woods institutions, in a reprise of the same argument made about the financial activities of the League of Nations in the 1920s.[8] But such legalistic claims often downplayed the vast differences in power that existed between creditors and debtors—particularly ones in extreme financial distress—and the consequences for the latter of rejecting the demands of the former. The leverage wielded by the IMF increased dramatically when private banks began to make their own loans conditional on recipients having a stand-by arrangement with the IMF, which became the ultimate "seal of approval" in international markets.[9] In effect, this turned the IMF into the final arbiter of many countries' credit and access to foreign capital. Agreeing to these sacrifices of sovereignty was often a useful strategy for domestic factions in their struggles for power. But once interference was invited, it could be very difficult to later escape.[10]

The gradual development of the powers of the Bretton Woods institutions to target domestic economic policies during the Cold War should be seen as the culmination of an important transformation in practices of international governance that had begun decades before. As the IMF innovated forms of conditional lending, it did not violate any clear rules about the limits of its jurisdictional reach established during the Second World War. Instead, it drew on its obvious latent powers, ones that the most influential US banks had always insisted it should wield. From the vantage point of the IMF, embedded liberalism was not a universal doctrine, if this meant guarantees of a robust degree of autonomy for all countries seeking its assistance.

The IMF made demands on the domestic policies and institutions of its members unevenly by design. While the gold standard had required fiscal and monetary discipline for its maintenance, the rules of gold applied to any country that adhered to it. International institutions, by contrast, could adjust the pressure they put on countries according to their perceived power, status, and strategic significance.[11] This was made clear in 1967, when Britain was granted a $1.4 billion stand-by arrangement with more lenient terms than most borrowers in the "developing world" enjoyed. Fearful of the political consequences of accepting conditions, British officials claimed that the United Kingdom was entitled to a degree of insulation that other countries were not. Conditionality was fine, one wrote, for "the Argentine or a lesser-developed African country," but not for a former hegemon.[12] While Britain had drawn on the IMF's resources on several occasions since the mid-1950s, these stand-by arrangements had come with fewer strings attached than those for other members, particularly in Latin America.[13] This differential treatment was criticized by representatives of countries subject to stricter policing. This dispute over impartiality led to clarification of the rules for conditional lending. But it also resulted in these powers being written into an amended Articles of Agreement, which had initially lacked clear guidance on conditionality.[14] By this point, there was no longer any question that Keynes's fears had come to pass. In 1976, the IMF applied much greater pressure on the British government, when the offer of a $3.9 billion loan to stabilize the pound came with demands that the Labour government of James Callaghan enact austere reforms over vocal opposition in London. While these conditions were still not as far-reaching as the IMF insisted on elsewhere, that they were being applied to an elected British government was a potent symbol of the culmination of a long-term process of British decline. After this episode, few countries in the Global North turned to the IMF for help.[15]

When the dollar's peg to gold was removed in 1971—inaugurating the breakdown of a Bretton Woods system that had only, in practice, been operational for a little over a decade—the IMF's conditional lending practices expanded in scope. This was opposed by the governments of Global South countries and their representatives, who objected to the restrictions that these practices imposed on domestic policies and the unevenness of their application. Throughout the Cold War, as many states gained independence from colonial empires, their governments invoked the old principle of non-interference to ensure that formal sovereignty translated into autonomy and economic self-determination. The Ghanaian intellectual and Prime Minister Kwame Nkrumah, for example, famously defined neo-colonialism as "foreign interference in the affairs of developing countries."[16] In the 1960s and 1970s, representatives of Third World countries in the United Nations successfully pushed for several resolutions to affirm the right of all states to non-intervention, whether this was to prevent the armed incursions of the Cold War superpowers or unwanted economic meddling.[17] The movement for a New International Economic Order of the early 1970s also made one of its principal aims the defense of the principle of "non-interference in the internal affairs of other States."[18] Instead of joining a Westphalian world of nation-states enjoying equal rights to autonomy, many of these new postcolonial states found themselves in an international order of highly unequal sovereignties, in which real economic self-determination was not secured by formal independence or legal status.[19] They shared obvious similarities to the successor states of the Ottoman, Austro-Hungarian, and Russian empires, which after the First World War had become workshops for the first interventionist experiments in global economic governance.

During the Third World sovereign debt crisis of the 1980s, the reach of the IMF and the World Bank into the domestic affairs of some member states broadened dramatically, moving beyond fiscal and monetary questions to include major structural reforms as well: privatization, trade liberalization, deregulation, the imposition of central bank independence, and changes to social policies and labor laws. Unlike the gold standard of an earlier era, which had also resulted in a narrowing of national "policy-space," the scope of this expanded form of IMF conditionality in principle knew no limits.[20] While the myth of the automatic adjustments made possible by the gold standard can be exaggerated, the gold standard did not rely on international institutions staffed by officials making decisions on the basis of inescapably political criteria. Moving from the painful regularity of a metallic standard to the uncertain judgments of these officials was, to be sure, a step that for some countries promised an escape from an international monetary regime that weakened labor, pre-vented national welfare programs or expansive macroeconomic policies, and enshrined the rule of bankers over elected governments. Abandoning gold was necessary to allow democracy to bloom and the power of labor to be realized more fully in national politics.

But leaving the gold standard did not, on its own, guarantee that the autonomy of all countries would be respected by institutions that, despite their claims to neutrality, exercised power in ways that reproduced and entrenched global hierarchies. Even with the Bretton Woods institutions' formal prohibitions on political lending, conditional lending was always marked by decisions that could not, by their very nature, be depoliticized. Judgments about a government's creditworthiness were inherently po-litical: how it raised and spent money, managed exchange rates and cur-rency, and handled private property. Making external sources of capital available to some sectors of an economy had distributional consequences and affected the balance of power among different domestic actors. Most of all, fiscal performance criteria targeted some of the most intimate in-ternal matters of a sovereign state. The Bretton Woods institutions were also mobilized for strategic aims soon after their creation. In particular, the World Bank played an important role in propping up US Cold War allies and encouraging countries to defect from the Soviet bloc.[21] In 1991, a seventy-seven-year-old Jacques Polak—who, after leaving the League of Nations, worked at the IMF until the late 1970s—admitted that there was an "unwritten rule" at the Fund that political decisions had to, as much as possible, be "dressed up in economic garb."[22]

Interference and Autonomy in the Twenty-First Century

By the end of the Cold War, the IMF—deeply involved in the transition of nearly every formerly communist country to capitalism—had become, as one scholar has put it, the "most powerful international institution in history."[23] During the 1997 Asian financial crisis, IMF-led bailouts came with demands for major domestic reforms, leading to a new groundswell of global criticism.[24] Afterward, many countries built up their dollar re-serves to insure themselves against financial instability without needing to turn to the IMF.[25] At the turn of the twenty-first century, as the aus-terity demanded by bailouts led to protests and even violent conflicts, and as more national governments refused to follow the IMF script, the global reputation of the Bretton Woods institutions plummeted. But predictions that they were on their last legs proved to be false. While there was less IMF lending in the 2000s than before, the loans that were made continued to come with strings attached. In the wake of the 2008 global financial crisis, the IMF oversaw austerity policies in countries like Greece. But notably it was not invited back to the countries where it had made such intrusive demands in the 1990s, including Russia, South Korea, Mexico, and Indonesia. The IMF's return to Europe was controversial. "The IMF is not for Europe," the French President Nicolas Sarkozy insisted in 2010, openly giving voice to a view that was more quietly held by others. "It's for Africa—it's for Burkina Faso!"[26] Mindful of the institution's poor reputation, some IMF officials now claimed that its help came with fewer conditions. But when conditions were made more lenient, it was usually because the country in receipt of loans had already undertaken the extensive liberalizing reforms that had previously been asked of it.[27]

Similar interventionist powers were also developed by the WTO, which had in 1995 replaced the more limited international trade regime of GATT. GATT had been designed to deal with outright barriers to trade in goods and was run by a weak secretariat. But the WTO was a powerful intergovernmental organization, whose scope extended to many domains of domestic regulation and law concerning health and safety issues, the environment, and business standards.[28] The institutions of the European Union also faced a steady drumbeat of criticisms for wielding powers that were not democratically legitimated.[29] Critics on the left and right argued that these institutions pressured representative governments into ceding control over a traditional act of sovereign power: regulating the economic livelihoods of the populations residing within their territorial borders.[30]

Not all of these diagnoses suggested the need to give up on global governance altogether. Instead, they pointed to the importance of searching for resolutions to the deep contradictions it has always involved. Insofar as international economic institutions continued to be linked to practices of informal empire, the internationalist visions they were supposed to embody were difficult for many to accept at face value. When they unevenly wielded more leverage over some governments than others, their proclamations of being universal institutions rang hollow. The already considerable task of legitimating international cooperation was made yet more difficult by the fact that these institutions clearly provided a way for some governments and private interests to pressure others into accepting their designs. A vision of global economic governance that embodied principles of impartiality, equality, and representative decision-making went unrealized. Asymmetries of power had been built into these institutions from the start.

The history told in this book suggests that the challenges of global governance in the early twenty-first century are more significant than what is implied by stylized histories of embedded liberalism and its collapse into neoliberalism. There was no stable era of mid-twentieth-century autonomy that can be easily recaptured. Since they first appeared in 1918, international economic institutions have always been accused of being meddlers. And they have always been closely linked to the prerogatives of empires. Unlike international bodies tasked with preventing squabbling foreign ministries from declaring war, their work involved reaching deeply into contentious domestic issues. Even when limits were placed on their power, these institutions tended over time to become more interventionist, as their decisions reverberated across many levels of the political, social, and economic life of states and empires. In part, this was due to the nature of capitalist interdependence itself. Economic decisions made on local levels produce macro effects in the aggregate, both national and global, and economic decisions taken on the grandest scales ramify on the most local levels through the forces of supply, demand, and prices. As global economic governance evolved, it continually involved moving beyond the borders of states and empires down to these local levels, touching intimate questions of distribution, politics, labor, production, and identity. The scope of this power made it very difficult to legitimate and ensured that this form of international governance was more likely to generate resistance than others. One of the greatest challenges for internationalists has always been to convince states to relinquish some sovereignty for the sake of international cooperation, while at the same time affirming the existence of a domain that belonged to the state alone. These efforts were continually jeopardized when this interior realm was chipped away at, not for collective purposes, but for the sake of private profits and the strategic aims of competing states. These efforts were also jeopardized by the fact that these sacrifices were not demanded of all states, but instead only of ones that occupied a subordinate position in the global order.

That this problem, in various forms, has persisted for more than a century suggests that tweaks to existing international institutions, like the IMF or World Bank, may be insufficient to produce a more stable reconciliation of global governance and democratic politics. But this very insufficiency might also spur ambitious thinking about how to design a new architecture of international cooperation that goes beyond the institutions of the twentieth century and the legacies of empire. A retreat to nation-alist policies is dangerously unsuitable for the global problems of the twenty-first century. But it is also clear that governing the world economy needs to be dramatically rethought if it is to be made fully compatible, for the first time, with real economic self-determination and democratic self-governance—and for all states, regardless of their histories of sovereignty and imagined standings in a hierarchical global order.

ABBREVIATIONS

NOTES

ACKNOWLEDGMENTS

INDEX

ABBREVIATIONS

In-text Abbreviations

BIS	Bank for International Settlements
CDFC	China Development Finance Corporation
FMS	Federated Malay States
GATT	General Agreement on Tariffs and Trade
IFC	International Financial Commission (Greece)
ILO	International Labour Organization
IMF	International Monetary Fund
ITC	International Tin Committee
NEC	National Economic Council (China)
OPEC	Organization of the Petroleum Exporting Countries
RSC	Refugee Settlement Commission
SEC	Supreme Economic Council
UN	United Nations
WTO	World Trade Organization

Archives

AEFP	Arthur Elliott Felkin Papers, King's College Archives, University of Cambridge
ASP	Arthur Sweetser Papers, Library of Congress, Washington, DC
AYP	Arthur Young Papers, Hoover Institution Library and Archives, Stanford, CA
AZP	Alfred Zimmern Papers, Bodleian Library, University of Oxford

BIS	Bank for International Settlements Archives, Basel
BOE	Bank of England Archives, London
BOF	Banque de France Archives, Paris
BSP	Benjamin Strong Papers, Federal Reserve Bank of New York
CAP	Chandler Anderson Papers, Library of Congress, Washington, DC
CHAR	Winston Churchill Archives, Churchill Archives Centre, University of Cambridge
CHP	Charles Howland Papers, Yale University Manuscripts and Archives, New Haven, CT
CSAP	Charles Stewart Addis Papers, School of Oriental and African Studies (SOAS) Archives, University of London
EGP	Edwin Gay Papers, Hoover Institution Library and Archives. Stanford, CA
EHP	Edward Hunt Papers, Hoover Institution Library and Archives. Stanford, CA
EMHLP	E. M. H. Lloyd Papers, London School of Economics Library Archives and Special Collections, London
FNA	French National Archives, Paris
GHP	George Harrison Papers, Federal Reserve Bank of New York
GSP	George Schuster Papers, Bodleian Library, University of Oxford
HMSP	Henry Morgenthau, Sr. Papers, Library of Congress, Washington, DC
HSBC	HSBC Archives, London
IAFC	Inter-Allied Food Council, Hoover Institution Library and Archives. Stanford, CA
ILO	International Labour Organization Archives, Geneva
IMF	Archives of the International Monetary Fund, Washington, DC
IOR	India Office Records, British Library, London
JMKP	John Maynard Keynes Papers, King's College Archives, University of Cambridge
JMP	Jean Monnet Papers, Fondation Jean Monnet pour l'Europe, Lausanne
LON	League of Nations Archives, United Nations Library, Geneva
LRP	Ludwik Rajchman Papers, Louis Pasteur Institute Archives, Paris
MEP	Marriner Eccles Papers, University of Utah, Salt Lake City, UT
NAI	National Archives of India, New Delhi
NARA	US National Archives and Records Administration, College Park, MD

NBP   Newton Baker Papers, Library of Congress, Washington, DC

RFA   Rockefeller Archive Center, Sleepy Hollow, NY

SALT   Arthur Salter Papers, Churchill Archives Centre, University of Cambridge

TLP   Thomas Lamont Papers, Baker Library, Harvard Business School, Cambridge, MA

TNA   British National Archives, London

WWP   Woodrow Wilson Papers, Library of Congress, Washington, DC

Publications

FRUS   *Foreign Relations of the United States*

FRUS PPC   *Foreign Relations of the United States, Paris Peace Conference*

LON OJ   *League of Nations, Official Journal*

LON OJ SS   *League of Nations. Official Journal, Special Supplement*

NOTES

Introduction

1. For histories of the Bretton Woods agreements, see Richard N. Gardner, *Sterling-Dollar Diplomacy: Anglo-American Collaboration in the Reconstruction of Multilateral Trade* (Oxford: Clarendon Press, 1956); Alfred J. Eckes, Jr., *A Search for Solvency: Bretton Woods and the International Monetary System, 1941–1971* (Austin, TX: University of Texas Press, 1975); Armand Van Dormael, *Bretton Woods: Birth of a Monetary System* (London: Macmillan, 1978); Harold James, *International Monetary Cooperation since Bretton Woods* (Washington, DC: International Monetary Fund, 1996); Elizabeth Borgwardt, *A New Deal for the World: America's Vision for Human Rights* (Cambridge, MA: Harvard University Press, 2005); Benn Steil, *The Battle of Bretton Woods: John Maynard Keynes, Harry Dexter White, and the Making of a New World Order* (Princeton, NJ: Princeton University Press, 2013); Eric Helleiner, *The Forgotten Foundations of Bretton Woods: International Development and the Making of the Postwar Order* (Ithaca, NY: Cornell University Press, 2014); Ed Conway, *The Summit: Bretton Woods, 1944: J. M. Keynes and the Reshaping of the Global Economy* (New York: Pegasus, 2015); Giles Scot-Smith and J. Simon Rofe, eds., *Global Perspectives on the Bretton Woods Conference and the Post-War World Order* (London: Palgrave Macmillan, 2017); Naomi Lamoreaux and Ian Shapiro, eds., *The Bretton Woods Agreements* (New Haven, CT: Yale University Press, 2019). For histories of GATT, see Thomas Zeiler, *Free Trade, Free World: The Advent of GATT* (Chapel Hill, NC: University of North Carolina Press, 1999); Richard Toye, "Developing Multilateralism: The Havana Charter and the Fight for the International Trade Organization, 1947–1948," *The International History Review* 25.2 (2003): 282–305; Petros C. Mavroidis, Douglas A. Irwin, and Alan O. Sykes, *The Genesis of the GATT* (Cambridge: Cambridge University Press, 2009); Francine McKenzie, *GATT and Global Order in the Postwar Era* (Cambridge: Cambridge University Press, 2020).

2. For the development of modern capitalism in light of the national political, legal, and institutional systems that gave it structure, particularly in the United States, see, for example, Sven Beckert, *The Monied Metropolis: New York City and the Consolidation of the American Bourgeoisie, 1850–1896* (Cambridge: Cambridge University Press, 2001); Bethany Moreton, *To Serve God and Wal-Mart: The Making of Christian Free Enterprise* (Cambridge: Harvard University Press, 2009); Julia Ott, *When Wall Street Met Main Street: The Quest for an Investors' Democracy* (Cambridge, MA: Harvard University Press, 2011); Jonathan Levy, *Freaks of Fortune: The Emerging World of Capitalism and Risk in America* (Cambridge, MA: Harvard University Press,

2012); Walter Johnson, *River of Dark Dreams: Slavery and Empire in the Cotton Kingdom* (Cambridge, MA: Harvard University Press, 2013); Jürgen Kocka and Marcel van der Linden, eds., *Capitalism: The Reemergence of a Historical Concept* (London: Bloomsbury, 2016); Noam Maggor, *Brahmin Capitalism: Frontiers of Wealth and Populism in America's First Gilded Age* (Cambridge: MA: Harvard University Press, 2017); Sven Beckert and Christine Desan, *American Capitalism: New Histories* (New York: Columbia University Press, 2018); Stefan Link and Noam Maggor, "The United States as a Developing Nation: Revisiting the Peculiarities of American History," *Past and Present* 246.1 (2020): 269–306. Relatedly, see Christof Dejung and Niels P. Petersson, eds., *The Foundations of Worldwide Economic Integration: Power, Institutions, and Global Markets, 1850–1930* (Cambridge: Cambridge University Press, 2013).

3. For recent additions to a vast literature on the rise of self-determination and nationalism out of the collapse of these empires, see, for example, Erez Manela, *The Wilsonian Moment: Self-Determination and the International Origins of Anticolonial Nationalism* (Oxford: Oxford University Press, 2007); Tara Zahra, *Kidnapped Souls: National Indifference and the Battle for Children in the Bohemian Lands, 1900–1948* (Ithaca, NY: Cornell University Press, 2011); Joshua A. Sanborn, *Imperial Apocalypse: The Great War and the Destruction of the Russian Empire* (Oxford: Oxford University Press, 2014); Eric. D. Weitz, "Self-Determination: How a German Enlightenment Idea Became the Slogan of National Liberation and a Human Right," *American Historical Review* 120.2 (2015): 462–496; Pieter M. Judson, *The Habsburg Empire: A New History* (Cambridge, MA: Harvard University Press, 2016); Volker Prott, *The Politics of Self-Determination: Remaking Territories and National Identities in Europe, 1917–1923* (Oxford: Oxford University Press, 2016); Dominique Kirchner Reill, *The Fiume Crisis: Life in the Wake of the Habsburg Empire* (Cambridge, MA: Harvard University Press, 2020); Larry Wolff, *Woodrow Wilson and the Reimagining of Eastern Europe* (Stanford: Stanford University Press, 2020); Tara Zahra, "Against the World: The Collapse of Empire and the Deglobalization of Interwar Austria," *Austrian History Yearbook* 52 (2021): 1–10.

4. See, above all, Charles S. Maier, *Recasting Bourgeois Europe: Stabilization in France, Germany, and Italy in the Decade after World War I* (Princeton, NJ: Princeton University Press, 1975).

5. See, especially, W. Arthur Lewis, *The Evolution of the International Economic Order* (Princeton, NJ: Princeton University Press, 1978); Kevin H. O'Rourke and Jeffrey G. Williamson, *Globalization and History: The Evolution of a Nineteenth-Century Atlantic Economy* (Cambridge, MA: MIT Press, 1999); Ronald Findlay and Kevin H. O'Rourke, *Power and Plenty: Trade, War, and the World Economy in the Second Millennium* (Princeton, NJ: Princeton University Press, 2009), 365–428; Jeffrey G. Williamson, *Trade and Poverty: When the Third World Fell Behind* (Cambridge, MA: MIT Press, 2013); Steven C. Topik and Allen Wells, *Global Markets Transformed 1870–1945* (Cambridge, MA: Harvard University Press, 2012). See also Kenneth Pomeranz, *The Great Divergence: China, Europe, and the Making of the Modern World Economy* (Princeton, NJ: Princeton University Press, 2000).

6. Friedrich Engels, "Outline of a Critique of Political Economy," in Lawrence S. Stepelevich, ed., *The Young Hegelians: An Anthology* (Cambridge: Cambridge University Press, 1983), 278–302, at 292.

7. On this point, see Adam McKeown, "Global Migration, 1846–1940," *Journal of World History* 15.2 (2004): 155–189; Adam Tooze and Ted Fertik, "The World Economy and the Great War," *Geschichte und Gesellschaft* 40.2 (2014): 214–238; Stefan Link, "How Might 21st-Century De-Globalization Unfold? Some Historical Reflections," *New Global Studies* 12.3 (2018): 343–365.

8. Richard Roberts, *Saving the City: The Great Financial Crisis of 1914* (Oxford: Oxford University Press, 2013), 195–227.

9. For this term, see Jeffry A. Frieden, *Global Capitalism: Its Fall and Rise in the Twentieth Century, and Its Stumbles in the Twenty-First* (New York: W. W. Norton, 2020).

10. For exemplary accounts, see Patricia Clavin, "Explaining the Failure of the London World Economic Conference" in Harold James, ed., *The Interwar Depression in an International Context* (Munich: R. Oldenbourg, 2002), 77–97; and Patricia Clavin, *The Failure of Economic Diplomacy: Britain, Germany, France and the United States, 1931–36* (London: Macmillan, 1996).

11. The literature on the related economic and security crises of the interwar period is vast. See, especially, W. Arthur Lewis, *Economic Survey 1919–1939* (London: George Allen and Unwin, 1949); Stephen Clarke, *Central Bank Cooperation, 1924–1931* (New York: Federal Reserve Bank, 1967); Carl P. Parinni, *Heir to Empire: United States Economic Diplomacy, 1916–1923* (Pittsburgh: University of Pittsburg Press, 1969); Richard Meyer, *Bankers' Diplomacy: Monetary Stabilization in the Twenties* (New York: Columbia University Press, 1970); Derek H. Aldcroft, *From Versailles to Wall Street 1919–1929* (London: Allen Lane, 1977); Walter A. McDougall, *France's Rhineland Policy, 1914–1924: The Last Bid for a Balance of Power in Europe* (Princeton, NJ: Princeton University Press, 1978); Marc Trachtenberg, *Reparation in World Politics: France and European Economic Diplomacy, 1916–1923* (New York: Columbia University Press, 1980); Kathleen Burk, "Economic Diplomacy between the Wars," *The Historical Journal* 24.4 (1981): 1003–1015; Dan P. Silverman, *Reconstructing Europe after the Great War* (Cambridge, MA: Harvard University Press, 1982); Frank Costigliola, *Awkward Dominion: American Political, Economic, and Cultural Relations with Europe, 1919–1933* (Ithaca, NY: Cornell University Press, 1984); Carole Fink, *The Genoa Conference: European Diplomacy, 1921–1922* (Chapel Hill, NC: University of North Carolina Press, 1984); Robert Boyce, *British Capitalism at the Crossroads 1919–1932: A Study in Politics, Economics, and International Relations* (Cambridge: Cambridge University Press, 1987) and *The Great Interwar Crisis and the Collapse of Globalization* (London: Palgrave Macmillan, 2009); Gilbert Ziebura, *World Economy and World Politics, 1924–1931: From Reconstruction to Collapse*, trans. Bruce Little (Oxford: Berg, 1990); Beth Simmons, *Who Adjusts? Domestic Sources of Economic Foreign Policy during the Interwar Years* (Princeton, NJ: Princeton University Press, 1994); Patricia Clavin, *The Great Depression in Europe, 1929–1939* (Houndmills, Basingstoke, Hampshire: Macmillan, 2000); Harold James, *The End of Globalization: Lessons from the Great Depression* (Cambridge, MA: Harvard University Press, 2001); Zara Steiner, *The Lights That Failed: European International History, 1919–1933* (Oxford: Oxford University Press, 2005); Patrick Cohrs, *The Unfinished Peace after World War I: America, Britain and the Stabilisation of Europe, 1919–1932* (Cambridge: Cambridge University Press, 2006); Liaquat Ahamed, *Lords of Finance: 1929, the Great Depression, and the Bankers Who Broke the World* (London: Windmill Books, 2009); Adam Tooze, *The Deluge: The Great War, America and the Remaking of the Global Order, 1916–1931* (London: Penguin, 2014); Stefan J. Link, *Forging Global Fordism: Nazi Germany, Soviet Russia, and the Contest over the Industrial Order* (Princeton, NJ: Princeton University Press, 2020).

12. The term "collapse of globalization" is from Boyce, *The Great Interwar Crisis and the Collapse of Globalization*.

13. Charles H. Feinstein, Peter Temin, and Gianni Toniolo, *The European Economy between the Wars* (Oxford: Oxford University Press, 1997), 204.

14. Barry Eichengreen, *Golden Fetters: The Gold Standard and the Great Depression, 1919–1939* (Berkeley, CA: University of California Press, 1992).

15. For other histories of the classical gold standard and its overturning during the interwar, see Karl Polanyi, *The Great Transformation* (New York: Farrar & Rinehart, 1944); D. E. Moggridge, *The Return to Gold, 1925: The Formulation of Economic Policy and Its Critics* (Cambridge: Cambridge University Press, 1969); Marcello de Cecco, *The International Gold Standard: Money and Empire* (London: Frances Pinter, 1984); Diane B. Kunz, *The Battle for Britain's Gold Standard in 1931* (Beckenahm: Croom Helm, 1987); Kenneth Mouré, *The*

Gold Standard Illusion: France, the Bank of France and the International Gold Standard, 1914–1939 (Oxford: Oxford University Press, 2002).

16. For a canonical statement of this shift, see League of Nations [Ragnar Nurkse and William Adams Brown, Jr.], *International Currency Experience: Lessons of the Inter-War Period* (Geneva: League of Nations, 1944), 229–232.

17. See, for example, Dani Rodrik's idea of the "political trilemma of the world economy" in Rodrik, *The Globalization Paradox: Democracy and the Future of the World Economy* (New York: W. W. Norton, 2011).

18. On this point, see Marc Flandreau and Harold James, "Introduction," in Marc Flandreau, Carl-Ludwig Holtfrerich, and Harold James, eds., *International Financial History in the Twentieth Century: System and Anarchy* (Cambridge: Cambridge University Press, 2003), 1–16, at 7.

19. On this point, particularly in regard to the adoption of the gold standard by Argentina and Japan, see Steven Bryan, *The Gold Standard at the Turn of the Twentieth Century: Rising Powers, Global Money, and the Age of Empire* (New York: Columbia University Press, 2010).

20. On long-term legacies of interwar internationalism, see, especially, Susan Pedersen, "Back to the League of Nations," *American Historical Review* 112.4 (2007): 1091–1117; J. W. Schot and V. C. Lagendijk. "Technocratic Internationalism in the Interwar Years: Building Europe on Motorways and Electricity Networks," *Journal of Modern European History* 6.2 (2008): 196–217; Mark Mazower, *No Enchanted Palace: The End of Empire and the Ideological Origins of the United Nations* (Princeton, NJ: Princeton University Press, 2009) and *Governing the World: The History of an Idea* (London: Penguin, 2012); Tara Zahra, *The Lost Children: Reconstructing Europe's Families After World War II* (Cambridge, MA: Harvard University Press, 2011); Daniel Gorman, *The Emergence of International Society in the 1920s* (Cambridge: Cambridge University Press, 2012); Bruno Cabanes, *The Great War and the Origins of Humanitarianism, 1918–1924* (Cambridge: Cambridge University Press, 2014); Glenda Sluga, *Internationalism in the Age of Nationalism* (Philadelphia: University of Pennsylvania Press, 2015); Daniel Laqua, *The Age of Internationalism and Belgium, 1880–1930: Peace, Progress and Prestige* (Manchester: Manchester University Press, 2015); Glenda Sluga and Patricia Clavin, eds. *Internationalisms: A Twentieth-Century History* (Cambridge: Cambridge University Press, 2017); Guy Fiti Sinclair, *To Reform the World: International Organizations and the Making of Modern States* (New York: Oxford University Press, 2017); Talbot Imlay, *The Practice of Socialist Internationalism; European Socialists and International Politics, 1914–1960* (Oxford: Oxford University Press, 2018); Simon Jackson and Alanna O'Malley, eds., *The Institution of International Order: From the League of Nations to the United Nations* (London: Routledge, 2018); Katharine Marino, *Feminism for the Americas: The Making of an International Human Rights Movement* (Chapel Hill: University of North Carolina Press, 2020); Patricia Owens and Katharina Rietzler, eds., *Women's International Thought: A New History* (Cambridge: Cambridge University Press, 2021).

21. Yann Decorzant, *La Société des Nations et la naissance d'une conception da la régulation économique internationale* (Brussels: Peter Lang, 2011). See also Decorzant, "Internationalism in the Economic and Financial Organisation of the League of Nations," in Daniel Laqua, ed., *Internationalism Reconfigured: Transnational Ideas and Movements between the World Wars* (London: I.B. Taurus, 2011), 115–134, and "Répondre à la demande sociale et à la demande du marché: les prémisses de la régulation économique dans les années 1920," *Les cahiers IRICE* 2 (2008): 107–126. For accounts of other innovations in interwar international governance see, on public health, Iris Borowy, *Coming to Terms with World Health: The League of Nations Health Organisation 1921–1946* (Frankfurt am Main: Peter Lang, 2009) and Heidi Tworek, "Communicable Disease: Information, Health, and Globalization

in the Interwar Period," *American Historical Review* 124.3 (2019): 813–842; on migration, Christopher Szabla, "Reimagining Global Migration Governance: From Insufficient Ideas to South-South Solutions," *Berkeley Journal of International Law* (forthcoming); on contraband, Steffen Rimner, *Opium's Long Shadow: From Asian Revolt to Global Drug Control* (Cambridge, MA: Harvard University Press, 2018); on the international oversight of colonial empire, Susan Pedersen, *The Guardians: The League of Nations and the Crisis of Empire* (Oxford: Oxford University Press, 2015); on anti-slavery work, Amala Ribi Forclaz, *Humanitarian Imperialism: The Politics of Anti-Slavery Activism, 1880–1940* (Oxford: Oxford University Press, 2015); on sanctions, Nicholas Mulder, *The Economic Weapon: The Rise of Sanctions as a Tool of Modern War* (New Haven, CT: Yale University Press, 2022); on international law, see Mark Lewis, *The Birth of the New Justice: The Internationalization of Crime and Punishment, 1919–1950* (Oxford: Oxford University Press, 2014); Scott Shapiro and Oona Hathaway, *The Internationalists: How a Radical Plan to Outlaw War Remade the World* (New York: Simon & Schuster, 2017); Natasha Wheatley, "Mandatory Interpretation: Legal Hermeneutics and the New International Order in Arab and Jewish Petitions to the League of Nations," *Past and Present* 227 (2015): 205–248; and "New Subjects in International Law and Order," in Sluga and Clavin, eds., *Internationalisms: A Twentieth-Century History*, 265–286; Mira Siegelberg, *Statelessness: A Modern History* (Cambridge, MA: Harvard University Press, 2020). For histories of ideas of international order, see David Armitage, *Foundations of Modern International Thought* (Cambridge: Cambridge University Press, 2013); Or Rosenboim, *The Emergence of Globalism: Visions of World Order in Britain and the United States, 1939–1950* (Princeton, NJ: Princeton University Press, 2017).

22. Patricia Clavin, *Securing the World Economy: The Reinvention of the League of Nations 1920–1946* (Oxford: Oxford University Press, 2013), 1. Clavin almost single-handedly rescued the League's economic functions from the obscurity to which they were relegated for decades after the Second World War. See, in addition to *Securing the World Economy*, her many other path-breaking publications on this topic, including Clavin and Jens-Wilhelm Wessels, "Another Golden Idol? The League of Nations' Gold Delegation and the Great Depression, 1929–1932," *The International History Review* 26.4 (2004): 765–795; "'Money Talks:' Competition and Cooperation with the League of Nations, 1929–40," in Marc Flandreau, ed., *Money Doctors: The Experience of International Financial Advising 1850–2000* (London: Routledge, 2003), 219–248; "What's in a Living Standard?: Bringing Society and Economy Together in the ILO and the League of Nations Depression Delegation, 1938–1945," in Sadrine Kott and Joëlle Droux, eds., *Globalizing Social Rights: The International Labour Organization and Beyond* (London: Palgrave Macmillan, 2013), 233–248; "The Austrian Hunger Crisis and the Genesis of International Organization after the First World War," *International Affairs* 90.2 (2014): 265–278; "Men and Markets: Global Capital and the International Economy," in Sluga and Clavin, eds., *Internationalisms: A Twentieth-Century History*, 85–112; "The Ben Pimlott Memorial Lecture 2019—Britain and the Making of Global Order after 1919," *Twentieth Century British History* 31.3 (2020): 340–359; For earlier attempts to draw suggestive links between the League's work and that of the IMF, see Louis W. Pauly, "The League of Nations and the Foreshadowing of the International Monetary Fund." *Essays in International Finance* 201 (Princeton, NJ: Princeton University Press, 1996), 1–52; *Who Elected the Bankers?" Surveillance and Control in the World Economy* (Princeton, NJ: Princeton University Press, 1997); and "International Financial Institutions and National Economic Governance: Aspects of the New Adjustment Agenda in Historical Perspective," in Flandreau, Holtfrerich, and James, eds., *International Financial History in the Twentieth Century*, 239–264.

23. On the League's role in dealing with international trade, see, especially, Mona Pinchis, "The Ancestry of 'Equitable Treatment' in Trade: Lessons from the League of Nations

during the Inter-War Period," *Journal of World Investment and Trade* 15.1–2 (2014): 13–72; Patricia Clavin and Madeleine Dungy, "Trade, Law, and the Global Order of 1919," *Diplomatic History* 44.4 (2020): 554–579; Madeleine Lynch Dungy, "Writing Multilateral Trade Rules in the League of Nations," *Contemporary European History* 30 (2021): 60–75. On the League and financial stabilization, see Nicole Pietri, *La Société des Nations et la reconstruction financière de l'Autriche 1921–1926* (Geneva: Centre européen de la Dotation Carnegie pour la paix internationale, 1970); Anne Orde, *British Policy and European Reconstruction after the First World War* (Cambridge: Cambridge University Press, 1990); Michel Fior, *Institution globale et marchés financiers: La Société des Nations face à la reconstruction de l'Europe, 1918–1931* (Bern: Peter Lang, 2008); Peter Berger, *Im Schatten der Diktatur: Die Finanzdiplomatie des Vertreters des Völkerbundes in Österreich, Meinoud Marinus Rost van Tonnignen 1931–1936* (Vienna: Böhlau, 2009); Frank Beyersdorf "'Credit or Chaos?' The Austrian Stabilisation Programme of 1923 and the League of Nations," in Laqua, ed., *Internationalism Reconfigured*, 135–157; Barbara Susan Warnock, "The First Bailout: The Financial Reconstruction of Austria 1922–1926," unpublished PhD dissertation, Birckbeck University of London (2016); Juan H. Flores Zendejas and Yann Decorzant, "Going Multilateral? Financial Markets' Access and the League of Nations Loans, 1923–8," *Economic History Review* 69.2 (2016): 653–678; Nathan Marcus, *Austrian Reconstruction and the Collapse of Global Finance, 1921–1931* (Cambridge, MA: Harvard University Press, 2018). On other aspects of the League's economic work, see Michele d'Alessandro, "Global Economic Governance and the Private Sector," in Dejung and Petersson, eds., *The Foundations of Worldwide Economic Integration*, 249–270; Marco Bertilorenzi, "Legitimising Cartels: The Joint Roles of the League of Nations and of the International Chamber of Commerce," in Susanna Fellman and Martin Shanahan, eds., *Regulating Competition: Cartel Registers in the Twentieth Century World* (Abingdon, UK: Routledge, 2016), 30–47; Ludovic Tournès, *Les États-Unis et la Société des Nations (1914–1946): Le Système International face à l'émergence d'une superpuissance* (Bern: Peter Lang, 2016), 333–374; Vanessa Ogle, "Archipelago Capitalism: Tax Havens, Offshore Money, and the State, 1950s–1970s," *American Historical Review* 122.5 (2017): 1431–1458.

24. Neil de Marchi with Peter Dohlmann, "League of Nations Economists and the Ideal of Peaceful Change in the Decade of the 'Thirties,'" in C. D. W. Goodwin, ed., *Economics and National Security: A History of their Interaction* (Durham, NC: Duke University Press, 1991), 143–178; Timothy Mitchell, "Fixing the Economy," *Cultural Studies* 12.1 (1998): 82–101; A. M. Endres and Grant Fleming, *International Organizations and the Analysis of Economic Policy, 1919–1950* (Cambridge: Cambridge University Press, 2002); Mauro Boianovsky and Hans-Michael Trautwein, "Haberler, the League of Nations, and the Quest for Consensus in Business Cycle Theory in the 1930s," *History of Political Economy* 38.1 (2006): 45–89. On the history of the idea of "the national economy," see Adam Tooze, "Imagining National Economies: National and International Economics Statistics 1900–1950," in G. Cubitt, ed., *Imagining Nations* (Manchester: Manchester University Press, 1998), 212–228; and Timothy Shenk, "Inventing the American Economy," unpublished PhD dissertation, Columbia University (2016).

25. Martin Bemmann, "Weltwirtschaftsstatistik: Internationale Wirtschaftsstatistik und die Geschichte der Globalisierung, 1850–1950," Habilitationsschrift, Albert-Ludwigs-Universität Freiburg (2020). On the history of the idea of the "world economy," see also Quinn Slobodian, "How to See the World Economy: Statistics, Maps, and Schumpeter's Camera in the First Age of Globalization," *Journal of Global History* 10.2 (2015): 307–332; Jamie Martin, "Time and the Economics of the Business Cycle in Modern Capitalism," in Dan Edelstein, Stefanos Geroulanos, and Natasha Wheatley, eds., *Power and Time: Temporalities in Conflict and the Making of History* (Chicago: University of Chicago Press, 2020), 317–334.

26. See Emily Rosenberg, *Financial Missionaries to the World: The Politics and Culture of Dollar Diplomacy, 1900–1930* (Cambridge, MA: Harvard University Press, 1999); and the essays in Flandreau, ed., *Money Doctors*.

27. Vanessa Ogle, *The Global Transformation of Time 1870–1950* (Cambridge, MA: Harvard University Press, 2015).

28. The only prewar international public union to which any real powers over a significant area of economic policy were delegated was a commission created in 1902 to oversee the trade in sugar between Western European countries—an exception that was unique in its powers to compel states to relinquish some freedom to an external organization on tariffs; even so, it had limited reach. On this anomalous institution and its powers, once an object of extensive debate by internationalists and international lawyers, see, for example, M. Jarousse de Sillac, "Periodical Peace Conferences," *American Journal of International Law* 5.4 (1911): 968–986; Francis Bowes Sayre, *Experiments in International Administration* (New York: Harper & Brothers, 1919), 119; Felix Morley, *The Society of Nations: Its Organization and Constitutional Development* (Washington, DC: The Brookings Institution, 1932), 231, 235. See also Michael Fakhri, *Sugar and the Making of International Trade Law* (Cambridge: Cambridge University Press, 2014), 21–32.

29. On these treaties, see Marc Flandreau and Olivier Accominotti, "Bilateral Treaties and the Most Favored-Nation Clause: The Myth of Trade Liberalization in the Nineteenth Century," *World Politics* 60.2 (2008): 147–188. When an international tariff commission was established in Brussels in 1890, it was authorized only to ask members for data, not to compel them to adjust their policies. See S. L. Lyons, *Internationalism in Europe 1815–1914* (Leyden: A. W. Sythoff, 1963), 103–110; Paul S. Reinsch, *Public International Unions: Their Work and Organization* (Boston: World Peace Foundation, 1911); L. S. Woolf, *International Government* (New York: Brentano's, 1916).

30. See, for example, Craig N. Murphy, *International Organization and Industrial Change: Global Governance since 1850* (New York: Oxford University Press, 1994), 46–118.

31. On the importance of these differences of scope and power, see Charles Henry Alexandrowicz, *International Economic Organisations* (London: Stevens & Sons Limited, 1952), 2–3. For more on these nineteenth-century contexts, see also Madeleine Herren, *Internationale Organisationen seit 1865: Eine Globalgeschichte der internationalen Ordnung* (Darmstadt: Wissenschaftliche Buchgesellschaft, 2009), 15–50; and "International Organizations, 1865–1945," in Jacob Katz, Ian Hurd, and Ian Johnstone, eds., *The Oxford Handbook of International Organizations* (Oxford: Oxford University Press, 2017), 91–111. On the jurisdictional barriers limiting the functions of the International Institute of Agriculture when it was established in 1905, for example—which was empowered to collect data but not touch controversial issues like tariffs or migration—see Wolfram Kaiser and Johan Schot, *Writing the Rules for Europe: Experts, Cartels, and International Organizations* (Basingstoke, UK: Palgrave MacMillan, 2014), 53–54.

32. On these institutions, see, for example, Şevket Pamuk, *The Ottoman Empire and European Capitalism, 1820–1913: Trade, Investment and Production* (Cambridge: Cambridge University Press, 1987); Roumen Avramov, "Advising, Conditionality, Culture: Money Doctors in Bulgaria, 1900–2000," in Flandreau, ed., *Money Doctors;* Murat Birdal, *The Political Economy of Ottoman Public Debt: Insolvency and European Financial Control in the Late Nineteenth Century* (London: I.B. Tauris, 2010); Adam Tooze and Martin Ivanov, "Disciplining the 'Black Sheep of the Balkans': Financial Supervision and Sovereignty in Bulgaria, 1902–1938," *Economic History Review* 64 (2011): 30–51; Ali Coşkun Tunçer, *Sovereign Debt and International Financial Control: The Middle East and the Balkans, 1870–1913* (Basingstoke, UK: Palgrave Macmillan, 2015); and the essays in Nicolas Barreyre and Nicolas Delalande, eds., *A World of Public Debts: A Political History* (Cham: Palgrave Macmillan, 2020). For older accounts, see,

for example, François Deville, *Les contrôles financiers internationaux et la souveraineté de l'État* (Saint-Nicolas: V. Arsant, 1912); André Andréadès, "Les Contrôles Financiers Internationaux," *Recueil des cours de l'Académie de droit international* 5 (1924): 1–108; Edwin Borchard and William Wynne, *State Insolvency and Foreign Bondholders* (New Haven, CT: Yale University Press, 1951). On contemporary portrayals of the "civilizational" status of the Balkans, see James Perkins, "The Congo of Europe: The Balkans and Empire in Early Twentieth-Century British Political Culture," *The Historical Journal* 58.2 (2015): 565–587. On informal empire, see, especially, A.G. Hopkins, "Informal Empire in Argentina: An Alternative View," *Journal of Latin American Studies* 26.2 (1994): 469–484; Deborah Cohen, "Love and Money in The Informal Empire: The British in Argentina, 1830–1930," *Past & Present* 245.1 (2019): 79–115.

33. As a new wave of scholarship has demonstrated, the creation of international economic institutions in the 1940s was shaped by the ideas and mobilization of actors from Asia and Latin America, particularly from China, India, and Mexico. But the financial backing for these institutions came primarily from Europe and the United States, which meant that the visions of these Global South actors were often resisted. See Helleiner, *The Forgotten Foundations of Bretton Woods*; Aditya Balasubramanian and Srinath Raghavan, "Present at the Creation: India, the Global Economy, and the Bretton Woods Conference," *Journal of World History* 29.1 (2018): 65–94; and Christy Thornton, *Revolution in Development: Mexico and the Governance of the Global Economy* (Berkeley: University of California Press, 2021).

34. For a theoretical account of the role of ideology in international institutions, see Erik Voeten, *Ideology and International Institutions* (Princeton, NJ: Princeton University Press, 2021).

35. See, especially, Melvyn P. Leffler, *The Elusive Quest: America's Pursuit of European Stability and French Security, 1919–1933* (Chapel Hill, NC; University of North Carolina Press, 1979).

36. On this point, see, in particular, P. J. Cain and A. G. Hopkins, "Gentlemanly Capitalism and British Expansion Overseas II: New Imperialism, 1850–1945," *Economic History Review* 40.1 (1987): 1–26. On transformations of the British Empire during this period, see, for example, Stephen Constantine, *The Making of British Colonial Development Policy 1914–1940* (London: Frank Cass, 1984); Anthony Clayton, *The British Empire as a Superpower* (London: Palgrave Macmillan, 1986); Ronald Hyam, *Britain's Declining Empire: The Road to Decolonisation, 1918–1968* (Cambridge: Cambridge University Press, 2006); John Darwin, *The Empire Project: The Rise and Fall of the British World-System, 1830–1970* (Cambridge: Cambridge University Press, 2009); P. J. Cain and A. G. Hopkins, *British Imperialism 1688–2015* (London: Routledge, 2016); David Edgerton, *The Rise and Fall of the British Nation: A Twentieth-Century History* (London: Allen Lane, 2018).

37. For characteristic statements of this view, see Wilhelm Kaufmann "Les unions internationales de nature économique," *Recueil des cours de l'Académie de droit international* 3 (1924): 179–288; Wallace McClure, *World Prosperity as Sought through the Economic Work of the League of Nations* (New York: Macmillan, 1933); F. E. Lawley, *The Growth of Collective Economy*, Vol. 2. (London: P. S. King & Son, 1938); Alexandrowicz, *International Economic Organisations*. For a related claim, see Niels P. Petersson, "Legal Institutions and the World Economy, 1900–1930," in Dejung and Petersson, eds., *The Foundations of Worldwide Economic Integration*, 21–39, especially at 39.

38. On this term, see Beth Lew-Williams, *The Chinese Must Go: Violence, Exclusion, and the Making of the Alien in America* (Cambridge, MA: Harvard University Press, 2018), especially 10. For a related approach, see Leyla Dakhli and Vincent Bonnecase, "Introduction: Interpreting the Global Economy through Local Anger," *International Review of Social History* 66, Special Issue S29 (2021): 1–21.

39. Emmerich de Vattel, *Le Droit des Gens* (London, 1758). On the question of the universality of Vattel's concept of non-interference, see Jennifer Pitts, *Boundaries of the International: Law and Empire* (Cambridge, MA: Harvard University Press, 2018), 68–91.

40. Immanuel Kant, "Perpetual Peace: A Philosophical Sketch," in H. S. Reiss, ed., *Kant: Political Writings* (Cambridge: Cambridge University Press, 1970), 93–115. For debates about global commerce and sovereignty from the late eighteenth and early nineteenth centuries, see Emma Rothschild, "Global Commerce and the Question of Sovereignty in the Eighteenth-century Provinces," *Modern Intellectual History* 1.1 (2004): 3–25; Istvan Hont, *Jealousy of Trade: International Competition and the Nation-State in Historical Perspective* (Cambridge, MA: Harvard University Press, 2010); Isaac Nakhimovsky, *The Closed Commercial State: Perpetual Peace and Commercial Society from Rousseau to Fichte* (Princeton, NJ: Princeton University Press, 2011).

41. Augustus Granville Stapleton, *Intervention and Non-Intervention; or, the Foreign Policy of Great Britain from 1790 to 1865* (London: J. Murray, 1865).

42. Charles K. Webster, *The Foreign Policy of Castlereagh, 1812–1815* (London: G. Bell and Sons, 1931).

43. See accounts of a characteristic House of Lords debate in *The Morning Post*, June 16, 1847.

44. See quote in "Confidential Minute of Lord Castlereagh on the Affairs of Spain," May 1820, HC Deb (21 April 1823), vol. 8, col. 1139.

45. The literature on the closely connected problems of intervention and interference from the late nineteenth and early twentieth centuries is vast. For general orientation, see the influential account of Ellery C. Stowell, *Intervention in International Law* (Washington, DC: John Byrne & Co., 1921), especially 317–446, and Stowell's extensive annotated bibliography. See also Henry G. Hodges, *The Doctrine of Intervention* (Princeton, NJ: Banner Press, 1915). For a broad nineteenth-century discussion, see, for example, Henry Wheaton, *Elements of International Law* (London: Sampson, Low, Son and Company, 1863). For a characteristic denunciation of interference from an international lawyer, in this case concerning questions of sovereign debt, see Michel Kebedgy, "De la protection des créanciers d'un État étranger," *Journal du droit international privé et de la jurisprudence comparée* 21 (1894): 59–72, 504–519. For context, see Goronwy J. Jones, *The United Nations and the Domestic Jurisdiction of States: Interpretations and Applications of the Non-Intervention Principle* (Cardiff: University of Wales Press, 1979), 1–13.

46. R.J. Vincent, *Nonintervention and International Order* (Princeton, NJ: Princeton University Press, 1974). See also Antony Anghie, "Finding the Peripheries: Sovereignty and Colonialism in Nineteenth-century International Law," *Harvard International Law Review* 40.1 (1999): 1–80.

47. For a critical history of the related conceptions of intervention and interference, see also P. H. Winfield, "The History of Intervention in International Law," *British Yearbook of International Law* 3 (1922–1923): 130–149. For a characteristic international legal account, see, for example, William Edward Hall, *A Treatise on International Law* (Oxford: Clarendon Press, 1895), 297–309.

48. See, for example, Henry Bonfils, *Manuel de Droit International Public* 3rd ed. (Paris: Librarie Nouvelle de Droit et da Jurisprudence, 1901), 158; C. G. Fenwick and Edwin M. Borchard, "The Distinction between Legal and Political Questions," *Proceedings of the American Society of International Law at Its Annual Meeting* 18 (1924): 44–57; C. G. Fenwick, "The Scope of Domestic Questions in International Law," *American Journal of International Law* 19.1 (1925): 143–147. On definitional questions, see also Hedley Bull, "Introduction," in Bull, ed., *Intervention in World Politics* (Oxford: Clarendon Press, 1984), 1–6. For a more recent theoretical account of the histories of intervention and sovereignty, see

Christian Reus-Smit, "The Concept of Intervention," *Review of International Studies* 39.5 (2013): 1057–1076.

49. Findlay and O'Rourke, *Power and Plenty,* 387. Relatedly, see Marc-William Palen, *The "Conspiracy" of Free Trade: The Anglo-American Struggle over Empire and Economic Globalisation, 1846–1896* (Cambridge: Cambridge University Press, 2016).

50. See, for example, articles in *The Times* (London) from March 28, 1885.

51. Stephen R. Platt. *Imperial Twilight: The Opium War and the End of China's Last Golden Age* (New York: Alfred A. Knopf, 2018), 344, 359, 398.

52. Richard S. Horowitz, "International Law and State Transformation in China, Siam, and the Ottoman Empire during the Nineteenth Century," *Journal of World History* 15.4 (2005): 445–486.

53. Jay Sexton, *The Monroe Doctrine: Empire and Nation in Nineteenth-Century America* (New York: Hill and Wang, 2011), 199–240.

54. Kris James Mitchener and Marc Weidenmier, "Empire, Public Goods, and the Roosevelt Corollary," *Journal of Economic History* 65.3 (2005): 658–692; Benjamin Coates, *Legalist Empire: International Law and American Foreign Relations in the Early Twentieth Century* (Oxford: Oxford University Press, 2016).

55. For an overview, see Karl Strupp, "L'intervention en matière financière," *Recueil des cours de l'Académie de droit international* 8 (1925): 1–124.

56. A. J. Thomas, Jr., and Ann Van Wynen Thomas, *Non-intervention: The Law and Its Import in the Americas* (Dallas: Southern Methodist University Press, 1956).

57. Amos S. Hershey, "The Calvo and Drago Doctrines," *American Journal of International Law* 1.1 (1907): 26–45; Luis S. Drago, "State Loans in Their Relation to International Policy," *American Journal of International Law* 1.3 (1907): 692–726. For broader context, see Dana Gardner Munro, *Intervention and Dollar Diplomacy in the Caribbean, 1900–1921* (Princeton, NJ: Princeton University Press, 1964); Cyrus Veeser, *A World Safe for Capitalism: Dollar Diplomacy and America's Rise to Global Power* (New York: Columbia University Press, 2002); Greg Grandin, *Empire's Workshop: Latin America, the United States, and the Making of an Imperial Republic* (New York: Metropolitan Books, 2006); Peter James Hudson, *Bankers and Empire: How Wall Street Colonized the Caribbean* (Chicago: University of Chicago Press, 2017); Kathryn Greenman, "Aliens in Latin America: Intervention, Arbitration and State Responsibility for Rebels," *Leiden Journal of International Law* 31.3 (2018): 617–639.

58. David Hunter Miller, *The Drafting of the Covenant,* Vol. 1 (New York: G.P. Putnam's Sons, 1928), 276, 331–332; Denna Frank Fleming, *The United States and the League of Nations, 1918–1920* (New York: G.P. Putnam's Sons, 1932), especially 133; Douglas A. Irwin, *Clashing over Commerce: A History of US Trade Policy* (Chicago: University of Chicago Press, 2017), 345–346. On the legal redefinition of immigration restrictions in the United States in the late nineteenth century, see also Lew-Williams, *The Chinese Must Go,* especially 192–193.

59. Edwin M. Borchard, *The Diplomatic Protection of Citizens Abroad: Or the Law of International Claims* (New York: The Banks Law Publishing Co., 1919), 314.

60. Adom Getachew, *Worldmaking after Empire: The Rise and Fall of Self-Determination* (Princeton, NJ: Princeton University Press, 2019); Antony Anghie, *Imperialism, Sovereignty, and the Making of International Law* (Cambridge: Cambridge University Press, 2004). For a theoretical account of sovereign equality and hierarchy in international law, see Gerry Simpson, *Great Powers and Outlaw States: Unequal Sovereigns in the International Legal Order* (Cambridge: Cambridge University Press, 2004). On questions of autonomy and global order during this period, see also Charles Bright and Michael Geyer, "Benchmarks of Globalization: The Global Condition, 1850–2010," in Douglas Northrop, ed., *A Companion to World History* (Oxford: Wiley-Blackwell, 2012), 285–300.

61. On the efforts of Mexican President Venustiano Carranza to ensure that the League of Nations respected the full sovereign equality of member states regarding their right to noninterference in domestic economic affairs, see Thornton, *Revolution in Development*, 18–38. See also Thomas Fischer, *Die Souveränität der Schwachen: Lateinamerika und der Völkerbund, 1920–1936* (Stuttgart: Franz Steiner, 2012).

62. Fenwick, "The Scope of Domestic Questions in International Law," 144.

63. Georg Schwarzenberger, *The League of Nations and World Order: A Treatise on the Principle of Universality in the Theory and Practice of the League of Nations* (Westport, CT: Hyperion Press, 1936), 92.

64. See, for example, "Lodge Predicts Loss of Independence if Nation Accepts Covenant of the League," *Boston Globe*, August 12, 1919.

65. See the congressional debates on this question in *Congressional Record. Proceeding and Debates of the Second Session of the Sixty-Sixth Congress* Vol. LIX, Part 5, especially at 4589–4590. For context, see William G. Ross, "Constitutional Issues Involving the Controversy over American Membership in the League of Nations, 1918–1920," *American Journal of Legal History* 53.1 (2013): 1–88.

66. J. L. Brierly, "Matters of Domestic Jurisdiction," *British Yearbook of International Law* 6 (1925): 8–19; Alfred Zimmern, *The League of Nations and the Rule of Law, 1918–1935* (London: Macmillan & Co, 1936), 244–245. See also J. Paulus, "Les 'Affaires Domestiques,' Alinéa 8 du Pacte de la Societé des Nations," *Revue de droit international de sciences diplomatiques, politiques et sociales* 115 (1924), 123–138; John Fischer Williams, *Some Aspects of the Covenant of the League of Nations* (London: Oxford University Press, 1934), 59–60, 146–147. For more on the legal history and legacies of the domestic jurisdiction clause, see also M. Rajan, *United Nations and Domestic Jurisdiction* (Bombay: Orient Longmans, 1958).

67. See, for example, Zimmern, *The League of Nations and the Rule of Law*, 300; Pierre Mamopoulos, "Le Déclin da la Souveraineté," *Revue Hellénique de Droit International* 31 (1948): 31–40.

68. Zimmern, *The League of Nations and the Rule of Law*, 200, 300.

69. On this point, see Philip Dehne, *After the Great War: Economic Warfare and the Promise of Peace in Paris 1919* (London: Bloomsbury Academic, 2019), 68.

70. Miller, *The Drafting of the Covenant*, Vol. 2, 387–392, 702–703. See Naoko Shimazu, *Japan, Race and Equality: The Racial Equality Proposal of 1919* (London: Routledge, 1998).

71. Mona Siegel, *Peace on Our Terms: The Global Battle for Women's Rights After the First World War* (New York: Columbia University Press, 2020), 23, 38. For a record of these discussions, see "Secretary's Notes of a Conversation Held in M. Pichon's Room at the Quai d'Orsay, Paris," February 13, 1919, *FRUS PPC*, vol. III.

72. On this point, see C. A. Macartney, *National States and National Minorities* (London: Oxford University Press, 1934), 295–308. For context, see, especially, Tara Zahra, "The 'Minority Problem' and National Classification in the French and Czechoslovak Borderlands," *Contemporary European History* 17.2 (2008): 137–165.

73. Carole Fink, "The League of Nations and the Minorities Question," *World Affairs* 157.4 (1995): 197–205, and *Defending the Rights of Others: The Great Powers, the Jews, and International Minority Protection, 1878–1938* (Cambridge: Cambridge University Press, 2006), especially 267–268; Mazower, *Governing the World*, 160–161. For contemporary debates about the nonuniversality of the minority rights regime, see Macartney, *National States and National Minorities*, 286–294; Howard B. Calderwood, "International Affairs: The Proposed Generalization of the Minorities Régime," *American Political Science Review* 28.6 (1934): 1088–1098. For a perspective on this problem from the end of the Second World War, see Oscar I. Janowsky, *Nationalities and National Minorities (With Special Reference to East-Central Europe)* (New York: Macmillan, 1945), 154–157. As Laura Robson has

shown, this treaty regime also represented an adaptation of prewar imperial arrangements, particularly the system of "capitulations" used by the British, French, and Russian empires to intervene on behalf of the non-Muslim populations of the Ottoman Empire. See Robson, "Capitulations Redux: The Imperial Genealogy of the Post–World War I 'Minority' Regimes," *American Historical Review* 126.3 (2021): 978–1000.

74. Sean Brawley, *The White Peril: Foreign Relations and Asian Immigration to Australasia and North America 1918–1978* (Sydney: University of New South Wales Press, 1995), 36–44; Rowland Brucken, *A Most Uncertain Crusade: The United States, the United Nations, and Human Rights, 1941–1953* (Ithaca. NY: Cornell University Press, 2013); Carol Anderson, "From Hope to Disillusion: African Americans, the United Nations, and the Struggle for Human Rights, 1944–1947," *Diplomatic History* 20.4 (1996): 531–563. Much later, the South African government also attempted to protect apartheid by reference to the domestic jurisdiction clause of the UN Charter. See Vincent, *Nonintervention*, 261–274.

75. Mark Mazower, "The Strange Triumph of Human Rights, 1933–1950," *Historical Journal* 47.2 (2004): 379–398; Samuel Moyn, *The Last Utopia: Human Rights in History* (Cambridge, MA: Harvard University Press, 2010). For a contemporary account, see D. J. Llewelyn Davies, "Domestic Jurisdiction: A Limitation on International Law," *Transactions of the Grotius Society* 32 (1946): 60–67. For a related argument about the jurisdictional transformation sparked by the International Labour Organization (ILO), see Jan Klabbers, "An Accidental Revolution: The ILO and the Opening Up of International Law," in Tarja Halonenn and Ulla Liukkunen, eds. *International Labour Organization and Global Social Governance* (Cham: Springer, 2021), 123–140. While the ILO did attempt to make domestic social and labor questions an object of international concern, it wielded limited powers of enforcement over its member states. There is a large literature on the history of the ILO. See, especially, Kott and Droux, eds., *Globalizing Social Rights*.

76. The first test of it was a dispute over the Åland Islands between Finland and Sweden. On this episode, see Leonard V. Smith, *Sovereignty at the Paris Peace Conference of 1919* (Oxford: Oxford University Press, 2018), 238.

77. Woolf, *International Government*, 113–114. This book was influential on British designs for the League of Nations. For another contemporary account of Austria-Hungary's interference in Serbia's affairs, see Hodges, *The Doctrine of Intervention*, 214–216. See also Christopher Clark, *The Sleepwalkers: How Europe Went to War in 1914* (New York: Harper Perennial, 2014), 455–457.

78. Jörn Leonhard, *Der überforderte Frieden: Versailles und die Welt 1918–1923* (Munich: C.H. Beck, 2018), 1269–1272.

79. See, above all, Moyn, *Last Utopia*.

80. Quinn Slobodian, *Globalists: The End of Empire and the Birth of Neoliberalism* (Cambridge, MA: Harvard University Press, 2018), 5–16. On questions of delegation to unelected national and international agencies, see Kathleen McNamara, "Rational Fictions: Central Bank Independence and the Social Logic of Delegation," *West European Politics* 25.1 (2002): 47–76; Darren G. Hawkins, David A. Lake, Daniel L. Nielson, and Michael J. Tierney, *Delegation and Agency in International Organizations* (Cambridge: Cambridge University Press, 2006); Paul Tucker, *Unelected Power: The Quest for Legitimacy in Central Banking and the Regulatory State* (Princeton, NJ: Princeton University Press, 2018).

81. This is not to say that the League did not have an impact on norms and rules of trade. As some historians have shown, it helped solidify practices and ideas about trade liberalization with lasting effects. See Dungy, "Writing Multilateral Trade Rules in the League of Nations;" Clavin and Dungy, "Trade, Law, and the Global Order of 1919; Slobodian, *Globalists*, 27–145." See also League of Nations, *Commercial Policy in the Interwar Period: International Proposals and National Policies* (Geneva: League of Nations, 1944). One of its signature accomplishments, the

1927 World Economic Conference, resulted in a loud affirmation of principles of freer trade and was followed by some progress in arresting the upward trend of tariffs. But coming just before the Depression, the conference fell short of its broader aims. The organizers of the conference attempted to upend a conception of tariffs as being solely matters of domestic interest, while conceding that they continued to fall squarely within states' sovereign jurisdictions. See Arthur Salter, "World Government," in Mary Adams, ed., *The Modern State* (New York: The Century Company, 1933), 253–316, at 268. For another contemporary account, see Robert Guillain, *Les Problèmes Douaniers Internationaux et la Société des Nations* (Paris: Librairie de la Société du Recueil Sirey, 1930).

82. On this hegemonic transition, see Charles Kindleberger, *The World in Depression, 1929–1939* (Berkeley, CA: University of California Press, 1973); Randall Bennett Woods, *A Changing of the Guard: Anglo-American Relations, 1941–1946* (Chapel Hill, NC: University of North Carolina Press, 1990); Giovanni Arrighi, *The Long Twentieth Century: Money, Power, and the Origins of Our Times* (London: Verso, 1994); Anne Orde, *The Eclipse of Great Britain, The United States and British Imperial Decline, 1895–1956* (New York: Palgrave Macmillan, 1996); Leo Panitch and Sam Gindin, *The Making Of Global Capitalism: The Political Economy Of American Empire* (London: Verso, 2013); Tooze, *The Deluge*.

83. The term, one of the most influential in the study of international political economy, is from John Gerard Ruggie, "International Regimes, Transactions, and Change: Embedded Liberalism in the Postwar Economic Order," *International Organization* 36.2 (1982): 379–415. The literature extending and applying the concept is vast. For a recent overview, see Eric Helleiner, "The Life and Times of Embedded Liberalism: Legacies and Innovations since Bretton Woods," *Review of International Political Economy* 26.6 (2019): 1112–1135. Ruggie himself admitted in passing that the compromise never applied to the "developing" world, given the austere IMF conditionality that was applied after the war to various member states in Latin America and elsewhere. While Ruggie admitted his model should not be seen as universally applicable to all sovereign countries, he did not expand on the meaning of this crucial limitation for his overall model. This important caveat is also seldom foregrounded in applications of his idea. See Ruggie, "International Regimes, Transactions, and Change," 407, n. 90 and 408, 413.

84. For skeptical accounts of the existence of a Bretton Woods "system," see, for example, Alan Milward, *The Reconstruction of Western Europe 1945–1951* (Berkeley, CA: University of California Press, 1984); and Francis J. Gavin, *Gold, Dollars, and Power: The Politics of International Monetary Relations, 1958–1971* (Chapel Hill, NC: University of North Carolina Press, 2004).

1. Managing the Global Economy during the First World War

1. See, for example, Ronald Findlay and Kevin H. O'Rourke, *Power and Plenty: Trade, War, and the World Economy in the Second Millennium* (Princeton, NJ: Princeton University Press, 2009), 429; Carl Strikwerda, "World War I in the History of Globalization," *Historical Reflections* 42.3 (2016): 112–132.

2. For overviews of the economics of the First World War, see Gerd Hardach, *The First World War, 1914–1918* (Hardmondsworth, UK: Penguin, 1987); Hew Strachan, *Financing the First World War* (Oxford: Oxford University Press, 2007); Stephen Broadberry, *The Economics of World War I* (Cambridge: Cambridge University Press, 2009). On the war's global nature, see, for example, Hew Strachan, "The First World War as a Global War," *First World War Studies* 1.1 (2010): 3–14; and Robert Gerwarth and Erez Manela, eds. *Empires at War, 1911–1923* (Oxford: Oxford University Press, 2014); Jamie Martin, "Globalizing the History of the First World War: Economic Approaches," *The Historical Journal* (2021). Available at: https://www.cambridge.org/core/journals/historical-journal/article/globalizing-the

-history-of-the-first-world-war-economic-approaches/7A8DD62C1D21C4689B0699CB4EA A99B6.

3. Nicholas A. Lambert, *Planning Armageddon: British Economic Warfare and the First World War* (Cambridge, MA: Harvard University Press, 2012), 1–60. On resources during the war, see, for example, *Avner Offer, The First World War: An Agrarian Interpretation* (Oxford: Oxford University Press, 1989); Tyler Priest, *Global Gambits: Big Steel and the U.S. Quest for Manganese* (Westport, CT: Praeger, 2003); Alison Frank, *Oil Empire: Visions of Prosperity in Austrian Galicia* (Cambridge, MA: Harvard University Press, 2005), 173–204; Ronald Limbaugh, *Tungsten in Peace and War, 1918–1946* (Reno: University of Nevada Press, 2010).

4. The two best strategic accounts of Allied economic cooperation are Elizabeth Greenhalgh, *Victory through Coalition: Britain and France during the First World War* (Cambridge: Cambridge University Press, 2005); and Meighan McCrae, *Coalition Strategy and the End of the First World War: The Supreme War Council and War Planning, 1917–1918* (Cambridge: Cambridge University Press, 2019), 186–236.

5. Yann Decorzant, *La Société des Nations et la naissance d'une conception da la régulation économique internationale* (Brussels: Peter Lang, 2011), 124–161; and "Internationalism in the Economic and Financial Organisation of the League of Nations," in Daniel Laqua, ed., *Internationalism Reconfigured: Transnational Ideas and Movements between the World Wars* (London: I.B. Taurus, 2011), 115–134; Patricia Clavin, *Securing the World Economy: The Reinvention of the League of Nations 1920–1946* (Oxford: Oxford University Press, 2013), 13–14; and Clavin, "The Ben Pimlott Memorial Lecture 2019—Britain and the Making of Global Order after 1919," *Twentieth Century British History* 31.3 (2020): 340–359, 6–8.

6. Wolfram Kaiser and Johan Schot, *Writing the Rules for Europe: Experts, Cartels, and International Organizations* (Houndmills, Basingstoke, UK: Palgrave MacMillan, 2014), 63–67; Adam Tooze, *The Deluge: The Great War, America and the Remaking of the Global Order, 1916–1931* (London: Penguin, 2014), 290.

7. David Engerman, "The Rise and Fall of Central Planning," in Michael Geyer and Adam Tooze, eds., *The Cambridge History of the Second World War*, Vol. 3 (Cambridge: Cambridge University Press, 2015), 575–598, at 577.

8. Robert D. Cuff, *The War Industries Board: Business-Government Relations during World War I* (Baltimore: Johns Hopkins University Press, 1973).

9. "Rapport Sur l'Origine et la Création des Différents Comités du Ravitaillement à Londres." JMP. AMB 1/1/77.

10. Jean-Baptiste Duroselle, "Strategic and Economic Relations during the First World War," in Neville Waites, ed., *Troubled Neighbours: Franco-British Relations in the Twentieth Century* (London: Weidenfeld, 1971), 40–66; Greenhalgh, *Victory through Coalition,* 102–132.

11. "Minutes of a Meeting of the War Cabinet, October 30, 1917, at 11:30 A.M." TNA CAB 23/4/34; "Minutes of a Meeting of the War Cabinet, October 31, 1917, at noon." TNA CAB 23/4/35.

12. Michael Miller, *Europe and the Maritime World: A Twentieth-Century History* (Cambridge: Cambridge University Press, 2012), 213–244.

13. C. Earnest Fayle, *Seaborne Trade,* Vol. 3 (London: John Murray, 1924), 235–246.

14. Arthur Salter, *Memoirs of a Public Servant* (London: Faber and Faber, 1961); Jean Monnet, *Memoirs,* trans. Richard Mayne (London: Collins, 1978). See also Eric Roussel, *Jean Monnet, 1888–1979* (Paris: Fayard, 1996); Sidney Aster, *Power, Policy and Personality: The Life and Times of Lord Salter, 1881–1975* (Scotts Valley, CA: CreateSpace Independent Publishers, 2016). On the collaboration of Monnet and Salter in the 1940s, see Th. W. Bottelier, "'Not on a Purely Nationalistic Basis:' The Internationalism of Allied Coalition Warfare in the Second World War," *European Review of History* 27.1–2 (2020): 152–175.

15. Report of the Special Representative of the United States Government. *FRUS* 1917, Supplement 2, The World War, Volume 1, Document 350; Raymond B. Stevens and George Rublee to Newton Baker, September 26, 1918. NBP. Box 15.

16. Edward N. Hurley, *The Bridge to France* (Philadelphia: J. B. Lippincott, 1927), 207; Jeffrey J. Safford, *Wilsonian Maritime Diplomacy 1913–1921* (New Brunswick, NJ: Rutgers University Press, 1978), 149.

17. George Rublee to Woodrow Wilson, June 20, 1918. See also Raymond Stevens to George Rublee, June 14, 1918. NBP. Box 15; and Raymond Stevens to Woodrow Wilson, May 4, 1918. IAFC. Box 20.

18. Statement for Mr. Gay via Mr. Rublee. May 29, 1918. EGP. Box 2.

19. *Allied Maritime Transport Council, 1918* (London: HMSO, 1919), 11.

20. Memo by James A. Field. January 10, 1919. EGP. Box 2.

21. *Allied Maritime Transport Council, 1918*, 52, 238–240.

22. Hurley, *The Bridge to France*, 196.

23. Arthur Salter, *Allied Shipping Control: An Experiment in International Administration* (London: Clarendon Press, 1921), 248.

24. American Shipping Mission, Statistical Division, "American Representation on Inter-Allied Bodies in London with Special Reference to the Organisation of the Allied Maritime Transport Council," December 1918. IAFC. Box 20.

25. Raymond Stevens to Edward Hurley, Edwin Gay, William McAdoo, Vance McCormick, and Herbert Hoover, May 25, 1918; Raymond Stevens to State Department, June 12, 1918. NBP. Box 15.

26. These committees have received little historical attention. For an account of the Anglo-French disputes over one of them, the Oil and Seeds Executive, see Marc Michel, *L'appel à l'Afrique: contributions et réactions à l'effort de guerre en A.O.F. (1914–1919)* (Paris: Publications de la Sorbonne, 1982), 270–273.

27. On Layton, see Alexander Zevin, *Liberalism at Large: The World According to the Economist* (London: Verso, 2019), 177–221.

28. H. W. W. Bird to Arthur Balfour. July 30, 1917. TNA MUN 4–2109; Bernard Baruch, *American Industry in the War* (Washington, DC: Government Printing Office, 1920), 390.

29. Letter for Robert Cecil. January 19, 1918. TNA T 1/12166.

30. Memorandum on the Nitrate of Soda Situation. TNA CAB 40/43.

31. Nitrate of Soda Executive. Memorandum of Agreement. TNA MUN 4/2109; Memorandum for the American Importers of Nitrates, January 21, 1918. CAP. Box 32.

32. "Memo on the Formation and Dealings of the Nitrate of Soda Executive," August 20, 1918. TNA MUN 4/6487.

33. Dupont Nitrate Company to Bernard Baruch. CAP. Box 32; Baruch, *American Industry in the War*, 159. See also Jordan Schwarz, *The Speculator: Bernard M. Baruch in Washington, 1917–1965* (Chapel Hill, NC: University of North Carolina Press, 1981), 89–98.

34. Memorandum for the American Importers of Nitrates, January 21, 1918. CAP. Box 32. For an overview of the powers of this and other executives, see the brief report by Chandler P. Anderson, who played a significant role in their creation at the War Industries Board: "International Executives," *American Journal of International Law* 13.1 (1919): 85–88.

35. Statement Showing Terms of Nitrate Executive Agreement. June 20, 1918. CAP. Box 33.

36. Draft of Instructions to Consul General Skinner in Regard to Nitrate of Soda Negotiations, November 22, 1917. CAP Box 32.

37. Pap A. Ndiaye, *Nylon and Bombs: DuPont and the March of Modern America*, trans. Elborg Forster (Baltimore: Johns Hopkins University Press, 2006), 111–113.

38. Chandler Anderson Diary, Nov. 8, 1917. CAP. Box 1, Reel 1.

39. Memo on the Formation and Dealings of the Nitrate of Soda Executive, August 20, 1918. TNA MUN 4/6487.

40. Nitrate of Soda Executive. Duties of Director of Purchases, November 6, 1918. CAP. Box 33.

41. Draft of Instructions to Consul General Skinner to Regard to Nitrate of Soda Negotiations. November 22, 1917. CAP. Box 32.

42. Chandler Anderson Diary, Nov. 7, 1917. CAP Box 1 Reel 1.

43. Lord Reading to Winston Churchill, February 15, 1918. TNA MUN 4/2109.

44. Winston Churchill to Charles Gordon, March 12, 1918; C. Gordon for C. J. Phillips, March 19, 1918. TNA MUN 4/2019.

45. Bill Albert, *South America and the First World War: The Impact of the War on Brazil, Argentina, Peru and Chile* (Cambridge: Cambridge University Press, 1988), 26, 48; Robert Greenhill, "The Nitrate and Iodine Trade 1880–1914," in D.C.M. Platt, ed., *Business Imperialism: An Inquiry Based on British Experience in Latin America* (Oxford: Clarendon Press, 1977), 231–283.

46. Michael Monteón, *Chile in the Nitrate Era: The Evolution of Economic Dependence, 1800–1930* (Madison: The University of Wisconsin Press, 1982), 108–124; Juan Ricardo Couyoumdjian, *Chile y Gran Bretaña durante la Primera Guerra Mundial y la postguerra, 1914–1921* (Santiago: Eicione Universidad Catolica de Chile, 1986), 127–131.

47. Robert Greenhill, "Managed Decline, Headlong Retreat or Entrepreneurial Failure? British Nitrate Producers and the Withdrawal from Chile, 1920–1930," in Manuel Llorca-Jaña, Rory M. Miller, and Diego Barría, eds., *Capitalists, Business and State-building in Chile* (Cham: Springer, 2019), 97–138, at 100–101.

48. Chandler Anderson Diary, November 7, 1917. CAP Box 1, Reel 1; Albert, *South America and the First World War*, 45–48, 95–100. See also United States Tariff Commission, *Chemical Nitrogen: A Survey of Processes, Organization, and International Trade, Stressing Factors Essential to Tariff Consideration* (Washington, DC: US Government Printing Office, 1937), 108. On the environmental toll, see Tait Keller, "The Ecological Edges of Belligerency: Toward a Global Environmental History of the First World War," *Annales* 71.1 (2016): 61–78. On economic warfare in South America, see Phillip Dehne, *On the Far Western Front: Britain's First World War in South America* (Manchester: Manchester University Press, 2009). On Argentina, see Roger Gravil, *The Anglo-Argentine Connection and the War of 1914–1918* (Boulder: Westview Press, 1985), 111–150.

49. Memorandum with reference to the organization of an International Committee to Control the Acquisition and Distribution of Certain Essential Materials for War Supplies. CAP. Box 33; Chandler Anderson to André Tardieu, March 14, 1918; Memorandum for Brigadier General P. E. Pierce, March 14, 1918; Chandler Anderson to Frank L. Polk, March 15, 1918; Memorandum of Conversation with Mr. Broderick of the British Embassy, Commerce Division, January 7, 1918. CAP. Box 32.

50. Agreement for Establishing an Inter-Allied Executive to Deal with Tungsten Ores and Tungsten Products. TNA MUN 4/845; Edward House to Robert Lansing, November 26, 1917. NARA WIB. Box 186.

51. Lord-Geoffrey Ores Co. to Chandler Anderson, March 30, 1918; Abrum Elkus to Chandler Anderson, March 20, 1918; Abrum Elkus to Clarence M. Woolley, March 4, 1918; Lord-Geoffrey Ores Co. to Chandler Anderson, July 22, 1918; Abrum Elkus to Bernard Baruch, August 6, 1918. NARA WIB. Box 186.

52. Alfred E. Eckes, *The United States and the Global Struggle for Minerals* (Austin: University of Texas Press, 1979), 18–19.

53. Frank Hess to H. W. Sanford, September 21, 1918. CAP. Box 33. On the Department of the Interior, see Megan Black, *The Global Interior: Mineral Frontiers and American Power* (Cambridge, MA: Harvard University Press, 2018).

54. Leland Summers to Bernard Baruch, September 12, 1918. CAP. Box 33; Agreement for Establishing an Inter-Allied Executive to Deal with Tungsten Ores and Tungsten Products. TNA MUN 4/845.

55. Conference with French and American Representatives re: tungsten. TNA MUN 4/3673; Wolfram, Draft Agreement, February 21, 1918. NARA WIB. Box 183.

56. Tin: French Government Requirements. CHAR 15/37.

57. Letter on Tin Executive, June 11, 1918. TNA MUN 4/684; Draft of Plan for Controlling the Procurement and Distribution of Tin to Meet the Requirements of the United States and the Allies, April 6, 1918. CAP. Box 33. LOC.

58. Telegram to Lord Reading, June 3, 1918. TNA MUN 4-6388.

59. Nicholas J. White, "Gentlemanly Capitalism and Empire in the Twentieth Century: The Forgotten Case of Malaya 1914–1965," in Raymond E. Dumett, ed., *Gentlemanly Capitalism and British Imperialism: The New Debate on Empire* (New York: Longman, 1999), 175–195, at 179.

60. Telegram to Lord Reading, June 3, 1918. TNA MUN 4/6388.

61. Foreign Office letter, June 1918. TNA MUN 4/6388. Relatedly, see Austen Chamberlain's Report, "Inter-Ally Council and Inter-Ally Executives," from May 15, 1918. TNA MUN 4/6582.

62. Memorandum of Decision of Conference of Representatives of the Non-Ferrous Metals Allocation Committee, May 17, 1918. TNA MUN 4/6388; Telegram to Lord Reading, June 8, 1918. TNA MUN 4/6388; Telegram to Lord Reading, July 6, 1918, and Letter to Lord Reading, June 22, 1918. TNA MUN 4/684; Tin. Cable Agreed upon at a Meeting of the Non Ferrous Metals Allocation Committee, July 4, 1918. TNA MUN 4/684.

63. See, above all, Georges-Henri Soutou, *L'or et le sang: Les buts de guerre économiques de la Première Guerre mondiale* (Paris: Fayard, 1989), 141–229.

64. "Conférence Économique des Gouvernements Alliés tenue à Paris." FNA F/12/8104.

65. Richard F. Kuisel, *Capitalism and the State in Modern France: Renovation and Economic Management in the Twentieth Century* (Cambridge: Cambridge University Press, 1981), 37–48; John F. Godfrey, *Capitalism at War: Industrial Policy and Bureaucracy in France, 1914–1918* (New York: Berg, 1987), 85–105.

66. In Germany, plans for a *Mitteleuropa* bloc provided a popular early vision of European integration. See David Stevenson, "The First World War and European Integration," *The International History Review* 34.4 (2012): 841–863. For broader context, see Sven Beckert, "American Danger: United States Empire, Eurafrica, and the Territorialization of Industrial Capitalism, 1870–1950," *American Historical Review* 122.4 (2017): 1137–1170.

67. After the war, Clémentel became the first head of the International Chamber of Commerce, an internationalist business lobbying-group established to encourage a return to freer trade.

68. Marc Trachtenberg, "'A New Economic Order': Etienne Clémentel and French Economic Diplomacy during the First World War," *French Historical Studies* 10.2 (1977): 315–341, see especially 320; and Trachtenberg, *Reparation in World Politics: France and European Economic Diplomacy, 1916–1923* (New York: Columbia University Press, 1980), 9–28; Walter MacDougall, *France's Rhineland Diplomacy, 1914–1924: The Last Bid for a Balance of Power in Europe* (Princeton, NJ: Princeton University Press, 1978), 31–32; David Stevenson, *French War Aims against Germany* (Oxford: Clarendon Press, 1982), 153–154, 165; Elisabeth Glaser, "The Making of the Economic Peace," in Manfred F. Boemeke, Gerald D. Feldman, and Elisabeth Glaser, eds., *The Treaty of Versailles: A Reassessment after 75 Years* (Cambridge: Cambridge University Press, 2006), 371–399, at 381–382. For his own recollections, see Étienne Clémentel, *La France et la Politique Économique Interalliée* (Paris: Les Presses universitaires de France, 1931).

69. "La conférence économique et l'opinion étrangère." FNA F/12/7988.

70. Carl P. Parinni, *Heir to Empire: United States Economic Diplomacy, 1916–1923* (Pittsburgh: University of Pittsburgh Press, 1969), 15–39.

71. Frank Trentmann, *Free Trade Nation: Commerce, Consumption, and Civil Society in Modern Britain* (Oxford: Oxford University Press, 2008), 249–258.

72. Robert E. Bunselmeyer, *The Cost of the War 1914–1919: British Economic War Aims and the Origins of Reparations* (Hamden, CT: Archon Books, 1975), 14–16.

73. For this term, see Henry Farrell and Abraham L. Newman, "Weaponized Interdependence: How Global Economic Networks Shape State Coercion," *International Security* 44.1 (2019): 42–79.

74. Lambert, *Planning Armageddon*, 1–60.

75. V. H. Rothwell, *British War Aims and Peace Diplomacy 1914–1918* (Oxford: Clarendon Press, 1971), 266–282; Bunselmeyer, *The Cost of War*, 56–59. For minutes and memoranda, see TNA CAB 27/15 and CAB 27/16.

76. Economic Offensive Committee. "Control of Raw Materials." November 16, 1917 CAB 24/4/26.

77. Paul Barton Johnson, *Land Fit for Heroes: The Planning of British Reconstruction 1916–1919* (Chicago: University of Chicago Press, 1968), 68–77, 118–127; Anne Orde, *British Policy and European Reconstruction after the First World War* (Cambridge: Cambridge University Press, 1990), 6; Roger Lloyd-Jones and M. J. Lewis, *Arming the Western Front: War, Business and the State in Britain 1900–1920* (Abingdon, UK: Routledge, 2016), 282–295.

78. Ministry of Reconstruction. Memorandum on the Problem of Raw Materials in the Transition Period after Peace, October 1917. TNA RECO 1/371; Ministry of Reconstruction, *Raw Materials and Employment* (London: HMSO, 1919).

79. Peter Cline, "Winding Down the War Economy: British Plans for Peacetime Recovery, 1916–19," in Kathleen Burk, ed. *War and the State: The Transformation of British Government 1914–1919* (London: Allen & Unwin, 1982), 157–181.

80. Ministry of Reconstruction. "Economic Pressure," November 20, 1917. TNA CAB 27/16. See also Orde, *British Policy and European Reconstruction*, 14–24.

81. Nicholas Mulder, *The Economic Weapon: The Rise of Sanctions as a Tool of Modern War* (New Haven, CT: Yale University Press, 2022); Philip Dehne, *After the Great War: Economic Warfare and the Promise of Peace in Paris 1919* (London: Bloomsbury Academic, 2019); Stevenson, *French War Aims against Germany*, 19; Roy MacLeod, "The Mineral Sanction," in Richard P. Tucker, Tait Keller, J. R. McNeill, and Martin Schmid, eds. *Environmental Histories of the First World War* (Cambridge: Cambridge University Press, 2018), 99–116.

82. Étienne Clémentel to Woodrow Wilson, October 6, 1917. FNA F12/7817.

83. "Differences between the United States, England, and France concerning Economic Policy." Records of the Inquiry. Economic Division. R.G. 256. Box 107. Peace Conference Document 242. NARA.

84. George W. Egerton, *Great Britain and the Creation of the League of Nations: Strategy, Politics, and International Organization, 1914–1919* (Chapel Hill, NC: University of North Carolina Press, 1979), 37–38; Peter Yearwood, *Guarantee of Peace: The League of Nations in British Policy, 1914–1925* (Oxford: Oxford University Press, 2009), 24–50; Henry R. Winkler, *The League of Nations Movement in Great Britain, 1914–1919* (New Brunswick, NJ: Rutgers University Press, 1952), 244–245.

85. J. L. Garvin, *The Economic Foundation of Peace: Or World-Partnership as the Truer Basis of the League of Nations* (London: MacMillan, 1919), 42.

86. On this point, see Jan Smuts's influential blueprint, *The League of Nations: A Practical Suggestion* (London: Hodder and Stoughton, 1918), 7–8. For other characteristic accounts in the British government, see Lord Northcliffe's letter to Balfour, June 10, 1918, in TNA CAB 27/44.

87. "Memorandum on the Inter-Allied Control of Raw Materials After the War." TNA CAB 27/16.

88. For a clear statement of official French views from December 1917, see, for example, "Question d'un contrôle international des matières premières." FNA F12 F/12/7988.

89. Jessie Hughan, *A Study of International Government* (New York: Thomas Y. Crowell, 1923), 97.

90. Maurice Hankey, "The League of Nations. Observations by the Secretary," January 16, 1918. TNA CAB 24/39/44. See also Peter Yearwood, "'Real Securities against New Wars': Official British Thinking and the Origins of the League of Nations, 1914–19," *Diplomacy and Statecraft* 9.3 (1998): 83–109, at 90.

91. See, for example, Étienne Clémentel to Georges Clemenceau, undated. FNA F12/8106. For a characteristic expression of French official views at war's end, see "L'union économique des alliés dans la guerre," *Bulletin de la Section d'Information du G[rand].Q[aurtier].G[énéral]* 69 (Oct. 27, 1918).

92. Stevenson, *French War Aims against Germany*, 148.

93. Bunselmeyer, *The Cost of War*, 59.

94. See also Robert Cecil, "Inter-Allied Control of Imports," September 10, 1918. TNA CAB 27/44.

95. James A. Field to Edwin Gay, September 11, 1918. EGP. Box 2.

96. G.C.V.H. to Hanson, November 12, 1918. TNA MUN 5/137.

97. "Differences between the United States, England, and France concerning Economic Policy." Records of the Inquiry. Economic Division. R.G. 256. Box 107. Peace Conference Document 242. NARA.

98. Baruch to Legge and Summers. November 16, 1918. CAP. Box 33. On this point, see Michael Hogan, *Informal Entente: The Private Structure of Cooperation in Anglo-American Economic Diplomacy, 1918–1928* (Columbia, MO: University of Missouri Press, 1977), 20–23.

99. Burl Noggle, *Into the Twenties: The United States from Armistice to Normalcy* (Urbana, IL: University of Illinois Press, 1974), 46–65. See also Soutou, *L'Or et le sang*, 807–840; Orde, *British Policy and European Reconstruction*, 24–31.

100. F. S. Marston, *The Peace Conference of 1919: Organization and Procedure* (London: Oxford University Press, 1944), 104; David M. Kennedy, *Over Here: The First World War and American Society* (Oxford: Oxford University Press, 1999), 296–347.

101. Ray Stannard Baker, *Woodrow Wilson and World Settlement*, Vol. II (Gloucester, MA: P. Smith, 1922), 335.

102. See, for example, the remarks of Albert Thomas, director of the International Labour Organization, in 1926. "Directeur du Bureau International du Travail, sur les problèmes du relèvement économique, vus du B.I.T. ILO." CAT 2–6. In the 1940s, similar views were common in the United States and Britain. See J. B. Condliffe, *Agenda for a Postwar World* (London: George Allen & Unwin, 1943), 58–61; William Diamond, *The Economic Thought of Woodrow Wilson* (Baltimore: Johns Hopkins University Press, 1943), 182–192; R. H. Tawney, "The Abolition of Economic Controls, 1918–1921," *Economic History Review* 13.1/2 (1943): 1–30, at 29; Albert O. Hirschman, *National Power and the Structure of Foreign Trade* (Berkeley: University of California Press, 1945), 67; David Thomson, *Patterns of Peacemaking* (London: K. Paul, Trench, Trubner, 1945), 32–33.

103. See, for example, Eugene Staley, "The Economic Implications of Lend-Lease," *American Economic Review* 33.1 Part 2 (1943): 362–376, at 375.

104. Herbert Hoover to J. P. Cotton, November 8. 1918. Reprinted in *FRUS* 1918. Supplement 1. The World War. Document 537.

105. On Anglo-American rivalry in Latin America, see Safford, *Wilsonian Maritime Diplomacy*, 149–156; Jonathan R. Barton, "Struggling against Decline: British Business in Chile,

1919–33," *Journal of Latin American Studies* 32.1 (2000): 235–264; Stefan Rinke, *Latin America and the First World War*, trans. Christopher W. Reid (Cambridge: Cambridge University Press, 2017), 170–177. On Chilean nitrate specifically, see Joseph S. Tulchin, *The Aftermath of War: World War I and U.S. Policy toward Latin America* (New York: New York University Press, 1971), 28–37.

106. Wessel, Duval & Co. to Chandler Anderson, November 19, 1918. CAP. Box 33. There was some private support, it should be noted, for the perpetuation of the Nitrate Executive. See Robert Skinner to Robert Lansing, November 8, 1918. CAP. Box 33.

107. Leland Summers to Chandler Anderson. December 18, 1918. CAP. Box 33.

108. Walter S. Tower to Edwin Gay. November 13, 1918. EGP. Box 2.

109. Frank Taussig to Woodrow Wilson. Letter reprinted in Eugene Staley, "Taussig on 'International Allotment of Important Commodities,'" *American Economic Review* 33 (1943): 877–881. See also William Smith Culbertson, "The 'Open Door' and Colonial Policy," *American Economic Review* 9.1 (1919): 325–340, at 339.

110. Eckes, *The United States and the Global Struggle for Minerals*, 20–24; C. K. Leith, "International Control of Minerals," in *Mineral Resources of the United States 1917. Part I: Metals* (Washington, DC: US Government Printing Office, 1921), 7A–17A.

111. Colonel E. M. House to the British Secretary of State for Foreign Affairs (Balfour), December 1, 1918. *FRUS PPC*, Vol. II, Document 535.

112. On the foundation of the SEC, see documents in TNA FO 608/76. For its minutes, see *FRUS PPC*, Vol. X. For an older but still useful account, see Seth Tillman, *Anglo-American Relations at the Paris Peace Conference of 1919* (Princeton, NJ: Princeton University Press, 1961), 263–279S; and Oscar Penn Fitzgerald, "The Supreme Economic Council and Germany: A Study of Inter-Allied Cooperation after World War I." Unpublished PhD thesis, Georgetown University (1971).

113. E. F. Wise to William Beveridge. June 19, 1919. LON R356. For a more conservative account of European economic distress in early 1919 and the revolutionary threat it was said to pose, see Robert Cecil, "The Economic Situation in Europe," March 2, 1919. TNA FO 608/170. See also Susan Armitage, *The Politics of Decontrol of Industry: Britain and the United States* (London: Wiedenfeld and Nicolson, 1969), 35–37.

114. "Notes on Draft Memorandum entitled 'International Food Control' by EF Wise." LON R356.

115. "Note on Clause in Treaty on Purchase and Distribution of Food and Raw materials." June 12, 1919. EMHLP 3/6. On the worldwide scope of inflation in 1918–1919, see Adam Tooze and Ted Fertik, "The World Economy and the Great War," *Geschichte und Gesellschaft* 40.2 (2014): 214–238; Mark Metzler, "The Correlation of Crises, 1918–20," in Urs Matthias Zachmann, ed., *Asia after Versailles: Asian Perspectives on the Paris Peace Conference and the Interwar Order, 1919–33* (Edinburgh: Edinburgh University Press, 2017), 23–54.

116. Kuisel, *Capitalism and the State in Modern France*, 51–58.

117. René Bazin to Walter Layton, November 7, 1918. TNA MUN 5/137.

118. David Hunter Miller, *The Drafting of the Covenant*, Vol. 2 (New York: G.P. Putnam's Sons, 1928), 247.

119. Eric Drummond to Arthur Salter, July 11, 1919. LON R291/10/243.

120. Eric Drummond to Arthur Salter, November 21, 1919. LON R293/10/2101/2101.

121. Eric Drummond to Arthur Salter, November 25, 1919. LON R293/10/2101/2101.

122. Arthur Salter to Eric Drummond, November 25, 1919. LON R293/10/2101/2101; Arthur Salter to Austen Chamberlain, November 17, 1919. TNA T 161/75.

123. See F. E. Lawley, *The Growth of Collective Economy*, Vol. 2. (London: P. S. King & Son, 1938), 20–30.

124. Alfred Zimmern, *Nationality and Government, with Other Wartime Essays* (London: Chatto & Windus, 1919), 289, 293–296. On Zimmern's wartime and postwar advocacy for

inter-Allied economic controls, see the many documents in AZP, Box 78–81. See also Tomohito Baji, *The International Thought of Alfred Zimmern: Classicism, Zionism and the Shadow of Commonwealth* (Cham: Palgrave Macmillan, 2021).

125. Printed in Labour Party, *Memoranda on International Labour Legislation: The Economic Structure of the League of Nations* (London: Labour Party, 1919), 31.

126. "Resolutions of the First International Congress of Working Women, Washington, DC, 1919," Mary van Kleeck Papers. Box 72, Folder 2. Sophia Smith Collection. Women's History Archive. On feminist internationalism in 1919, see Glenda Sluga, "Women, Feminisms and Twentieth-Century Internationalisms," in Glenda Sluga and Patricia Clavin, eds., *Internationalisms: A Twentieth-Century History* (Cambridge: Cambridge University Press, 2017), 61–84; and Mona Siegel, *Peace on Our Terms: The Global Battle for Women's Rights after the First World War* (New York: Columbia University Press, 2020).

127. Siegel, *Peace on Our Terms*, 142–144.

128. Karl Kapp, "Memorandum on the Efforts Made By the League of Nations towards a Solution of the Problem of Raw Materials," in *International Studies Conference, Tenth Session, June 28–July 3, 1937* (Paris: International Institute of Intellectual Co-operation, 1937), 37.

129. Miller, *Drafting of the Covenant*, Vol. 1, 272–273.

130. James A. Field to Edwin Gay, October 22, 1918. EGP. Box 2. For context, see Douglas J. Forsyth, *The Crisis of Liberal Italy: Monetary and Financial Policy, 1914–1922* (Cambridge: Cambridge University Press, 1993).

131. Quoted in Kapp, "Memorandum on the Efforts Made By the League of Nations towards a Solution of the Problem of Raw Materials," 40.

132. League of Nations, "The Records of the First Assembly. Plenary Meetings." November 15—December 18, 1920, 169–170. LON.

133. League of Nations, "Records of the First Assembly," 178–179.

134. League of Nations, "Records of the First Assembly," 362.

135. On Gini's hire by the League, see "Proposal Involving Expenditure. Personnel." LON S778/10028/10028.

136. League of Nations [Corrado Gini], *Report on the Problem of Raw Materials and Foodstuffs* (Geneva: League of Nations, 1921), 25–26. For brief mention of this overlooked episode, see Mats Ingulstad, "Regulating the Regulators: The League of Nations and the Problem of Raw Materials," in Andreas R. Dugstad Sanders, Pål R. Sandvik, and Espen Storli, eds., *The Political Economy of Resource Regulation: An International and Comparative History, 1850–2015* (Vancouver: UBC Press, 2019), 231–258, at 238. For the appropriation of the ideas of Gini's report by the fascist government in its later colonial claims, see Elisabetta Tollardo, *Fascist Italy and the League of Nations, 1922–1935* (London: Palgrave Macmillan, 2016), 26–27.

137. "Supplies of Foodstuffs and Raw Materials. Questionnaire to the Governments." ILO L 5/3; F. H. Nixon to Corrado Gini. 13 April 1921. LON S778/10028/10028; League of Nations, *Report on the Problem of Raw Materials and Foodstuffs*, 11.

138. "Note on the Future of the Supreme Economic Council." TNA CAB 24/93/36; "Proposed Organisation for Carrying into Effect International Consultation in Economic Matters Pending the Formation of the League of Nations." TNA FO 608/76; "Relations of the Supreme Economic Council to the League of Nations and the Reparation Commission." TNA T 1/12311. While the US government did not respond to a request to transform the SEC into this international council, the idea was backed by some US diplomatic officials, who attempted to win Wilson's support for it. See letters in WWP, Reel 377, Series 4.

139. General Note as to Immediate Work and Requirements of the Economic and Financial Section. LON R291/10/243.

140. On the formation of the Secretariat, see Karen Gram-Skjoldager and Haakon A. Ikonomou, "The Construction of the League of Nations Secretariat: Formative Practices of Au-

tonomy and Legitimacy in International Organizations," *International History Review* 41.2 (2019): 257–279.

141. On Lloyd's technocratic orientation in comparison with the more orthodox liberalism of some of his other early League colleagues, see, in particular, the diary kept by Per Jacobsson on the first months of their work together, particularly the entry for July 23, 1920. Per Jacobsson Diary Volume 1: 1911–1925, held in the London School of Economics Library Archives and Special Collections, London.

142. "The Technical Organisations of the League." EMHLP 3 / 9.

143. Trentmann, *Free Trade Nation*, 261–262, 267–269.

144. List of International Bodies Concerned with Economic Questions Already in Existence; Economic Organisation under the League of Nations. EMHLP 3 / 3. See also "Economic Foundation of the League of Nations." EMHLP 3 / 4.

145. EMH Lloyd to Eric Drummond. March 23, 1920. EMHLP 3 / 5.

146. Salter, *Allied Shipping Control*, 265, 252.

147. Salter, *Allied Shipping Control*, 253, 279.

148. See, for example, Dwight Morrow, *The Society of Free States* (New York: Harper & Brothers, 1919); and H. R. G. Greaves, *The League Committees and World Order* (London: Oxford University Press, 1931), 21. Salter has even been credited with all but inventing the "functionalist" tradition of international relations. See Leonie Holthaus and Jens Steffek, "Experiments in International Administration: The Forgotten Functionalism of James Arthur Salter," *Review of International Studies* 42 (2016): 114–135.

149. Felix Morley, *The Society of Nations: Its Organization and Constitutional Development* (Washington, DC: The Brookings Institution, 1932), 227–260.

150. Alfred Zimmern, *The League of Nations and the Rule of Law, 1918–1935* (London: Macmillan & Co, 1936), 149–150. On Salter's reputation in some circles for having effectively won the war for the Allies, see Felix Frankfurter, "Review of Arthur Salter, 'Allied Shipping Control,'" *Harvard Law Review* 35.8 (1922): 975–977, at 975.

151. Leo Chiozza Money, *The Triumph of Nationalization* (London: Cassel and Company, 1920), 236–241.

152. For this term, see Adom Getachew, *Worldmaking after Empire: The Rise and Fall of Self-Determination* (Princeton, NJ: Princeton University Press, 2019), 54.

2. Enforcing Austerity in Postwar Europe

1. For overviews, see Derek H. Aldcroft, *From Versailles to Wall Street 1919–1929* (London: Allen Lane, 1977), 55–77; W. Arthur Lewis, *Economic Survey 1919–1939* (London: Routledge, 1949), 16–37.

2. See League of Nations, *Commercial Policy in the Postwar World* (Geneva: League of Nations, 1945), 11–12.

3. Michael Hogan, *Informal Entente: The Private Structure of Cooperation in Anglo-American Economic Diplomacy, 1918–1928* (Columbia, MO: University of Missouri Press, 1977), 24–28.

4. "Note Submitted by Lord Robert Cecil on the General Economic Position," April 5, 1919. EMHLP. 3 / 1.

5. "Memorandum on the Technical Organisations of the League." EMHLP 3 / 9.

6. Quincy Wright, "Effects of the League of Nations Covenant," *American Political Science Review* 13.4 (1919): 556–576.

7. During the organization of a League-sponsored international financial conference in Brussels in 1920, for example, French officials attempted to remove nearly all topics from the agenda on the grounds that they were purely internal matters that could not to be subjected

to international debate. See Dan P. Silverman, *Reconstructing Europe after the Great War* (Cambridge, MA: Harvard University Press, 1982), 275.

8. On Article 23e, see Mona Pinchis, "The Ancestry of 'Equitable Treatment' in Trade: Lessons from the League of Nations during the Inter-War Period," *Journal of World Investment and Trade* 15.1–2 (2014): 13–72; Patricia Clavin and Madeleine Dungy, "Trade, Law, and the Global Order of 1919," *Diplomatic History* 44.4 (2020): 554–579; and Madeleine Lynch Dungy, "Writing Multilateral Trade Rules in the League of Nations," *Contemporary European History* 30 (2021): 60–75.

9. For an account of this disappointment from a free trader who was also director of the Mandates Section of the Secretariat of the League of Nations, see William Rappard, *Postwar Efforts for Freer Trade* (Geneva: Geneva Research Centre, 1938). For a more optimistic assessment of the breadth of the League's economic mandate, see H. R. G. Greaves, *The League Committees and World Order* (London: Oxford University Press, 1931).

10. Robert Gerwarth, *The Vanquished: Why the First World War Failed to End, 1917–1923* (London: Penguin, 2017).

11. See, above all, Charles S. Maier, *Recasting Bourgeois Europe: Stabilization in France, Germany, and Italy in the Decade after World War I* (Princeton, NJ: Princeton University Press, 1975).

12. J. A. Salter. "Present Position with Regard to the Supreme Economic Council and Economic Co-operation under the League," December 10, 1919. TNA T 1/12348.

13. Report of Meeting Held at King's College, Cambridge, December 20–21, 1919. JMKP F1/4.

14. In the Free City of Danzig, political authorities still protested against the League's financial control. See, for example, Vice-President of the Danzig Senate to the High Commissioner, December 19, 1922. LON C.11.1923 I.

15. Franz Borkenau, *Socialism: National or International* (London: George Routledge & Sons, 1942), 148.

16. See, for example, Juan H. Flores Zendejas and Yann Decorzant, "Going Multilateral? Financial Markets' Access and the League of Nations Loans, 1923–8," *Economic History Review* 69.2 (2016): 653–678; Juan H. Flores Zendejas, "Financial Markets, International Organizations and Conditional Lending: A Long-Term Perspective," in Grégoire Mallard and Jérôme Sgard, eds., *Contractual Knowledge: One Hundred Years of Legal Experimentation in Global Markets* (Cambridge: Cambridge University Press, 2016), 61–91. Relatedly, see Marc Flandreau and Juan H. Flores, "Bondholders versus Bond-Sellers? Investment Banks and Conditionality Lending in the London Market for Foreign Government Debt, 1815–1913," *European Review of Economic History* 16.4 (2012): 356–383. For an older account of the League loans, see, for example, Corina Cosoiu, *Le rôle de la Société des nations en matière d'emprunts d'état* (Paris: Domat-Montchrestien, 1934).

17. Louis W. Pauly, "The League of Nations and the Foreshadowing of the International Monetary Fund." *Essays in International Finance* 201 (Princeton, NJ: Princeton University Press, 1996), 1–52; *Who Elected the Bankers? Surveillance and Control in the World Economy* (Princeton, NJ: Princeton University Press, 1997); Harold James, "From Grandmotherliness to Governance: The Evolution of IMF Conditionality," *Finance & Development: A Quarterly Magazine of the IMF* 35.4 (1998); Patricia Clavin, "Men and Markets: Global Capital and the International Economy," in Glenda Sluga and Patricia Clavin, eds., *Internationalisms: A Twentieth-Century History* (Cambridge: Cambridge University Press, 2017), 85–112.

18. Marc Flandreau, ed., *Money Doctors: The Experience of International Financial Advising 1850–2000* (London: Routledge, 2003); Emily Rosenberg, *Financial Missionaries to the World: The Politics and Culture of Dollar Diplomacy, 1900–1930* (Cambridge, MA: Harvard University Press, 1999), 4–96.

19. League of Nations [Corrado Gini], *Report on the Problem of Raw Materials and Foodstuffs* (Geneva: League of Nations, 1921), 72.

20. League of Nations [Corrado Gini], *Report on the Problem of Raw Materials and Foodstuffs*, 48.

21. "Memorandum à Sir Eric Drummond." LON R356/14697/14697.

22. See J. Melot to Paternotte, December 7 1921, with draft contract attached. LON R356/18330/14697.

23. "Report to the Council on Certain Aspects of the Raw Materials Problem by the Economic Section of the Provisional Economic and Financial Committee." LON R369.

24. Minutes of the Financial Committee. February 1922. Attached to Note by the Secretariat, "Technical Advisers on Commercial & Financial Administration." LON R356/14697/14697.

25. "Note sur l'état actuel de l'enquête relative aux conseillers techniques." LON R356/25380/14697.

26. Devawongse Varoprakar to Eric Drummond, August 9, 1922. LON R356/23674/14697. Siam would ultimately employ League experts on public health, opium control, and human trafficking measures. See Stefan Hell, *Siam and the League of Nations: Modernisation, Sovereignty and Multilateral Diplomacy, 1920–1940* (Bangkok: River Books, 2010).

27. Olivier Accominotti, Marc Flandreau, and Riad Rezzik, "The Spread of Empire: Clio and the Measurement of Colonial Borrowing Costs," *Economic History Review* 64.2 (2011): 385–407. See also Leigh Gardner, "Colonialism or Supersanctions: Sovereignty and Debt in West Africa, 1871–1914," *European Review of Economic History* 21.2 (2017) 236–257. See also Susan Pedersen, "Empires, States and the League of Nations," in Sluga and Clavin, eds., *Internationalisms: A Twentieth-Century History*, 113–138, at 126, n. 25.

28. See, especially, Ali Coşkun Tunçer, *Sovereign Debt and International Financial Control: The Middle East and the Balkans, 1870–1913* (Basingstoke, UK: Palgrave Macmillan, 2015). For US institutions of control, see Rosenberg, *Financial Missionaries to the World*. On questions of sovereignty in French Tunisia, see also Mary Lewis, *Divided Rule: Sovereignty and Empire in French Tunisia, 1881–1938* (Berkeley, CA: University of California Press, 2014).

29. Juan Cole, *Colonialism & Revolution in the Middle East: Social and Cultural Origins of Egypt's 'Urabi Movement* (Cairo: The American University in Cairo Press, 1999); Aaron G. Jakes, *Egypt's Occupation: Colonial Economism and the Crises of Capitalism* (Stanford, CA: Stanford University Press, 2020).

30. Kris James Mitchener and Marc D. Weidenmier, "Supersanctions and Sovereign Debt Repayment," *Journal of International Money and Finance* 29 (2010): 19–36. For an alternative view, see Michael Tomz, *Reputation and International Cooperation: Sovereign Debt across Three Centuries* (Princeton, NJ: Princeton University Press, 2007), especially 114–157.

31. On the extensive powers wielded by this commission, see Francis Bowes Sayre, *Experiments in International Administration* (New York: Harper & Brothers, 1919), 56–62.

32. Owen Pearson, *Albania in the Twentieth Century: A History. Volume One: Albania and King Zog: Independence, Republic and Monarchy 1908–1939* (London: Centre for Albanian Studies/I.B. Taurus, 2004), 157–184.

33. F. H. Nixon to Albert Calmes, July 28, 1922; Count Moltke to Major Abraham, September 20, 1922. LON S137; G. H. F. Abraham, "The Albanian Question." ASP. Box 13. MSS42085.

34. Arthur Salter to M. L. Gwyer, August 31, 1923. LON S115.

35. Unsigned letter to H. A. L. Fisher, May 29, 1922. LON R374.

36. F. H. Nixon to Albert Calmes, July 28. 1922. LON S137.

37. F. H. Nixon to Albert Janssen, October 18, 1922. LON S137.

38. F. H. Nixon to Marcus Wallenberg, September 29, 1922. LON S137.

39. Abraham to F. H. Nixon, November 11, 1922. LON S137.

40. F. H. Nixon to Bernardo Attolico, November 24, 1922. LON S137.

41. R. S. Patterson to Major Abraham, with curriculum vitae, December 1, 1922. LON S137.

42. Bernardo Attolico to F. H. Nixon, November 29, 1922. LON S137.

43. H. Wilson Harris, "The League at Its Worst: A New Cloak for Old Vices." LON R374.

44. A Swedish adviser was ruled out immediately for this reason. Marcus Wallenberg to F. H. Nixon, August 15, 1922. LON S137.

45. F. H. Nixon to Bernardo Attolico, November 30, 1922. LON S137.

46. C. E. Ter Meulen Secretary to F. H. Nixon, November 29, 1922 and F. H. Nixon to C. E. Ter Meulen, November 30, 1922. LON S137.

47. "Translation of a Letter from Mr. J. G. Moojen to the Dutch Colonial Minister," December 12, 1922. LON S137.

48. F. H. Nixon to Marcus Wallenberg, January 6, 1922. LON S137.

49. F. H. Nixon to Marcus Wallenberg, June 15, 1922. LON R374.

50. Marcus Wallenberg to F. H. Nixon, March 11, 1923. LON R374.

51. Marcus Wallenberg to F. H. Nixon, March 11, 1923. LON R374.

52. In the Financial Committee, it was noted that the existence of a parliament clearly limited the executive powers Hunger would be able to wield. See extract of Minutes of the Financial Committee, September 5, 1922. LON S147.

53. "First Report by the Financial Adviser to the Albanian Government" and "Second Report of the Financial Adviser to the Albanian Government." *LON OJ* 5.1 (January 1924): 162–168.

54. Major Abraham to Eric Drummond, August 17, 1923; Alexander Loveday to Arthur Salter, August 20, 1923. LON R375.

55. Major Abraham to Eric Drummond, August 17, 1923. LON R375.

56. Record of Interview with Benoit Blinishti, August 21, 1923. LON R375.

57. *Fourth Yearbook of the League of Nations, January 1–December 31, 1923* (Brooklyn: Brooklyn Daily Eagle, 1924), 69.

58. Record of Interview with Benoit Blinishti, August 21, 1923. LON R375.

59. Paul Mantoux to Eric Drummond, August 17, 1923. LON R375.

60. Adriaan Joost van Van Hamel to Walters, August 24, 1923. LON R375.

61. Eric Drummond Memorandum, August 24, 1923. LON R375. Salter also conceded that having the government's procedure for awarding concessions discussed at the Council was inappropriate. Arthur Salter Memorandum, August 23, 1923. LON R375.

62. In the case of the creation of an Albanian central bank, for example, Morocco was the explicit precedent. See Financial Committee, "Draft Law for Albanian Bank of Issue," August 16, 1923. LON R375.

63. "Second Report of the Financial Adviser to the Albanian Government," *LON OJ* (January 1924): 162–168.

64. "Fourth Report of the Financial Adviser to the Albanian Government," *LON OJ* 5.4 (April 1924): 727–728.

65. Alessandro Roselli, *Italy and Albania: Financial Relations in the Fascist Period* (London: I.B. Tauris, 2006), 21–32.

66. Robert C. Austin, *Founding a Balkan State: Albania's Experiment with Democracy, 1920–1925* (Toronto: University of Toronto Press, 2012), 132–136; Pearson, *Albania and King Zog*, 212, 217–218.

67. "Fourteenth Plenary Meeting," *LON OJ SS* No. 23 (1924): 101.

68. "Fourteenth Plenary Meeting," *LON OJ SS* No. 23 (1924): 97.

69. Barbara Jelavich, *Modern Austria; Empire and Republic, 1815–1986* (Cambridge: Cambridge University Press, 1987), 151–176; Walter Goldinger, *Geschichte der Republik Österreich 1918–1938* (Vienna: Verlag für Geschichte und Politik, 1992), 84–133. On Anschluss, see also Erin R. Hochman, *Imagining a Greater Germany: Republican Nationalism and the Idea of Anschluss* (Ithaca, NY: Cornell University Press, 2017). For a contemporary account from someone involved, see Jan van Walré de Bordes, *The Austrian Crown: Its Depreciation and Stabilization* (London: P. S. King & Son, 1924).

70. For a critical account, see Karl Bachinger and Herbert Matis, *Der Österreichische Schilling: Geschichte einer Währung* (Graz: Verlag Styria, 1974).

71. Karl Polanyi, *The Great Transformation* (New York: Farrar & Rinehart, 1944), 25.

72. Nathan Marcus, *Austrian Reconstruction and the Collapse of Global Finance, 1921–1931* (Cambridge, MA: Harvard University Press, 2018). For a brief summary of this argument, see pp. 8–16.

73. See, for example, Gunnar Myrdal, *Warnung vor Friedensoptimismus*, trans. Werner Arpe (Zürich: Europa, 1945), 180.

74. R. Calomfiresco, *L'Organisation et l'Œuvre économique de la Société des Nations* (Paris: Les Presses Universitaires de France, 1929), 222; League of Nations [J. B. Condliffe], *World Economic Survey* 1931–32 (Geneva: League of Nations, 1932), 73.

75. See Marcus, *Austrian Reconstruction and the Collapse of Global Finance, 1921–1931,* and "Austria, the League of Nations, and the Birth of Multilateral Financial Control," in Peter Becker and Natasha Wheatley, eds. *Remaking Central Europe: The League of Nations and the Former Habsburg Lands* (Oxford: Oxford University Press, 2021), 127–144. See also Barbara Susan Warnock, "The First Bailout—The Financial Reconstruction of Austria 1922–1926," unpublished PhD dissertation, Birkbeck College, University of London (2015); Frank Beyersdorf "'Credit or Chaos?' The Austrian Stabilisation Programme of 1923 and the League of Nations," in Daniel Lacqua, ed., *Internationalism Reconfigured: Transnational Ideas and Movements between the World Wars* (London: I.B. Tauris, 2011), 135–157; Peter Berger, "The League of Nations and Interwar Austria: Critical Assessment of a Partnership in Economic Reconstruction," in Günter Bischof, Anton Pelinka, and Alexander Lassner, eds., *The Dollfuss/Schuschnigg Era in Austria* (New Brunswick, NJ: Transaction, 2003), 73–92; Anne Orde, *British Policy and European Reconstruction after the First World War* (Cambridge: Cambridge University Press, 1990), 108–145; Nicole Piétri, *La Société des Nations et la reconstruction financière de l'Autriche 1921–1926* (Geneva: Centre européen de la Dotation Carnegie pour la paix internationale, 1970).

76. Marcus emphasizes this as the key difference from nineteenth-century practices, especially in "Austria, the League of Nations, and the Birth of Multilateral Financial Control."

77. Patricia Clavin, "The Austrian Hunger Crisis and the Genesis of International Organization after the First World War," *International Affairs* 90.2 (2014): 265–278.

78. For a characteristic expression of this view, see F. O. Lindley to George Curzon, November 3, 1920. TNA T 160/57.

79. Austria. Rapport par M. Loucheur. LON S117

80. See, for example, "Deutschlands Schicksalstunde," *Neues Wiener Abendblatt,* July 26, 1920. See also Adam Tooze, *The Deluge: The Great War, America and the Remaking of the Global Order, 1916–1931* (London: Penguin, 2014), 370; Stefan Ihrig, *Atatürk in the Nazi Imagination* (Cambridge, MA: Harvard University Press, 2014), 26.

81. Robert Boyce, *The Great Interwar Crisis and the Collapse of Globalization* (London: Palgrave Macmillan, 2009), 115.

82. British Secretary's Notes of an Allied Conference Held in the Salle de l'Horloge, Quai d'Orsay, January 25, 1921. TNA T 160/57.

83. "Report of the Committee on Austria," January 29, 1921. TNA T 160/57.

84. British Secretary's Notes of Meeting Held in Boardroom, Treasury, March 12, 1921. TNA T 160/57.

85. H. A Siepmann, "The International Financial Conference at Brussels," *The Economic Journal* 30 (1920): 436–459, at 451. See also W. Gordon Brown, "Opinion," June 7, 1921. LON S144.

86. Van Hamel to Colonel Schuster, November 9, 1921. LON S144.

87. International Credits. Report to End of February 1922. LON S144.

88. György Péteri, "Central Bank Diplomacy: Montagu Norman and Central Europe's Monetary Reconstruction after World War," *Contemporary European History* 1.3 (1992): 233–258.

89. Montagu Norman to Benjamin Strong, June 19, 1921. BOE. OV 28/52.

90. Montagu Norman to C. E. Ter Meulen, June 16, 1921. BOE OV 28/52.

91. "Extract from *The Economist,* May 6, 1922," LON S144.

92. F. H. Nixon. "Control of Austria," April 15, 1922. LON S103.

93. "The Austrian Scheme and Genoa." LON S106.

94. Jean Monnet [F. H. Nixon] to Dwight Morrow, March 16, 1922. LON S106.

95. F. H. Nixon. "Control of Austria," April 15, 1922. LON S103.

96. F. H. Nixon. "Control of Austria," April 15, 1922. LON S103.

97. F. H. Nixon to John Maynard Keynes, April 6, 1922; For similar points, see also F. H. Nixon to Marcus Wallenberg, March 21, 1922. LON S116.

98. "Conversation between Monsieur Monnet and Sir Basil Blackett," February 24, 1922. LON S103.

99. F. H. Nixon to John Maynard Keynes, April 6, 1922. LON S116.

100. Jean Monnet [F. H. Nixon] to Dwight Morrow, March 16, 1922. LON S106.

101. F. H. Nixon, "Financial Intervention in Austria," May 1922. *Manchester Guardian.* In LON S106.

102. Jean Monnet [F. H. Nixon] to Dwight Morrow, March 16, 1922. LON S106.

103. "Note by the Secretariat on the International Controls Established in China," and "The Various Systems for the Control of Public Finance. Note by the Secretariat." LON S107.

104. "Financial Committee. Minutes. 9th Session, 10th Meeting. (Second Half)." September 16, 1922. LON S107.

105. F. H. Nixon. "Control of Austria," April 15, 1922; "Austrian Finances. Suggested Lines of Action of Controller Nominated by Financial Committee." LON S103.

106. F. H. Nixon. "Control of Austria," April 15, 1922. LON S103.

107. "Reply of the Financial Committee to Four Questions Reported by the Austrian Committee of the Council of September 8th." LON S107.

108. "Financial Committee. Minutes. 9th Session, 10th Meeting. (Second Half). September 16, 1922. LON S107.

109. Financial Committee. 9th Session, 16th Meeting. September 26, 1922. LON S107.

110. See, for example, the letter from Austrian businessman Julius Meinl to the British banker Harry Goschen, February 10, 1922. BOE OV 28/52.

111. Marcus, *Austrian Reconstruction and the Collapse of Global Finance,* 111–112.

112. See, for example, "Finanzkontrolle," *Neues Wiener Tagblatt* (September 24, 1922); "Der Genfer Sanierungsplan," *Tages-Post* (September 22, 1922). For an earlier expression of such anxieties, see, for example, "Die Verpfändung der Gobelins," *Neue Freie Presse* (December 29, 1921).

113. See, for example, "Austria Puzzled How to Spend Its Allied Loan," *Los Angeles Evening Express,* March 21, 1922.

114. "Revue des commentaries de la presse sur la question autrichienne." LON S97.

115. Minutes of Council, September 6, 1922. *LON OJ* 11.3 (November 1922): 1449.

116. Walter Rauscher, *Die verzweifelte Republik: Österreich 1918–1922* (Vienna: Kremayr & Scheriau, 2017), 192–202.

117. "For Sir Arthur Salter from Mr. Pelt," October 13, 1922. LON S109.

118. Basil Blackett to Arthur Salter, October 18, 1922. LON S109.

119. John Fischer Williams, "L'entr'aide financière," *Recueil des cours de l'Académie de droit international* 5 (1924): 109–158, at 151.

120. André Andréadès, "Les Contrôles Financiers Internationaux," *Recueil des cours de l'Académie de droit international* 5 (1924): 1–108.

121. For an overview, see Lea Heimbeck, "Legal Avoidance as Peace Instrument: Domination and Pacification through Asymmetric Loan Transactions," in Thomas Hippler and Miloš Vec, eds., *Paradoxes of Peace in Nineteenth Century Europe* (Oxford: Oxford University Press, 2015), 111–130.

122. Amos S. Hershey, "The Calvo and Drago Doctrines," *American Journal of International Law* 1.1 (1907): 6–22.

123. See, for example, Edwin Dickinson, *The Equality of States in International Law* (Cambridge, MA: Harvard University Press, 1920), 256–279.

124. See, for example, Henry Wheaton, *Elements of International Law* (London: Sampson, Low, Son and Company, 1863).

125. Steven C. Topik, "When Mexico Had the Blues: A Transatlantic Tale of Bonds, Bankers, and Nationalists, 1862–1910," *American Historical Review* 105.3 (2000): 714–738.

126. Karl Strupp, "L'intervention en matière financière," *Recueil des cours de l'Académie de droit international* 8 (1925): 1–124; François Deville, *Les Contrôles Financiers Internationaux et la souveraineté de l'État* (Paris: Limoges Charles-Lavauzelle, 1913), especially at 7. See also Charles Dupuis, *Le droit des gens et les rapports des grandes puissances avec les autres états avant le pacte de la Société des nations* (Paris: Paris, Plon-Nourrit et cie, 1921), 270–309.

127. Henry Carter Adams, *Public Debts: An Essay in the Science of Finance* (New York: D. Appleton & Company, 1895), 29.

128. See, for example, Panagiotis B. Dertilis, *La Reconstruction Financière de la Grèce et la Société des Nations* (Paris: Jouve, 1928), 142–162.

129. Andréadès, "Les Contrôles Financiers Internationaux," 10.

130. "Note du Secrétariat sur quelques précédents d'Actes Internationaux de garantie d'intégrité territoriale, etc." LON S107.

131. John Deak, "Dismantling Empire: Ignaz Seipel and Austria's Financial Crisis, 1922–1925," in Peter Berger, Günter Bischof, and Fritz Plasser, eds., *From Empire to Republic: Post-World War I Austria* (New Orleans: University of New Orleans Press, 2010), 123–141, at 136.

132. See, for example, Miklós Lojkó, *Meddling in Middle Europe: Britain and the 'Lands Between' 1919–1925* (Budapest: Central European University Press, 2006); Zoltán Peterecz, *Jeremiah Smith, Jr. and Hungary, 1924–1926: The United States, the League of Nations, and the Financial Reconstruction of Hungary* (Boston: Walter De Gruyter, 2013).

133. Printed in Harold G. Moulton, *The Reparation Plan: An Interpretation of the Reports of the Expert Committees Appointed by the Reparation Commission, November 30, 1923* (New York: McGraw-Hill, 1924), 139.

134. Max Sering, *Germany under the Dawes Plan: Origin, Legal Foundations, and Economic Effects of the Reparation Payments*, translated by S. Milton Hart (London: P. S. King & Son, 1929), 61, 65. For a similar account, see Walter Brodbeck, *International Finanzkontrollen und ihre politischen Grenzen* (Berlin: Junker und Dünnhaupt Verlag, 1935), 49–64.

135. On this point, see, for example, Edmund C. Mower, *International Government* (Boston: Heath & Company, 1931), 516–517.

136. Bulgarian National Assembly, 71st–72nd Meetings, April 9–10, 1928. BOE OV9/413; H. A. Siepmann "Note on Conversation with Monsieur Ivanof," February 27, 1928. BOE OV 9/161. See also Adam Tooze and Martin Ivanov, "Disciplining the 'Black Sheep of the Balkans': Financial Supervision and Sovereignty in Bulgaria, 1902–38," *Economic History Review* 64.1 (2011): 30–51.

137. Owen O'Malley to Otto Niemeyer, April 1, 1930. BOE OV 9/256.

138. Neville Henderson to Arthur Henderson, March 13, 1930. BOE OV 9/256.

139. This generated considerable anxiety at the Bank of England. See Montagu Norman to Dwight Morrow, December 24, 1926. BOE G1/43; Henry Strakosch to Montagu Norman, June 17, 1927. BOE OV 110-33.

140. Richard Meyer, *Bankers' Diplomacy: Monetary Stabilization in the Twenties* (New York: Columbia University Press, 1970), 58–99; Frank Costigliola, "The Politics of Financial Stabilization: American Reconstruction Policy in Europe 1924–30," PhD dissertation, Columbia University (1973); Piotr S. Wandycz, *The United States and Poland* (Cambridge, MA: Harvard University Press, 1980), 196–208; Neal Pease, *Poland, the United States, and the Stabilization of Europe, 1919–1933* (Oxford: Oxford University Press, 1986), 55–100.

141. Financial Committee, "Financial Reconstruction of Portugal," March 10, 1928. BOE OV 62-29.

142. Exposé from Liga de Defesa da República to the President of the Council of the League of Nations. LON 490.

143. Bernardino Machado to Eric Drummond, undated. LON R490.

144. Bernardino Machado to Eric Drummond, February 20, 1928. LON R490.

145. Portuguese Stabilisation Loan, Extracts from the Portuguese Press, March 20, 1928. LON R2927.

146. Louis Araquistan, "Dictatorship in Portugal," *Foreign Affairs* (January 1, 1928): 41–53, at 49.

147. "Portugal." BOE G1-391.

148. Note of Conversation with Monsieur de Bordes on the 12th and 13th July, 1928, Otto Niemeyer, July 17, 1928; Otto Niemeyer note, September 17, 1928. BOE OV 9/256.

149. Otto Niemeyer to Júlio Dantas, March 20, 1928. TNA T 188/296. The difference made by Portugal's membership in the League was similarly emphasized by the Bank of England. See letter to Benjamin Strong, September 29, 1927. BOE G1/391; Alb. d'Oliveira to the President of the Council, June 5, 1928. LON R2927.

150. "120 Millionen Pfund—und der stolze Portugiese!" *Kladderadatsch* 26.81 (June 24, 1928).

151. "Portuguese Stabilisation—Introduction." BOE OV 62–29; Carl Melchior to Arthur Salter, July 9, 1929. LON R2927.

152. Walter C. Opello, *Portugal: From Monarchy to Pluralist Democracy* (Boulder: Westview Press, 1991), 60–61; Leonor Freire Costa, Pedro Lains, and Susan Münch Miranda, *An Economic History of Portugal, 1143–2010* (Cambridge: Cambridge University Press, 2019), 298.

153. Montagu Norman to Benjamin Strong, January 21, 1928. BOE G1-39.

154. Arthur Salter, *Memoirs of a Public Servant* (London: Faber, 1961), 182; Arthur Salter to Montagu Norman, June 2, 1927. SALT 1/4; Note of Conversation between Governor Strong and Sir Arthur Salter," May 25, 1928. LON P141.

155. Benoy Kumar Sarkar, *A Scheme of Economic Development for Young India* (Calcutta: Oriental Library, 1926), 3–13. On the concerns of Mexican diplomats that the US State Department planned something similar for Latin American states, see Christy Thornton, *Revolution in Development: Mexico and the Governance of the Global Economy* (Berkeley, CA: University of California Press, 2021), 44.

156. Nnamdi Azikiwe, *Liberia in World Politics* (London: Arthur H. Stockwell, 1934), 136–137. On Azikiwe, see Adom Getachew, *Worldmaking after Empire: The Rise and Fall of Self-Determination* (Princeton, NJ: Princeton University Press, 2019), 135–137.

157. Request for Assistance Submitted by the Liberian Government, May 21, 1932. LON C. 469. M. 238. 1932. VII.

158. W. E. Burghardt Du Bois, "Liberia, the League and the United States," *Foreign Affairs* 11 (1932–1933): 682–695, at 693.

159. Ibrahim Sundiata, *Brothers and Strangers: Black Zion, Black Slavery, 1914–1940* (Durham, NC: Duke University Press, 2004), 97–184.

160. See, for example, J. B. Condliffe, *Agenda for a Postwar World* (London: George Allen & Unwin, 1943), 173–182; J. J. Polak, "Raw Materials and Inflation." LON C1726.

161. Julio A. Santaella, "Stabilization Programs and External Enforcement. Experience from the 1920s," *IMF Staff Papers* 40.3 (1993): 584–621.

162. For this claim, see, for example, Pauly, "The League of Nations and the Foreshadowing of the International Monetary Fund."

163. For a related argument about the border between the European world of settled laws and rules and the non-European world of "war capitalism," see Sven Beckert, *Empire of Cotton: A Global History* (New York: Vintage, 2014), especially at 38.

164. Salter, "General Survey," in League of Nations, *The Financial Reconstruction of Austria: General Survey and Principal Documents* (Geneva: League of Nations, 1926), 82.

3. An Independent International Bank

1. Dan P. Silverman, *Reconstructing Europe after the Great War* (Cambridge, MA: Harvard University Press, 1982), 282–284.

2. Liaquat Ahamed, *Lords of Finance: 1929, the Great Depression, and the Bankers Who Broke the World* (London: Windmill Books, 2009).

3. Norman to Strong, April 17, 1927. Correspondence with Great Britain—Montagu Norman, Governor, Bank of England (1927) pt. 2. BSP.

4. Assen Tzankov, "Contre le Contrôle étranger," *Zora*, January 29, 1928.

5. Paul W. Drake, *The Money Doctor in the Andes: The Kemmerer Missions, 1923–1933* (Durham, NC: Duke University Press, 1989), 94–96; Emily Rosenberg, *Financial Missionaries to the World: The Politics and Culture of Dollar Diplomacy, 1900–1930* (Cambridge, MA: Harvard University Press, 1999), 155–166. For a defense of this practice in relation to the Austrian case, see Nathan Marcus, "Les conseillers étrangers à la Banque nationale d'Autriche 1923–1929: contrôle ou coopération?," *Histoire, Économie et Société* 35.4 (2016): 8–20.

6. See Montagu Norman to Robert C. Vansittart, November 26, 1930, for his explanation of his change of mind. He did not mention the rivalry with the Banque de France. BOE OV G1/391.

7. For accounts of the foundations of the BIS in relation to the history of central bank cooperation and German reparations, see Frank Costigliola, "The Other Side of Isolationism: The Establishment of the First World Bank, 1929–1930," *Journal of American History* 59.3 (1972): 602–620; Bruce Kent, *The Spoils of War: The Politics, Economics, and Diplomacy of Reparations, 1918–1932* (Oxford: Oxford University Press, 1989), 287–321; Beth Simmons, "Why Innovate? Founding the Bank for International Settlements," *World Politics* 45.3 (1993): 361–405; Paolo Baffi, *The Origins of Central Bank Cooperation: The Establishment of the Bank for International Settlements* (Rome: Bank of Italy, 2002); Harold James, "The Creation of a World Central Bank? The Early Years of the Bank for International Settlements," in Harold James, ed., *The Interwar Depression in International Context* (Munich: Olden-

bourg, 2002), 159–170; Gianni Toniolo, *Central Bank Cooperation at the Bank for International Settlements, 1930–1973* (Cambridge: Cambridge University Press, 2005); Frédéric Clavert, "La Fondation de la Banque des Règlements Internationaux," *Histoire, économie & société* 4.30 (2011): 11–17; Kazuhiko Yago, *The Financial History of the Bank for International Settlements* (London: Routledge, 2012).

8. For an exemplary account of this later context, see, for example, Alasdair Roberts, *The Logic of Discipline: Global Capitalism and the Architecture of Government* (Oxford: Oxford University Press, 2010).

9. The historiography on German reparations is vast. For overviews, see, for example, Sally Marks, "The Myths of Reparations," *Central European History* 11.3 (1978): 231–255; Gerald Feldman, "The Reparations Debate," *Diplomacy and Statecraft* 16.3 (2005): 487–498; Robert Yee, "Reparations Revisited: The Role of Economic Advisers in Reforming German Central Banking and Public Finance," *Financial History Review* 27.1 (2020): 45–72.

10. Others included international commissions to control plebiscites in territories like Schleswig. See Edwin D. Dickinson, "The Execution of Peace with Germany: An Experiment in International Organization," *Michigan Law Review* 18.6 (1920): 484–507. See also Nicholas Mulder, "'A Retrograde Tendency': The Expropriation of German Property in the Versailles Treaty," *Journal of the History of International Law* 22 (2020): 507–535.

11. On the Dawes Plan, see Stephen Schuker, *The End of French Predominance in Europe: The Financial Crisis of 1924 and the Adoption of the Dawes Plan* (Chapel Hill, NC: University of North Carolina Press, 1976); Adam Tooze, *The Deluge: The Great War, America and the Remaking of the Global Order, 1916–1931* (London: Penguin, 2014), 452–461; Melvyn P. Leffler, *The Elusive Quest: America's Pursuit of European Stability and French Security, 1919–1933* (Chapel Hill, NC; University of North Carolina Press, 1979), 90–111; Patricia Clavin, *The Great Depression in Europe, 1929–1939* (Houndmills, Basingstoke, Hampshire: Macmillan, 2000), 36–39.

12. On the Austrian precedent, see Thomas Lamont letter, March 21, 1930. TLP. Box 181.

13. "Germany's Attitude toward Supervision," April 22, 1925. Trip to Europe (July–September 1925). BSP.

14. For accounts of the short-term stabilizing effects of the Dawes Plan, despite its shortcomings, see Robert Boyce, *British Capitalism at the Crossroads 1919–1932: A Study in Politics, Economics, and International Relations* (Cambridge, MA: Cambridge University Press, 1987), 54–59; Patrick Cohrs, *The Unfinished Peace after World War I: America, Britain and the Stabilisation of Europe, 1919–1932* (Cambridge: Cambridge University Press, 2006), 129–153, 187–200.

15. William Phillip Bradley, "The Deutschnationale Volkspartei and the Dawes Plan, 1923–1924," unpublished master's thesis, College of William and Mary (1978). For a theoretical account of the Weimar Republic under the Dawes Plan as an ideal type of a "penetrated system," which allowed external actors to determine its internal conditions, see Werner Link, "Der amerikanische Einfluß auf die Weimarer Republik in der Dawesplanphase (Elemente eines 'penetrierten Systems')," in Hans Mommsen, Dietmar Petzina, and Bernd Weisbrod, eds., *Industrielles System und politische Entwicklung in der Weimarer Republik* (Düsseldorf: Droste Verlag, 1974), 485–498.

16. Moritz Julius Bonn, *Der Neue Plan als Grundlage der deutschen Wirtschaftspolitik* (Munich and Leipzig: Verlag von Duncker & Humblot), 77, 103.

17. In a 1922 House of Commons debate about the powers of the Reparation Commission, the Liberal MP John Simon put this point in terms of moral hazard and personal responsibility: "you never can, and never do, raise the credit of your debtor when you are giving the debtor time to pay if at the same time you insist upon putting in a receiver and manager of his affairs." HC Deb (14 December 1922), vol. 159, col. 3227.

18. Pierre Quesnay note, October 23, 1929. BIS B2489.

19. "Report of the Agent General for Reparation Payments," December 10, 1927. In *Federal Reserve Bulletin* 14 (1928): 28–46, at 28. For context, see William C. McNeil, *American Money and the Weimar Republic: Economics and Politics on the Eve of the Great Depression* (New York: Columbia University Press, 1986), 163–196.

20. George A. Finch, "Report of the Secretary on Progress in International Law during the year 1929–1," *Proceedings of the American Society of International Law at Its Annual Meeting* (1921–1969) 24 (1930): 1–14, at 5. See also H. L. Lutz, "Inter-Allied Debts, Reparations, and National Policy," *Journal of Political Economy* 38.1 (1930): 29–61, at 52.

21. "Report of the Committee of Experts, June, 7, 1929," printed in Denys P. Myers, *The Reparation Settlement, 1930* (Boston: World Peace Foundation, 1930), 948.

22. "Dr Schacht on Paris Conference of the Experts." TLP. Box 180. See also Hans Luther, *Vor dem Abgrund, 1930–1933: Reichsbankpräsident in Krisenzeiten* (Berlin: Propyläen Verlag, 1964), 91.

23. Werner Link, *Die amerikanische Stabilisierungspolitik in Deutschland 1921–32* (Düsseldorf: Droste, 1970), 255–259.

24. Extrait de comptes-rendus de Pierre Quesnay sur les discussions au Comité des Experts (Paris, Comité Young) relatives à la future Banque des Règlements Internationaux. March 8, 1929. BIS B2489. A similar term was used in German (*entpolitisieren*) to describe the promise of the BIS. See Bonn, *Der Neue Plan*, 93.

25. Paul M. Warburg, "Political Pressure and the Future of the Federal Reserve System," *Annals of the American Academy of Political and Social Science* 99 (1922): 70–74, at 74.

26. Alec Cairncross, "The Bank of England: Relationships with the Government, the Civil Service, and Parliament," in Gianni Toniolo, ed., *Central Banks' Independence in Historical Perspective* (Berlin: De Grutyer, 1988), 39–72. For a recent overview of the bank's history, see David Kynaston, *Till Time's Last Sand: A History of the Bank of England 1694–2013* (London: Bloomsbury Publishing, 2017).

27. Quoted in Peter Clarke, *The Keynesian Revolution in the Making, 1924–1936* (Oxford: Clarendon Press, 1990), 35.

28. On this point, see Marc Flandreau, Jacques Le Cacheux, Frédéric Zumer, Rudi Dornbusch, and Patrick Honohan, "Stability without a Pact? Lessons from the European Gold Standard, 1880–1914," *Economic Policy* 13.26 (1998): 115–162, at 130–131. See also Forrest Capie, "Central Bank Statutes: The Historical Dimension," in *Die Bedeutung der Unabhängigkeit der Notenbank für die Glaubwürdigkeit der europäischen Geldpolitik* (Vienna: Oesterreichischen Nationalbank, 1997), 42–55.

29. See also Beth A. Simmons, "Rulers of the Game: Central Bank Independence during the Interwar Years," *International Organization* 50.3 (1996): 407–443.

30. John Maynard Keynes, *The Economic Consequences of Mr. Churchill* (London: L. & V. Woolf, 1925).

31. D. E. Moggridge, *The Return to Gold 1925: The Formulation of Economic Policy and Its Critics* (Cambridge: Cambridge University Press, 1969).

32. T. E. Gregory, *The Present Position of Central Banks* (London: University of London Athlone Press, 1955), 7–12; Richard Sayers, *The Bank of England, 1891–1944, Volume 1* (Cambridge: Cambridge University Press, 1976), 110–152; John Singleton, *Central Banking in the Twentieth Century* (Cambridge: Cambridge University Press, 2011), 50–109.

33. Kenneth Mouré, *The Gold Standard Illusion: France, the Bank of France, and the International Gold Standard, 1914–1939* (Oxford: Oxford University Press, 2002); Jean Bouvier, "The Banque de France and the State from 1850 to the Present Day," in Toniolo, ed., *Central Banks' Independence in Historical Perspective*, 73–104.

34. Allan H. Metzler, *A History of the Federal Reserve Volume 1: 1913–1951* (Chicago: University of Chicago Press, 2004).

35. Paul Einzig, *The Bank for International Settlements* (London: Macmillan, 1932), 126.

36. On this point, see also György Péteri, *Global Monetary Regime and National Central Banking: The Case of Hungary, 1921–1929* (Boulder, CO: Social Science Monographs, 2002), 27–37.

37. See Simon James Bytheway and Mark Metzler, *Central Banks and Gold: How Tokyo, London, and New York Shaped the Modern World* (Ithaca, NY: Cornell University Press, 2015), especially 101–102.

38. Charles Conant, *A History of Modern Banks of Issue* (New York: G.P. Putnam's Sons, 1927), 758.

39. C. H. Kisch and W. A. Elkin, *Central Banks: A Study of the Constitutions of Banks of Issue, With an Analysis of Representative Charters* (London: Macmillan, 1929), 16–39; Carl-Ludwig Holtfrerich, "Relations between Monetary Authorities and Governmental Institutions: The Case of Germany from the 19th Century to the Present," in Toniolo, ed., *Central Banks' Independence in Historical Perspective*, 105–159, at 115–118; Simone Reinhardt, *Die Reichsbank in der Weimarer Republik* (Frankfurt: Peter Lang, 2000), 85–98; Simon Mee, *Central Bank Independence and the Legacy of the German Past* (Cambridge: Cambridge University Press, 2019), 45–50.

40. Boyce, *British Capitalism at the Crossroads*, 186–216; Kent, *Spoils of War*, 307; G. C. Peden, *The Treasury and British Public Policy, 1906–1959* (Oxford: Oxford University Press, 2000), 235–236; Sayers, *The Bank of England*, 354.

41. Philip Snowden to Warren Fisher, September 14, 1929. TNA T 172/1656.

42. Jeremiah Smith Jr. to Thomas Lamont, September 9, 1929. TLP. Box 180.

43. S. D. Waley. "Bank for International Settlements and the League of Nations," September 13, 1929. TNA T 172/1656. See also Frederick Leith-Ross to Fischer Williams, July 15, 1929. TNA T/160/1393.

44. Note for Philip Snowden on Bank for International Settlements. TNA T 172/1656.

45. Note of Conversation with the Prime Minister on Sept. 4th. TNA T 172/1656.

46. Note for Philip Snowden on Bank for International Settlements. TNA T 172/1656.

47. "Relations between the Bank for International Settlement and the League of Nations. Draft Resolution proposed by the Danish, Norwegian and Polish Delegations." TNA T 160/1393.

48. "Extracts from the Minutes of the Eleventh Meeting of the Second Committee of the Assembly, September 21, 1929." Copy in BOE OV 4/10.

49. Philip Snowden to Arthur Henderson, September 18, 1929. TNA T 172/1656.

50. Olivier Feiertag, "Pierre Quesnay et les réseaux de l'internationalisme monétaire en Europe (1917–1937)," in Michel Dumoulin, ed., *Réseaux économiques et construction européenne* (Brussels: Peter Lang, 2004), 331–350; Renaud Boulanger, "La question du rapprochement financier et bancaire entre la France et les États-Unis à la fin des années 1920. L'entremise de Pierre Quesnay," *Histoire@Politique* 1.19 (2013): 52–65.

51. Note Pierre Quesnay. "Quelques réponses aux critiques adressées à la Banque des Règlements Internationaux." BOF. Box 24.

52. "Compte-Rendu de la visite de M. Quesnay à la Banque d'Angleterre les 13 & 14 septembre 1929." BOF. Box 26. For Quesnay's and Moreau's earlier views of Norman, see Andrew Boyle, *Montagu Norman: A Biography* (London: Cassell & Company, 1967), 198–206.

53. "Some Reflections on the Reparations Bank," *The Economist*, July 6, 1929.

54. Boyle, *Montagu Norman*, 247.

55. See also S. Parker Gilbert to Thomas Lamont and Owen Young, September 3, 1929. TLP. Box 181.

56. Montagu Norman to A. H. E. Moreau, September 10, 1929. BOF Box 26; Philip Snowden to Warren Fisher, September 14, 1929. TNA T 172/1656.

57. "Évolution des faits concernant la B. R. I. de juin 1929 (après le Comité des Experts de Paris à octobre 1929 (Baden-Baden) BIS B2489; "Compte-Rendu de la visite de M. Quesnay à Lausanne les 19 et 20 septembre pour y rencontrer les représentants de la Banque d'Italie." BOF Box 26; "The BIS and Baden-Baden," December 4, 1929. BOE OV 4/11.

58. Marcello de Cecco, "Central Bank Cooperation in the Inter-War Period: A View from the Periphery," in Jaime Reis, ed. *International Monetary Systems in Historical Perspective* (London: Macmillan, 1995), 113–134; Giandomenico Piluso, "Adjusting to Financial Instability in the Interwar Period: Italian Financial Elites, International Cooperation, and Domestic Regulation, 1919–1939," in Youssef Cassis and Giuseppe Telesca, eds., *Financial Elites and European Banking: Historical Perspectives* (Oxford: Oxford University Press, 2018), 61–91.

59. Karin Priester, "Fascism in Italy between the Poles of Reactionary Thought and Modernity," in Helmut Konrad and Wolfgang Maderthaner, eds., *Routes into the Abyss: Coping with Crises in the 1930s* (New York: Berghahn Books, 2013), 55–75, at 65.

60. Gian Giacomo Migone, *The United States and Fascist Italy: The Rise of American Finance in Europe,* trans. Molly Tambor (New York: Cambridge University Press, 2015).

61. Eleanor Dulles, *The Bank for International Settlements at Work* (New York: Macmillan, 1932), 83.

62. Joan Hoff Wilson, *American Business & Foreign Policy, 1920–1933* (Lexington, KY: University of Kentucky Press, 1971), 124.

63. George Harrison conversation with Ogden Mills, April 18, 1930. GHP 2013.1.

64. J. P. Morgan to Thomas Lamont, August 6, 1929; Thomas Lamont to Pierre Quesnay, August 19, 1929. TLP. Box 180.

65. Thomas Lamont to Philip Snowden, August 20, 1929. TNA T172/1656; Thomas Lamont to Ramsay MacDonald, August 19, 1929. TLP. Box 180.

66. Philip Snowden to Thomas Lamont, August 23, 1929. TLP Box 180.

67. S. Parker Gilbert to Thomas Lamont, September 10, 1929; Jeremiah Smith Jr. to Thomas Lamont, September 9, 1929. TLP. Box 181.

68. Zoltán Peterecz, *Jeremiah Smith, Jr. and Hungary, 1924–1926: The United States, the League of Nations, and the Financial Reconstruction of Hungary* (Boston: Walter De Gruyter, 2013), 99–100.

69. Comité d'Organisation de la Banque des Règlements Internationaux. XXVII—Séance du 23 October 1929. BIS B2489.

70. Roberta Allbert Dayer, *Finance and Empire: Sir Charles Addis, 1861–1945* (Houndmills, Basingstoke, Hampshire: Macmillan, 1988), 186–232.

71. "The BIS and Baden-Baden," December 4, 1929. BOE OV 4/11.

72. "L'oeuvre du Comité d'Organisation da la B.R.I." BIS B2489.

73. "Reasons which prompted the British Delegation to propose the Separation of Constitution and Statutes." BIS COBRI 7.16.1.1.

74. "Reasons which prompted the British Delegation to propose the Separation of Constitution and Statutes." BIS COBRI 7.16.1.1.

75. Dîner Layton. Conversations du 3 et du 4 Octobre 1929. BIS B2489.

76. The British Treasury regarded the strategy of the "Latin bankers" to keep the statues from being submitted for government approval with unease. See Frederick Leith-Ross to Philip Snowden, October 10, 1929. BOE OV 4/1.

77. "L'oeuvre du comité d'organisation de la Banque des Règlements Internationaux I." BIS B2489.

78. Dîner Layton. Conversations du 3 et du 4 Octobre 1929. BIS B2489.

79. "L'oeuvre du comité d'organisation de la Banque des Règlements Internationaux I"; Conversation du 5 Octobre 1929 avec M. Beneduce. BIS B2489.

80. Note Pierre Quesnay. "Quelques réponses aux critiques adressées à la Banque des Règlements Internationaux." BOF. Box 24.

81. Pierre Quesnay to Robert Coulondre, October 19, 1929. BIS B2489.

82. Dîner Layton. Conversations du 3 et du 4 Octobre 1929. BIS B2489.

83. Holtfrerich, "Relations between Monetary Authorities and Governmental Institutions," 121–129.

84. "Dr Schacht on Paris Conference of the Experts." TLP. Box 180.

85. Harold James, *The Reichsbank and Public Finance in Germany: 1924–1933* (Frankfurt am Main: Fritz Knapp, 1985); Pierpaolo Barbieri, *Hitler's Shadow Empire: Nazi Economics and the Spanish Civil War* (Cambridge, MA: Harvard University Press, 2015), 74–104.

86. After the Nazi seizure of power in 1933, Schacht returned to the presidency of the Reichsbank and then served as minister of economics, though his falling out with Hermann Göring and opposition to financial aspects of the Nazi rearmament program led to his dismissal from the Reichsbank in 1939. See Adam Tooze, *The Wages of Destruction: The Making and Breaking of the Nazi Economy* (London: Penguin, 2008).

87. See, for example, C. H. Lambert, "The Schacht Affair," *The Nation & Athenaeum*, March 22, 1930, 852.

88. Josiah Stamp, *Reparation Payments and Future International Trade* (Paris: International Chamber of Commerce, 1925), 47–55; E. G. Burland, "The Trend of Economic Restoration Since the Dawes Reparation Settlement," *International Conciliation* 215 (1925): 5–36, at 12.

89. Another influential advocate of this conception of the BIS was the Belgian internationalist and futurist Paul Otlet, who called for a world bank to finance global infrastructural development in line with his larger aims of creating a global network of communication, what he called the "Mundaneum" or "world brain." The idea was pitched to the Paris Conference attendees. See Paul Otlet, *La Banque internationale; économie mondiale et société financière des nations* (Brussels: L'Églantine, 1929).

90. Hjalmar Schacht, *My First Seventy-Six Years: The Autobiography of Hjalmar Schacht*, trans. Diana Pyke (London: Allan Wingate, 1955), 249–251. However, Schacht was alone among the founders of the BIS in later becoming a development adviser. After being tried and acquitted at Nuremberg for his role in the Third Reich, he spent much of the 1950s and early 1960s as a private consultant to the governments of countries like the Philippines and Indonesia.

91. See, for example, "The Young Plan Bank," *Manchester Guardian*, October 4, 1929.

92. Comité Young; Memorandum No. 3, La Banque Internationale, February 25, 1929. BIS B2489; "Capital de la Banque Internationale," March 11, 1929. BIS B2489.

93. On this point, see also Georg Schwarzenberger, *Die Internationalen Banken für Zahlungsausgleich und Agrarkredite* (Berlin: Junker und Dünnhaupt, 1932), 72.

94. For details, see Clive M. Schmitthoff, "The International Corporation (Legal Organization of a Planned World Economy)," *Transactions of the Grotius Society* 30 (1944): 165–183.

95. John Fischer Williams, "The Legal Character of the Bank for International Settlements," *American Journal of International Law* 24.4 (1930): 665–673. See also Manley O. Hudson, "The Bank for International Settlements," *American Journal of International Law* 24.3 (1930): 561–566; Mario Giovanoli, "The Role of the Bank for International Settlements in International Monetary Cooperation and Its Tasks Relating to the European Currency Unit," *The International Lawyer* 23.4 (1989): 841–864; David J. Bederman, "The Unique Legal Status of the Bank for International Settlements Comes into Focus," *Leiden Journal of International Law* 16 (2003): 787–794; Roland Portmann, *Legal Personality in International Law* (Cambridge: Cambridge University Press, 2014), 228–232.

96. Williams, "The Legal Character of the Bank for International Settlements," 667.

97. On this point, see Benvenuto Griziotti, "La Banque des Règlements Internationaux," *Recueil des cours de l'Académie de droit international* 42 (1932): 359–466, at 394–395.

98. Quoted in *Bulletin périodique de la press allemande* 374, March 7, 1929, 2.

99. Jonathan Mitchell, "The World Bank as an Aid to Peace," *St. Louis Post-Dispatch*, January 30, 1930. See also "Memorandum Submitted to the French Government and the French Parliament Concerning the Establishment of a Monetary Federation." ILO CAT 11A; "Projet de Résolution présenté au Comité Fédéral de Coopération Européenne." ILO CAT 6B-7-2-1. For a characteristic account of the bank as a "pacifier," see the Associated Press article "The World Bank," March 20, 1929, which was widely printed in US newspapers.

100. Tobias Straumann, *1931: Debt, Crisis, and the Rise of Hitler* (Oxford: Oxford University Press, 2019), 32–38; Larry Eugene Jones, *The German Right, 1918–1930: Political Parties, Organized Interests, and Patriotic Associations in the Struggle against Weimar Democracy* (Cambridge: Cambridge University Press, 2020), 486–494.

101. Characteristic views are documented in *Bulletin périodique de la presse allemande*. See, for example, editions from October 31, 1929, and April 16, 1931.

102. See, especially, Thomas Lamont to Louis McFadden, March 20, 1930, and other documentation in TLP. Box 181.

103. HC Deb (20 February 1930), vol. 235, col. 1610; HC Deb (27 May 1930), vol. 239.

104. "La Banque des Règlements Internationaux après Baden-Baden et jusqu'après la 2ème Conférence de La Haye (nov. 1929–fin janv. 1930). BIS B2489.

105. Ahamed, *Lords of Finance*, 247–254; Kenneth Mouré, "The Bank of France and the Gold Standard, 1914–1928," in Marc Flandreau, Carl-Ludwig Holtfrerich, and Harold James, eds., *International Financial History in the Twentieth Century: System and Anarchy* (Cambridge: Cambridge University Press, 2003), 95–124. See also Jean-Noël Jeanneney, *Leçon d'histoire pour une Gauche au pouvoir: la faillite du cartel, 1924–1926* (Paris: Éditions du Seuil, 1977).

106. Chambre des Députés. 3éme Séance du 28 Décembre 1929. BOF. Box 34.

107. Chambre des Députés. 3éme Séance du 28 Décembre 1929. BOF Box 34. On the French reception of the bank plans, see also Constantin Karanikas, *La Banque des règlements internationaux* (Paris, Domat-Montchrestian, 1931).

108. "New Reparation Bank," *Manchester Guardian*, March 12, 1929.

109. Chambre des Députés. 3éme Séance du 28 Décembre 1929. BOF. Box 34; "La Banque des Règlements Internationaux après Baden-Baden et jusqu'après la 2ème Conférence de La Haye" (nov. 1929–janv. 1930). BIS B2489.

110. Jean Lacouture, *Pierre Mendès France*, trans. George Holoch (New York: Holmes & Meier, 1984), 176.

111. Pierre Mendès France, *La Banque Internationale: contribution à l'étude du problème des État-Unis d'Europe* (Paris: Valois, 1930), 215.

112. There is a large literature on this hinge point in the *annus terribilis* of 1931. See, for example, Stephen Clarke, *Central Bank Cooperation, 1924–1931* (New York: Federal Reserve Bank, 1967), 183–201; Aurel Schubert, *The Credit-Anstalt Crisis of 1931* (Cambridge: Cambridge University Press, 1991), 13–14, 158–167; Iago Gil Aguado, "The Creditanstalt Crisis of 1931 and the Failure of the Austro-German Customs Union Project," *Historical Journal* 44.1 (2001): 199–221; Toniolo, *Central Bank Cooperation at the Bank for International Settlements*, 84–114; Tooze, *The Deluge*, 494–495; Straumann, *1931*, 171–201.

113. Simon Banholzer and Tobias Straumann, "Why the French Said 'Non': A New Perspective on the Hoover Moratorium of June 1931," *Journal of Contemporary History* 56.4 (2021): 1040–1060.

114. Boyle, *Montagu Norman*, 265.

115. Kindersley Plan, February 2, 1931. TNA T 160/398/6.

116. Frederick Leith-Ross note on Kindersley scheme, January 30, 1931. TNA T 160/398/6.

117. Montagu Norman to Gates McGarrah, February 2, 1931. BIS. 7.16; Frederick Leith-Ross, "International Credit Scheme," April 16, 1931. TNA T 160/398; H. A. Siepmann, "Sir Robert Kindersley's Scheme," February 13, 1931. BOE OV 4/84.

118. Gates McGarrah to J. P. Morgan, T. W. Lamont, S. Parker Gilbert, March 12, 1931. BIS Bo519; Clément Moret to Gates McGarrah, March 1931. BIS 7.16.

119. Leon Fraser to Ivan Kreuger, July 16, 1931. BIS 7.16.

120. J. P. Morgan, T. W. Lamont, S. Parker Gilbert to Gates McGarrah, March 13, 1931. BIS Bo519.

121. Rapport présenté par M. Francqui; "Report on the Meetings of the Bank for International Settlements Committee Held in Brussels on June 3 and 4, 1931." BIS 7.16.

122. S. Parker Gilbert to Gates McGarrah, April 18, 1931; J. P. Morgan and S. Parker Gilbert to Gates McGarrah, May 15, 1931; Gates McGarrah to J. P. Morgan and S. Parker Gilbert, May 18, 1931. BIS Bo519.

123. Montagu Norman to Émile Francqui, April 27, 1931. BOE OV 4-84.

124. See, for example, James, "The Creation of a World Central Bank?"

125. Diane Kunz, *The Battle for Britain's Gold Standard in 1931* (London: Croom Helm, 1987).

126. David Blaazer, "Finance and the End of Appeasement: The Bank of England, the National Government and the Czech Gold," *Journal of Contemporary History* 40.1 (2005): 25–39; Toniolo, *Central Bank Cooperation at the Bank for International Settlements*, 204–213. The BIS president at the time, Johan W. Beyen (later executive director of the IMF and member of the Board of Directors of the International Bank for Reconstruction and Development) blamed the British and French governments, and their policies of appeasement, for not halting the transaction. See Johan W. Beyen, *Money in a Maelstrom* (New York: Macmillan, 1949), 137–139.

127. On a similar point, see also Griziotti, "La Banque des Règlements Internationaux," 456.

128. John Maynard Keynes, *A Treatise on Money*, Volume 2 (London: Macmillan, 1930), 388–408. For the BIS as model for Mexican plans for an international financial institution during the Depression, see Christy Thornton, *Revolution in Development: Mexico and the Governance of the Global Economy* (Berkeley, CA: University of California Press, 2021), 59–61.

129. Vincent Lagendijk, *Electrifying Europe: The Power of Europe in the Construction of Electricity Networks* (Amsterdam: Aksant, 2008), 74–106; Pierre Tilly and Michel Dumoulin, "Interwar Plans for European Integration," in Natalie J. Doyle and Lorenza Sebesta, eds. *Regional Integration and Modernity: Cross-Atlantic Perspectives* (Lanham, MD: Lexington Books, 2014), 1–20. For contemporary views, see, for example, Wladimir Woytinsky, "International Measures to Create Employment: A Remedy for the Depression," *International Labour Review* 25.1 (1932): 1–22. On the afterlife of some of these ideas in Nazi Germany, see Richard Vahrenkamp, *The German Autobahn 1920–1945: Hafraba Visions and Mega Projects* (Cologne: EUL, 2010).

130. "Les travaux publics devant la Commission pour l'Union Européenne et Assemblée de la Société des Nations." ILO CAT 11B; "Procès-Verbal de la séance de la Commission Agricole et des Travaux Publics du Comité Fédéral de Coopération Européenne," January 30, 1931. ILO CAT 11C; Francqui note on "Immediate Practical Methods of Alleviating the Economic Position in Europe." ILO CAT 11A; Annex to Francqui Plan. BIS 6/27. See also Francis Delaisi, *Les deux Europes* (Paris: Payot, 1929). Delaisi, the intellectual inspiration for many of these ideas, also suggested that the BIS help finance them.

131. J. E. Meade, *Public Works in Their International Aspect* (London: New Fabian Research Bureau, 1933), 4–5.

4. The Origins of International Development

1. The literature on international development is vast. For comprehensive historio-graphical overviews, see Joseph Hodge, "Writing the History of Development (Part 1: The First Wave)," *Humanity* 6.2 (2015): 429–463 and "Writing the History of Development (Part 2: Longer, Deeper, Wider)," *Humanity* 7.1 (2016): 125–174.

2. The interwar history of international development is understudied. For histories of development that mention these precedents, see especially Gilbert Rist, *The History of Development: From Western Origins to Global Faith*, trans. Patrick Camiller (London: Zed Books, 1997); Eric Helleiner, *The Forgotten Foundations of Bretton Woods: International Development and the Making of the Postwar Order* (Ithaca, NY: Cornell University Press, 2014), 72–78; Christy Thornton, *Revolution in Development: Mexico and the Governance of the Global Economy* (Berkeley, CA: University of California Press, 2021), 58–78. On other interwar precursors, see also Daniel Maul, *Human Rights, Development and Decolonization: The International Labour Organization, 1940–1970* (New York: Palgrave Macmillan, 2012).

3. For an official statement of this view, see "Work of the Financial Committee During Its Thirty-Ninth Session: Report of the Committee, Submitted to the Council on September 24th, 1930," *LON OJ* 11.11 (November 1930): 1553–1562, at 1561.

4. Otto Niemeyer, "The Sphere of the League Financial Committee," March 28, 1928. OV 9/281.

5. Otto Niemeyer, "The Sphere of the League Financial Committee," March 28, 1928. OV 9/281.

6. Thirty-Seventh Council Session, Extract from Minutes of 13th Meeting (private). December 14, 1925. OV 9/281.

7. Otto Niemeyer, "The Sphere of the League Financial Committee," March 28, 1928. OV 9/281. On the peculiarities of Danzig, see also Marcus M. Payk, "'Emblems of Sovereignty:' The Internationalization of Danzig and the Polish Post Office Dispute, 1919–25," in Marcus M. Payk and Roberta Pergher, eds., *Sovereignty, Legitimacy, and the Formation of New Polities after the Great War* (Bloomington: Indiana University Press, 2019), 215–235.

8. Otto Niemeyer to O. G. Sargent, April 30, 1929. BOE G1/391.

9. Otto Niemeyer to O. G. Sargent, January 14, 1929. BOE G1/391.

10. Statement submitted by the Zionist Organisation for the consideration of His Majesty's Government. January 31, 1928; S. D. Waley to Otto Niemeyer, March, 16, 1928; Otto Niemeyer to S. D. Waley, March 16, 1928; Otto Niemeyer to Richard Hopkins, March 28, 1931; "The Sphere of the League Financial Committee," March 28, 1928. OV 9/281. BOE OV 9/281.

11. Statement submitted by the Zionist Organisation for the consideration of His Majesty's Government. Ch. Weizmann, January 31, 1928. BOE OV9/281.

12. See, for example, Eliot Grinnell Mears, *Greece Today: The Aftermath of the Refugee Impact* (Stanford, CA: Stanford University Press, 1929); Stephen P. Ladas, *The Exchange of Minorities: Bulgaria, Greece and Turkey* (New York: MacMillan, 1932); Dimitri Pentzopoulos, *The Balkan Exchange of Minorities and Its Impact upon Greece* (Paris: Mouton, 1962); Claudena M. Skran, *Refugees in Inter-War Europe* (Oxford: Clarendon Press, 1995); Anastasia N. Karakasidou, *Fields of Wheat, Hills of Blood: Passages to Nationhood in Greek Macedonia, 1870–1990* (Chicago: University of Chicago Press, 1997); Renée Hirschorn, ed., *Crossing the Aegean: An Appraisal of the 1923 Compulsory Population Exchange between Greece and Turkey* (New York: Berghahn Books, 2003); Onur Yıldırım, *Diplomacy and Displacement: Reconsidering the Turco-Greek Exchange of Populations, 1922–1934* (New York and London: Routledge, 2006); Bruce Clark, *Twice a Stranger: The Mass Expulsions That Forged Modern Greece and Turkey* (Cambridge, MA: Harvard University Press, 2006);

Sarah Shields, "Forced Migration as Nation-Building: The League of Nations, Minority Protection, and the Greek-Turkish Population Exchange," *Journal of the History of International Law* 18 (2016): 120–145; Laura Robson, *States of Separation: Transfer, Partition, and the Making of the Modern Middle East* (Berkeley, CA: University of California Press, 2017); A. Dirk Moses, *The Problems of Genocide: Permanent Security and the Language of Transgression* (Cambridge: Cambridge University Press, 2021), 332–363.

13. A few accounts have mentioned in passing how the problem of Greek refugee settlement offered a kind of prelude to later international development schemes. See, for example, Mark Mazower, *Greece and the Inter-War Economic Crisis* (Oxford: Clarendon Press, 1991), 72; Peter Gatrell, *The Making of the Modern Refugee* (Oxford: Oxford University Press, 2013), 66; Matthew Frank, *Making Minorities History: Population Transfer in Twentieth-Century Europe* (Oxford: Oxford University Press, 2017), 81–85. For a broader history of ideas of economic development in Greece, see Andreas Kakridis, "*Deus ex machina*? Truman/Marshall Aid, Engineers, and Greece's Post-war Development Discourse," *Journal of Modern Greek Studies* 27.2 (2009): 241–274.

14. On the Bulgarian refugee loan, see Theodora Dragostinova, "Competing Priorities, Ambiguous Loyalties: Challenges of Socioeconomic Adaptation and National Inclusion of the Interwar Bulgarian Refugees," *Nationalities Papers* 34.5 (2006): 549–574.

15. Otto Niemeyer to Under Secretary of State, Foreign Office. May 30, 1925. OV 9/281.

16. For details, see, especially, Ionna Pepelasis Minoglu, "The Greek State and the International Financial Community, 1922–1932: Demystifying the 'Foreign Factor.'" Unpublished PhD dissertation, London School of Economics and Political Science (1993), especially 64–93. See also Anne Orde, *British Policy and European Reconstruction after the First World War* (Cambridge: Cambridge University Press, 1990), 284–288. For an early but still useful account by a member of the League's Economic and Financial Organization, and the earliest chronicler of its history, see Martin Hill, "The League of Nations and the Work of Refugee Settlement and Financial Reconstruction in Greece, 1922–1930," *Weltwirtschaftliches Archiv* 3 (1931): 265–283.

17. On the economic aspects of the problem, see André Rodocanachi, *Les Finances de la Grèce et l'Établissement des Réfugiés* (Paris: Librairie Dalloz, 1934); Elisabeth Kontogiorgi, *Population Exchange in Greek Macedonia; The Rural Settlement of Refugees 1922–1930* (Oxford: Clarenon Press, 2006), especially 297–329; George Kritikos, "The Agricultural Settlement of Refugees: A Source of Productive Work and Stability in Greece, 1923–1930," *Agricultural History* 79.3 (2005): 321–346. For context, see Mazower, *Greece and the Inter-War Economic Crisis*, 41–112.

18. Alexander Betts, Louise Bloom, Josiah Kaplan, and Naohiko Omata, *Refugee Economies: Forced Displacement and Development* (Oxford: Oxford University Press, 2017), 14–15; Gatrell, *The Making of the Modern Refugee*, 64–67; Pentzopoulos, *The Balkan Exchange of Minorities*, 111.

19. E. J. Tsouderos, *Le Relèvement économique de la Grèce* (Paris: Berger-Levrault, 1920), 23–31; John Levandis, *The Greek Foreign Debt and the Great Powers, 1821–1898* (New York: Columbia University Press, 1944), 88–116; George J. Andreopoulos, "The International Financial Commission and Anglo-Greek Relations (1928–1933)," *The Historical Journal* 31.2 (1988): 341–364; Korinna Schönhärl, *European Investment in Greece in the Nineteenth Century: A Behavioural Approach to Financial History,* trans. Katharine Thomas (Abingdon: Routledge, 2021), 296–330.

20. Otto Niemeyer to Under Secretary of State, Foreign Office, May 30, 1925. BOE OV 9/281.

21. Socrates D. Petmezas, "The Modernisation of Agriculture in Greece (c. 1920–1970): Variation of a European Mediterranean Model?," in Peter Moser and Tony Varley, eds.,

Integration Through Subordination: The Politics of Agricultural Modernisation in Industrial Europe (Turnhout: Brepols, 2013), 109–131, at 115–118.

22. On these efforts, see Davide Rodogno, "The American Red Cross and the International Committee of the Red Cross' Humanitarian Politics and Policies in Asia Minor and Greece (1922–1923)," *First World War Studies* 5.1 (2014): 83–99.

23. A. S. Pennell to C. H. Bentinck, February 28 and March 8, 1924. TNA FO 286/910.

24. "Greek Refugee Loan," July 27, 1923. BOE C44/127; Montagu Norman to Alexandros Diomedes, August 1, 1923. BOE C44/127.

25. George Mavrogordatos, *Stillborn Republic: Social Coalitions and Party Strategies in Greece, 1922–1936* (Berkeley, CA: University of California Press, 1983), 25–54, 183–185, 198–206.

26. For details, see Minoglu, "The Greek State and the International Financial Community," 64–93.

27. Dertilis, *La Reconstruction Financière de la Grèce,* 132.

28. On interwar innovations in legal personality, see Mira Siegelberg, *Statelessness: A Modern History* (Cambridge, MA: Harvard University Press, 2020) and Natasha Wheatley, "Spectral Legal Personality in Interwar International Law: On New Ways of Not Being a State," *Law and History Review* 35.3 (2017): 753–787.

29. On Morgenthau's role, see, in particular, Louis P. Cassimatis, *American Influence in Greece 1917–1929* (Kent, OH: Kent State University Press, 1988).

30. See, for example, Hill, "The League of Nations and the Work of Refugee Settlement and Financial Reconstruction in Greece," 273.

31. "Arrangement between the Greek Government and the Refugee Settlement Commission;" Joost Adriaan Van Hamel, "Note on Legal Questions, Refugee Settlement Commission," September 9, 1925. LON C132-No. 6. 25.

32. Henry Morgenthau, *I Was Sent to Athens* (Garden City: Doubleday, Doran & Company, 1929), 251.

33. See, for example, Frederick J. Haskin, "American Friends of Greece," *The Independent-Record,* January 30, 1925.

34. "Refugees obligations towards the RSC," December 30, 1923. LON C129. No. 1. 23–26.

35. On the innovation of such protocols and their binding force, see Juan H. Flores Zendejas, "Financial Markets, International Organizations and Conditional Lending: A Long-Term Perspective," in Grégoire Mallard and Jérôme Sgard, eds., *Contractual Knowledge: One Hundred Years of Legal Experimentation in Global Markets* (Cambridge: Cambridge University Press, 2016), 81–82.

36. See, for example, letter to Henry Morgenthau, December 5, 1924. HMSP. Box 31. Reel 25.

37. Mavrogordatos, *Stillborn Republic,* 208–209; Mazower, *Greece and the Inter-War Economic Crisis,* 32.

38. S. Papadakis to Henry Morgenthau, June 20, 1924. HMSP. Box 10. Reel 9.

39. John Campbell to Henry Morgenthau, December 25, 1924. HMSP. Box 31. Reel 25.

40. Henry Morgenthau to Alexandros Papanastasiou, May 13, 1924. LON C130-No. 2. 23–30.

41. John Campbell to Arthur Salter, July 11, 1924. LON C129-No. 1. 23–26.

42. Charles Howland to Arthur Felkin, July 14, 1925. LON C129-No.1. 23–26.

43. "Greece and the Refugees." LON. C129-No. 1. 23–26.

44. Greek Refugee Settlement Commission. Report to the Council by the Financial Committee. LON C132-No. 6. 25.

45. John Campbell to A. E. Felkin, July 3, 1925. LON C129-No. 1. 23–26.

46. Charles Howland to Arthur Salter, August 12, 1925. CHP. Box 7.

47. John Campbell to A. E. Felkin, July 3, 1925. LON C129-No. 1. 23–26; Charles Howland to Etienne Delta, July 2, 1925. LON C123-No. 4. 25–29. For context, see David Close, "Conservatism, authoritarianism and fascism in Greece, 1915–45," in Martin Blinkhorn, ed., *Fascists and Conservatives: The Radical Right and the Establishment in Twentieth-Century Europe* (London: Unwin Hyman, 1990), 200–217.

48. "Warrant of Incarceration;" "Statement by the Chairman of the Greek Refugees [sic] Settlement Commission Relating to the Questions Presented by It to the Council of the League of Nations on the Basis of the Commission's Special Report Presented Herewith." LON C129.-No. 1. 23–26.

49. Charles Howland to Arthur Salter, August 12, 1925. CHP. Box 7.

50. Décret-Loi of July 20, 1925. Copy in LON C132-No. 6.25.

51. Charles Howland to Arthur Felkin, July 14, 1925. LON C129-No. 1. 23–26.

52. Charles Howland to Arthur Salter, August 25, 1925. CHP. Box 7; Pamboukas to RSC Council, August 25, 1925. LON C130-No. 2. 23–30; Note juridique préparée à la demande du Comité grec du Conseil de la Société des Nations, September 9, 1925. LON C129. No. 1. 23–26.

53. Charles Howland to Theodoros Pangalos, July 24, 1925. LON C130-No. 2. 23–30.

54. Charles Howland to Theodoros Pangalos, August 22 and August 26, 1925. LON C132-No 6. 25.

55. Emmanouil Tsoudéros to Charles Howland, August 25, 1925. CHP. Box 7.

56. Charles Howland to Arthur Salter, August 25, 1925. CHP. Box 7.

57. Charles Howland to Arthur Salter, November 12, 1925. CHP. Box 7.

58. Otto Niemeyer to H. Nicholson, July 31, 1925. BOE. C44/127.

59. Etienne Delta. Translation of three articles in *Eleutheron Vema*. August 1925. CHP Box 7.

60. League of Nations. Greek Refugee Settlement Commission. Report to the Council by the Financial Committee; Joost Adriaan Van Hamel, "Note on Legal Questions, Refugee Settlement Commission." September 9, 1925. LON C132-No. 6. 25.

61. Charles Howland to Arthur Salter, November 12, 1925. CHP. Box 7.

62. Charles Howland to Arthur Salter, August 20, 1925; Charles Howland to A. E. Felkin, September 23, 1925; Charles Howland to Arthur Salter, October 13, 1925; Charles Howland to A. E. Felkin, December 2, 1925; Charles Howland to Arthur Salter, January 19, 1926. CHP. Box 7.

63. Charles Howland, "Memorandum for the Financial Committee on the Factors Bearing on the Possibility of a New Greek Refugee Loan," May 1926. Howland. BOE. OV9/423.

64. Myrsini Pichou and Chrysoula Kapartziani, "Thirty Centimetres above the Ground: The Regulation Length for Greek Skirts during the Dictatorship of General Theodoros Pangalos, 1925–1926," *Clothing Cultures* 3.1 (2016): 55–65. For context, see also Thanos Veremis, "The Greek State and Economy during the Pangalos Regime, 1925–1926," *Journal of the Hellenic Diaspora* 7.2 (1980): 43–50.

65. Charles Howland to Montagu Norman, September 25, 1925; Arthur Salter to Eric Hambro, December 21, 1925; Milne Cheetham to Austen Chamberlain, December 17, 1925. TNA. FO 286/945. Charles Howland to Arthur Salter, August 12, 1925; Charles Howland to A.E. Felkin, December 2, 1925. CHP. Box 7; Otto Niemeyer to Charles Howland, August 3, 1926. BOE OV9/423.

66. "Eleventh Quarterly Report of the Refugee Settlement Commission," September 4, 1926, printed in *LON OJ* 7 (1926): 1330.

67. Charles Howland to John Campbell, August 25 and September 3, 1926. LON C129. No. 1. 23–26.

68. Charles Howland to John Campbell, July 30, 1926. LON C129-No. 1. 23–26.

69. Arthur Salter to John Campbell, June 16, 1926; John Campbell to Charles Howland, June 30, 1926. LON C129-No. 1. 23–26.

70. John Campbell to Demetre Tantalidès, June 30, 1926. LON C130-No. 2. 23–30.

71. See Commission report in LON C123-No. 7. 26–30; Note on an interview with Mr. Tantalidès, Minister of Finance, June 9, 1926. LON C129-No. 1. 23–26.

72. "Confidential Note on the Question of the Dime," June 7, 1926. LON C129-No. 1. 23–26.

73. Charles Howland to John Campbell, June 29, 1926. LON C129-No 1. 23–26.

74. John Campbell to Governor of National Bank of Greece, March 9, 1926. LON C133-No.1. 24–29.

75. Otto Niemeyer to Arthur Salter, August 24, 1926. BOE. OV9/423.

76. "Preparatory Work for the Organisation of the 'Service for the Collection of the Refugee Debts,'" October 15, 1925. LON C133-No. 1. 24–29.

77. "Refugees Obligations towards the RSC," December 30, 1923. LON C129-No. 1. 23–26.

78. Letter to Eric Hambro, October 30, 1925. LON C133-No. 1. 24–29.

79. John Campbell to Arthur Salter, February 25, 1925. LON C129-No. 1. 23–26. On the politics of the compensation issue, see Mavrogordatos, *Stillborn Republic,* 188–191, 209–212.

80. "Measures of the Government against the Refugees. Yesterday's Refugee Manifestation." *Scrip* May 25, 1925. CHP. Box 7.

81. Greek Communist Party pamphlet. LON C123-No. 4. 25–29.

82. Charles Howland to John Campbell, June 9, 1925; Charles Howland to John Campbell, June 11, 1925; Charles Howland to Etienne Delta, July 2, 1925. LON C123-No. 4. 25–29.

83. Charles Howland to Arthur Salter, June 12, 1925. CHP. Box 7.

84. Charles Howland to Andreas Michalakopoulos, June 9, 1925. LON C130-No 2. 23–30.

85. Charles Howland to Arthur Salter, June 12, 1925. CHP. Box 7.

86. Charles Howland to Arthur Felkin, July 14, 1925. LON C129-No.1. 23–26.

87. On this point, see also an extract from a letter to Arthur Salter from March 23, 1926. BOE. OV 9/423.

88. Charles Howland, "Outline of a Plan for the Collection of Refugee Debts," March 1926. BOE OV9/423.

89. Otto Niemeyer to Eric Hambro, July 6, 1927; Otto Niemeyer to Charles Eddy, July 14, 1927. BOE OV 9//423.

90. International Financial Commission. Dissolution of the Refugee Settlement Commission. May 12, 1929. LON C123. No 7. 26–30.

91. International Financial Commission. Dissolution of the Refugee Settlement Commission. May 12, 1929. LON C123. No 7. 26–30.

92. On the issue of repayment after the RSC's end, see Mark Mazower, "The Refugees, the Economic Crisis, and the Collapse of Venizelist Hegemony," *Bulletin of the Centre for Asia Minor Studies* 9 (1992): 119–134, at 125–126.

93. "Communiqué to the Press on Meeting between the RSC and Representatives of the Refugees Residing in the Quarters of the Commission in Athens, on February 12th, 1929;" John Hope Simpson to Eleftherios Venizelos, January 15, 1929. LON C125-No. 6.

94. John Hope Simpson, February 12, 1929. LON C123-No. 2. 27–30.

95. Procés-Verbal of Meeting at RSC, May 15, 1929. LON C125-No.6. 26–30.

96. John Hope Simpson. Undated Note from 1929. LON C123-No. 2. 27–30.

97. Procés-Verbal of a Meeting at the Petit Palais, January 2, 1929. LON C125-No. 6. 26–30.

98. On the long-term effects of this scheme on Greek agriculture, see Socrates D. Petmezas, "The Policy of Wheat Self-Sufficiency and Its Impact upon Rural Modernization in Greece, 1928–1960," in Carin Martiin, Juan Pan-Montojo, and Paul Brassley, eds., *Agriculture in Capitalist Europe, 1945–1960: From Food Shortages to Food Surpluses* (London: Routledge, 2016), 87–106, especially 92.

99. On attempts to evade control, see Minoglu, "The Greek State and the International Financial Community," 133–170.

100. Mazower, *Greece and the Inter-War Economic Crisis*, 102–107, and "Banking and Economic Development in Interwar Greece," in Harold James, Håkan Lindgren, and Alice Teichova, eds., *The Role of Banks in the Interwar Economy* (Cambridge: Cambridge University Press, 1991), 206–232, at 215–220; Olga Christodoulaki, "The Origins of Central Banking in Greece," unpublished PhD dissertation, London School of Economics and Political Science (2015). For context, see also George B. Dertilis and Constantine Costis, "Banking, Public Finance, and the Economy: Greece, 1919–1933," in Charles H. Feinstein, ed., *Banking, Currency, and Finance in Europe Between the Wars* (Oxford: Oxford University Press, 1995), 458–471.

101. Charles Howland to A. E. Felkin, April 6, 1926. LON C122-No 7. 27–30.

102. Otto Niemeyer to S. D. Waley, March 16, 1928. BOE OV 9 / 281.

103. Eric Vernon Francis, *Britain's Economic Strategy* (London: J. Cape, 1939), 96.

104. Iris Borowy, *Coming to Terms with World Health: The League of Nations Health Organisation 1921–1946* (Frankfurt am Main: Peter Lang, 2009), 305–324.

105. See, above all, Margherita Zanasi, *Saving the Nation: Economic Modernity in Republican China* (Chicago: University of Chicago Press, 2006), and "Exporting Development: The League of Nations and Republican China," *Comparative Studies in Society and History* 49.1 (2007): 143–169. See also James T. Watkins, "China's Role in the League of Nations 1920–1935," unpublished PhD dissertation, Stanford University (1941); James C. Thomson Jr., *While China Faced West: American Reformers in Nationalist China 1928–1937* (Cambridge, MA: Harvard University Press, 1969), 114–115, 197–200; Arthur N. Young, *China's Nation Building Effort, 1927–1937: The Financial and Economic Record* (Stanford, CA: Stanford University Press, 1971), 342–349; Ernst Neugebauer, *Anfänge pädagogischer Entwicklungshilfe unter dem Völkerbund in China, 1931 bis 1935* (Hamburg: Institute für Asienkunde, 1971); Ann Trotter, *Britain and East Asia, 1933–1937* (Cambridge: Cambridge University Press, 1975); Jürgen Osterhammel, "'Technical Cooperation' between the League of Nations and China," *Modern Asian Studies* 13.4 (1979): 661–680; Ian Nish, *Japan's Struggle with Internationalism: Japan, China, and the League of Nations, 1931–3* (London: Kegan Paul International, 1993), 16–22; William C. Kirby, "Engineering China: Birth of the Developmental State, 1928–1937," in Wen-hsin Ye, ed., *Becoming Chinese: Passages to Modernity and Beyond* (Berkeley, CA: University of California Press, 2000), 137–160; Susanne Kuß, *Der Völkerbund und China: Technische Kooperation und deutsche Berater, 1928–34* (Münster: Lit, 2005); Donald A. Jordan, "China's National Economic Council and the League of Nations Experts, 1929–1937," in Susanne Weigelin-Schwierzik, Agnes Schick-Chen, and Sascha Klotzbücher, eds., *As China Meets the World: China's Changing Position in the International Community* (Vienna: Verlag der Österreichischen Akademie der Wissenschaften, 2006), 123–132; Paul B. Trescott, "Western Economic Advisers in China, 1940–1949," *Research in the History of Economic Thought and Methodology* 28 (2010): 1–37; Harumi Goto-Shibata, "The League of Nations as an Actor in East Asia: Empires and Technical Cooperation with China," *International Relations of the Asia-Pacific* 17 (2017): 435–461.

106. Stefan Hell, *Siam and the League of Nations: Modernisation, Sovereignty and Multilateral Diplomacy, 1920–1940* (Bangkok: River Books, 2010).

107. Ibrahim Sundiata, *Brothers and Strangers: Black Zion, Black Slavery, 1914–1940* (Durham, NC: Duke University Press, 2004), 97–169.

108. On this point, see Megan Donaldson, "The League of Nations, Ethiopia, and the Making of States," *Humanity* (May 14, 2020). Available at: http://humanityjournal.org /issue11-1/the-league-of-nations-ethiopia-and-the-making-of-states/.

109. On this point, see "The Financial Reconstruction of China," in J. B. Condliffe, ed., *Problems of the Pacific: Proceedings of the Third Conference of the Institute of Pacific Relations, Nara and Kyoto, Japan, October 23 to November 9, 1929* (Chicago: University of Chicago Press, 1930), 141–153, at 143.

110. Xu Guoqi, *China and the Great War: China's Pursuit of a New National Identity and Internationalization* (Cambridge: Cambridge University Press, 2005), and *Strangers on the Western Front: Chinese Workers in the Great War* (Cambridge, MA: Harvard University Press, 2011).

111. Erez Manela, *The Wilsonian Moment: Self-Determination and the International Origins of Anticolonial Nationalism* (Oxford: Oxford University Press, 2007), 177–183.

112. "Mission of Dr. Rajchman in the Far East." LRP. Racj. C1.

113. David Hunter Miller, *The Drafting of the Covenant* (New York: G. P. Putnam's Sons, 1928), Vol. 1, 331–332. On Koo, see Stephen G. Craft, *V. K. Wellington Koo and the Emergence of Modern China* (Lexington, KY: University of Kentucky Press, 2004).

114. Maggie Clinton, "Ends of the Universal: The League of Nations and Chinese Fascism on the Eve of World War II," *Modern Asian Studies* 48.6 (2014): 1740–1768; Liang Pan, "National Internationalism in Japan and China," in Glenda Sluga and Patricia Clavin, eds. *Internationalisms: A Twentieth-Century History* (Cambridge: Cambridge University Press, 2017), 170–190. For a contemporary explanation of this point, see Prentiss B. Gilbert, "Report on League of Nations Work in China," January 31, 1933. NARA RG59. Box 7231.

115. H. W. Arndt, *Economic Development: The History of an Idea* (Chicago: University of Chicago Press, 1987), 16; Eric Helleiner, "Sun Yat-sen as a Pioneer of International Development," *History of Political Economy* 50 (S1) (2018): 76–93.

116. Jürgen Osterhammel, "Semi-Colonialism and Informal Empire in Twentieth-Century China: Towards a Framework of Analysis," in Wolfgang J. Mommsen, ed., *Imperialism and After: Continuities and Discontinuities* (London: Allen & Unwin, 1986), 290–314.

117. On the Maritime Customs Service, see Hans van de Ven, *Breaking with the Past: The Maritime Customs Service and the Global Origins of Modernity in China* (New York: Columbia University Press, 2014), at 172.

118. Trotter, *Britain and East Asia, 1933–1937*, 8–20; Stephen Lyon Endicott, *Diplomacy and Enterprise: British China Policy 1933–1937* (Manchester: University of Manchester Press, 1975).

119. For a comprehensive account of the confluence of pressures that forced this change of policy, see Phoebe Chow, *Britain's Imperial Retreat from China, 1900–1931* (Abingdon, UK: Routledge, 2017), 147–200. See also William James Megginson, "Britain's Response to Chinese Nationalism, 1925–1927: The Foreign Office Search for a New Policy," Ph.D. Dissertation, George Washington University, 1973; Peter Clarke, "Britain and the Chinese Revolution, 1925–1927." Unpublished PhD dissertation, University of California, Berkeley (1973).

120. Speech by Sir Charles Addis at Banquet given to Council of the Consortium for China, October 19, 1925. TNA FO 228/3068.

121. Quoted in V. H. Rothwell, "The Mission of Sir Frederick Leith-Ross to the Far East, 1935–1936," *The Historical Journal* 18.1 (1975): 147–169, at 162.

122. See, above all, Felix Boecking, *No Great Wall: Trade, Tariffs and Nationalism in Republican China, 1927–1945* (Cambridge, MA: Harvard University Press, 2017). See also Edmund S. K. Fung, "Britain, Japan and Chinese Tariff Autonomy," *Proceedings of the British Association for Japanese Studies* 6.1 (1981): 23–36.

123. William Roger Louis, *British Strategy in the Far East 1919–1939* (Oxford: Clarendon Press, 1971), 17–49; Edmund S. K. Fung, *The Diplomacy of Imperial Retreat: Britain's South China Policy, 1924–1931* (Oxford: Oxford University Press, 1991).

124. Roberta Dayer, *Bankers and Diplomats in China 1917–1925 Anglo-American Relationship* (London: Cass, 1981); P. J. Cain and A. G. Hopkins, *British Imperialism 1688–2015* (London: Routledge, 2016), 636–660.

125. For a synthesis, see Chow, *Britain's Imperial Retreat from China*, 236–240.

126. Cain and Hopkins, *British Imperialism*, 646–647; Niv Horesh, *British Banks, Banknote Issuance, and Monetary Policy in China, 1842–1937* (New Haven, CT: Yale University Press, 2009), 128–129. See also Elizabeth Köll, *Railroads and the Transformation of China* (Cambridge, MA: Harvard University Press, 2019).

127. Austin Dean, "The Shanghai Mint and U.S.–China Monetary Interactions, 1920–1933," *Journal of American-East Asian Relations* 25.1 (2018): 7–32.

128. For overviews, see Theodore William Overlach, *Foreign Financial Control in China* (New York: Macmillan, 1919); Frederick V. Field, *American Participation in the China Consortiums* (Chicago: University of Chicago Press, 1931); Anthony B. Chan, "The Consortium System in Republican China, 1912–1913," *Journal of European Economic History* 6 (1977): 597–640; Clarence B. Davis, "Financing Imperialism: British and American Bankers as Vectors of Imperial Expansion in China, 1908–1920," *Business History Review* 56.2 (1982): 236–264; van de Ven, *Breaking with the Past*, 168–170.

129. J. T. Pratt, "Memorandum respecting the China Consortium," August 21, 1929. TNA FO 371/13956. See also K. C. Chan, "British Policy in the Reorganization Loan to China," *Modern Asian Studies* 5.4 (1971): 355–372; Hirata Koji, "Britain's Men on the Spot in China: John Jordan, Yuan Shikai, and the Reorganization Loan, 1912–1914," *Modern Asian Studies* 47.3 (2013): 895–934; Ghassan Moazzin, "Investing in the New Republic: Multinational Banks, Political Risk, and the Chinese Revolution of 1911," *Business History Review* 94 (2020): 507–534. For context on the late Qing period, see Dong Yan, "The Domestic Effects of Foreign Capital: Public Debt and Regional Inequalities in Late Qing China," in Nicolas Barreyre and Nicolas Delalande, eds., *A World of Public Debts: A Political History* (Cham: Palgrave Macmillan, 2020), 201–230.

130. Roy W. Curry, *Woodrow Wilson and Far Eastern Policy, 1913–1921* (New York: Octagon Books, 1957), 23.

131. "Memorandum on the China Consortium," TNA FO 228/3068. See also Carl P. Parinni, *Heir to Empire: United States Economic Diplomacy, 1916–1923* (Pittsburgh: University of Pittsburg Press, 1969), 172–184. Lamont also played a central role in organizing a similar banking consortium to handle lending to Mexico in 1919, the International Committee of Bankers on Mexico. In the late 1920s, he collaborated closely on Mexican debt issues with Dwight Morrow, a former adviser to the Allied Maritime Transport Council and J.P. Morgan partner, who became US ambassador to Mexico in 1927. See Robert Freeman Smith, *The United States and Revolutionary Nationalism in Mexico, 1916–1932* (Chicago: The University of Chicago Press, 1972).

132. Warren I. Cohen, "America's New Order in East Asia: The Four Power Financial Consortium and China, 1919–1946," in Kwan Wai So and Warren I. Cohen, eds., *Essays in the History of China and Chinese-American Relations* (East Lansing, MI: Asian Studies Center, 1982), 41–74; Mark Metzler, *Lever of Empire: The International Gold Standard and the Crisis of Liberalism in Prewar Japan* (Berkeley, CA: University of California Press, 2006), 98–101, 124–129; Michael Schiltz, *The Money Doctors from Japan: Finance, Imperialism, and the Building of the Yen Bloc, 1895–1937* (Cambridge, MA: Harvard University Press, 2012), 121–154.

133. Thomas W. Lamont, "The Economic Situation in the Orient," *Proceedings of the Academy of Political Science* 9.2 (1921): 68–75; and Addis quote in Joan Hoff Wilson, *American*

Business and Foreign Policy: 1920–1933 (Lexington, KY: University Press of Kentucky, 1971), 203. For other accounts of the Consortium as a "League of Nations," see, for example, Edward Alexander Powell, *Asia at the Crossroads: Japan, Korea, China, Philippine Islands* (New York: The Century Co., 1922), 257; and "The China Consortium," *The Nation* 111.2886 (Oct 27, 1920).

134. Charles Addis, "Memorandum on the China Consortium," September 1, 1924. TNA FO 228/3068. Addis had long claimed that China could not be placed under international control like Egypt or Turkey, despite the relative ease with which he thought this could be done. See, for example, Charles Addis, Memorandum, November 1, 1921. TNA FO 371/6660.

135. On the frustration of US businesses and the Department of Commerce regarding the Consortium, for example, see Wilson, *American Business and Foreign Policy*, 201–206.

136. E. T. Minute on F.O. Telegram No. 129, July 2, 1924. TNA FO 228/3068.

137. R. Macleay to F.O. Telegram No. 186, July 5, 1924. TNA FO 228/3068.

138. Report of the Meeting of the Consortium Council, July 14, 1924. TNA FO 228/3068.

139. Miles Lampson to Austen Chamberlain, April 2, 1929. TNA FO 371/13951.

140. Miles Lampson to Austen Chamberlain, April 2, 1929. TNA FO 371/13951.

141. Miles Lampson to Arthur Henderson, December 5, 1929. TNA FO 371/14690.

142. J. T. Pratt, "The China Consortium," August 21, 1929. FO 371/13956.

143. Miles Lampson to Arthur Henderson, December 5, 1929. TNA FO 371/14690.

144. Otto Niemeyer, October 1, 1929. BOE OV 9–8.

145. See, for example, G. E. Hubbard, "Financial Reconstruction for China," *Journal of the Royal Institute of International Affairs* 9.5 (1930): 636–651; and "A Practical Program of Reconstruction in China," April 2, 1925. HSBC LOH I 8.2.

146. Charles Addis to Colonel Young, May 22, 1925. HSBC LOH. I 8.2; Charles Addis to Thomas Lamont, April 28, 1932. Lamont thought an Austrian-style loan to China was an unrealistic idea. See Thomas Lamont to Henry L. Stimson, July 11, 1932. TLP. Box 184. On this point, see also the influential book by Herbert Feis, *Europe the World's Banker 1870–1914: An Account of European Foreign Investment and the Connection of World Finance with Diplomacy Before World War I* (New Haven, CT: Yale University Pres, 1930), 458–459.

147. Josef Avenol to Arthur Salter, February 9, 1929. LON P 16; Miles Lampson to Austen Chamberlain, April 2, 1929. TNA FO 371/13951.

148. Gaimusho, ed., *Nihon gaiko bunsho* [Documents on Japanese Foreign Policy], Showa Era, Series I (1931), Part 1, Volume 5 (Tokyo: Gaimusho, 1995), 680–681. I am grateful to Toshihiro Higuchi for bringing my attention to this source and for translating the relevant passage for me.

149. Conversation with Mr. Joseph Avenol, April 26, 1929. GHP NYF. 2011.1.

150. "The Financial Reconstruction of China," and Wu Ding-Chang, "International Economic Co-operation in China," in Condliffe, ed., *Problems of the Pacific*, 151 and 368–376.

151. Arthur Henderson to Edward Ingram, February 6, 1931. TNA FO 371/15479.

152. Reconstruction in China with special relation to foreign assistance. TNA FO 371–14744.

153. P. J. Noel Baker, June 21, 1930. TNA FO 371/14744.

154. Eric Drummond to Arthur Salter, February 5, 1931. IOR/L/E/9/262.

155. Cecil Kisch to E. J. Turner. IOR R/L/E/9/262.

156. Note for C. W. Orde, January 30, 1931. TNA FO 371/15479.

157. J. T. Pratt, January 30, 1931. TNA FO 371/15479.

158. Arthur Henderson to Edward Ingram, February 6, 1931. TNA FO 371/15479.

159. F. W. Leith-Ross to Otto Niemeyer, September 27, 1929. BOE OV 9/8; F. W. Leith-Ross to Montagu Norman, February 18, 1931. BOE OV 104/66.

160. Montagu Norman to F. W. Leith-Ross. March 5, 1931; Leith-Ross to Norman, March 7, 1931. BOE OV 104/66.

161. See, for example, Arthur Salter to Montagu Norman, June 2, 1927. SALT 1/4.

162. Notes as to Information Given and Opinions Expressed by J.A.S. in Conversation on April 26th, 1931." SALT 1/10. See also Arthur Salter, "Supplementary Note on China," June 2, 1931; Miles Lampson to Arthur Henderson, April 30, 1931; and "Economic Situation in China and visit of Sir A. Salter," May 28, 1931. TNA FO 371/15479.

163. George Sokolsky to Arthur Young, July 31, 1931. AYP. Box 52.

164. "A Suggestion for a National Development Council in China." AEFP. AEF/3/1/110.

165. Zanasi, Saving the Nation, 4–83.

166. Herman Finer, Representative Government and a Parliament of Industry. A Study of the German Federal Economic Council (London: G. Allen and Unwin, 1923); Karl Loewenstein, "Occupational Representation and the Idea of an Economic Parliament," Social Science 12.4 (1937): 420–431, 529–530; Edith C. Bramhall, "The National Economic Council of France," American Political Science Review 20.3 (1926): 623–630; Carmen Haider, "The Italian Corporate State," Political Science Quarterly 46.2 (1931): 228–247; Joachim Lilla, ed., Der Vorläufige Reichswirtschaftsrat 1920 bis 1933/34. Zusammensetzung—Dokumentation—Biographien (Düsseldorf: Droste, 2012); Charles S. Maier, Recasting Bourgeois Europe: Stabilization in France, Germany, and Italy in the Decade after World War I (Princeton, NJ: Princeton University Press, 1975), 75 and 138–150, and "Between Taylorism and Technocracy: European Ideologies and the Vision of Industrial Productivity in the 1920s," Journal of Contemporary History 5.2 (1970): 27–61, at 51–54; Susan Howson and Donald Winch, The Economic Advisory Council, 1930–1939: A Study in Economic Advice during Depression and Recovery (Cambridge: Cambridge University Press, 1977); E. Pendleton Herring, "The Czechoslovak Advisory Board for Economic Questions," American Political Science Review 24 (1930): 439–450, at 439–440.

167. Daniel Ritschel, The Politics of Planning: The Debate on Economic Planning in Britain in the 1930s (Oxford: Oxford University Press, 1997), 176–178.

168. Arthur Salter, Recovery: The Second Effort (London: Bell, 1932), 245–246. Salter supported the creation of an Economic Consultative Council a few years earlier for similar reasons. See Arthur Salter to Georges Theunis, November 28, 1927; Arthur Salter to Ernesto Belloni, April 12, 1928; and Arthur Salter to Walter Layton, April 13, 1928. SALT 1/5.

169. See, for example, Minutes of Sixth Meeting of the Second Committee of the Assembly, September 18, 1931. LON OJ SS 1 (1931), 30. For context, see Jens Steffek, "Fascist Internationalism," Millennium: Journal of International Studies 44.1 (2015): 3–22.

170. League of Nations [Elli Lindner], Review of the Economic Councils in the Different Countries of the World (Geneva: League of Nations, 1932). See also Elli Lindner, Die Wirtschaftsräte in Europa: Ein Beitrag zur Frage der Schaffung einer europäischen Wirtschaftsunion (Berlin: E. S. Mitter, 1931).

171. Walter Layton to George Schuster, April 11, 1930; George Schuster to Arthur Salter, March 21, 1930 GSP. Box 27.

172. "Report on India" and Mission to India: Jan 9th—Feb. 15th, 1931. Collaboration of India and the League. Report by Sir Arthur Salter. AEFP. AEF/3/1/109; George Schuster to Louis Kershaw, November 10, 1930. IOR. L/E/9/262. On India and the League, see J. C. Coyajee, India and the League of Nations (Madras: Waltair, 1932); Lanka Sundaram, India in World Politics—A Historical Analysis and Appraisal (New Delhi: Sultan Chand & Co., 1944).

173. "Notes," File No. 2002-C; "Appendix IV," File No 15-I-F, 1930. NAI. Salter's report was published as A Scheme for an Economic Advisory Organisation in India (Delhi: Government of India Press, 1931). I am grateful to Mircea Raianu for finding these documents for me.

174. See, for example, Gyan Chand, India's Teeming Millions: A Contribution to the Study of the Indian Population Problem (London: G. Allen & Unwin, 1939), 216–231; H. L. Dey,

"Scope and Method of Economic Planning in India," *Indian Journal of Economics* 15.56–59 (1934–1935): 573–587; S. C. Mitter, *A Recovery Plan for Bengal* (Calcutta: Book Co., 1934), esp. 7–9; Khagendra Sen, *Economic Reconstruction of India: A Study in Economic Planning* (Calcutta: University of Calcutta, 1939); N. S. Subba Rao, *Some Aspects of Economic Planning: Being Sir William Meyer Lectures, 1932–33, University of Madras* (Bangalore: Bangalore Press, 1935), 199–201. For context, see Raghabendra Chattopadhyay, "The Idea of Planning in India, 1930–1951," unpublished PhD dissertation, Australian National University (1985), 29–71; and "An Early British Government Initiative in the Genesis of Indian Planning," *Economic and Political Weekly* 22.5 (1987): 19–29. Salter's proposal for an Indian economic council also had a strange afterlife elsewhere. In a striking instance of the global circulation of economic planning ideas in the early Depression, it was studied by advocates of a US national economic council, as congressional hearings were held on a Republican-led effort to renovate the economic powers of the state shortly before Roosevelt's election and the beginning of the New Deal. See Edward Hunt to A. W. Shaw, July 4, 1931. EHP. Box 17; "Hearings before a Subcommittee of the Committee on Manufacturers. United States Senate. Seventy-Second Congress. First session on S. 6215 (71st Congress). A Bill to Establish a National Economic Council." October 22 to December 19, 1931. (Washington, DC, 1932). See also "Salter Maps Guide for India's Economy," *New York Times,* June 28, 1931.

175. Manu Goswami, *Producing India: From Colonial Economy to National Space* (Chicago: University of Chicago Press, 2004).

176. Zanasi, *Saving the* Nation, 93–97, 102–129. For more on Chinese capitalists during the Republican era, see Parks Coble, *The Shanghai Capitalists and the Nationalist Government, 1927–1937* (Cambridge, MA: Harvard University Press, 1986).

177. On Sino-foreign ventures from this era, see Jürgen Osterhammel, "Imperialism in Transition: British Business and the Chinese Authorities, 1931–37," *China Quarterly* 98 (1984): 260–286.

178. Kirby, "Engineering China," 137–160.

179. "Proposed Return of Dr. Rajchman to China on Behalf of League of Nations." TNA FO 371/17127. On Avenol's attempt to bring Japan back into the League and its impact on the technical assistance project, see James Barros, *Betrayal from Within: Joseph Avenol, Secretary-General of the League of Nations, 1933–1940* (New Haven, CT; Yale University Press, 1969), 40–47.

180. On this point, see the recollections of a member of the Kemmerer mission. Young, *China's Nation-Building Effort,* 342; A. Holman to M. B. Ingram, February 2, 1934. TNA FO 371–18052.

181. ETW note, June 2, 1933; Nelson Trusler Johnson to Cordell Hull, May 27, 1933; Nelson Trusler Johnson note on meeting with René Charron, April 19, 1933. NARA RG 59. Box 7231; Minute, March 6, 1934. TNA FO 371–18047; Selskar Gunn. Travel Diary, December 12, 1932, April 13, 1933. RFA. RF.RG1.601.12.129; C. Y. W. Meng, "China Goes to Geneva for Technical Assistance in Reconstruction Program," *China Weekly Review,* July 29, 1933; Memorandum of Conversation, December 27, 1933. NARA RG 59. Box 7232.

182. Ron Chernow, *The House of Morgan: An American Banking Dynasty and the Rise of Modern Finance* (New York: Grove Press, 1990), 336–345.

183. Memorandum respecting League of Nations Technical Assistance to China, May 8, 1934. TNA FO 371/18090.

184. See Louis Beale to Alexander Cadogen, June 6, 1934, and "Aims of New Development Corporation." TNA FO 371-18078; "Regulations Governing the China Development Finance Corporation." JMP. AMD 1-1.

185. Jean Monnet, *Memoirs,* trans. Richard Mayne (London: Collins, 1978), 112. See also Hungdah Su, "The Father of Europe in China: Jean Monnet and Creation of the C.F.D.C.

(1933–1936), *Journal of European Integration History* 13.1 (2007), 9–24; Eric Roussel, *Jean Monnet, 1888–1979* (Paris: Fayard, 1996), 137–164.

186. Louis Beale, "Finance Corporation," March 6, 1934. TNA FO 371-18078.

187. David Drummond to F. O. Lindley, April 27, 1934. TNA FO 371/18078.

188. Notes on the China Development Finance Corporation, May 28, 1937. JMP. ADS 3-1; J. Pratt, "Proposed scheme for reform of Chinese railways," April 21. 1934. TNA FO 371/18047.

189. J. Pratt, "Sir A. Salter's report on China," May 28, 1934. TNA FO 371/18047.

190. S. Harcourt Smith, record of conversation with David Drummond, October 11, 1934. TNA FO 371/1807; C.D. May 7, 1934. TNA FO 3781/18078; Letter to Addis, January 8, 1934; Montagu Norman to Charles Addis, July 8, 1933. CAP. Box 39.

191. John Pratt, May 25, 1934. TON FO 371/18090.

192. John Pratt, "Dr. Rajchman's visit to China," May 14, 1934. TNA FO 371/18090. On this point, see Dorothy Borg, *The United States and the Far Eastern Crisis of 1933–1938: From the Manchurian Incident through the Initial Stage of the Undeclared Sino-Japanese War* (Cambridge, MA: Harvard University Press, 1964), 77–78. See also Michael A. Barnhart, *Japan Prepares for Total War: The Search for Economic Security, 1919–1941* (Ithaca, NY: Cornell University Press, 2013), 116.

193. Charles Cheney Hyde, "Legal Aspects of the Japanese Pronouncement in Relation to China," *American Journal of International Law* 28.3 (1934): 431–443. For context, see Schiltz, *The Money Doctors from Japan*, 205–206; Jeremy Yellen, *The Greater East Asia Co-Prosperity Sphere: When Total Empire Met Total War* (Ithaca, NY: Cornell University Press, 2019).

194. William Kirby, *Germany and Republican China* (Stanford, CA: Stanford University Press, 1984).

195. On economic diplomacy in China during the mid-1930s, see, for example, Stephen L. Endicott, "British Financial Diplomacy in China: The Leith-Ross Mission, 1935–1937," *Pacific Affairs* 46.4 (1973–1974): 481–501 and *Diplomacy and Enterprise,* 102–185; Roberta Allbert Dayer, *Finance and Empire: Sir Charles Addis, 1861-1945* (Houndmills, Basingstoke, Hampshire: Macmillan, 1988), 274–306; Gill Bennett, "British Policy in the Far East 1933–1936: Treasury and Foreign Office," *Modern Asian Studies* 26.3 (1992): 545–568; Niv Horesh, "Whitehall vs Old China Hands: The 1935–36 Leith-Ross Mission Revisited," *Asian Studies Review* 33.2 (2009): 211–227; Antony Best, "The Leith-Ross Mission and British Policy towards East Asia, 1934–7," *International History Review* 35.4 (2013): 681–701.

196. See, for example, Lewis Lorwin, *International Economic Development: Public Works and Other Problems* (Washington, DC: United States Printing Office, 1942).

197. Greg Grandin, *Empire's Workshop: Latin America, the United State, and the Making of an Imperial Republic* (New York: Metropolitan Books, 2006), 44–47; Thornton, *Revolution in Development*, 39–57. On the role of US bankers and diplomats like Lamont and Morrow in calling for a move away from violent practices of debt diplomacy in the 1920s, see also G. M. Joseph, *Revolution from Without: Yucatán, Mexico, and the United States 1880–1924* (Cambridge: Cambridge University Press, 1982), 280–281.

198. Department of Overseas Trade to John Anderson, November 4, 1943. TNA T 247/32.

199. Helleiner, *Forgotten Foundations of Bretton Woods*, 186–200.

5. Controlling Commodities

1. For an overview, see Derek H. Aldcroft, *From Versailles to Wall Street 1919–1929* (London: Allen Lane, 1977), 218–238.

2. For overviews, see Ervin Hexner, *International Cartels* (Chapel Hill, NC: University of North Carolina Press, 1946); Clemens Wurm, *Business, Politics and International Relations:*

Steel, Cotton and International Cartels in British Politics, 1924–1939, trans. Patrick Salmon (Cambridge: Cambridge University Press, 1993); Marco Bertilorenzi, *The International Aluminum Cartel: The Business and Politics of a Cooperative Industrial Institution (1886–1978)* (London: Routledge, 2015). Some of these international cartels were important political players during these years. On this point in regard to Franco-German rapprochement, see especially Conan Fischer, *A Vision of Europe: Franco-German Relations during the Great Depression, 1929–1932* (Oxford: Oxford University Press, 2017). For a theoretical account, see Debora Spar, *The Cooperative Edge: The Internal Politics of International Cartels* (Ithaca, NY: Cornell University Press, 1994).

3. For overviews, see the extensive literature from the mid-twentieth century, especially P. Lamartine Yates, *Commodity Control: A Study of Primary Products* (London: Cape, 1943); International Labour Office, *Intergovernmental Commodity Control Agreements* (Montreal: International Labour Office, 1943); Joseph S. Davis, "Experience under Intergovernmental Commodity Agreements, 1902–45," *Journal of Political Economy* 54 (1946): 193–220; Klaus Knorr, "The Problem of International Cartels and Intergovernmental Commodity Agreements," *Yale Law Journal* 55 (1946): 1097–1126; Bernard Haley, "The Relation between Cartel Policy and Commodity Agreement Policy," *American Economic Review* 36.2 (1946): 717–734; Edward Mason, *Controlling World Trade: Cartels and Commodity Agreements* (New York: McGraw Hill, 1946); J. W. F. Rowe, *Primary Commodities in International Trade* (London: Cambridge University Press, 1965), 120–220.

4. On questions of raw materials being seen as exclusively domestic ones, legally speaking, see, for example, Lynn R. Edminster, "Control of Exports of Raw Materials: An International Problem," *Annals of the American Academy of Political and Social Science* 150.1 (1930): 89–97, at 96.

5. For exemplary accounts, see Patricia Clavin, *The Failure of Economic Diplomacy: Britain, Germany, France and the United States, 1931–36* (Basingstoke, UK: Macmillan Press, 1996); and Robert Boyce, *The Great Interwar Crisis and the Collapse of Globalization* (London: Palgrave Macmillan, 2009).

6. On the International Tea Agreement, see V. D. Wickizer, *Tea under International Regulation* (Stanford, CA: Food Research Institute, 1944), 72–96.

7. On the history of OPEC as an international organization of sovereign states, and not a private cartel, as it would be commonly but mistakenly referred to (as would earlier intergovernmental schemes), see Giuliano Garavini, *The Rise & Fall of OPEC in the Twentieth Century* (Oxford: Oxford University Press, 2019), especially at 123.

8. It was common at the time to see commodity agreements as one of the only sources of enthusiasm for international economic cooperation during the Depression and one of the only immediate practical results of the otherwise failed 1933 World Economic Conference. See, for example, H. V. Hodson, *Slump and Recovery 1929–1937* (London: Oxford University Press, 1938), 230–257.

9. See, for example, Maurice Dobb, *Studies in the Development of Capitalism* (Oxford: Oxford University Press, 1945), 383. On the broader aims of intergovernmental control schemes, their durability, and the trend toward them and away from private international cartels during the interwar period, see Hexner, *International Cartels*, 115–117; Mason, *Controlling World Trade*, 16–17, 152; and Charles Henry Alexandrowicz, *International Economic Organisations* (London: Stevens & Sons Limited, 1952), 34–47. For example, although the 1931 Chadbourne Agreement to regulate sugar prices was a private affair, the 1937 International Sugar Agreement involved governments directly. See Michael Fakhri, *Sugar and the Making of International Trade Law* (Cambridge: Cambridge University Press, 2014), 92–138.

10. Ian M. Drummond, *Imperial Economic Policy 1917–1939: Studies in Expansion and Protection* (London: George Allen & Unwin, 1974), 442–444.

11. E. M. H. Lloyd, "International Schemes for Regulation of Supply," in *Proceedings of the Third International Conference of Agricultural Economists* (London: Oxford University Press, 1935), 435–445, at 436.

12. On the unique success of the tin scheme, see, for example, Alfred Plummer, *Raw Materials or War Materials?* (London: Victor Gollancz, 1937), 49–53.

13. The most in-depth treatments of the International Tin Agreement can be found in the many publications of John Hillman on this topic. See, most notably, *The International Tin Cartel* (London: Routledge, 2010). See also "Malaya and the International Tin Cartel," *Modern Asian Studies* 22.2 (1988): 237–261; "Bolivia and the International Tin Cartel, 1931–1941," *Journal of Latin American Studies*, 21.1 (1988): 83–110; "The Freerider and the Cartel: Siam and the International Tin Restriction Agreements, 1931–1941," *Modern Asian Studies* 24.2 (1990): 297–321. See also Elizabeth May, "The International Tin Cartel," in William Yandell Elliott, Elizabeth S. May, J. W. F. Rowe, Alex Skelton, and Donald H. Wallace, eds. *International Control in the Non-Ferrous Metals* (New York: Macmillan, 1937), 277–346; K. E. Knorr, *Tin under Control* (Stanford, CA: Food Research Institute, 1945); William Fox, *Tin: The Working of a Commodity Agreement* (London: Mining Journal Books, 1974); William L. Baldwin, *The World Tin Market: Political Pricing and Economic Competition* (Durham, NC: Duke University Press, 1983). For accounts of individual producing countries and colonies, see Li Dun-jen, *British Malaya: An Economic Analysis* (New York: American Press, 1956), 49–58; William Leef Lofstrom, "Attitudes of an Industrial Pressure Group in Latin America, the Asociación de Industriales Mineros de Bolivia, 1925–1935." Unpublished MA thesis, Columbia University (1968), 65–73; Yip Yat Hoong, *The Development of the Tin Mining Industry of Malaya* (Kuala Lumpur: University of Malaya Press, 1969); Bill Freund, *Capital and Labour in the Nigerian Tin Mines* (Atlantic Highlands, NJ: Humanities Press, 1981); Jean-Jacques van Helten and Geoffrey Jones, "British Business in Malaysia & Singapore since the 1870s," in R. P. T. Davenport-Hines and Geoffrey Jones, eds., *British Business in Asia since 1860* (Cambridge: Cambridge University Press, 1989), 157–188; Antonio Mitre, *Bajo un Cielo de Estaño: Fulgor y Ocaso del Metal en Bolivia* (La Paz, Bolivia: Asociación Nacional de Mineros Medianos, 1993); John H. Drabble, *An Economic History of Malaysia, c. 1800–1990* (Houndsmills, UK: Macmillan, 2000), 127–132.

14. J. H. Drabble, *Rubber in Malaya, 1876–1922: The Genesis of the Industry* (Kuala Lumpur: Oxford University Press, 1973), 162–198; Lim Teck Ghee, *Peasants and their Agricultural Economy in Colonial Malaya 1874–1941* (Kuala Lumpur: Oxford University Press, 1977), 143–154; John Tully, *The Devil's Milk: A Social History of Rubber* (New York: Monthly Review Press, 2011), 190–193.

15. Mark R. Finlay, *Growing American Rubber: Strategic Plants and the Politics of National Security* (New Brunswick, NJ: Rutgers University Press, 2009), 45–73; Greg Grandin, *Fordlandia: The Rise and Fall of Henry Ford's Forgotten Jungle City* (London: Icon, 2010). For context, see also Daniel Immerwahr, *How to Hide an Empire: A History of the Greater United States* (New York: Farrar, Straus and Giroux, 2019), 262–277.

16. The idea was widely discussed. See, for example, the account of a public debate about the League of Nations in the United States in 1919, in "League of Nations Plan Criticised and Defended at Liberal Culture Club," *Anaconda Standard,* March 14, 1919.

17. On this point, see Rupert Emerson, "The United Nations and Colonialism," in Kenneth Twitchett, ed., *The Evolving United Nations: A Prospect for Peace?* (London: Europa for the David Davies Memorial Institute of International Studies, 1971), 83–99, at 89.

18. Susan Pedersen, *The Guardians: The League of Nations and the Crisis of Empire* (Oxford: Oxford University Press, 2015), 233–260.

19. Mark Mazower, "The Strange Triumph of Human Rights, 1933–1950," *Historical Journal* 47.2 (2004): 379–398, at 389.

20. For an influential account, see League of Nations [Bertil Ohlin], *The Course and Phases of the World Economic Depression* (Geneva: League of Nations, 1931). See also W. Arthur Lewis, *Economic Survey, 1919–1939* (London: Allen and Unwin, 1947).

21. Kathleen M. Stalhl, *Metropolitan Organization of British Colonial Trade* (London: Faber, 1951), 11–121; C. D. Cowan, *Nineteenth-Century Malaya: The Origins of British Political Control* (London: Oxford University Press, 1961); Hillman, "Malaya and the International Tin Cartel," 246–247.

22. E. B. Yeap, "Tin and Gold Mineralizations in Peninsular Malaysia and Their Relationships to the Tectonic Development," *Journal of Southeast Asian Earth Sciences* 8.1 (1993): 329–348; J. K. Eastham, "Rationalisation in the Tin Industry," *Review of Economic Studies* 4.1 (1936): 13–32.

23. Wong Lin Ken, *The Malayan Tin Industry to 1914* (Tucson, AZ: University of Arizona Press, 1965); Anthony Webster, *Gentlemen Capitalists: British Imperialism in Southeast Asia, 1770–1890* (London: Taurus, 1998), 167–201. For global histories of the tin industry, see Mats Ingulstad, Andrew Perchard, and Espen Storli, eds., *Tin and Global Capitalism: A History of the Devil's Metal, 1850–2000* (New York: Routledge, 2015).

24. "Memorandum Regarding the Tin Industry in Malaya." TNA CO 323/1108/8.

25. "'Inverted Triangle' Plan of Regulating the Output of Tin-Ore in Malaya." TNA CO 323/1108/8.

26. J. Norman Parmer, *Colonial Labor Policy and Administration: A History of Labor in the Rubber Plantation Industry in Malaya, c. 1910–1941* (New York: J. J. Augustin Incorporated, 1960), 243.

27. Lok Kok Wah, "From Tin Mine Coolies to Agricultural Squatters: Socio-Economic Change in the Kinta District during the Inter-war Years," in Peter J. Rimmer and Lisa M. Allen, eds., *The Underside of Malaysian History: Pullers, Prostitutes, Plantation Workers* (Singapore: Singapore University Press, 1990), 72–96, at 86.

28. Federated Malay States. "Report on the Administration of the Mines Department and on the Mining Industries for the Year 1930." Supplement to the *FMS Government Gazette*, June 5, 1931, 4.

29. James Lawrence, *The World's Struggle with Rubber 1905–1931* (New York: Harper & Brothers, 1931), 37.

30. Note of Conference at the Colonial Office on the 23rd December, 1930. TNA CO 323/1108/9. See also "Tin—Voluntary Curtailment of Output," December 19, 1930. TNA CO 323/1108/8.

31. John Campbell minute, November 28, 1930. TNA CO 323/1108/8; Colonial Office Note. TNA CO 323/1154/9.

32. "Official Stenographic Record of the Proceedings in the Federal Council Held on the 13th April, 1931, Relating to the Passing of the Bill to Give Effect to the International Tin Restriction Scheme." TNA CO 323/54/11.

33. Minutes of meeting, International Tin Committee, April 1, 1931. CO 323/1154/11.

34. On this analogy regarding sugar controls, see also Fakhri, *Sugar and the Making of International Trade Law,* 117.

35. Beelaerts von Blokland to Odo Russell, February 7, 1931. TNA CO 323/1154/11.

36. Jagjit Singh Sidhu, *Administration in the Federated Malay States* (Oxford: Oxford University Press, 1980), 1–36; Lynn Hollen Lees, *Planting Empire, Cultivating Subjects: British Malaya, 1786–1941* (Cambridge: Cambridge University Press, 2017).

37. "An Enactment to Restrict, Regulate and Control the Production, Possession, Sale, Purchase, and Export of Tin and Tin-Ore." TNA CO 323/1154/11.

38. Yip, *The Development of the Tin Mining Industry of Malaya,* 199–200.

39. Federated Malay States. Enactment No. 257 of 12 April 1931. TNA CO 323/1154/11.

40. G. E. Greig, *Mining in Malaya* (London: Malayan Information Agency, 1924), 32; A. Azmi Abdul Khalid, "The Social Organization of the Mining Industry during the Depression, 1929–1933, in Malaya," *Journal of the Malaysian Branch of the Royal Asiatic Society* 65.2 (1992): 85–98; Amarjit Kaur, "Race, Gender and the Tin Mining Industry in Malaya, 1900–1950," in Kuntala Lahiri-Dutt and Martha Macintyre, eds., *Women Miners in Developing Countries: Pit Women and Others* (Abingdon, UK: Routledge, 2006), 73–88, at 82–83. For data on the falling number of *dulang* passes issued from 1928 to 1930 in the Federated Malay States, see Federated Malay States, *Report on the Administration of the Mines Department and on the Mining Industries for the Year 1930.* Supplement to the *FMS Government Gazette*, June 5, 1931.

41. See, for example, Cecil Clementi to Philip Cunliffe-Lister, June 19, 1932. TNA CO 323/1196/14.

42. Minutes of Tin Restriction Committee, February 13, 1931. TNA CAB 27/447.

43. See, for example, the comments of William Peat in "Note of a Meeting on 15th January [1931] with Representatives of the Tin Producers' Association." TNA CO 323/1154/8.

44. Philip Cunliffe-Lister to Samuel H. Wilson, January 4, 1931. TNA CO 322/99.

45. D. K. Fieldhouse, "Metropolitan Economics of Empire," in Judith Brown and Wm Roger Louis, eds., *The Oxford History of the British Empire: Volume IV: The Twentieth Century* (Oxford: Oxford University Press, 1999), 88–114.

46. Secretary of State for the Colonies Memorandum, March 19, 1931. TNA CAB 24/220/23.

47. Knorr, *Tin under Control*, 89; Yip, *The Development of the Tin Mining Industry of Malaya*, 182–183; Wong, *The Malayan Tin Industry to 1914*, 21, 113; Lim *Peasants and their Agricultural Economy in Colonial Malaya*; Daniel R. Headrick, *The Tentacles of Progress: Technology Transfer in the Age of Imperialism, 1850–1940* (Oxford: Oxford University Press, 1988), 259–268; van Helten and Jones, "British Business in Malaysia & Singapore since the 1870s," 164–167; William Tai Yuen, *Chinese Capitalism in Colonial Malaya* (Bangi, Malaysia: Penerbit Universiti Kebangsaan Malaysia, 2013), 106; Corey Ross, *Ecology and Power in the Age of Empire: Europe and the Transformation of the Tropical World* (Oxford: Oxford University Press, 2017), 136–163; Sivachandralingam Sundara Raja, *The Economy of Colonial Malaya: Administrators versus Capitalists* (Abingdon, UK: Routledge, 2018).

48. Knorr, *Tin Under Control*, 89–91; Yip, *The Development of the Tin Mining Industry of Malaya*, 182–183.

49. "Summary of Case against Tin Restriction." TNA CO 323/1154/8; Colonial Office Note, July 1930. TNA CO 717/73/7.

50. "Tin Restriction Scheme." TNA CO 323/1108/9.

51. For an account of these conflicts in terms of business structure, see, for example, Hillman, "Malaya and the International Tin Cartel," 237, and *The International Tin Cartel*, 142–148; Eastham, "Rationalisation in the Tin Industry," 26.

52. "Times Comments on Quota Scheme: Supply and Demand Too Strong." *Straits Times*, February 9, 1931.

53. "More Haste Less Speed." *The Mining Journal.* CLXXII.4976. January 3, 1931. CO 323/1154/8.

54. Federated Malay States, *Proceedings of the Federal Council of the Federated Malay States for the Year 1931* (Kuala Lumpur: Federated Malay States, 1932), B47–B48.

55. *Proceedings of the Federal Council of the Federated Malay States for the Year 1931*, 49.

56. *Proceedings of the Federal Council of the Federated Malay States for the Year 1931*, B30.

57. John Campbell minute, July 15, 1931. TNA CO 323/1155/1.

58. Tin Control. Questions and Answers at Meetings at Ipoh, January 7, 1931. TNA CO 323/1154/9.

59. John Campbell to Sidney Caine, and Sidney Caine minute, October 30, 1931. TNA CO 323/1155/4.

60. "Interpretation and Application of Treaties: 1895, 1909, 1927 Treaties Relating to the Federated Malay States," in S. Jayakumar, *Public International Law Cases from Malaysia and Singapore* (Singapore: Singapore University Press, 1974), 284–298.

61. "Order made on appeal: Pahang Company Limited v. State of Pahang." TNA CO 717/94/5.

62. Nicholas J. White, "The Frustrations of Development: British Business and the Late Colonial State in Malaya, 1945–57," *Journal of Southeast Asian Studies* 28.1 (1997): 103–119, at 107.

63. "Pahang Consolidated: Serious Effects of Tin Restriction," *Financial News*, December 12, 1932.

64. Colonial Office to Foreign Office memo, January 2, 1933. TNA CO 717/94/5.

65. See, for example, "Mining Companies Badly Misled: Consumers Displaying Little Interest," *Straits Times*, May 4, 1931.

66. Mitre, *Bajo un Cielo de Estaño*, 50; Burton C. Hallowell, "Administration of Tin Control in Bolivia, 1931–1939," *Inter-American Economic Affairs* 3.2 (1949): 3–24.

67. Minutes of Tin Restriction Committee, February 17, 1931. TNA CAB 27/447.

68. Telegram from Cecil Clementi to Sidney Webb, December 28, 1930. TNA CO 323/1108/9.

69. Phoebe Chow, *Britain's Imperial Retreat from China, 1900–1931* (Abingdon, UK: Routledge, 2017), 173.

70. Nicholas J. White, "Gentlemanly Capitalism and Empire in the Twentieth Century: The Forgotten Case of Malaya 1914–1965," in Raymond E. Dumett, ed., *Gentlemanly Capitalism and British Imperialism: The New Debate on Empire* (New York: Longman, 1999), 175–195, at 179, 190.

71. "FMS Excess Production;" J. A. Calder, "Memorandum: Malayan Excess Tin Production," September 1, 1931. TNA CO 323/1155/3; Cecil Clementi to Sidney Webb, July 24 and August 14, 1931. TNA CO 323/1155/2.

72. "Unemployed as Tin-Mine Detectives! Comments from League of Nations," *Straits Times*, March 9, 1931.

73. "Should Malaya Withdraw? A Serious Position. Defects of the Quota Scheme," *Straits Times* May 20, 1931.

74. Sidney Webb to Cecil Clementi, July 29, 1921. TNA CO 323/1155/2; John Henry Thomas to Cecil Clementi, September 17, 1931. TNA CO 323/1155/3.

75. John Campbell to J. A. Calder, September 17, 1931. TNA CO 323/1155/3.

76. Cecil Clementi to Sidney Webb, August 5, 1931. TNA CO 323/1155/2; "FMS Excess Production." TNA CO 323/1155/3. In September 1931, more than 7,500 Chinese workers were repatriated. See Cecil Clementi to John Henry Thomas, September 28, 1931. TNA CO 323/1155/2.

77. Kernial Singh Sandhu, *Indians in Malaya: Some Aspects of Their Immigration and Settlement (1786–1957)* (Cambridge: Cambridge University Press, 1969), 106; Lees, *Planting Empire, Cultivating Subjects*, 214–217. See also Sunil S. Amrith, "Indians Overseas? Governing Tamil Migration to Malaya 1870–1941," *Past & Present* 208 (2010): 231–261.

78. W. G. Huff, "Entitlements, Destitution, and Emigration in the 1930s Singapore Great Depression," *Economic History Review* 54.2 (2001): 290–323, at 312.

79. Parmer, *Colonial Labor Policy and Administration*, 236–243; Tak Ming Hoh, *Ipoh: When Tin was King* (Ipoh: Perak Academy, 2009), 552–564. See also Khoo Kay Kim, *The*

History of South-East, South, and East Asia: Essays and Documents (Oxford: Oxford University Press, 1977), 81–88.

80. John H. Drabble, "Some Thoughts on the Economic Development of Malaya under British Administration," *Journal of Southeast Asian Studies* 5.2 (1974): 199–208, at 207; and T. N. Harper, *The End of Empire and the Making of Malaya* (Cambridge: Cambridge University Press, 1999), 28.

81. K. Nadaraja, "Malay Reactions to the 1930s Economic Depression in Malaya," *Malaysian Journal of History, Politics & Strategic Studies* 43.1 (2016): 46–64; Huff, "Entitlements, Destitution, and Emigration," 318.

82. Federated Malay States, "Report on the Administration of the Mines Department and on the Mining Industries for the Year 1930." Supplement to the *FMS Government Gazette*, June 5, 1931, 5, 15.

83. Lees, *Planting Empire, Cultivating Subjects*, 214–217.

84. "FMS Excess Production;" Cecil Clementi to James Henry Thomas, September 20, 1931. TNA CO 323/1155/3.

85. J. A. Calder minute, September 16, 1931. TNA CO 323/1155/3. See also HC Deb (16 September 1931), vol. 256, col. 827. Campbell had been anxious to avoid "rushing" the Malayan and Nigerian colonial governments when the scheme was being proposed. See "International Scheme to Regulate the Production and Export of Tin, Meeting in London," February 27, 1931. TNA CO 323/1154/10.

86. John Campbell minute, September 29, 1931. TNA CO 323/1155/3.

87. Bolivian Delegation to the International Tin Committee to John Campbell, September 14, 1931; A. Groothoff to John Campbell, September 10, 1931; John Shuckburgh to Netherland East Indies Delegation of the International Tin Committee, September 18, 1931. TNA CO 323/1155/3.

88. John Campbell to J. A. Calder, September 14, 1931. TNA CO 323/1155/3.

89. James Henry Thomas to Cecil Clementi, September 30, 1931. TNA CO 323/1155/3.

90. John G. Butcher, *The British in Malaya 1880–1941: The Social History of a European Community in Colonial South-East Asia* (Oxford: Oxford University Press, 1979), 4–22; Simon C. Smith, *British Relations with the Malay Rulers from Decentralization to Malayan Independence 1930–1957* (Oxford: Oxford University Press, 1995), 22–29.

91. Two telegrams from Cecil Clementi to James Henry Thomas, October 1, 1931; James Henry Thomas to Cecil Clementi, October 2, 1931. TNA CO 323/1155/3.

92. J. A. Calder minute, September 3, 1931. TNA CO 323/1155/3.

93. J. A. Calder minute, March 11, 1931. TNA CO 323/1156/1.

94. Agreement between British and Dutch syndicates. HSBC 192/035.

95. Cecil Clement to James Henry Thomas, September 15, 1931. TNA CO 323/1155/3.

96. "History of the Tin Pool Negotiations." TNA CO 323/1156/2.

97. *Proceedings of the Federal Council of the Federated Malay States for the Year 1931*, B131; John Campbell minute, July 23, 1931; John Campbell to J. A. Calder, July 27, 1931. TNA CO 323/1156/1. See also Philip Cunliffe-Lister to Nigerian Colonial Government, May 23, 1933. TNA CO 323/1242/4.

98. Sidney Webb to Cecil Clementi, August 4, 1931. TNA CO 323/1156/2; John Howeson to Reginald McKenna, August 11, 1931. HSBC, 192/037; Cecil Clementi to Sidney Webb, July 17, 1931. TNA CO 323/1156/1; J. A. Calder to R. M. Vargas, June 5, 1931. TNA CO 323/1156/1; J. A. Calder to A. Groothoff, June 5, 1931. TNA CO 323/1156/1; John Howeson to Reginald McKenna, August 11, 1931. HSBC 192/037.

99. John Howeson to John Campbell, June 18, 1931. TNA CO 323-1156.

100. Officer Administering the Government of Nigeria to Sidney Webb, June 12, 1931. TNA CO 323/1156/1; "History of the Tin Pool Negotiations." TNA CO 323/1156/2.

101. Petition from Nigerian Tin Mining Companies to British Colonial Office. TNA CO 323/1156/1.

102. Gazetteers of the Northern Provinces of Nigeria. *Volume IV: The Highland Chieftaincies (Plateau Province)* (London: Frank Cass, 1972), 305; Moses Ochonu, "Conjoined to Empire: The Great Depression and Nigeria," *African Economic History* 34 (2006): 103–145; and *Colonial Meltdown: Northern Nigeria in the Great Depression* (Athens, OH: Ohio University Press, 2009), 72–73; Freund, *Capital and Labour in the Nigerian Tin Mines*, 122–123.

103. "Tekka, Ltd.: Tin Restriction Producing a Stalemate," reprinted from *The Mining Journal*, November 28, 1931. TNA CO 717/79/6.

104. *Proceedings of the Federal Council of the Federated Malay States for the Year 1931*, B131. See also "Increase of Investment Buying: Uninspiring News from U.S.A.," *Straits Times*, September 28, 1931. John Campbell to J. A. Calder. February 17, 1932. TNA CO 323/1196/12;A.C.J. Towers to FMS Government, October 1, 1931. TNA CO 323/1155/5.

105. W. E. Pepys to A. C. J. Towers, October 7, 1931. TNA CO 323/1155/5; John Howeson to John Campbell, January 13, 1932. HSBC 192/036; A. Groothoof to Reginald McKenna. August 20, 1931. HSBC 192/037.

106. Ian Phimister, "Corners and Company-Mongering: Nigerian Tin and the City of London, 1909–12," *Journal of Imperial and Commonwealth History* 28.2 (2000): 23–41.

107. John Howeson to John Campbell, January 4, 1932. TNA CO 323/1197/5.

108. Cecil Clementi to Philip Cunliffe-Lister, May 10, 1932. TNA CO 323/1196/14.

109. Cecil Clementi to Philip Cunliffe-Lister, April 30, 1932. TNA CO 323/1196/13.

110. Yuen, *Chinese Capitalism in Colonial Malaya*, 116–119; Nicholas J. White, "The Trouble with Tin: Governments and Businesses in Decolonizing Malaya," in Ingulstad, Perchard, and Storli, eds., *Tin and Global Capitalism*, 169–201, at 170.

111. *Proceedings of the Federal Council of the Federated Malay States for the year 1931*, B52.

112. John Campbell to J. A. Calder, May 10, 1932. TNA CO 323/1196/13.

113. Cecil Clementi to Philip Cunliffe-Lister, May 10, 1932. TNA CO 323/1196/14.

114. John Campbell to Sidney Caine, April 13, 1932. TNA CO 323/1197/5; John Howeson to Reginald McKenna, April 18, 1932. HSBC 192/036.

115. S.H.G. to Philip Cunliffe-Lister, April 22, 1932. TNA CO 323/1196/13.

116. Cecil Clementi to Philip Cunliffe-Lister, May 10, 1932. TNA CO 323/1196/14.

117. Reginald McKenna to Philip Cunliffe-Lister, April 21, 1932. HSBC 192/035.

118. On this point, see Malcom MacDonald memorandum, July 1938. TNA CO 852/140/1.

119. John Campbell minute, June 8, 1938. TNA CO 852/140/1; See also John Howeson to John Campbell, February 15, 1932. TNA CO 323/1196/12.

120. After the Second World War, competition continued between low-cost European firms that opposed restriction and high-cost firms who backed restriction on the grounds that it protected sterling and neutralized growing anti-colonial resistance. See White, "Gentlemanly Capitalism and Empire in the Twentieth Century," 186. See also Ian A. Mallory, "Conduct Unbecoming: The Collapse of the International Tin Agreement," *American University International Law Review* 5.3 (1990): 835–892.

121. W. Y. Elliott, "Political Implications," in Elliott, May, Rowe, Skelton, and Wallace, eds., *International Control in the Non-Ferrous Metals*, 22–55, at 35.

122. Sidney Caine to Frederick Leith-Ross, January 13, 1941. TNA T 188/247.

123. John H. Drabble, *Malayan Rubber: The Interwar Years* (Houndmills, UK: Macmillan, 1991), 171–184.

124. World Peace Foundation, *The Program for the World Economic Conference: The Experts' Agenda and Other Documents*, Volume 25 (Boston: World Peace Foundation, 1933),

73. League of Nations, Monetary and Economic Conference. Economic Commission. Sub-Commission II. Co-ordination of Production and Marketing. Report by the Sub-Committee on Tin to Sub-Commission II of the Conference. TNA FCO 141/16515/2; "Exécution des décisions de la Conférence: Étain." LON 10D/6186/6186. See also H. R. G. Greaves, *Raw Materials and International Control* (London: Methuen & Co., 1936), 143–164.

125. Owen Chalkley to Frederick Leith-Ross, January 29, 1941. TNA T 188/247.

126. Eugene Staley, *World Economy in Transition: Technology vs. Politics, Laissez Faire vs. Planning, Power vs. Welfare* (New York: Council on Foreign Relations, 1939), 263–265, 184–185. See also Herbert Feis, *The Sinews of Peace* (New York: Harper & Bros., 1944), 229–252. Friedrich A. Hayek used the example of markets efficiently transmitting information about global tin prices to criticize economic planning in his influential article "On the Use of Knowledge in Society," *The American Economic Review* 35.4 (1945): 519–530, at 526.

127. See, for example, F. E. Lawley, *The Growth of Collective Economy*, Vol. 2 (London: P. S. King & Son, 1938), 155–247.

128. *LON OJ SS* 138 (1935): 43–46.

129. Mats Ingulstad, "Regulating the Regulators: The League of Nations and the Problem of Raw Materials," in Andreas R. Dugstad Sanders, Pål R. Sandvik, and Espen Storli, eds. *The Political Economy of Resource Regulation: An International and Comparative History, 1850–2015* (Vancouver: UBC Press, 2019), 244–250; Patricia Clavin, *Securing the World Economy: The Reinvention of the League of Nations 1920–1946* (Oxford: Oxford University Press, 2013), 183–184. For contemporary discussions, see the proceedings of the 1937 International Studies Conference, *Peaceful Change; Procedures, Population, Raw Materials, Colonies. Proceedings of the Tenth International Studies Conference, Paris, June 28–July 3, 1937* (Paris: International Institute of Intellectual Co-operation, League of Nations, 1938).

130. On the evolution of these arrangements from Anglo-Dutch imperial tools to the United Nations Conference on Trade and Development and the New International Economic Order, see Kabir-ur-Rahman Khan, *The Law and Organisation of International Commodity Agreements* (The Hague: M. Nijhoff, 1982). On intergovernmental commodity agreements and the New International Economic Order, see Vanessa Ogle "State Rights against Private Capital: The 'New International Economic Order' and the Struggle over Aid, Trade, and Foreign Investment, 1962–1981," *Humanity: An International Journal of Human Rights, Humanitarianism, and Development* 5.2 (2014): 211–234; and Nils Gilman, "The New International Economic Order: A Reintroduction," *Humanity: An International Journal of Human Rights, Humanitarianism, and Development* 6.1 (2015): 1–16.

131. Rowe, *Primary Commodities in International Trade*, 155 ff.

132. HC Deb (2 February 1943), vol. 386, col. 846.

133. John Maynard Keynes, "The Policy of Government Storage of Foodstuffs and Raw Materials," *Economic Journal* 48 (1938): 449–460. He also had a personal stake in their success: Keynes lost a great deal of money when the Stevenson Plan collapsed in 1928. *Collected Writings of John Maynard Keynes*, Vol. 12, eds. Austin Robinson and Donald Moggridge (Cambridge: Cambridge University Press, 2012), 15.

134. John Maynard Keynes to Hurst, February 1, 1943. TNA T 247/10.

135. Goronwy J. Jones, *The United Nations and the Domestic Jurisdiction of States: Interpretations and Applications of the Non-Intervention Principle* (Cardiff: University of Wales Press, 1979), 65–115.

136. Christopher R. W. Dietrich, *Oil Revolution: Anticolonial Elites, Sovereign Rights, and the Economic Culture of Decolonization* (Cambridge: Cambridge University Press, 2017), 24–25.

6. Sovereignty and the IMF

1. Jamie Martin, "The Global Crisis of Commodity Glut during the Second World War," *International History Review* 43.6 (2021): 1273-1290.

2. David Edgerton, *Britain's War Machine: Weapons, Resources, and Experts in the Second World War* (Oxford: Oxford University Press, 2011), 2.

3. For this quote, commonly used throughout the war, see, for example, Alan P. Dobson, "'A Mess of Pottage for Your Economic Birthright?' The 1941–42 Wheat Negotiations and Anglo-American Economic Diplomacy," *The Historical Journal* 28.3 (1985): 739–750; and, for a detailed account of Lend-Lease, see Dobson, *U.S. Wartime Aid to Britain, 1940–1946* (New York: St. Martin's Press, 1986). For an account of some of the political dynamics of the conditions of Lend-Lease, also explored in this chapter, see Randall Woods, *A Changing of the Guard: Anglo-American Relations, 1941–1946* (Chapel Hill, NC: University of North Carolina Press, 1990).

4. For exemplary histories, see the essays in Naomi Lamoreaux and Ian Shapiro, eds., *The Bretton Woods Agreements* (New Haven, CT: Yale University Press, 2019); and Giles Scot-Smith and J. Simon Rofe, eds., *Global Perspectives on the Bretton Woods Conference and the Post-War World Order* (London: Palgrave Macmillan, 2017); Eric Helleiner, *The Forgotten Foundations of Bretton Woods: International Development and the Making of the Postwar Order* (Ithaca, NY: Cornell University Press, 2014); Ed Conway, *The Summit: Bretton Woods, 1944: J. M. Keynes and the Reshaping of the Global Economy* (New York: Pegasus, 2015); Benn Steil, *The Battle of Bretton Woods: John Maynard Keynes, Harry Dexter White, and the Making of a New World Order* (Princeton, NJ: Princeton University Press, 2013); Harold James, *International Monetary Cooperation since Bretton Woods* (Washington, DC: International Monetary Fund, 1996); Armand Van Dormael, *Bretton Woods: Birth of a Monetary System* (London: Macmillan, 1978); Alfred J. Eckes, Jr., *A Search for Solvency: Bretton Woods and the International Monetary System, 1941–1971* (Austin, TX: University of Texas Press, 1975); Richard N. Gardner, *Sterling-Dollar Diplomacy: Anglo-American Collaboration in the Reconstruction of Multilateral Trade* (Oxford: Clarendon Press, 1956). For alternative accounts of postwar planning, see Samuel Moyn, *Not Enough: Human Rights in an Unequal World* (Cambridge, MA: Harvard University Press, 2018), 89–118, and Stephen Wertheim, *Tomorrow, the World: The Birth of U.S. Global Supremacy* (Cambridge, MA: Harvard University Press, 2020).

5. See, for example, J. Keith Horsefield, *The International Monetary Fund 1945–1965: Twenty Years of International Monetary Cooperation, Volume I: Chronicle* (Washington, DC: International Monetary Fund, 1969), which to date still offers arguably the most thorough account of the complex debates about interpreting the IMF's Articles of Agreement and their relation to questions of domestic fiscal and monetary policies, as well as the slow evolution of formal doctrine at the early IMF toward "conditionality." See also, for example, Manuel Guitián, "Conditionality: Past, Present, Future," *IMF Staff Papers* 42.4 (1995): 792–835; Jacques J. Polak, *The Changing Nature of IMF Conditionality* (Princeton, NJ: Princeton University Press, 1991); James M. Boughton, "The Universally Keynesian Vision of Bretton Woods," in Lamoreaux and Shapiro, eds., *The Bretton Woods Agreements,* 77–94.

6. Sarah Babb, "Embeddedness, Inflation, and International Regimes: The IMF in the Early Postwar Period," *American Journal of Sociology* 113.1 (2007): 128–164.

7. For an early influential account, see H. W. Arndt, *The Economic Lessons of the Nineteen-Thirties* (London: Oxford University Press, 1944). See also Harold James, *The End of Globalization: Lessons from the Great Depression* (Cambridge, MA: Harvard University Press, 2001); and Robert Boyce, *The Great Interwar Crisis and the Collapse of Globalization* (London: Palgrave Macmillan, 2009).

8. Patricia Clavin, *The Failure of Economic Diplomacy: Britain, Germany, France and the United States, 1931–36* (London: Macmillan, 1996), 189. See also Max Harris. *Monetary War and Peace: London, Washington, Paris, and the Tripartite Agreement of 1936* (Cambridge: Cambridge University Press, 2021).

9. On this point, see Herbert Feis, *The Sinews of Peace* (New York: Harper & Brothers, 1944), 55.

10. On the US wartime push for decartelization and how it related to problems of intergovernmental commodity agreements, see Wyatt Wells, *Antitrust and the Formation of the Postwar World* (New York: Columbia University Press, 2002).

11. Patricia Clavin, *Securing the World Economy: The Reinvention of the League of Nations 1920–1946* (Oxford: Oxford University Press, 2013), 267–340; Ludovic Tournès, *Les États-Unis et la Société des Nations (1914–1946): Le Système International face à l'émergence d'une superpuissance* (Bern: Peter Lang, 2016).

12. The postwar planning of Latin American, Canadian, and Chinese governments, as well as some European governments-in-exile, is the subject of a new wave of scholarship. See Christy Thornton, *Revolution in Development: Mexico and the Governance of the Global Economy* (Berkeley, CA: University of California Press, 2021); Aditya Balasubramanian and Srinath Raghavan, "Present at the Creation: India, the Global Economy, and the Bretton Woods Conference," *Journal of World History* 28.1 (2018): 65–94; Smith and Rofe, eds., *Global Perspectives on the Bretton Woods Conference and the Post-War World Order*, and Helleiner, *The Forgotten Foundations of Bretton Woods*.

13. Charlie Whitham, *Bitter Rehearsal: British and American Planning for a Post-War West Indies* (Westport, CT: Praeger, 2002). See also Ian Drummond and Norman Hillmer, *Negotiating Freer Trade: The United Kingdom, the United States, Canada and the Trade Agreements of 1938* (Waterloo, Ontario: Wilfried Laurier University Press, 1989).

14. See, for example, Austen Chamberlain's defense of the British Empire's right to non-interference concerning preferential imperial trade arrangements in a 1919 parliamentary debate. HC Deb (7 May 1919), vol. 115, col. 963.

15. See, for example, C. G. Fenwick, "The Scope of Domestic Questions in International Law," *American Journal of International Law* 19.1 (1925): 143–147, at 146.

16. See, for example, "Parley Success May Be Delayed," *Calgary Herald*, July 23, 1932.

17. On a similar point, see Susan Pedersen, *The Guardians: The League of Nations and the Crisis of Empire* (Oxford: Oxford University Press, 2015), 345–346.

18. On this point, see Dobson, "'A Mess of Pottage for Your Economic Birthright?'" 748.

19. "Winston Churchill to Roosevelt, February 7, 1942," in Warren Kimball, ed., *Churchill & Roosevelt: The Complete Correspondence* (Princeton, NJ: Princeton University Press, 1984), 351. For an excellent account of the power, persistence, and broad cultural and ideological resonance of ideas of imperial preference, and its relationship to anxieties about Britain's international standing, see Francine McKenzie, *Redefining the Bonds of Commonwealth, 1939–1948: The Politics of Preference* (Basingstoke, UK: Palgrave Macmillan, 2002).

20. "Export Surpluses and Their Importance to the Producing Countries," November 14, 1940. TNA CAB 72/27.

21. On Wallace, see Norman Markowitz, *The Rise and Fall of the People's Century: Henry A. Wallace and American Liberalism, 1941–1948* (New York: Free Press, 1973); J. Samuel Walker, *Henry A. Wallace and American Foreign Policy* (Westport, CT: Greenwood Press, 1976).

22. Owen Chalkley to Frederick Leith-Ross, January 29, 1941. TNA T 188/247.

23. War Cabinet. Official Committee on Export Surpluses. Wheat Sub-Committee, May 27, 1941. T 161/1432/1; Report on the State of Negotiations with the U.S. Governments on Surplus Primary Products and Post-war Supplies. T 188/247.

24. John Maynard Keynes to Frederick Leith-Ross, July 10, 1941. See also Frederick Leith-Ross to Noel Hall, July 15, 1941; and Noel Hall to Leith-Ross, July 4, 1941. T 188/247.

25. Donald Fergusson to Frederick Leith-Ross, May 9, 1941. TNA T 161/1432/1.

26. "Note on Draft International Wheat Agreement." See also H. D. Henderson, "Notes on the International Wheat Scheme," August 22, 1941. TNA T 161/1432/2; and "Meeting in Chancellor of the Exchequer's Room on International Wheat Agreement," September 15, 1941. TNA T 161/1432/3. For some of the other disputes around the agreement, see "Draft International Wheat Agreement. Report by the Official Committee on Export Surpluses," September 2, 1941. T 161/1432/3; "International Wheat Policy," December 16, 1941. TNA MAF 83/568; "War Cabinet. Official Committee on Export Surpluses. Wheat Sub-Committee," May 27, 1941. TNA T 161/1432/1; "Report on the State of Negotiations with the U.S. Government on Surplus Primary Products and Post-war Supplies." TNA T 188/247.

27. Paul de Hevesy, *World Wheat Planning and Economic Planning in General* (London: Oxford University Press, 1940), especially 156–157.

28. J. M. Keynes to G. S. Dunnett, August 26, 1941. TNA T 161/1432/2.

29. G. S. Dunnett to Philip Dennis Proctor, August 27, 1941. TNA T 161/1432/2.

30. Minutes of the thirty-second session of Washington wheat meeting, October 28, 1941. TNA FO 371/32411.

31. See minutes of discussions in TNA FO 371/32411, 32412, and 32413.

32. On the high stakes of the wheat agreement, see, for example, J. W. F. Rowe, "Amendment to Draft Report of the Committee on the International Wheat Agreement," August 28, 1942. TNA T 161/1432/2.

33. J. M. Keynes to G. S. Dunnett, August 26, 1941. TNA T 161/1432/2.

34. On this almost completely forgotten episode and its high stakes, see the pathbreaking work by Dobson, "'A Mess of Pottage for Your Economic Birthright?' and *U.S. Wartime Aid to Britain*, 93–125.

35. Anthony Eden to Lord Halifax, August 18, 1941. TNA T 161/1432/2.

36. Their intellectual lineage, influences, and drafts and edits have been chronicled at length. For an excellent synthesis, see Donald Markwell, *John Maynard Keynes and International Relations: Economic Paths to War and Peace* (Oxford: Oxford University Press, 2006), 233–247, and Stefan Eich, *The Currency of Politics: The Political Theory of Money from Aristotle to Keynes* (Princeton, NJ: Princeton University Press, 2022), chapter 5.

37. See, for example, Matthew C. Klein and Michael Pettis, *Trade Wars Are Class Wars: How Rising Inequality Distorts the Global Economy and Threatens International Peace* (New Haven, CT: Yale University Press, 2020). In the compromise plans, the so-called "scarce-currency" clause provided a limited means of encouraging surplus countries to adjust. It would end up being one of the most controversial aspects of the Bretton Woods agreements in the United States.

38. H. D. H. to John Maynard Keynes, March 24, 1942. TNA T 247/33.

39. Donald Moggridge, ed., *The Collected Writings of John Maynard Keynes. Volume 25, Activities 1940–1944: Shaping the Post-war World* (Cambridge: Cambridge University Press, 1980), 143.

40. Keynes, *Collected Writings*, Vol. 25, 73.

41. Keynes, *Collected Writings*, Vol. 25, 57.

42. See, for example, Wilfred Eady note, November 21, 1942. TNA T 160/1281/2.

43. On this point, see Woods, *A Changing of the Guard*, 72.

44. See, for example, accounts in the various biographies of Keynes, such as Robert Skidelsky, *John Maynard Keynes, Volume 3, Fighting for Britain, 1937–1946* (New York: Viking, 2000); D. E. Moggridge, *Maynard Keynes: An Economist's Biography* (London: Routledge, 1992); R. F. Harrod, *The Life of John Maynard Keynes* (New York: St. Martin's Press, 1951).

45. See Frederick Phillips to Treasury, February 24, 1943. TNA CAB 117/71.

46. Washington to Foreign Office, June 23, 1943. TNA CAB 115/575.

47. On Wall Street's opposition, see, in particular, Eric Helleiner, *States and the Reemergence of Global Finance: From Bretton Woods to the 1990s* (Ithaca, NY: Cornell University Press, 1994), 25–50.

48. John Francis Neylan, "World Credit Plan Dangers Revealed: Neylan Asserts Governing Board Could Meddle in Our Internal Affairs," *San Francisco Examiner,* May 3, 1943.

49. "The Gold Standard," *New York Times,* September 29, 1943; "A 'New' World Currency?" *The New York Times,* March 30, 1943. This last opinion piece was regarded with great apprehension by British officials. See Treasury from Phillips, April 1, 1943. TNA. CAB 115/575.

50. See, for example, J. H. Riddle, *British and American Plans for International Currency Stabilization* (New York: National Bureau of Economic Research, 1943), 31.

51. Redvers Opie and Frank Graham, "Discussion," *American Economic Review* 34.1 Part 2 (1944): 396–401, at 400. Graham was a founding member of the Mont Pelerin Society. See Ben Jackson, "At the Origins of Neo-Liberalism: The Free Economy and the Strong State, 1930–1947," *The Historical Journal* 53.1 (2010): 129–151.

52. Harold James, "The Historical Development of the Principle of Surveillance," *IMF Staff Papers* 42.4 (1995): 762–791.

53. Howard S. Ellis, "Can National and International Monetary Policies Be Reconciled?," *The American Economic Review* 34.1, Part 2 (1944): 385–395.

54. "Warns of Dangers in Currency Plans," *New York Times,* October 7, 1943.

55. J. H. Riddle, "International Financial Organization," April 12, 1944. TNA T 160/1287/4.

56. On Burgess and the BIS, see Gianni Toniolo, *Central Bank Cooperation at the Bank for International Settlements, 1930–1973* (Cambridge: Cambridge University Press, 2005), 53–54.

57. On Kemmerer and Dewey in Poland, see Emily Rosenberg, *Financial Missionaries to the World: The Politics and Culture of Dollar Diplomacy, 1900–1930* (Cambridge, MA: Harvard University Press, 1999), 176–183.

58. See, for example, S. D. Waley, April 18, 1944. TNA 160/1287/4.

59. Keynes, *Collected Writings,* Vol. 25, 234–235.

60. HC Deb (12 May 1943), vol. 389, col. 657. See also Andrew Bailey, Gordon Bannerman, and Cheryl Schonhardt-Bailey, "The Parliamentary Debates in the United Kingdom," in Lamoreaux and Shapiro, eds., *The Bretton Woods Agreements,* 95–120.

61. HC Deb (12 May 1943), vol. 389, col. 712.

62. HC Deb (12 May 1943), vol. 389, col. 719.

63. HC Deb (12 May 1943), vol. 389, col. 686.

64. HC Deb (12 May 1943), vol. 389, col. 761.

65. John Balfour to Anthony Eden, December 25, 1943. TNA T 160/1281/9.

66. See documents in TNA T 160/1281/8.

67. Keynes, *Collected Writings,* Vol. 25, 260.

68. Keynes, *Collected Writings,* Vol. 25, 317–318.

69. Extract from W.M. (43) 121st. Conclusions of meeting held on September 2, 1943. TNA CAB 115/575. See also Washington to Foreign Office, June 23, 1943. TNA CAB 115/575; Sir Alfred Hurst. C.U. & S.F. TNA CAB 117/71.

70. He used the term on several occasions. See, for example, Donald Moggridge, ed., *The Collected Writings of John Maynard Keynes. Volume 24, Activities 1944–1946: The Transition to Peace* (Cambridge: Cambridge University Press, 1980), 404.

71. See, for example, O.T.P. to John Maynard Keynes, September 22, 1943. TNA CAB 117/76/1.

72. See documents from September 1943 in CAB 117/71; Extract from W.M. (43) 121st. Conclusions of meeting held on September 2, 1943. TNA CAB 115/575. See also Washington to Foreign Office, June 23, 1943. TNA CAB 115/575; Sir Alfred Hurst. C.U. & S.F. TNA CAB 117/71.

73. Note of a Conversation with Mr. Bernstein of the U.S. Treasury on September 25, 1943. TNA T 247/76. See also Albert Baster to Alfred Hurst, October 5, 1943. TNA CAB 117/76/1.

74. See, for example, Horsefield, *The International Monetary Fund, 1945–1965*, Vol. 1, 67–77; John Spraos, "IMF Conditionality: Ineffectual, Inefficient, Mistargeted," *Princeton Essays in International Finance* 1 (Princeton, NJ: Princeton University Press, 1986); Joseph Gold, *Conditionality* (Washington, DC: International Monetary Fund, 1979).

75. Minutes, Discussion on Agenda under Article VII at U.S. Treasury, October 4, 1943. TNA T 160/1281/8.

76. Quoted in Horsefield, *International Monetary Fund 1945–1965*, Vol. 1, 77.

77. Albert Baster to Alfred Hurst, October 16, 1943. CAB 117/76/1.

78. Albert Baster to Alfred Hurst, October 16, 1943. CAB 117/76/1.

79. Donald Moggridge, ed., *The Collected Writings of John Maynard Keynes. Volume 23, Activities 1940–1943: External War Finance* (Cambridge: Cambridge University Press, 1980), 46.

80. Minutes, Discussion on Agenda under Article VII at U.S. Treasury, October 4, 1943. TNA T 160/1281/8.

81. Keynes, *Collected Writings*, Vol. 25, p. 345. Other postwar economic planners at the State Department, like Herbert Feis, shared Keynes's view that the fund had to avoid excessive monitoring of the policies of member countries, on the grounds that this risked "interfering with the behavior of individual nations." See Feis, *Sinews of Peace*, 191.

82. Minutes, Discussion on Agenda under Article VII at U.S. Treasury, October 4, 1943. TNA T 160/1281/8.

83. On similar points, see also Jacqueline Best, *The Limits of Transparency: Ambiguity and the History of International Finance* (Ithaca, NY: Cornell University Press, 2005), 33–61; and "Ambiguity and Uncertainty in International Organizations: A History of Debating IMF Conditionality," *International Studies Quarterly* 56.4 (2012): 674–688.

84. S. D. Waley, "Monetary Conversation," January 17, 1944. TNA T 247/27.

85. Keynes, *Collected Writings*, Vol. 25, 404–405.

86. "A World Monetary Plan," *The New York Times*, April 24, 1944.

87. HL Deb (23 May 1944), vol. 131, col. 837.

88. HC Deb (10 May 1944), vol. 399, col. 837.

89. See, for example, Alice Bourneuf to Burke, June 24, 1944, and Walter Gardner to M.S. Szymczak, June 19, 1944. RG82, Box 42 Atlantic City, 2nd Folder, Drafting Committee. NARA.

90. "Meeting of 12 Americans with British. June 26, 1944." RG82, Box 42 Atlantic City, 2nd Folder, Drafting Committee. NARA. On a related point, see also John Morton Blum, *From the Morgenthau Diaries: Years of War 1941–1945* (Boston: Houghton Mifflin Company, 1967), 267–268.

91. Article VII Discussions with Representatives of the Dominions and India, March 8, 1944. TNA T 160/1287/3.

92. Thornton, *Revolution in Development*, 90–92.

93. Kurt Schuler and Andrew Rosenberg, eds. *The Bretton Woods Transcripts* (New York: Center for Financial Stability, 2012), Kindle Edition, Location 7319.

94. Schuler and Rosenberg, *The Bretton Woods Transcripts*, Location 10784.

95. "Draft Minutes of a Meeting held at 10.45 a.m. on Tuesday, 29th February [1944], in the Offices of the War Cabinet." TNA T 247/25. See John Winant to Cordell Hull, March 5, 1944, *FRUS*, Economic and Social Matters, Volume II, 20.

96. "The White Paper on the International Monetary Fund," April 16, 1944. TNA T 160/1287/4.

97. E. A. Goldenweiser, "Bretton Woods," November 22, 1944. MEP. Box 36, Folder 11, Item 3.

98. Edward E. Brown, "The International Monetary Fund: A Consideration of Certain Objections," *Journal of Business of the University of Chicago* 17.4 (1944): 199–208, at 204.

99. "International Currency Stabilization," December 21, 1944. MEP. Box 34, Folder 16.

100. On congressional debates, see, especially, Kathryn C. Lavelle, *Legislating International Organization: The US Congress, the IMF, and the World Bank* (Oxford: Oxford University Press, 2012), 39–61; Eckes, *A Search for Solvency*, 165–209. A good overview of the congressional context also remains Blum, *From the Morgenthau Diaries: Years of War 1941–1945*, 427–436. For advocates in Congress, see Richard Hedlund, "Brent Spence and the Bretton Woods Legislation," *The Register of the Kentucky Historical Society* 79.1 (1981): 40–56.

101. *Bretton Woods Agreements Act. Hearings before the Committee on Banking and Currency, United States Senate, Seventy-ninth Congress June 12, 13, 14, 15, 16,18, 19, 20, 21, 22, 25, and 28, 1945* (Washington, DC: Government Printing Office, 1945), 636–637. On this group, see Glen Jeansonne, *Women of the Far Right: The Mothers' Movement and World War II* (Chicago: University of Chicago Press, 1996), 98–151.

102. *Bretton Woods Agreements Act. Hearings before the Committee on Banking and Currency, House of Representatives, Seventy-ninth Congress, First Session. March 7, 8, 9, 12, 13, 14, 15, 16, 19, 20, 21, 22, and 23, 1945* (Washington, DC: Government Printing Office, 1945), 546.

103. *Bretton Woods Agreements Act*, Senate Hearings, 413–414.

104. Elizabeth Borgwardt, *A New Deal for the World: America's Vision for Human Rights* (Cambridge, MA: Harvard University Press, 2005), 135; Quinn Slobodian, *Globalists: The End of Empire and the Birth of Neoliberalism* (Cambridge, MA: Harvard University Press, 2018), 144.

105. *Bretton Woods Agreements Act*, House of Representatives Hearings, 1093.

106. *Bretton Woods Agreements Act*, House of Representatives Hearings, 376.

107. *Bretton Woods Agreements Act*, House of Representatives Hearings, 349. See also American Bankers Association, *Practical International Financial Organization, through Amendments to Bretton Woods Proposals* (New York, American Bankers Association, 1945).

108. *Bretton Woods Agreements Act*, Senate Hearings, 414.

109. *Bretton Woods Agreements Act*, Senate Hearings, 219.

110. See this argument made by Edward Brown, inserted as a statement to the record of the House of Representatives hearings. *Bretton Woods Agreements Act*, House of Representatives Hearings, 212.

111. For what remains one of the best accounts of this still wholly understudied episode, see E. F. Penrose, *Economic Planning for the Peace* (Princeton, NJ: Princeton University Press, 1953), 63–86.

112. See Francine McKenzie, *GATT and Global Order in the Postwar Era* (Cambridge: Cambridge University Press, 2020); Douglas A. Irwin, Petros C. Mavroidis, and Alan O. Sykes, *The Genesis of the GATT* (Cambridge: Cambridge University Press, 2008); Slobodian, *Globalists*, 121–145.

113. *Bretton Woods Agreements Act*, House of Representatives Hearings, 348.

114. *Bretton Woods Agreements Act*, House of Representatives Hearings, 181.

115. Borgwardt, *A New Deal for the World*, 166.

116. Quoted in R. J. Vincent, *Nonintervention and International Order* (Princeton, NJ: Princeton University Press, 1974), 236. On Article 2(7), see M. S. Rajan, "United States Attitude toward Domestic Jurisdiction in the United Nations," *International Organization*

13.1 (1959): 19–37. On the evolution of economic policy-making at the United Nations, see John Toye and Richard Toye, *The UN and Global Political Economy* (Bloomington, IN: Indiana University Press, 2004).

117. See, for example, House of Commons Debate (12 and 13 December 1945). Vol. 417.

118. On Keynes's aggravation about the likely defeat of his views on conditionality at the inaugural meeting of the Board of Governors of the IMF in Savannah in 1946, and the role that the stress of this conference may have played in his death, see Roy Harrod, *Reforming the World's Money* (New York: St. Martin's Press, 1965), 120–127.

119. "From Washington to Foreign Office," May 27, 1946. TNA T 236/1162.

120. A. P. Grafftey Smith to G. L. F. Bolton, July 8, 1946. TNA T 236/1162.

121. Quoted in Sidney Dell, "On Being Grandmotherly: The Evolution of IMF Conditionality," *Essays in International Finance* 144 (1981), 8.

122. "The Future of the Bretton Woods Organisations," September 23, 1949. TNA T 236/5706.

123. E. Rowe Dutton to G. L. F. Bolton, March 5, 1947; G. L. F. Bolton to A. T. K. Grant, April 14, 1947. TNA T 236/5706.

124. A. T. K. Grant to E. Rowe-Dutton, April 15, 1947. TNA T 236/5706.

125. G. L. F. Bolton to A.T.K. Grant, April 14, 1947. TNA T 236/5706.

126. Fred L. Block, *The Origins of International Economic Disorder: A Study of United States International Monetary Policy from World War II to the Present* (Berkeley: University of California Press, 1977), 110–113.

127. Catherine R. Schenk, *The Decline of Sterling: Managing the Retreat of an International Currency, 1945–1992* (Cambridge: Cambridge University Press, 2010), 37–82.

128. G. L. F. Bolton to E. Rowe-Dutton, January 6, 1948. TNA T 236/5706.

129. "Automaticity," January 8, 1948. T 236/5706; Rowe-Dutton to Bolton, April 17, 1948. TNA T 236/5736.

130. "Policies and Work of the Fund," January 5, 1948. TNA T 233/5706.

131. "Policies and Work of the Fund," January 5, 1948. TNA T 233/5706.

132. Note, February 13, 1948. TNA T 236/5706.

133. Foreign Office to Washington, January 10, 1948. TNA T 236/5706.

134. Horsefield, *The International Monetary Fund 1945–1965*, Vol. 1, 192.

135. Note of Telephone Conversation with Mr. Tansley, March 12, 1948; Foreign Office to Washington, March 15, 1948; G. L. F. Bolton to E. Rowe-Dutton, March 31, 1948. TNA T 236/5706.

136. EBS/49/67, Use of Fund's Resources by Mexico, May 23, 1949. IMF.

137. Thornton, *Revolution in Development*, 157–159.

138. Joseph Gold, "Mexico and the Development of the Practice of the International Monetary Fund," *World Development* 16.10 (1988): 1127–1142.

139. Statement by U.S. Executive Director, printed in telegram from Washington to Foreign Office, May 20, 1949. TNA T 236/5706. For Southard's account of the early years of the IMF and the confusion about Article V of the Articles of Agreement, which set conditions for use of the Fund's resources, but lacked any real guidance about conditionality, see Frank A. Southard, Jr., *The Evolution of the International Monetary Fund* (Princeton, NJ: Princeton University Press, 1979), 16–21. Southard played an important role in the evolution of conditionality but was disappointed that the IMF struggled to play the role of "policeman."

140. Quoted in James, *International Monetary Cooperation*, 94.

141. From Washington to Foreign Office, June 4, 1949. TNA T 236/5706.

142. R.W.B.C., June 9, 1949. TNA T 236/5706.

143. "The Future of the Bretton Woods Organisations," September 23, 1949. TNA T 236/5706.

144. See, for example, Francis J. Gavin, *Gold, Dollars, and Power: The Politics of International Monetary Relations, 1958–1971* (Chapel Hill, NC: University of North Carolina Press, 2004), especially 28–29. Gavin exaggerates the IMF's "emasculation" in the 1940s–1950s. Alan Milward has argued that if there ever was a Bretton Woods "System," it collapsed during the international payments crisis of 1947. See Alan Milward, *The Reconstruction of Western Europe 1945–1951* (Berkeley, CA: University of California Press, 1984), 44.

145. Block, *The Origins of International Economic Disorder*, 113.

146. From Washington to Foreign Office, October 22, 1949. TNA T 236/5706.

147. From Washington to Foreign Office, October 30, 1949. TNA T 236/5706.

148. See, for example, Sarah Babb's pathbreaking "Embeddedness, Inflation, and International Regimes" and Babb and Ariel Buira, "Mission Creep, Mission Push and Discretion: The Case of IMF Conditionality," in Ariel Buira, ed., *The IMF and the World Bank at Sixty* (London: Anthem, 2006), 59–84. See also Sarah Babb, *Behind the Development Banks: Washington Politics, World Poverty, and the Wealth of Nations* (Chicago: University of Chicago Press, 2009), 100–103.

149. John Gerard Ruggie, "International Regimes, Transactions, and Change: Embedded Liberalism in the Postwar Economic Order," *International Organization* 36.2 (1982), 379–415, at 413.

150. Lavelle, *Legislating International Organizations*, especially at 61.

151. Erica R. Gould, *Money Talks: The International Monetary Fund, Conditionality, and Supplementary Financiers* (Stanford, CA: Stanford University Press, 2006), 41–42.

152. See an exemplary quote from US diplomatic official Douglas Dillon in Cheryl Payer, *The Debt Trap: The IMF and the Third World* (New York: Monthly Review Press, 1974), 31.

153. On legal interpretation of the IMF's powers during the evolution of conditionality, see Kenneth W. Dam, *The Rules of the Game: Reform and Evolution in the International Monetary System* (Chicago: University of Chicago Press, 1982), 117–127.

154. Southard, *The Evolution of the International Monetary Fund*, 19.

155. Andreas F. Lowenfeld, "Jurisdiction to Prescribe and the IMF," in Colin B. Picker, Isabella D. Bunn, and Douglas W. Arner, eds., *International Economic Law: The State and Future of the Discipline* (Portland, OR: Hart Publishing, 2008), 313–330, at 316.

156. A. L. Burgess to J. G. Owen, February 6, 1950. TNA T 236/5706.

157. As a long-time legal adviser at the IMF pointed out in 1970, making funds available through the stand-by arrangement was the "most effective technique by which the Fund has been able to persuade members to pursue the policies it favors," and made up for the fact that the Articles of Agreement lacked clear guidance on this question. Joseph Gold, *The Stand-By Arrangements of the International Monetary Fund: A Commentary on Their Formal, Legal, and Financial Aspects* (Washington, DC: International Monetary Fund, 1970), 4–5.

Conclusion

1. Ludwell Denny, *America Conquers Britain* (New York: A. A. Knopf, 1930), 168.

2. Matthias Schmelzer, *The Hegemony of Growth: The OECD and the Making of the Economic Growth Paradigm* (Cambridge: Cambridge University Press, 2017).

3. Erin Jacobsson, *A Life for Sound Money: Per Jacobsson: His Biography* (Oxford: Clarendon Press, 1979).

4. Subimal Mookerjee, "Policies on the Use of Fund Resources," *Staff Papers* 13.3 (International Monetary Fund, 1966): 421–442; Sidney Dell, "On Being Grandmotherly: The Evolution of IMF Conditionality," *Essays in International Finance* 144 (1981): 1–38.

5. J. Keith Horsefield, *The International Monetary Fund 1945–1965: Twenty Years of International Monetary Cooperation, Volume I: Chronicle* (Washington, DC: International

Monetary Fund, 1969), 428–433; Sarah L. Babb and Bruce G. Carruthers, "Conditionality: Forms, Function, and History," *Annual Review of Law and Social Science* 4 (2008): 13–29.

6. David A. Baldwin, "The International Bank in Political Perspective," *World Politics* 18.1 (1965): 68–81. See also Michele Alacevich, *Political Economy of the World Bank: The Early Years* (Stanford, CA: Stanford University Press, 2008).

7. For a theoretical account of how states can compromise their own sovereignty by "invitation," particularly in relation to conditional lending, see Stephen D. Krasner, *Sovereignty: Organized Hypocrisy* (Princeton, NJ: Princeton University Press, 1999), 127–151.

8. See, for example, A. J. Thomas, Jr. and Ann Van Wynen Thomas, *Non-intervention: The Law and Its Import in the Americas* (Dallas: Southern Methodist University Press, 1956). 97.

9. Margaret Garritsen de Vries, *The International Monetary Fund 1972–1978: Cooperation on Trial, Volume I: Narrative and Analysis* (Washington, DC: International Monetary Fund, 1985), 493–494.

10. Mary C. Tsai, "Globalization and Conditionality: Two Sides of the Sovereignty Coin," *Law and Policy in International Business* 31.4 (2000): 1317–1329.

11. On this point, see Randall W. Stone, "The Scope of IMF Conditionality," *International Organization* 62.4 (2008): 589–620; Stephen C. Nelson, "Playing Favorites: How Shared Beliefs Shape the IMF's Lending Decisions," *International Organization* 68 (2014): 297–328; Axel Dreher, Jan-Egbert Sturm, and James Raymond Vreeland, "Politics and IMF Conditionality," *Journal of Conflict Resolution* 59.1 (2015): 120–148.

12. For an account of this episode, and the source of the quote, see Jacqueline Best, "Ambiguity and Uncertainty in International Organizations: A History of Debating IMF Conditionality," *International Studies Quarterly* 56.4 (2012): 674–688, at 680. See also Margaret Garritsen de Vries, *The International Monetary Fund 1966–1971: The System under Stress, Volume I: Narrative* (Washington, DC: International Monetary Fund, 1976), 338–348

13. Sarah Babb, "Embeddedness, Inflation, and International Regimes: The IMF in the Early Postwar Period," *American Journal of Sociology* 113.1 (2007): 128–164, at 147.

14. de Vries, *The International Monetary Fund 1972–1978*, Vol. I, 482–486.

15. Kathleen Burk and Alec Cairncross, *Goodbye, Great Britain: The 1976 IMF Crisis* (New Haven, CT: Yale University Press, 1992); Mark D. Harmon, *The British Labour Government and the 1976 IMF Crisis* (Houndmills, UK: Macmillan, 1997); Ben Clift and Jim Tomlinson, "Negotiating Credibility: Britain and the International Monetary Fund, 1956–1976," *Contemporary European History* 17.4 (2008): 545–566. For a theoretical account, see also Ben Clift and Jim Tomlinson, "When Rules Started to Rule: the IMF, Neo-liberal Economic Ideas and Economic Policy Change in Britain," *Review of International Political Economy* 19.3 (2012): 477–500.

16. Kwame Nkrumah, *Neo-Colonialism, the Last Stage of Imperialism* (London: Nelson, 1965).

17. These included the 1962 resolution on Permanent Sovereignty over Natural Resources; the 1965 Declaration on the Inadmissibility of Intervention in the Domestic Affairs of States and Protection of Their Independence and Sovereignty; and the 1974 Charter of Economic Rights and Duties of States.

18. Declaration on the Establishment of a New International Economic Order, General Assembly Resolution 3201 (S-VI), May 1, 1974. Available at https://digitallibrary.un.org/record/218450?ln=en.

19. On this point, see also Adom Getachew, *Worldmaking after Empire: The Rise and Fall of Self-Determination* (Princeton, NJ: Princeton University Press, 2019); Susan Pedersen, *The Guardians: The League of Nations and the Crisis of Empire* (Oxford: Oxford University Press, 2015), 203, 235, 260.

20. Ha-Joon Chang, "Policy Space in Historical Perspective with Special Reference to Trade and Industrial Policies," *Economic and Political Weekly* 41.7 (2006): 627–633.

21. Ngaire Woods, *The Globalizers: The IMF, the World Bank, and Their Borrowers* (Ithaca, NY: Cornell University Press, 2006), 33–38, 76.

22. Jacques J. Polak, *The Changing Nature of IMF Conditionality* (Princeton Essays in International Finance 184) (Princeton, NJ: Princeton University Press, 1991), 31–32.

23. Randall W. Stone, *Lending Credibility: The International Monetary Fund and the Post-Communist Transition* (Princeton, NJ: Princeton University Press, 2002), 1.

24. Ben Thirkell-White, *The IMF and the Politics of Financial Globalization: From the Asian Crisis to a New International Financial Architecture?* (Houndmills, UK: Palgrave Macmillan, 2005).

25. For discussion of this point, see Eric Helleiner, "Understanding the 2007–2008 Global Financial Crisis: Lessons for Scholars of International Political Economy," *Annual Review of Political Science* 14 (2011): 67–87, at 79–80.

26. Adam Tooze, *Crashed: : How a Decade of Financial Crises Changed the World* (New York: Viking, 2018), 7, 261, 333.

27. Alexander E. Kentikelenis, Thomas H. Stubbs, and Lawrence P. King, "IMF Conditionality and Development Policy Space, 1985–2014," *Review of International Political Economy* 23.4 (2016): 543–582. There were, however, important changes in economic thinking in the institution. See Ben Clift, *The IMF and the Politics of Austerity in the Wake of the Global Financial Crisis* (Oxford: Oxford University Press, 2018).

28. Nitsan Chorev, "The Institutional Project of Neo-Liberal Globalism: The Case of the WTO," *Theory and Society* 34.3 (2005): 317–355; Nitsan Chorev and Sarah Babb, "The Crisis of Neoliberalism and the Future of International Institutions: A Comparison of the IMF and the WTO," *Theory and Society* 38 (2009): 459–484; Andrew Lang, *World Trade Law after Neoliberalism: Reimagining the Global Economic Order* (Oxford: Oxford University Press, 2014).

29. The literature on this topic is vast. See Vivien Schmidt, *Europe's Crisis of Legitimacy* (Oxford: Oxford University Press, 2020).

30. See, for example, David Singh Grewal, *Network Power: The Social Dynamics of Globalization* (New Haven, CT: Yale University Press, 2008); and "Three Theses on the Current Crisis of International Liberalism," *Indiana Journal of Global Legal Studies* 25.2 (2018): 595–621.

ACKNOWLEDGMENTS

This book was a collective effort that benefited enormously from the support, feedback, and encouragement of a large number of people. First, I owe a very special debt of gratitude to my advisers and mentors at Harvard University who saw this project emerge in its earliest form. Peter Gordon, David Blackbourn, Patrice Higonnet, Maya Jasanoff, and Mary Lewis all played important roles in my training in modern European history. Emma Rothschild encouraged me to turn to the history of political economy. Samuel Moyn was and remains a source of support in many endeavors and has always pushed me to refine and clarify the stakes of my arguments. Charles Maier taught me how to think expansively about international history, and Adam Tooze shaped this project at many key stages. His engagement and feedback had a major impact on its final form. I am particularly grateful to David Armitage for helping me to turn an earlier version into a project that allowed me to push my ideas in new directions.

I began the challenging process of transforming a draft into a book while I was a postdoctoral fellow at the University of Sydney in the Laureate Research Program in International History. I owe an enormous debt of gratitude to Glenda Sluga for making possible one of the best years of my life. Her mentorship, friendship, and intellectual engagement have meant the world to me. At the University of Sydney, I also benefitted from the comments and advice of Thomas Adams, Mike Beggs, Gareth Bryant, David Brophy, Marco Duranti, Sheila Fitzpatrick, Chris Hilliard, and Dirk Moses, and from the friendship and support of the other fellows: Philippa Hetherington, Sophie Loy-Wilson, and Natasha Wheatley.

This book took further shape at the Safra Center for Ethics at Harvard University. I would like to thank Danielle Allen for three wonderful semesters in a very stimulating intellectual community. I owe particular thanks to Turkuler Isiksel for her invaluable feedback on an early draft of a chapter at the Monday seminar. During this time in Cambridge, I counted on the support and solidarity of many very special friends, including Laura Adler, Tim Barker, Alyssa Battistoni, Jon Connolly,

Maggie Doherty, Hande Inanc, Aaron Kerner, Jeffrey Lenowitz, Quinn Slobodian, Michelle Sterling, Ben Tarnoff, Simon Torracinta, Moira Weigel, and Kirsten Weld.

Many people read chapter drafts of this book, some at very early stages. I am grateful for the feedback of Atossa Abrahamian, Peter Becker, Martin Bemmann, Freddy Foks, Julian Gewirtz, Georgios Giannakopoulos, Alexander Kentikelenis, Hélder Macedo, Nathan Marcus, George Th. Mavrogordatos, Ghassan Moazzin, Nicholas Mulder, Tim Shenk, Mira Siegelberg, Natasha Wheatley, and Tara Zahra. I owe a deep debt of gratitude to Stefan Eich, Adom Getachew, Diana Kim, and Dong Yan for reading multiple chapters (or multiple drafts of the same chapter). Numerous colleagues also read an entire early draft of the manuscript. I owe enormous thanks to Elizabeth Cross, Stefan Eich, Toshihiro Higuchi, Diana Kim, Meredith McKittrick, John McNeill, Thomas Meaney, Jim Millward, David Painter, Aviel Roshwald, Joseph Sassoon, Quinn Slobodian, Adam Tooze, and John Tutino. Thanks to Abraham Newman and the Mortara Center for International Studies for sponsoring a workshop held (remotely) at Georgetown University shortly after the outbreak of the COVID-19 pandemic in the spring of 2020 and for supporting my research, more broadly. I am extremely grateful to John McNeill for organizing this event and for his sage guidance on many matters over the last few years.

At Georgetown, many other people were indispensable to this project. Particular gratitude is owed to Gregory Afinogenov, Mustafa Aksakal, Anthony Arend, Carol Benedict, Katie Benton-Cohen, Dagomar Degroot, Erick Langer, Bryan McCann, Kathleen McNamara, and Adam Rothman. Thank you also to Charles King for helping me to strategize a title for the book and to Irfan Nooruddin for encouraging me to present an early chapter draft at the Political Economy Seminar. I am extremely grateful to Abraham Newman for his comments on a draft chapter and for making the Mortara Center a base for me at Georgetown. I'm also grateful to the other Mortara Faculty Fellows for their feedback: Jenny Guardado, Shiloh Krupar, Ken Opalo, Jessica Roda, and Elizabeth Saunders. I owe a special debt to Anna von der Goltz for many things, not least for making Washington, DC, such a wonderful home. Nico von der Goltz, who passed away while this book was being finished, and who is deeply missed, engaged me in some of the most challenging and intellectually stimulating conversations about the stakes of global governance that I've ever had.

Over the years, this book has greatly benefitted from the engagement of many friends, readers, and commenters at workshops and seminars, including Grey Anderson, Nicolas Barreyre, Sven Beckert, Duncan Bell, Joanna Biggs, Patricia Clavin, Madeleine Dungy, David Edgerton, Ted Fertik, Patrick Fridenson, Stefanos Geroulanos, Udi Greenberg, Eric Helleiner, Liane Hewitt, Joel Isaac, Duncan Kelly, Richard Kuisel, Jonathan Levy, Kristen Loveland, Erez Manela, Małgorzata Mazurek, Francine McKenzie, Paul Myerscough, Susan Pedersen, Camille Robcis, Or Rosenboim, Andrew Sartori, Tehila Sasson, Sarah Shortall, Alice Spawls, Joshua Specht, Elizabeth Thompson, Christy Thornton, Vanessa Ogle, Stephen Wertheim, and Alden Young.

At Harvard University Press, several people made this book possible. In particular, I would like to thank the three editors I worked with: Thomas LeBien for supporting the project at its beginning; James Brandt for providing a helpful source of backing and advice through its middle phases; and Ian Malcolm for seeing it through to completion. Olivia Woods has been extremely helpful and patient throughout the process, and Sharmila Sen provided an important source of support at a key moment of transition. The anonymous peer reviewers gave me some of the best feedback I have ever received. Their advice pushed the book in exciting directions. I'm also grateful to John Palatella for editing a draft of the manuscript and to Derek Gottlieb for indexing.

Many archivists helped me to track down and make sense of the documents on which this book is based. I would like to extend a particularly hearty thanks to Jacques Oberson at the United Nations in Geneva. I was also lucky to be shown warm hospitality while doing research for this book in Europe, particularly by Irene Abrahamian and Fulvio Honegger. I've also counted on the help of an extremely talented set of research assistants, including Susanne Bauda, Tatjana Eichert, Chloe-Alexandra Laird, Ranjith Kumar Pindiga, Anna Polishchuk, Maggie Rymsza, David Schaefer, and Viswanathan Venkataraman.

There are two people to whom I would like to express a very special acknowledgement for the crucial roles they played in making this book what it is. For years, Quinn Slobodian has talked me through every detail and turn of argument, read draft after draft after draft and, most of all, been a loyal friend. David Armitage has pushed me both to think big and to be precise, in equal measure. I am so grateful for his steadfast support, encouragement, and ideas.

There are many other friends who helped to sustain life and sanity as this book was being completed. I would like to mention especially Atossa Abrahamian, Anna Altman, Joe Bernstein, Anastatia Curley, Stefan Eich, Mark Fisher, David Frank, Arik Gabbai, Adom Getachew, Mike Konczal, Sarah Leonard, Daniel Luban, Katy MacLellan, Durba Mitra, Asher Mullokandov, Priya Rajana, Kendra Salois, Tim Shenk, Mira Siegelberg, Jose Soegaard, Todd Tucker, and Gabriel Winant. Dimitri Kennedy-Kavouras and Alix Mauclère Kavouras provided a home (in more ways than one) during the summer of 2020, at the height of the pandemic, while major edits were being done on this book. I am so grateful to them—and to Rose Kennedy—for their generous hospitality and support.

My family has been more kind, encouraging, and supportive than I could ever do justice to in the brief words of gratitude I can show them here. In addition to reading an entire draft of this book, Lisa Appignanesi has been a mainstay over the last few years, through ups and downs. Before his death, John Forrester was the best interlocuter I could have hoped for—always pushing my argument but with a smile and a wink and an endless supply of curiosity and laughter. Not a day goes by that we don't miss him. The Atlantic Ocean has felt wider than ever over the last two years, but I'm so thankful that Josh, Devorah, and the boys have been so close in spirit. I am, as ever, deeply grateful to Denise Martin for making New York City a home away from home for so many years. My sister Sara Martin, Phil, and all of the Darwin gang have always been a source of joy, support, and love. I miss the days when we were only separated by the expanse of a single continent. Most of all, my parents, Janet Whelan and Roger Martin, have made all that I have ever done possible, in more ways than they realize. I owe them everything.

ACKNOWLEDGMENTS

It's difficult for me to find the proper words to express how grateful I am to the person who has been by my side, with love and patience, for every moment of this book—from the invigorating ones to the doldrums—and who has understood its arguments better than I have. Thank you, Katrina Forrester, for being my closest intellectual companion, my best friend, and my partner. Not only have you read every word of this book—and made the vast majority of them significantly better—but you also inspire me, every day, in more ways than you know. I'm so excited for our next adventure together.

INDEX

Note: Page numbers in *italics* indicate figures and tables.